SINCE THE
BEGINNING

SINCE THE BEGINNING

Interpreting Genesis 1 and 2 through the Ages

EDITED BY KYLE R. GREENWOOD

Baker Academic

a division of Baker Publishing Group
Grand Rapids, Michigan

Published by Baker Academic
a division of Baker Publishing Group
PO Box 6287, Grand Rapids, MI 49516-6287
www.bakeracademic.com

Printed in the United States of America

Library of Congress Cataloging-in-Publication Data
Names: Greenwood, Kyle, editor.
Title: Since the beginning : interpreting Genesis 1 and 2 through the ages / Kyle R. Greenwood, ed.
Description: Grand Rapids : Baker Publishing Group, 2018. | Includes bibliographical references and index.
Identifiers: LCCN 2017052470 | ISBN 9780801030697 (pbk. : alk. paper)
Subjects: LCSH: Bible. Genesis, I–II—Criticism, interpretation, etc.—History.
Classification: LCC BS1235.52 .S558 2018 | DDC 222/.110609—dc23
LC record available at https://lccn.loc.gov/2017052470

Chapter 7 is adapted from Joel S. Allen, *Jewish Biblical Legends: Rabbinic Wisdom for Christian Readers* (Eugene, OR: Cascade Books, 2013). Used by permission of Wipf and Stock Publishers. www.wipfandstock.com.

18 19 20 21 22 23 24   7 6 5 4 3 2 1

For Karen

עֶצֶם מֵעֲצָמַי וּבָשָׂר מִבְּשָׂרִי

(Gen. 2:23)

Contents

Sidebars

Acknowledgments

The impetus for this book was a course I taught half a decade ago on the history of interpretation of Genesis 1. At the time there was no single volume of primary source texts and certainly no individual commentary available on these source texts to help undergraduate students make sense of the subject matter. I was out of my depth beyond the biblical material and realized in short order that a resource like the one here was very much in need. Needless to say, the book you are holding is a result of recognizing both my own deficiencies in the vernacular of the various interpreters and the need for the voices of these interpreters to have a broader audience.

Attempting to teach a course with only limited background in many of the periods up for discussion was a daunting, even foreboding, task. Though I had a deep interest in the subject and a profound understanding of the importance for the topic for the students, it took some encouragement from my former dean Sid Buzzell, as well as some kind words from my former colleagues Megan Devore, Johann Kim, Ryan Murphy, Aaron Smith, and Kevin Turner to garner the necessary courage to put the course on the schedule. They were also generous in directing me toward primary sources and providing me with helpful insights for constructing the course. The students in that section were stellar and also deserve mention: Jacob Balbas, Brooke Brundy, Ben Fisher, Taylor Gray, Neil Heitmann, Zack McMurren, Mandy Paleczny, and Jeremy Schmitz. Despite my inadequacies as their instructor, these students carefully read from the primary sources and through engaging and lively discussion arrived at a cogent understanding of the significance of the interpretive diversity through the ages. The questions pondered in the seminar were instrumental in helping me identify the four central themes addressed throughout the eleven chapters of this book.

It is also important for me to recognize and thank the ten contributors, some of whom I have known for years, while others I have only had the privilege of acquaintance through this project. Either way, I count each of them as friends. They have demonstrated charity with me as their editor, have been respectful of deadlines, and were generously patient with me when the project took some unforeseen detours. I could not have asked for a finer group of men and women with whom to collaborate, especially for my first effort as editor.

Jim Kinney has been a true professional as the chief editor at Baker Academic. When I pitched the idea of this book to him in a rather informal setting, he saw the potential in the project and helped craft the scope of the book and fine-tune its essential components. I should also add that James Ernest—now the vice president and editor-in-chief at Eerdmans—played an important role in the early stages to help me establish a team of contributors.

Many other individuals have helped in multiple facets, large and small. Carl Pace and Ken Way graciously read early versions of my chapter. (Jeff Cooley and Chris Hays read such an early version of the chapter that it is no longer part of the book!) Unnamed countless others—family, friends, neighbors, church members, work colleagues, and students—have asked penetrating questions, showed various levels of interest in the project, made seemingly innocuous remarks that have sparked new ideas, and have in many unseen ways contributed to the final product. I am grateful to each for their friendship, their wisdom, their interjections (and occasional objections), and their investment.

Finally, I offer my gratitude to my wife, Karen, to whom this book is dedicated, for helping me to be a more critical thinker and—especially in the spirit of this book—for helping me see things from more than one perspective. As providence would have it, *Since the Beginning* is scheduled for release on the date of our twenty-fifth wedding anniversary, a fitting tribute to mark the many ways we ourselves have evolved together over the ages.

Abbreviations

General

†	died
a.	answer
ANE	ancient Near East(ern)
art.	article
BCE	before the Common Era
c.	century
ca.	*circa*, about
CE	Common Era
cf.	*confer*, compare
chap(s).	chapter(s)
col(s).	columns
comm.	commentary
dist.	*distinctio*, a discrimination
DSS	Dead Sea Scrolls
ed.	edition, edited by, editor
e.g.	*exempli gratia*, for example
enl.	enlarged
esp.	especially
ET	English translation
et al.	and others
etc.	*et cetera*, and the rest
fig(s).	figure(s)
fn.	footnote
frag.	fragment
Gk.	Greek
Heb.	Hebrew
i.e.	*id est*, that is
inq.	*inquisitio*, inquisition
lit.	literal, literally

LXX	Septuagint (Greek version of the Jewish Scriptures)
MT	Masoretic Text (Hebrew)
n.	note
no(s).	number(s)
NT	New Testament
OT	Old Testament
p(p).	page(s)
pl.	plural
q.	question(s)
R.	Rabbi
repr.	reprint
rev.	revised
sc.	*scilicet*, one may know
t.	tome = volume
trans.	translated by, translation, translator
v(v).	verse(s)
vol(s).	volume(s)

Modern Versions

ASV	American Standard Version
CEB	Common English Bible
ESV	English Standard Version
JB	Jerusalem Bible
KJV	King James Version
NAB	New American Bible (2010)
NASB	New American Standard Bible
NEB	New English Bible
NET	New English Translation

NIV   New International Version (2011)
NJPS *Tanakh: The Holy Scriptures: The New JPS Translation according to the Traditional Hebrew Text* (1985)
NLT   New Living Translation (2007)
NRSV New Revised Standard Version (1989)
REB   Revised English Bible
RSV   Revised Standard Version

Old Testament

Gen.	Genesis
Exod.	Exodus
Lev.	Leviticus
Num.	Numbers
Deut.	Deuteronomy
Josh.	Joshua
Judg.	Judges
Ruth	Ruth
1–2 Sam.	1–2 Samuel
1–2 Kings	1–2 Kings
1–2 Chron.	1–2 Chronicles
Ezra	Ezra
Neh.	Nehemiah
Esther	Esther
Job	Job
Ps./Pss.	Psalm/Psalms
Prov.	Proverbs
Eccles.	Ecclesiastes
Song	Song of Songs
Isa.	Isaiah
Jer.	Jeremiah
Lam.	Lamentations
Ezek.	Ezekiel
Dan.	Daniel
Hosea	Hosea
Joel	Joel
Amos	Amos
Obad.	Obadiah
Jon.	Jonah
Mic.	Micah
Nah.	Nahum
Hab.	Habakkuk
Zeph.	Zephaniah
Hag.	Haggai
Zech.	Zechariah
Mal.	Malachi

New Testament

Matt.	Matthew
Mark	Mark
Luke	Luke
John	John
Acts	Acts
Rom.	Romans
1–2 Cor.	1–2 Corinthians
Gal.	Galatians
Eph.	Ephesians
Phil.	Philippians
Col.	Colossians
1–2 Thess.	1–2 Thessalonians
1–2 Tim.	1–2 Timothy
Titus	Titus
Philem.	Philemon
Heb.	Hebrews
James	James
1–2 Pet.	1–2 Peter
1–3 John	1–3 John
Jude	Jude
Rev.	Revelation

Old Testament Apocrypha and Pseudepigrapha

2 Bar.	2 Baruch
1 En.	1 Enoch
2 En.	2 Enoch
4 Ezra	4 Ezra
Jub.	Jubilees
Let. Arist.	Letter of Aristeas
Sib. Or.	Sibylline Oracles
Sir.	Sirach
Tob.	Tobit

Dead Sea Scrolls and Related Texts

CD	Damascus Document
1QM	Milḥamah or War Scroll
4Q252	4QGenesis Pesher[a]
4Q253	4QGenesis Pesher[b]
4Q265	4QMiscellaneous Rules

4Q317	4QPhases of the Moon
4Q319–30	Calendrical Documents
4Q335–37	Astronomical Fragments
4Q422	Paraphrase of Gen. and Exod.
6Q17	Calendrical Document
11Q5	11QPsalms[a]
11Q13	11QMelchizedek

Rabbinic Sources

b.	Babylonian Talmud
Gen. Rab.	Genesis Rabbah
Hag.	Hagigah
Lev. Rab.	Leviticus Rabbah
m.	Mishnah
Rab.	Rabbah
Sanh.	Sanhedrin

Josephus and Philo

Josephus

| Ant. | Jewish Antiquities |

Philo

Alleg. Interp.	Allegorical Interpretation
Cherubim	On the Cherubim
Creat.	On the Creation of the World
Heir	Who Is the Heir?
Worse	That the Worse Attacks the Better

Apostolic Fathers

| Barn. | Barnabas |
| 1 Clem. | 1 Clement |

Church Fathers

An.	Tertullian, On the Soul
Autol.	Theophilus, To Autolycus [Ad Autolycum]
C. Ar.	Athanasius, Orations against the Arians
Cels.	Origen, Against Celsus
Comm. Matt.	Origen, Commentary on the Gospel of Matthew
Comm. Rom.	Origen, Commentaries on Romans

Comm. Song	Origen, Commentary on the Song
Conf.	Augustine, Confessions
Dial.	Justin, Dialogue with Trypho
Epid.	Irenaeus, Demonstration of the Apostolic Preaching
Exh. cast.	Tertullian, Exhortation to Chastity
1 Apol.	Justin, First Apology
Gen. litt.	Augustine, On Genesis Literally Interpreted
Gen. Man.	Augustine, Two Books On Genesis against the Manichaeans
Haer.	Irenaeus, Against Heresies
Herm.	Tertullian, Against Hermogenes
Hex.	Ambrose, Six Days of Creation
Hist. eccl.	Eusebius, Ecclesiastical History
Hom.	Basil, Homily [in Hexaemeron]
Hom. Exod.	Origen, Homilies on Exodus
Hom. Gen.	John Chrysostom, Homilies on Genesis
Hom. Gen.	Origen, Homilies on Genesis
Inst.	Lactantius, The Divine Institutes
Marc.	Tertullian, Against Marcion
Misc.	Clement, Miscellanies
Or. Graec.	Tatian, Oration to the Greeks
Pasc.	Melito of Sardis, Paschal Homily
Princ.	Origen, On First Principles
Res.	Tertullian, The Resurrection of the Flesh
Sat.	Juvenal, Satires
Virg.	Tertullian, The Veiling of Virgins

Other Greek and Latin Works

Hist. Tacitus, *Histories*
LAB Liber antiquitatum biblicarum
     (Pseudo-Philo)
Rep. Cicero, *The Republic*
Tim. Plato, *Timaeus*

Secondary Sources and Collections

AB Anchor Bible
ABD *Anchor Bible Dictionary*. Ed.
       D. N. Freedman. 6 vols. New
       York: Doubleday, 1992.
ACCS Ancient Christian Commen-
       tary on Scripture
AJSL *American Journal of Semitic
        Languages and Literatures*
AJSR *Association for Jewish Studies
        Review*
ALGHJ Arbeiten zur Literatur und
       Geschichte des hellenistischen
       Judentums
AnBib Analecta Biblica
ANESSup Ancient Near Eastern Studies
         Supplement Series
ANET *Ancient Near Eastern Texts
        Relating to the Old Testa-
        ment*. Ed. J. B. Pritchard. 3rd
        ed. Princeton: Princeton Uni-
        versity Press, 1969.
ANF *Ante-Nicene Fathers*. Ed. Al-
       exander Roberts and James
       Donaldson. Peabody, MA:
       Hendrickson, 2004.
AOAT Alter Orient und Altes
       Testament
AUSS *Andrews University Seminary
        Studies*
BASOR *Bulletin of the American
         Schools of Oriental Research*
BBR *Bulletin for Biblical Research*
Bib *Biblica*
BJS Brown Judaic Studies
BT *The Bible Translator*
BTB *Biblical Theology Bulletin*
BZAW Beihefte zur Zeitschrift für die
       alttestamentliche Wissenschaft

CBET Contributions to Biblical Ex-
       egesis and Theology
CBQ *Catholic Biblical Quarterly*
CBQMS Catholic Biblical Quarterly
        Monograph Series
CCSL Corpus Christianorum: Series
       Latina. Turnhout: Brepols,
       1953–.
CCT Corpus Christianorum in
       Translation
COS *The Context of Scripture*.
       Ed. W. W. Hallo and K. L.
       Younger Jr. 3 vols. Leiden:
       Brill, 1997–2003.
CSEL Corpus Scriptorum Ecclesias-
       ticorum Latinorum
DDD *Dictionary of Deities and
        Demons in the Bible*. Ed.
        K. van der Toorn, B. Beck-
        ing, and P. W. van der Horst.
        Leiden: Brill, 1995. 2nd rev.
        ed. Grand Rapids: Eerdmans,
        1999.
DOTP *Dictionary of the Old Testa-
        ment: Pentateuch*. Ed. T. D.
        Alexander and D. W. Baker.
        Downers Grove, IL: IVP Aca-
        demic, 2003.
DPL *Dictionary of Paul and His
        Letters*. Edited by G. F. Haw-
        thorne, R. P. Martin, and
        D. G. Reid. Downers Grove,
        IL: InterVarsity, 1993.
DSD *Dead Sea Discoveries*
DULAT *Dictionary of the Ugaritic
         Language in the Alphabetic
         Tradition*. G. del Olmo Lete
         and J. Sanmartín. Trans. and
         ed. W. G. E. Watson. 2 vols.
         3rd rev. ed. Leiden and Bos-
         ton: Brill, 2015.
EncJud *Encyclopaedia Judaica*. Ed.
          C. Roth and G. Wigoder. Je-
          rusalem: Keter Publishing
          House, 1971.
ErIsr *Eretz-Israel*
EvQ *Evangelical Quarterly*
FC Fathers of the Church

FRLANT   Forschungen zur Religion
         und Literatur des Alten und
         Neuen Testaments
Greg   Gregorianum
HALOT   The Hebrew and Aramaic
         Lexicon of the Old Testament.
         L. Koehler, W. Baumgartner,
         and J. J. Stamm. Trans. and
         ed. under the supervision of
         M. E. J. Richardson. 5 vols.
         Leiden: Brill, 1994–2000.
HDR   Harvard Dissertations in
         Religion
HeyJ   Heythrop Journal
HTR   Harvard Theological Review
IBC   Interpretation: A Bible Com-
         mentary for Teaching and
         Preaching
JAOS   Journal of the American Ori-
         ental Society
JBL   Journal of Biblical Literature
JBQ   Jewish Bible Quarterly
JBS   Jerusalem Biblical Studies
JECS   Journal of Early Christian
         Studies
JETS   Journal of the Evangelical
         Theological Society
JGRChJ   Journal of Greco-Roman
         Christianity and Judaism
JHebS   Journal of Hebrew Scriptures
JPS   Jewish Publication Society
JSJSup   Journal for the Study of Juda-
         ism in the Persian, Hellenistic
         and Roman Periods Supple-
         ment Series
JSNT   Journal for the Study of the
         New Testament
JSNTSup Journal for the Study of the
         New Testament Supplement
         Series
JSOT   Journal for the Study of the
         Old Testament
JSOTSup Journal for the Study of the
         Old Testament Supplement
         Series
JTI   Journal of Theological
         Interpretation

JTS   Journal of Theological Studies
JTSA   Journal of Theology for
         Southern Africa
KAI   Kanaanäische und aramäische
         Inschriften. Ed. H. Donner
         and W. Röllig. 2nd ed. Wiesba-
         den: Harrassowitz, 1966–69.
KTU   Die keilalphabetischen Texte
         aus Ugarit. Ed. M. Dietrich,
         O. Loretz, and J. Sanmartín.
         Münster: Ugarit-Verlag, 2013.
         3rd enl. ed. of KTU: The
         Cuneiform Alphabetic Texts
         from Ugarit, Ras Ibn Hani,
         and Other Places. Münster:
         Ugarit-Verlag, 1995 (= CTU)
LNTS   The Library of New Testa-
         ment Studies
LW   Luther's Works. Ed. J. Pelikan
         and H. T. Lehmann. American
         Edition. 55 vols. Philadelphia:
         Fortress, 1955–86.
NICOT   New International Commen-
         tary on the Old Testament
NIDB   The New Interpreter's Dic-
         tionary of the Bible. Ed. K. D.
         Sakenfeld. 5 vols. Nashville:
         Abingdon, 2006–9.
NTL   New Testament Library
NTS   New Testament Studies
OEANE   The Oxford Encyclopedia of
         Archaeology in the Near East.
         Ed. E. M. Meyers. 5 vols. New
         York: Oxford University Press,
         1997.
OTL   Old Testament Library
PAAJR   Proceedings of the American
         Academy of Jewish Research
PACS   Philo of Alexandria Com-
         mentary Series
PG   Patrologia Graeca [= Patrolo-
         giae Cursus Completus: Series
         Graeca]. Ed. J.-P. Migne. 162
         vols. Paris, 1857–86.
PL   Patrologia Latina [= Patrolo-
         giae Cursus Completus: Series
         Latina]. Ed. J.-P. Migne. 217
         vols. Paris, 1844–64.

RB	*Revue biblique*	UCOP	University of Cambridge Oriental Publications
RCS	Reformation Commentary on Scripture	*VC*	*Vigiliae Christianae*
SBL	Society of Biblical Literature	*VT*	*Vetus Testamentum*
SBLDS	Society of Biblical Literature Dissertation Series	VTSup	Supplements to Vetus Testamentum
ScEs	*Science et esprit*	WBC	Word Biblical Commentary
SCJ	*Stone-Campbell Journal*	*WTJ*	*Westminster Theological Journal*
SHBC	Smyth & Helwys Bible Commentary	*WW*	*Word and World*
SIL	Summer Institute of Linguistics	ZAC	*Zeitschrift für Antikes Christentum / Journal of Ancient Christianity*
Spec	*Speculum*		
TBN	Themes in Biblical Narrative	ZAW	*Zeitschrift für die alttestamentliche Wissenschaft*
TJ	*Trinity Journal*		
TynBul	*Tyndale Bulletin*		

Preface

KYLE R. GREENWOOD

Joining the Conversation

God asked Job, "Where were you when I laid the foundation of the earth?" (Job 38:4). Job was not present to record the proceedings. From the Aztecs to the Xin, peoples from vast and varied origins have consistently expressed a general fascination with their beginnings: beginnings of the cosmos, beginnings of humanity, beginnings of civilization, and beginnings of evil. These stories of beginnings provide a context for the present state of existence. They often explain such things as why there are mountains, seas, and stars; why women and men look and behave differently and are tasked with different cultural roles; why blood is essential to animal life; why suffering persists.

Genesis 1–2, likewise, addresses many of the same sorts of questions as the origin stories from other civilizations. However, there is a common misconception that the questions humanity raises today are the same questions that hearers of the text have posed throughout its history. There is a popular perception that the way one's pastor or rabbi interprets Gen. 1–2 is the way these chapters have always been interpreted. This approach is the unfortunate by-product of a diminished appreciation (at best) or willful ignorance (at worst) of any sense of historical consideration. In so doing, modern readers tend to turn a deaf ear to the interpretive inquiries of their forebears, assuming today's questions naturally would have been the questions raised 500, 1000, or 2000 years ago.

While many today are enamored with what Gen. 1–2 has to say about history, what is unfortunately missed by our present biases is that Gen. 1–2 also has a history. Ronald Hendel speaks to the history of Genesis in terms of its "afterlife," that is, the life the text appropriates after the text was breathed into Scripture.

> A text's afterlife inevitably affects one's reading of it, even if one is trying to attend to its plain or native senses. How difficult is it to read the Garden of Eden story without importing later interpretations, such as Original Sin, Eve as erotic temptress, or the snake as Satan? These are products of Genesis's afterlife, which are hard to see around. The life and afterlife are perpetually in a tangled relationship with each other, which is to say that Genesis has a complicated biography.[1]

This so-called afterlife of Gen. 1–2 is the subject at hand for this present volume.

By attending to the biography of these foundational chapters in the Hebrew and Christian Scriptures, the contributors to *Since the Beginning* lead us to new sights and insights. They enrich our understanding of the Genesis creation narratives as we eavesdrop on conversations from Moses to Marsden, and from Aquinas to the Zohar. We will incline our ears to Christian theologians, Greek sophists, and Jewish rabbis, sometimes in dialogue with each other, and other times with no one in particular. In other words, we will hear the words of prophets, philosophers, and preachers "since the beginning" to the present day.

Perhaps most importantly, however, attentive listening to past conversations about a text helps us become better conversationalists ourselves. Without a context for communication, the likelihood for miscommunication increases greatly. If this is true for conversations minutes old, how much more is this the case for conversations millennia old? As we enter into the dialogue of Gen. 1–2, then, it is essential that we take time to familiarize ourselves with the kinds of discussions that have already taken place. The aim of this volume is to provide readers with the context necessary to enter the dialogical fray to equip them to read Gen. 1–2 intelligently and interactively, honestly and humbly. If we neglect the biography of Gen. 1–2 as expressed through the voices of the past, we run the risk of merely attending to our concerns, rather than the concerns of the text. We run the risk of thinking that the questions raised today are the same questions that have always been raised.

---

1. Ronald Hendel, *The Book of Genesis: A Biography*, Lives of Great Religious Books (Princeton: Princeton University Press, 2013), 5–6.

More importantly, we run the risk of assuming that the answers we provide to those questions are the only right answers, an egregious error that places our interpretations on a level higher than Scripture itself.

Following the Conversation

To help you follow the conversation, ten scholars have joined me in recounting the biography of Gen. 1–2 over the course of its afterlife, surveying both Jewish and Christian readings from the earliest interpreters to the present day. All contributors have specialization in their assigned chapter, and many of them have published on some aspect of creation in their given era. The authors not only bring a wealth of knowledge to the project but also bring unique and assorted perspectives, coming from various regions of the world and diverse faith commitments.

One of the challenges faced when compiling a book such as this is defining parameters. An argument could certainly be made that Gen. 1 should stand alone, or that if Gen. 2 is included then so should Gen. 3 or Gen. 3–11. Regardless of the merits for those options, Gen. 1–2 has pride of place as the focal point of creation theology. These chapters introduce the concepts and ideas that are foundational to interpretations and misinterpretations of our own beginnings. Therein, Scripture invites us to tour the cosmos from the highest heavens to the depths of the sea, from birds in the sky to the beasts of the field. It establishes the six-day work week followed by a Sabbath rest. It introduces us to the human species and to a man and a woman naked and unashamed. It invites us into a garden blissfully bountiful, yet deceptively deadly.

A second parameter requiring definition is which topics to address. Genesis 1–2 is replete with interpretive issues. Across the millennia of interpretation, however, four issues recur with frequency, at least in broad generalities. Thus readers of *Since the Beginning* will notice that each chapter has a similar structure. While not every chapter is identical in format, great pains were made to achieve some semblance of consistency for the sake of cohesion. Following an introduction to the interpreters from the era under discussion, each chapter will deal with four explicit issues: (1) treatment of days; (2) cosmology; (3) creation and nature of humanity; and (4) garden of Eden. In a few cases the authors have found it necessary to combine two of the categories into one discussion when the interpreters themselves made little effort to distinguish them. In two chapters (9 and 11) one of the topics was abandoned altogether, as (in both cases) the garden of Eden elicited little comment. With those rare exceptions understood, readers will be able to make a straightforward comparison of interpretations throughout the ages. Some authors have also found it necessary to add a fifth category, "Interpretive Peculiarities," in which they have the liberty to address important interpretive issues that fall outside the commissioned parameters. At the end of each chapter, the authors provide a summary of their findings and help the readers draw some conclusions regarding their interpretations. Following each chapter, a short bibliography has been provided for further reading, along with resources for locating primary texts, enabling the book to be used in the classroom by instructors who, like most, are out of their depth in many of the interpretive eras.

A third parameter involves the selection of interpreters treated within the book. Among many mainline Christians and Jews, issues of origins and of science and faith are nonthreatening and pose no inherent challenges to their understanding of divine revelation and faithful obedience to the God revealed in Scripture. For others, however, science poses an apparent constant threat to biblical authority. Although readers of all faith commitments (or none at all) will benefit from hearing the millennia-old conversation regarding biblical beginnings, it is the latter group who would likely most benefit from an awareness of engagement with the wisdom of the sages, past and present. It is especially (though not solely) with those readers in mind that the broad but selective interpreters and commentators have been chosen for inclusion in the book. There is wisdom in recognizing that, out of a theological commitment to Gen. 1–2 as sacred writ, authors and exegetes from bygone eras have adopted interpretive methods that would seem quite foreign in current contexts. Moreover, since Gen. 1–2 were Jewish Scriptures long before they were appropriated as Christian Scriptures, this book interacts with interpreters from both *Jewish* and *Christian* perspectives.

However, attentive readers will notice that this book does not provide an overview of Jewish interpretation after the Reformation. This is because the Reformation was transformational for Christianity but not for Judaism since it had always engaged the Hebrew text of the Bible. This new Christian interest did, however, open the door for engagement with Jewish scholars and writers as teachers of Hebrew and rabbinic traditions about the Bible. Within the development of Jewish interpretation in this later period, much of the work was a reengagement with earlier rabbinic, mystical, and philosophical traditions outlined in the earlier chapters. In the modern period, Jews and Christians alike who adopted critical scholarship relied on similar archaeological discoveries and advances in linguistic and higher-critical methods, which yielded similar results.[2]

---

2. I am indebted to Jason Kalman for the content of this paragraph.

One final word of clarification remains. Whenever one discusses Gen. 1–2, inevitably one must define "literal." For some, a "literal" translation entails a plain-sense reading of the text. For others, "literal" refers to the text's intended usage given the word's context and the genre of the literature in which it appears. Let us take as an example God's communication in Gen. 1. According to the first definition of "literal," God's speech would naturally refer to the issuance of an audible voice, and, if pressed, would also involve exhalation, phonation, and articulation requiring various physiological and anatomical features resulting in a sound wave that is detected and translated by something capable of such a task. According to the second definition, God's speech acts in Genesis are "literal" in the sense that God is not a human and does not speak like a human, so God's "literal" speech is not the same as a human's literal speech. Some might argue, then, that God's speech in Gen. 1 is literally metaphorical or literally analogous, but not literally "literal." Unfortunately, some modern interpreters have hijacked the word "literal" as a way of usurping biblical authority for their pet doctrines. However, as we follow the conversation, we will bear witness to the fact that it was the insistence of a "literal" interpretation of Gen. 1–2 that led some interpreters to read these chapters christologically or eschatologically, some interpreters to read them allegorically or typologically, others metaphysically or philosophically, others as midrash, and still other interpreters to read them scientifically. What will inevitably become clear by following the conversation is that a "literal" reading rarely meant a univocal reading, where one word is assigned one and only one meaning.

1

Old Testament Reverberations
of Genesis 1–2

KYLE R. GREENWOOD

With the emergence of narrative criticism as a methodology of biblical exegesis in the last quarter of the twentieth century, greater interest has been placed on how and to what degree biblical texts are in communication with each other. This stands in stark contrast to the historical-critical method, which tends to fragment the biblical text. Drawing on the insights gleaned from modern literary criticism, narrative criticism invites its readers to participate in the interpretive process, albeit in varying degrees. Discrepancies abound, however, regarding the very nature of the methods espoused within the discipline. As such, scholars have tried their hand at various terms to communicate the idea of connections among biblical texts, such as allusion, echo, inner-biblical exegesis, inner-biblical interpretation, and intertextuality.[1] Regardless of the

---

1. For a detailed discussion of this field and the methodological challenges related to it, see Joseph Ryan Kelly, "Identifying Literary Allusions: Theory, and the Criterion of Shared Language," in *Subtle Citation, Allusion, and Translation in the Hebrew Bible*, ed. Ziony Zevit (Sheffield: Equinox, 2017), 22–40; see also Michael Fishbane, *Biblical Interpretation in Biblical Israel* (Oxford: Clarendon, 1985).

terminology, the generally stated objective of each is to demonstrate the directional communication from one text to another.

As we embark on our survey of the history of interpretation of Gen. 1–2, the appropriate place to start is with the OT itself. After all, it was the authors of these thirty-nine books who first had interaction with these texts. Questions immediately arise, however, regarding the diachronic development of the opening chapters of the Hebrew Bible. According to the Documentary Hypothesis articulated by Julius Wellhausen, Gen. 1 was a Priestly document written during the Persian period, while Gen. 2 was written in Judah around 750 BCE.[2] While OT scholars today are widely divided on the precise number and scope of sources within the Pentateuch, there is broad consensus that it is "a literary collage," composed and edited over a span of many centuries.[3] Thus we are right to ask to what extent other biblical writers might have had opportunity to engage these pivotal chapters.

Given the challenges of identifying "source texts" for the themes and concepts of Gen. 1–2, it is not my objective to identify the direction of intertextual allusions in the Hebrew Bible. Nor will I try to state whether there was a direct allusion at all, except in a few rare cases. Rather, the goal of this chapter is to demonstrate the ways in which the four major themes addressed in this volume—treatment of days, cosmology, creation and nature of humanity, garden of Eden—are treated throughout the OT, noting especially consonance and dissonance with respect to Gen. 1–2.

Treatment of Days

> In the beginning God created the heaven and the earth. (Gen. 1:1 KJV)

The opening verse in Genesis is among the most recognizable in the Bible. Its status as the codified entry into sacred Scripture is reflected in the fact that nearly every modern English translation simply follows the tradition of the King James Version. With simple clarity, Gen. 1:1 establishes a central theological tenet of the Bible: God is the sovereign creator of the entire cosmos and all its inhabitants. However, this familiar translation, which dates back to the Septuagint (ca. 225 BCE) and was followed by the Vulgate (390–405 CE), has been challenged in recent decades, thanks in large measure to advances in linguistic studies of Biblical Hebrew. Arguments over translation theory are too technical and tedious to detail here, but the crux of the discussion is

---

2. Julius Wellhausen, *Prolegomena zur Geschichte Israels* (Berlin: G. Reimer, 1899).
3. T. Desmond Alexander, "Authorship of the Pentateuch," in *DOTP*, 61–72, here 63.

worth summarizing.[4] In essence, modern translators consider three renderings of Gen. 1:1 as viable options, each of which is represented in the NRSV, either in the text or in a footnote.

1. In the beginning when God created the heavens and the earth . . . (text)
2. [In the beginning] when God began to create [the heavens and the earth] . . . (fn. 1)
3. In the beginning God created [the heavens and the earth]. (fn. 2)

The interpretive issue revolves around the relationship between the first two Hebrew words. The first word, *bərē'šît*, is composed of two elements, the preposition *b* ("in, with, by, when"), and the noun *rē'šît* ("beginning, starting point, first"). The second word, *bārā'*, is the finite verb, "he created." Following a linguistic analysis of similar syntactic structures in the Hebrew Bible, Robert Holmstedt concludes that Gen. 1:1 refers not to a specific beginning of known chronology but to the beginning of the particular act "from which the rest of the story as we know it unfolds."[5] In other words, Gen. 1:1 does not give us an account of the beginning of everything but an account of the commencement of one particular act of God.

The literary structure of Gen. 1 has been well documented, dating back at least as far as Thomas Aquinas,[6] and formalized by W. H. Griffith Thomas.[7]

Forming	Filling
Day 1: Light and Dark	Day 4: Lights of Day and Night
Day 2: Sea and Sky	Day 5: Creatures of Water and Air
Day 3: Fertile Earth	Day 6: Creatures of the Land

Although "evening and morning" mark the boundaries for each of days 1–6, it is unlikely the author of Gen. 1 had in mind twenty-four-hour solar days, given the fact that the sun was not created until day 4 (Gen. 1:16). A day

4. On the syntactical complexities of Gen. 1:1, see J. M. Powls Smith, "The Syntax and Meaning of Genesis 1:1–3," *AJSL* 44, no. 2 (1928): 108–15; William P. Brown, *Structure, Role, and Ideology in the Hebrew and Greek Texts of Genesis 1:1–2:3*, SBLDS 132 (Atlanta: Scholars Press, 1993), 62–73.
5. Robert D. Holmstedt, "The Restrictive Syntax of Genesis 1:1," *VT* 58 (2008): 56–66, here 66; for a linguistic defense of the traditional translation of Gen. 1:1, see Barry Bandstra, *Genesis 1–11: A Handbook on the Hebrew Text* (Waco: Baylor University Press, 2008), 41–44.
6. Thomas Aquinas, *Summa Theologiae* I, q. 70, art. 1. Aquinas refers to days 1–3 as "form," and days 4–6 as "fulness."
7. W. H. Griffith Thomas, *Genesis: A Devotional Commentary* (Grand Rapids: Eerdmans, 1946), 29.

defined by the earth's position relative to the sun would be nonsense in the absence of that greater light. The days of Gen. 1, then, are presented literarily, not scientifically.[8] The emphasis on literary structure is further demonstrated by two additional features. First, each day has a recurring, formulaic structure:[9]

> Then God said . . . let there be / let X do . . . , and it was so.
> Then God saw that it was (very) good.[10]
> There was evening and there was morning, day *n*.

The highly stylistic prose of Gen. 1 indicates to the reader/hearer that the interests of its author lie in the theological message of its contents, not in its scientific precision. Second, the way in which each day concludes varies to a degree in the Hebrew text, a point generally glossed over in English translations. In the Hebrew text, only days 6 and 7 are rendered definite. The first diurnal period is marked as "day one," while days 2–5 read, "a second day, a third day," and so on. Since the parameters of days 1–6 are somewhat vague ("evening and morning") and day 7 is without end (lacking an "evening and morning"), Herman Bavinck calls these days "God's workdays."[11] For C. John Collins, the days of Gen. 1 are analogous but not equivalent to human workdays, so that their duration is irrelevant to the original hearers of the text.[12]

A third indication that the days in Gen. 1 are literary devices rather than solar days is how the creation of the cosmos is recounted elsewhere in the Hebrew Bible. Although the creation event is described in numerous places throughout the OT, the days of creation are only relevant in two other passages, Exod. 20:8–11 and 31:17. Elsewhere, not only are the days inconsequential, the order of creation is often altered.[13] In Ps. 74, for example, God defeats the sea monster Leviathan, cuts openings for the springs, establishes celestial luminaries, fixes the boundaries of the earth, and then fashions summer and

8. For a detailed analysis of the stylistic nature of Gen. 1, see C. John Collins, *Genesis 1–4: A Linguistic, Literary, and Theological Commentary* (Philipsburg, NJ: P&R, 2006).

9. Gordon Wenham observes "that although there are ten announcements of the divine words and eight commands actually cited, all the formulae are grouped in sevens." *Genesis 1–15*, WBC 1 (Waco: Word, 1987), 6.

10. Only on day 6 is creation declared "very good" (*ṭôb məʾōd*) (Gen. 1:31).

11. Herman Bavinck, *In the Beginning: Foundations of Christian Theology*, ed. John Bolt, trans. John Vriend (Grand Rapids: Baker, 1999), 126.

12. C. John Collins, "Reading Genesis 1–2 with the Grain: Analogical Days," in *Reading Genesis 1–2: An Evangelical Conversation*, ed. J. Daryl Charles (Peabody, MA: Hendrickson, 2013), 73–92, here 88.

13. See Job 38:2–11; Pss. 74:12–17; 104:1–17; 136:1–9; Prov. 8:22–31; Isa. 40:12; 42:5–9; Neh. 9:6.

winter. Since most of these other accounts are written as poetry, it is difficult to say how precisely we should consider the order of the events. What we can say, however, is that the various authors were not bound to a canonized doctrine of the order or duration of the creative process.

However, both Exod. 20:8–11 and 31:17 are predicated on the six-day creation week. The fourth commandment of the Decalogue unambiguously commands Israel to remember the Sabbath "for in six days the LORD made heaven and earth, the sea, and all that is in them, but rested the seventh day; therefore the LORD blessed the Sabbath day and consecrated it" (Exod. 20:11). On the face of it, Exod. 20:11 appears to vindicate a solar-day reading of Gen. 1. Three factors must be taken into consideration, however. First, it is likely more accurate to speak of an underlying Sabbath tradition behind Gen. 1 than to suppose that Gen. 1 prescribes Sabbath law.[14] That is, Sabbath observance would have likely already been in place before its codification in the Ten Commandments or Gen. 1. Second, the order of creation in Exod. 20 (heavens, earth, sea) does not follow that of Gen. 1 (sea, heavens, earth). So, while Exod. 20 appeals to a seventh day of divine rest as justification for Sabbath observance, it is not bound to the creative order of the rest of the creation week. A third factor is that in the second giving of the law (Deut. 5:12–15), the rationale given for keeping the Sabbath has a different point of reference. In Exodus, Sabbath observance is grounded in cosmological-theological language, made explicit by the inclusion of "sea," rounding out the three-tiered cosmic structure (see "Cosmology" below).[15] By contrast, the motive provided for Sabbath rest in Deuteronomy is God's deliverance from Egyptian bondage.[16] The fact that this version of Sabbath law does not depend on a seven-day creation week is further indication that the days of creation were not imperative to a robust creation theology in the Hebrew Bible.

Cosmology

As I have argued elsewhere, biblical cosmology is ANE cosmology.[17] Observing the world from an earthbound perspective, the ancients deduced that they—whether in Alexandria, Babylonia, or Canaan—were at the center of

14. Brevard Childs, *The Book of Exodus*, OTL (Philadelphia: Westminster, 1974), 416.

15. William Johnstone, *Exodus 20–40*, SHBC 2b (Macon, GA: Smyth and Helwys, 2014), 34.

16. For further discussion on the differences between the two versions of the fourth commandment, see Josiah Derby, "The Fourth Commandment," *JBQ* 22 (1994): 26–31; and Asher Eder, "The Sabbath Commandment: Its Two Versions," *JBQ* 25 (1997): 188–91.

17. Kyle Greenwood, *Scripture and Cosmology: Reading the Bible between the Ancient World and Modern Science* (Downers Grove, IL: IVP Academic, 2015).

the cosmos, a cosmos composed of three tiers: heaven, earth, and seas. For these ancients, the earth was a flat disk, which either floated on the cosmic sea or was supported by foundational pillars. Within the bosom of the earth lay caverns and catacombs, the dark realm of the dead, as well as subterranean rivers, chthonic deities, and demons. Suspended over the earth was a vaulted ceiling supported by pillars, tent poles, or lead ropes. This "firmament" sepa-rated the heavens below from the heavens above, both of which composed the heavenly tier. The lower heavens were occupied by the celestial bodies, while the upper heavens belonged to the divine. Besides separating the lower and upper heavens, windows in the firmament also regulated the flow of rain, hail, and snow from the watery reservoirs above. The waters surrounded the earth, formed oceans, and were the source of springs, rivers, streams, and lakes. These cosmic waters together constituted the seas. Together, the three tiers—heavens, earth, and seas—provided the basic structural model neces-sary for explaining the entire cosmos.

The first creation account in Genesis is bound together by the use of *inclusio*—a type of literary bracketing—namely, the merismatic[18] phrase, "heavens and earth" (Gen. 1:1; 2:4a), used by the author of Gen. 1 as a refer-ence to "the totality of cosmic phenomena."[19] The nature of this early cosmos is expressed by the phrase *tōhû wābōhû*, "formless void," meaning it was "unproductive and empty, uninhabited,"[20] or "nonproductive, nonfunctional, and of no purpose."[21] The earth was incapable of being productive because it was engulfed in the cosmic ocean, the Deep (*təhôm*).[22] In these first verses of Genesis, the vision of the cosmos includes the entirety of an uninhabitable

18. A merism is a literary or rhetorical device used to encompass the entirety of something by pairing the extreme opposites of that entity, like "near and far," or "young and old."

19. Nahum Sarna, *Genesis: The Traditional Hebrew Text with the New JPS Translation* (Philadelphia: JPS, 1989), 5. In light of the obvious merism, Scott B. Noegel ("God of Heaven and Sheol," *Hebrew Studies* 58 [2017]: 119–44) has recently argued that *ereṣ* ("earth") is best understood in Gen. 1:1 as the netherworld, a common connotation of the word in the Semitic world, including in the Hebrew Bible.

20. David T. Tsumura, "Genesis and Ancient Near Eastern Stories of Creation and Flood: An Introduction," in *"I Studied Inscriptions from before the Flood": Ancient Near Eastern, Literary, and Linguistic Approaches to Genesis 1–11*, ed. R. S. Hess and D. T. Tsumura (Winona Lake, IN: Eisenbrauns, 1994), 27–57, here 33.

21. John H. Walton, *Genesis 1 as Ancient Cosmology* (Winona Lake, IN: Eisenbrauns: 2011), 141.

22. On the earlier predominant view that the preordered state represents chaos, see Brevard S. Childs, *Old Testament Theology in a Canonical Context* (London: SCM, 1985), 223–24; Her-mann Gunkel, *Creation and Chaos in the Primeval Era and the Eschaton: A Religio-historical Study of Genesis 1 and Revelation 12*, trans. K. William Whitney Jr. (Grand Rapids: Eerdmans, 2006); Gerhard von Rad, *Genesis: A Commentary*, rev. ed., trans. J. H. Marks, OTL (Philadel-phia: Westminster, 1973), 51.

earth as submerged in a dark abyss, which only God can make hospitable to life and productivity. At this point, the cosmos is merely one tier: sea.

On day 2 of creation, the upper tier—the heavens—was created. God separated "the waters from the waters" (Gen. 1:6) by placing a dome (*rāqîaʿ*) in the heavens. The word *rāqîaʿ* occurs only seventeen times in the Hebrew Bible.[23] At its etymological core, the verbal form of the root *rqʿ* refers to the hammering of metal (e.g., Exod. 39:3; Job 37:18; Jer. 10:9),[24] a notion supported by both the Septuagint (*stereōma* = firmness) and the Vulgate (*firmamentum* = something held strong), which treat the *rāqîaʿ* as a solid structure.[25] Found almost exclusively in so-called Priestly texts,[26] the *rāqîaʿ* forms the rigid ceiling from which the temple lamps (*məʾōrōt*) hang.[27] Luis Stadelmann concludes, "The impression most likely left on the modern mind by a survey of these ancient ideas about the shape of the firmament is that of a solid bowl put over the earth, like a vault or heavenly dome."[28] When God set the *rāqîaʿ* in place, some of the waters were pushed upward, thus separating "the waters from the waters" (Gen. 1:6), presumably creating a bubble of air beneath the canopy of the dome.[29] The firmament is then given the name "heaven" (*šāmayim*).

The third day of creation involved the gathering of the watery deep below the firmament "into one place" to reveal land. The gathering of these waters into one place only makes sense if "one place" stands "in contrast to an implied 'every place' when the waters covered the whole earth."[30] With the taming of these primordial waters, God has consequently created earth. At the conclusion of day 3, then, the cosmic structure is in place: heaven, earth, and seas. This tripartite structure is confirmed when humanity is given charge

23. Gen. 1:6, 7 (3×), 8, 14, 15, 17, 20; Pss. 19:1 (19:2 MT); 150:1; Ezek. 1:22, 23, 25, 26; 10:1; Dan. 12:3.

24. The word is also attested in the Phoenician text *KAI* 38:1 as the substantive *mrqʿ*, referring to an object made of beaten gold. Herbert Donner and Wolfgang Röllig, *KAI* 1 (Wiesbaden: Harrassowitz, 2002), 9.

25. On the interpretation that *rāqîaʿ* refers not to a solid dome but to the expanse of sky, see Randall W. Younker and Richard M. Davidson, "The Myth of the Solid Heavenly Dome: Another Look at the Hebrew רקיע (*rāqîaʿ*)," in *The Genesis Creation Account and Its Reverberations in the Old Testament*, ed. Gerald A. Klingbeil (Berrien Springs, MI: Andrews University Press, 2015), 31–56.

26. Gen. 1:6–8, 14–15, 17, 20; Pss. 19:1 (19:2 MT); 150:1; Ezek. 1:22–23, 25–26; 10:1; Dan. 12:3.

27. Jeffrey L. Cooley, "Psalm 19: A Sabbath Song," *VT* 64 (2014): 177–95, here 185–86.

28. Luis Stadelmann, *The Hebrew Conceptions of the World*, AnBib 39 (Rome: Pontifical Biblical Institute, 1970), 60.

29. See Umberto Cassuto, *A Commentary on the Book of Genesis: From Adam to Noah* (1944; repr., Jerusalem: Magnes, 1961), 31–32.

30. Wenham, *Genesis 1–15*, 20.

over the inhabitants of each cosmically categorized creature: beasts of the
earth; birds of the heaven (*šāmayim*); fish of the sea (Gen. 1:28).

Although different metaphors are employed to communicate this cosmology,[31] the tripartite cosmic structure evident in Gen. 1 is the assumed
cosmology throughout the remainder of the OT. According to the second
commandment, it is forbidden to make an idol that has the form of "anything
that is in *heaven* above, or that is on the *earth* beneath, or that is in the *water*
under the earth" (Exod. 20:4). When Ezra renewed Israel's covenant at the
Water Gate, he prayed, "You are the LORD, you alone; you have made *heaven*,
the heaven of heavens, with all their host, the *earth* and all that is on it, the
seas and all that is in them" (Neh. 9:6). Multiple hymns of creation in the
Psalter either are organized according to the tripartite structure or reference
this cosmic structure as the entirety of God's creation (see sidebar 1.1).[32] In
the book of Proverbs it is the substance that God created with Lady Wisdom.

> The LORD by wisdom founded the *earth*;
>   by understanding he established the *heavens*;
> by his knowledge the *deeps* broke open,
>   and the clouds drop down the dew. (Prov. 3:19–20)

In short, the cosmology of the OT is the cosmology of Gen. 1.

One particular facet of Gen. 1 cosmology that requires some canonical
teasing out is the nature of the cosmic order. What type of cosmos did God
create? The portrait in the opening chapter of the Bible seems to be that of an
orderly world, in which God brings the cosmos and its inhabitants into being
by divine fiat, and all creation is either good or very good. Even in Gen. 2,
where we encounter the first "not good" in God's creation (Gen. 2:18) and
the first hint of evil (Gen. 2:9), we find a garden with exceptional order and
functionality. Elsewhere in the OT, however, there are apparent vestiges of a
perspective in which God's creative act was one of cosmic and predacious
struggle, and the resultant created world is one of strife and conflict.

On day 5 (Gen. 1:21), God created the sea monsters (*tannînim*). There
is nothing distinctive about these creatures. They are merely one of the
various types of animals brought forth from the waters. A survey of the
thirteen additional uses of *tannîn* (singular) in the OT[33] suggests that these

31. For example, in some places, the idea of a solid dome (*rāqîaʿ*) is replaced by tent imagery
(Ps. 104:2; Isa. 40:22). In cognate literature from the ANE, the earth is sometimes depicted as
floating on the cosmic seas rather than as supported by foundation pillars.
32. See, e.g., Pss. 74:12–17; 95:3–5; 104:2–6; 136:5–6.
33. Exod. 7:9, 10, 12; Deut. 32:33; Job 7:12; Pss. 74:13; 91:13; 148:7; Isa. 27:1; 51:9; Jer.
51:34; Ezek. 29:3; 32:2.

Psalm 8

To the leader: according to The Gittith. A Psalm of David.

¹O Lᴏʀᴅ, our Sovereign,
   how majestic is your name in all the earth!

You have set your glory above the heavens.
   ²Out of the mouths of babes and infants
you have founded a bulwark because of your foes,
   to silence the enemy and the avenger.
³When I look at your heavens, the work of your fingers,
   the moon and the stars that you have established;
⁴what are human beings that you are mindful of them,
   mortals that you care for them? ·
⁵Yet you have made them a little lower than God,
   and crowned them with glory and honor.
⁶You have given them dominion over the works of your hands;
   you have put all things under their feet,
⁷all sheep and oxen,
   and also the beasts of the field,
⁸the birds of the air, and the fish of the sea,
   whatever passes along the paths of the seas.

⁹O Lᴏʀᴅ, our Sovereign,
   how majestic is your name in all the earth!

---

creatures are somehow related to mythological sea dragons, often associated with Rahab and Leviathan.[34] In Ps. 104:26 Leviathan was created as a domesticated beast with whom Yahweh would frolic in the sea.[35] In several of these passages conjuring mythological imagery, the *tannînim* are portrayed as cosmic foes of Yahweh. In Job 7:12, Job wonders if he has become one of God's enemies like Sea (*yām*)[36] or the *tannînim*.[37] In Ps. 74:13–14, Yahweh

34. Walter Vogels, "'And God Created the Great *Tanninim*' (Gen. 1:21)," *ScEs* 63 (2011): 349–65, here 349; see also Mary K. Wakeman, *God's Battle with the Monster: A Study in Biblical Imagery* (Leiden: Brill, 1973), 55–82.

35. Brian R. Doak, *Consider Leviathan: Narratives of Nature and Self in Job* (Minneapolis: Fortress, 2014), 163.

36. The Hebrew word *yām* (sea) is anarthrous in Job 7:12, indicating that it is a reference to the personified cosmic waters, rather than a large body of saltwater. In ANE mythology, primordial Sea was a deity who generally served as the epics' antagonist.

37. John E. Hartley, *The Book of Job*, NICOT (Grand Rapids: Eerdmans, 1988), 149.

shatters Sea (*yām*), breaks the heads of the *tannînim*, and crushes the heads of Leviathan, a primordial sea-serpent usually representing the cosmic waters encircling the earth.[38] In Isaiah, the *tannîn* is both Rahab, a cosmic sea creature already defeated by Yahweh (Isa. 51:9–10),[39] and Leviathan, who will ultimately be defeated on the day of the Lord (Isa. 27:1). In Ps. 104, Leviathan has already been tamed. Following Hermann Gunkel, many scholars have viewed these divine battles with *yām* as indicative of primordial combat motifs.[40] By contrast, David Tsumura has argued on etymological and contextual grounds that these conflicts are best understood as destruction-soteriological scenes (rather than creation scenes), whereby Yahweh strikes down chaos in order to bring about salvation.[41] Whether creation or destruction, the contrast with Gen. 1:21 is nonetheless salient. Whereas in Gen. 1 the *tannînim* are one of the various populations of sea creatures, in the rest of the OT these sea creatures stand in direct opposition to Yahweh's purposes.

On the sixth day, "God made the wild animals of the earth of every kind, and the cattle of every kind, and everything that creeps upon the ground of every kind. And God saw that it was good" (Gen. 1:25). Since Gen. 1:25 portrays the origins of all living land creatures as good, one may wonder why alligators have crushing jaws, why grizzly bears have massive claws, and why cougars have fangs. One may wonder: How is this a "good" cosmos? Some interpreters, relying on a particular reading of Rom. 5:12, discount the possibility of predatory animals constituting a good creation. Because death was not introduced until the man and the woman ate from the tree of knowledge, animals were incapable of carnivorous diets. However, this position does not coincide with the biblical testimony itself. First, there is the issue of the taxonomy of Gen. 1:24–25. As Iain Provan has attempted to demonstrate, the word translated as "creeping things" (*remeś*) might best be understood as "prowlers" (e.g., Ps. 104:20), indicating a distinction, not

38. See Christoph Uehlinger, "Leviathan," *DDD*, 511–15.

39. See Klass Spronk, "Rahab," *DDD*, 684–86.

40. Gunkel, *Creation and Chaos*, 12; John Day, *God's Conflict with the Dragon and the Sea: Echoes of a Canaanite Myth in the Old Testament*, UCOP 35 (Cambridge: Cambridge University Press, 1985); Mark S. Smith, *The Priestly Vision of Genesis 1* (Minneapolis: Fortress, 2010); Bernard F. Batto, *In the Beginning: Essays on Creation Motifs in the Ancient Near East and the Bible*, Siphrut 9 (Winona Lake, IN: Eisenbrauns, 2013).

41. David T. Tsumura, *Creation and Destruction: A Reappraisal of the* Chaoskampf *Theory in the Old Testament* (Winona Lake, IN: Eisenbrauns, 2005); Tsumura, "The Creation Motif in Psalm 74:12–14? A Reappraisal of the Theory of the Dragon Myth," *JBL* 134 (2015): 547–55. For a critique of Gunkel's position, see Rebecca S. Watson, *Chaos Uncreated: A Reassessment of the Theme of "Chaos" in the Hebrew Bible*, BZAW 34 (Berlin: de Gruyter, 2005).

between large and small, but between predatory and nonpredatory.[42] Second, the biblical tradition itself does not speak of a good, vegetarian creation but of a good, predacious creation.[43] While Isa. 11:1–9 envisions a future messianic hope in which prey will one day live at peace with predator (see Isa. 65:25), it appeals not to a bygone era to which creation will return but to "the restoration of creation by a new act of God through the vehicle of a righteous ruler."[44] Within a hymn to the Creator, the psalmist rejoices that God provides grass for the cattle, wine for human enjoyment, nests for birds, and prey for lion cubs, who seek "their food from God" (Ps. 104:14–23). Another psalmist praises Yahweh for feeding animals and ravens (Ps. 147:9), omnivorous scavengers who also prey on small animals and insects. In the book of Job, Eliphaz argues that if not for God's sustenance, even the ferocious lion would die and the lioness's cubs would scatter in search of a meal (Job 4:10–11; see also Ps. 58:6). Later in Job, God speaks out of the whirlwind and asks Job why he is unable to hunt for the lions or bring prey to the ravens (Job 38:39–41). Throughout the OT, then, animal predation is not a mark of the fall but the mark of a "good" creation. We observe this "good" creation even today, as predation in the animal kingdom provides balance in the ecosystem. In Job, at least, "God's world is filled with scavengers and predators, even monsters (cf. Gen. 1:21), all coexisting, though never peacefully. The lions eat their prey; the vultures feast on the slain. This world is God's wild kingdom."[45]

Creation and Nature of Humanity

God's creative activity reaches its zenith with the creation of humanity on the sixth day. Here both male and female are said to be created "in the image [ṣelem] of God" (Gen. 1:26–27). Aside from its three occurrences in Gen. 1:26–27, this particular phrase is found elsewhere only in Gen. 9:6 as the impetus for the Noachian covenant.[46] Including three instances in Gen. 1:26–27,

---

42. Iain Provan, *Discovering Genesis: Content, Interpretation, Reception*, Discovering Biblical Texts (Grand Rapids: Eerdmans, 2015), 120–24.

43. Ronald E. Osborn, *Death before the Fall: Biblical Literalism and the Problem of Animal Suffering* (Downers Grove, IL: IVP Academic, 2014).

44. Brevard Childs, *Isaiah*, OTL (Louisville: Westminster John Knox, 2001), 104.

45. William P. Brown, *The Seven Pillars of Creation: The Bible, Science, and the Ecology of Wonder* (Oxford: Oxford University Press, 2010), 129.

46. There also seems to be an allusion to the *imago Dei* concept in Gen. 5:3, where Adam's son Seth was born in Adam's likeness.

the Hebrew word ṣelem appears only seventeen times in the Bible,[47] usually representing an idol fashioned according to the craftsman's image of a god. Here, however, God does not call for the desolation of the image but elevates humanity to the very likeness of its Creator. The prohibitions against making divine images (e.g. Deut. 5:8; Exod. 20:4–6; Ps. 97:7; Isa. 44:9–17) find their theological counterpart in the conviction that God has created his image in humanity. While any attempt to represent God with cast metal or carved wood would merely misrepresent God, Gen. 1:26–27 identifies humanity as God's royal inheritance, representations on earth as benevolent royalty, tending to the welfare of the kingdom (Gen. 1:28).[48]

The creation of humanity is found in two separate iterations, the first of which is the aforementioned "image of God" reference in Gen. 1:26–27. Humankind is there defined as male and female (Gen. 1:27). In this creation account, 'ādām refers to the pool of humanity, composed of members from both genders. However, in Gen. 2 'ādām refers not to the entirety of humanity but to one specific male member of humanity. "Then the LORD God formed man [hā'ādām] from the dust of the ground, and breathed into his nostrils the breath of life; and the man [hā'ādām] became a living being" (Gen. 2:7). In this second instance, 'ādām signifies a single male individual, the progenitor of all humanity, from whom his female companion will soon be fashioned (Gen. 2:21–22).[49] Eventually this lone 'ādām will be given the name Adam (Gen. 2:20b). We see, then, that within the first two chapters of Genesis, Hebrew 'ādām has three distinct meanings: (a) classification—all of humanity; (b) title ("the man")—a specific male member within that pool of humanity; and (c) proper name—Adam.

The point in Genesis at which titular 'ādām becomes the proper name Adam is a complicated issue, due to the ambiguity of the Hebrew language itself.[50] The confusion lies in how Hebrew differentiates between "the man" and Adam. When Hebrew writers wanted to indicate a particular male from among all of humanity, the authors identified him by means of the definite

47. Gen. 1:26–27 (3×); 5:3; 9:6; Num. 33:52; 1 Sam 6:5 (2×), 11; 2 Kings 11:18; 2 Chron. 23:17; Pss. 39:6 (39:7 MT); 73:20; Ezek. 7:20; 16:17; 23:14; Amos 5:26.

48. For a detailed discussion of the divine image, see Catherine L. McDowell, *The Image of God in the Garden of Eden: The Creation of Humankind in Genesis 2:5–3:24 in Light of the* mīs pî pīt pî *and* wpt-r *Rituals of Mesopotamia and Ancient Egypt*, Siphrut 15 (Winona Lake, IN: Eisenbrauns, 2015).

49. Recent studies by John H. Walton and Seth D. Postell argue that Adam was not the first living human but an archetype for all humanity and also a typology for the nation Israel. Walton, *The Lost World of Adam and Eve: Genesis 2–3 and the Human Origins Debate* (Downers Grove, IL: IVP Academic, 2015); Postell, *Adam as Israel: Genesis 1–3 as the Introduction to the Torah and Tanakh* (Eugene, OR: Wipf & Stock, 2011).

50. Richard S. Hess, "Splitting the Adam: The Usage of 'ADAM in Genesis I–V," in *Studies in the Pentateuch*, ed. J. A. Emerton, VTSup 41 (Leiden: Brill, 1990), 1–15.

article.[51] Where it gets confusing, however, certain Hebrew prepositions affix directly to the noun to which they are syntactically connected, with the definite article only apparent in the pronunciation, not in the consonantal spelling. So, *'ādām* may mean "Adam" or "a human." While *lǝ'ādām* can mean "to/for Adam," "to/for a human," or "to/for humanity," *lā'ādām* must denote "to/for the man." This ambiguity is reflected quite clearly among modern commentators and major English translations, where at least seven interpretations have emerged regarding the introduction of Adam in Gen. 2: (1) 2:19;[52] (2) 2:20;[53] (3) 3:17;[54] (4) 3:20;[55] (5) 3:21;[56] (6) 4:1;[57] and (7) 4:25.[58]

Throughout Gen. 2–4, though, the male creation is accompanied by the definite article (*ha-*) twenty-one times, suggesting that *hā'ādām* is not considered the proper name Adam but is one male member among the population of humanity, thus translated as "the man." Nowhere in Gen. 2–3 is *'ādām* unprefixed. It is bound either to the definite article or to the inseparable preposition *lamed* (Gen. 2:20; 3:17, 21). According to the vocalization of the MT, *l'dm* should be read in each instance as *lǝ'ādām* (to Adam), rather than *lā'ādām* (to the man). If the oral tradition is to be followed, then the first occurrence of the proper name Adam occurs at Gen. 2:20b, leading to an inconsistent treatment of *'ādām* within this one verse. At first (Gen. 2:20a) *hā'ādām* is one particular but anonymous male member of the human race, who names all the cattle, birds, and beasts. But for Adam (*lǝ'ādām*), there was not found a helper suitable as his partner (Gen. 2:20b). So Gen. 2:20 treats *'ādām* both as a specific but unnamed male *and* as the man called Adam. If, however, one maintains the consonantal text of the MT, but reads *lā'ādām*, rather than *lǝ'ādām*, then the Hebrew text remains consistent throughout, until finally Adam obtains his name in Gen. 4:25. As Wenham succinctly states, "This fluidity between the definite and indefinite form makes it difficult to know when the personal name 'Adam' is first mentioned."[59]

---

51. There are a few exceptions to this rule (e.g., Gen. 1:27; 6:1), but context generally reveals its proper use.

52. KJV, following Jerome's *Vulgate*.

53. ESV, NASB, NIV; Collins, *Genesis 1–4*, 135–36; Marvin H. Pope, "Adam (אָדָם)," *EncJud* 1:371–72; Sarna, *Genesis*, 22.

54. RSV.

55. NLT; John Ellington, "Man and Adam in Genesis 1–5," *BT* 30 (1979): 201–5.

56. NEB.

57. CEB; Howard N. Wallace, "Adam (Person)," in *ABD* 1:62–64.

58. JB, NRSV, NAB; Julius Boehmer, "Wieviel Menschen sind am letzten Tage des Hexaëmerons geschaffen worden?," *ZAW* 34 (1914): 31–35; Hess, "Splitting the Adam," 4; Ernest Lussier, "'ADAM in Genesis 1,1–4,24," *CBQ* 18 (1956): 137–39; E. A. Speiser, *Genesis: A New Translation with Introduction and Commentary*, AB 1 (New York: Doubleday, 1964), 18.

59. Wenham, *Genesis 1–15*, 32.

For many translators, Gen. 4:25 provides the most compelling case for the appearance of Adam. As Richard Hess argues, "The lack of an article in iv 25, coupled with certain differences in the material that follows in the remainder of the verse and in [chap.] v, suggests that this is not the same title as was used before, but that here for the first time *'dm* is used as a personal name."[60] Other interpreters, on source-critical grounds, posit Gen. 5:1 as the first occurrence of Adam, since Gen. 5 is a P source, while Gen. 2–4 are J sources.[61] According to source critics, it is unlikely that both a J source and a P source would introduce Adam independently. Therefore, not only do they revocalize the Hebrew text at Gen. 2:20; 3:17; and 3:21 to read "to the man," they also prefer to emend the text of Gen. 4:25 to read "the man." A third suggestion is to keep the text as it stands, despite the apparent internal discrepancy. According to this view, the sudden switch in Gen. 2:20 actually works well for the narrative movement, as the scene shifts from the ground (*hā'ădāmâ*) to the man (*hā'ādām*) to Adam (*'ādām*). Just as *'ādām* has come from the dust of the ground, so too will Adam return to the dust of the ground (Gen. 3:17–19).

The ambiguity of Adam's origins is paralleled by the ambiguity of Adam's role in the origin of sin. If Adam is the man in Gen. 2–3 who partakes of the fruit of the tree of the knowledge of good and evil, then Adam was surely complicit in his and the woman's expulsion from the garden. However, as the narrative of the OT unfolds, there is strikingly little to implicate Adam for the misdeeds of his descendants.[62] While the propensity to sin—to seek the desires of self above God or others—is self-evident, the OT seldom, if ever, lays culpability at the feet of Adam.

Outside of Gen. 1–5, the proper name Adam appears at most six times: Deut. 4:32; Josh. 3:16; 1 Chron. 1:1; Job 31:33; Eccles. 7:29; and Hosea 6:7. In 1 Chron. 1:1, Adam is merely listed as the first member of humanity's genealogical roots, thus having no bearing on the issue of humanity's sin. The context of Deut. 4:32 is unclear whether *'ādām* should be rendered Adam or humanity. Most modern English translations prefer the latter, likely having Gen. 1:26–27 in mind. This seems especially likely given that the passage

60. Hess, "Splitting the Adam," 4.
61. Brevard Childs, *Introduction to the Old Testament as Scripture* (Philadelphia: Fortress, 1979), 148; Hermann Gunkel, *Genesis: Translated and Interpreted*, trans. M. E. Biddle, foreword E. W. Nicholson (Macon, GA: Mercer University Press, 1997), 54; Gerhard von Rad does not state unequivocally that the first instance of Adam is at 5:1. However, he does note that the proper noun is not found in Gen. 2–3, but neither does he comment at 4:1 or 4:25 regarding the interpretation of *'ādām. Genesis*, 70.
62. See Claus Westermann, *What Does the Old Testament Say about God?*, ed. Friedemann W. Golka (Atlanta: Westminster John Knox, 1979), 53–64.

refers to people (*'ām*) in Deut. 4:33. Regardless of the rendering, Deut. 4:32 provides no commentary on Adam's guilt.

Two of the four remaining Adam passages are likely references to the toponym Adam, located in the Transjordanian river valley and identified as Tell ed-Dāmiyeh.[63] In Josh. 3:16, Adam is explicitly described as "the city that is beside Zerethan" (i.e., Tell es-Saʿidiyeh),[64] the place where the waters began to heap as the ark-bearing priests entered the Jordan River. Less explicit is the reference to Adam in Hosea 6:7. Collins sees in this text a clear reference to the first man, Adam, whose covenant transgression serves as the paradigm for Israel's covenant failures.[65] One challenge for this interpretation, though, is that the adverb "there" (*šām*), which is found in Hosea 6:7, almost exclusively refers to a place—like Gilead (Hosea 6:8), Shechem (Hosea 6:9), Ephraim (Hosea 6:10), and Judah (Hosea 6:11)—rather than a time.[66] A second challenge is that Adam's disobedience in Gen. 3 is not portrayed as the transgression of a covenant. Covenant language does not make an appearance until Gen. 6:18, the so-called Noachian covenant. It seems unlikely that Hosea's concern is with the transgression of the first man. Rather, his concern is with Israel's failure to keep the covenant.[67] In Hosea 6:7, then, Adam undoubtedly refers to a toponym alongside the other covenant-breaking cities of Israel.

Interpretations vary vastly on whether *'ādām* in Job 31:33 should be rendered as Adam or "a man."[68]

> If I have concealed my transgressions as others [lit., "like *'ādām*"] do,
>   by hiding my iniquity in my bosom . . .

Even if we follow the translations that treat *'ādām* as the first man Adam (ASV, KJV, NASB, NJPS), Job 31:33 does not suggest an Adamic sin gene. While it may point to Adam as one who transgressed, it certainly does not ascribe to his transgression the root of all human transgression. Rather, with most modern translations (ESV, JPS, NET, NIV, NLT, NRSV, RSV), Job 31:33

63. Mark J. Fretz, "Adam (Place)," *ABD* 1:64.
64. Jonathan N. Tubb, "Saʿidiyeh, Tell es-," *OEANE* 4:452–55.
65. C. John Collins, "Adam and Eve in the Old Testament," in *Adam, the Fall, and Original Sin: Theological, Biblical, and Scientific Perspectives*, ed. Hans Madueme and Michael Reeves (Grand Rapids: Baker Academic, 2014), 3–32, here 26.
66. For possible temporal uses of *šām*, see *HALOT* 2:1547.
67. A third interpretation of *'ādām* in Hosea 6:7 has been suggested by Douglas Stuart, who reads it as "dirt" (from *'ādāmâ*, "ground"). According to Stuart, "By treating the covenant 'like dirt,' the nation has betrayed Yahweh himself." *Hosea–Jonah*, WBC 31 (Waco: Word, 1987), 111.
68. For a summary of interpretations, see David J. A. Clines, *Job 21–37*, WBC 18A (Nashville: Nelson, 2006), 971, 1029–30.

states that even though humans possess the proclivity to hide iniquity, Job
would openly declare his missteps to the Almighty.

Following Yehudah Kiel, Collins argues that Eccles. 7:29 alludes to Adam's
disobedience in Gen. 3.

> See, this alone I found, that God made *man* [*ha-'ādām*, humankind]
>   upright
> but *they* [*hémmâ*] have sought out many schemes.[69]

Collins sees in this passage a "likely echo of Genesis-3-read-as-a-fall-story."[70]
Matthew Seufert concurs with this view, arguing that Eccles. 7:29 and the
adjoining verses evoke the sin of Adam and Eve in Gen. 3.[71] They contend that
upright *'ādām* reflects the prefallen Adam, while the "many schemes" allude
to his disobedience in the garden of Eden. This view seems to be punctuated
by the fact that *'ādām* is definite, suggesting a particular member of humanity
whom God made upright. However, Choon-Leong Seow has rightly noted that
when the author of Ecclesiastes has a particular individual in mind, he uses the
Hebrew word *'îš*. By contrast, *'ādām* signifies one or any human.[72] Moreover,
Eccles. 7:29b employs the plural pronoun "they" (*hémmâ*), indicating that
hā'ādām in verse 29a is the human population, not an individual. Despite these
matters, whether Eccles. 7:29 alludes to Gen. 1–3 is of little consequence to
the question of Adam's role in original sin. There is nothing inherent in the
text that indicts Adam for the guilt of all humanity. Humans were created
straight (*yšr*), but humans ("they") sought the crooked (cf. Eccles. 7:13).

While the penchant for sin is universal (e.g., Prov. 20:9; Isa. 53:6), the OT is
reticent to place that blame on a single individual. Rather, the authors of the
Hebrew Bible were intent on placing blame squarely on the shoulders of the
individual or community complicit in the iniquity. A certain proverb circulated
among the people of ancient Israel that sought to place blame elsewhere:

> The parents have eaten sour grapes,
>   and the children's teeth are set on edge. (Ezek. 18:2)

Between the second (597 BCE) and third (586 BCE) deportations to Babylon, the Judahites continued to turn a deaf ear to the prophetic warnings of

---

69. Collins, "Adam and Eve," 25.
70. Collins, "Adam and Eve," 25.
71. Matthew Seufert, "The Presence of Genesis in Ecclesiastes," *WTJ* 78 (2016): 75–92, here 91.
72. Choon-Leong Seow, *Ecclesiastes: A New Translation with Introduction and Commentary*,
AB 18C (New York, Doubleday, 1997), 274.

God's impending judgment. Rather than assume blame for that judgment, they assigned blame to their ancestors. Unconvinced, Ezekiel corrected their self-righteous theology: "When the righteous turn away from their righteousness and commit iniquity, they shall die for it" (Ezek. 18:26). A variant of the same proverb is also cited by Jeremiah with a message that is consistent with Ezekiel: "But all shall die for their own sins; the teeth of everyone who eats sour grapes shall be set on edge" (Jer. 31:30). The OT prophets showed little patience for those who cast culpability of sin on anyone other than themselves.

Garden of Eden

The garden of Eden makes its first appearance in Gen. 2 as an oasis created by the Lord God that would eventually flow with streams and teem with life. After forming *'ādām* from the dust, God breathed life into him and placed him in Eden (v. 7). Eden was located "in the east" (v. 8), was filled with "every tree that is pleasant to the sight and good for food" (v. 9), and was the source of four major rivers (vv. 10–14). Most prominent among these trees were the tree of life and the tree of the knowledge of good and evil. Not wishing for *'ādām* to be alone, the Lord God formed out of the ground "every animal of the field and every bird of the air" (vv. 18–19), which the man then named (v. 20). Finally, God took a portion of the man's side and created his companion, woman (vv. 21–22).

At first blush, Eden may evoke images of a botanical and zoological paradise. In fact, a few biblical authors emphasized this aspect of Eden (Gen. 13:10; Ezek. 31:9). While several of the prophets drew on the analogy of its lush state to strike a contrast between Eden and desolate wilderness (Isa. 51:3; Ezek. 36:35; Joel 2:3), it seems evident that the author of Gen. 2 was intentionally drawing our attention to its function as the holy of holies in the divine cosmic sanctuary (Isa. 66:1).[73] Lifsa Schachter succinctly summarizes the apparent allusions to the tabernacle and temple in Gen. 2–3.[74] First, the sanctuary was designated as the locus of God's presence with his people (Exod. 25:8; Deut. 12:5). In Eden God communicated directly with humanity (Gen.

---

73. See Peter T. Lanfer, *Remembering Eden: The Reception History of Genesis 3:22–24* (Oxford: Oxford University Press, 2012), 127–57.

74. See Lifsa Schachter, "The Garden of Eden as God's First Sanctuary," *JBQ* 41 (2013): 73–77; see also Elizabeth Bloch-Smith, "'Who Is the King of Glory?': Solomon's Temple and Its Symbolism," in *Scripture and Other Artifacts: Essays on the Bible and Archaeology in Honor of Philip J. King*, ed. Michael D. Coogan, J. Cheryl Exum, and Lawrence E. Stager (Louisville: Westminster John Knox, 1994), 18–31; Lawrence E. Stager, "Jerusalem and the Garden of Eden," *ErIsr* 26 (1999): 183–94.

2:16–17; 3:9–19) and walked among them (3:8). Second, God's movement in Eden (*mithallēk*, Gen. 3:8) corresponded to his movement in the tabernacle (*hithallēk*, Lev. 26:12; *mithallēk*, Deut. 23:14 [23:15 MT]; *mithallēk*, 2 Sam. 7:6; *hithallēk*, 2 Sam. 7:7). Third, Eden had an easterly orientation, a typical feature of ANE temples (Gen. 2:8; 3:24; Exod. 26:22–27; Num. 3:38; Ezek. 47:1).[75] Moreover, Eden is depicted as being on a mountaintop—the typical location of temples—as indicated by the downward flow of the four rivers from their singular Edenic source (cf. Ezek. 47:1–12). The tradition of Eden's mountaintop location is also preserved in Ezek. 28:14. Fourth, each of the ninety occurrences of cherubim outside of Gen. 3:24 (and metaphorically in Ezek. 28:14–16) appear in sanctuary contexts as guardians of the sacred tree (1 Kings 6:29–35; Ezek. 41:18–25) or bearers of Yahweh's throne (Exod. 25:18–22; Ezek. 10:20).[76] Fifth, *'ādām*'s job in Eden is "to work [*'ābad*] it and keep [*šāmar*] it" (Gen. 2:15 ESV). These are the same verbs used to describe the priestly duties of the Levites (Num. 3:7–8). Sixth, in the same way that Eden was purged from the transgression of the human pair, so was the sanctuary to be purged from the transgressions of the people (Lev. 16:16). Finally, Schachter notes the vast references to garden imagery in descriptions of the temple. Even the seven-branched menorah with its floral imagery (Exod. 25:31–40) is suggestive of the tree of life (Gen. 2:9).[77] Given the title of the present chapter, one could easily get the impression that Gen. 2 provided the design for the tabernacle and temple. However, the general consensus among Bible scholars is that the direction of influence should be understood the other way. Rather than the tabernacle/temple finding its impetus in the garden, the author of Gen. 2 draws on temple architecture from Israel and the ANE intentionally to demonstrate Eden's status as sacred space.[78]

Reverberations of Eden are not extensive in the OT, but it has by no means been forgotten. Besides isolated references to a geographical place name (2 Kings 19:12; cf. Isa. 37:12; Ezek. 27:23) and a personal name (2 Chron. 31:15), Eden represents a primordial garden, known both as "the garden of God" (*gan 'ĕlohîm*, Ezek. 28:13; 31:8–9) and "the garden of the LORD" (*gan yhwh*, Gen. 13:10; Isa. 51:3). The most fully articulated echo of the Edenic tradition is preserved by the exilic prophet Ezekiel, first in an oracle

75. Although Exod. 26:22 does not explicitly state an easterly orientation of the tabernacle, one may infer from the text that the open end is facing east since the rear portion is situated to the west.

76. See Tryggve N. D. Mettinger, "Cherubim," *DDD*, 189–92.

77. See also Carol L. Meyers, *The Tabernacle Menorah: A Synthetic Study of a Symbol from the Biblical Cult* (Missoula, MT: Scholars Press, 1976).

78. See Gordon J. Wenham, "Sanctuary Symbolism in the Garden of Eden Story," in Hess and Tsumura, *"I Studied Inscriptions from Before the Flood,"* 399–404.

against the King of Tyre (Ezek. 28), then in an allegory concerning Pharaoh (Ezek. 31).

In the case of the former, the King of Tyre serves as a type of Edenic *'ādām*. Tyre's king claimed to be a god (Ezek. 28:2, 9), who was once "the signet of perfection, full of wisdom and perfect in beauty" (v. 12; see sidebar 1.2). He dwelled in Eden, "the holy mountain of God" (vv. 13–14). He was even created blameless, until the Lord found iniquity in him (v. 15). So, the Lord expelled the king from Eden with cherubim (v. 16). Somewhat ironically, the King of Tyre is depicted in terms consistent with a cult statue, garnered in precious metals and stones and guarded by a cherub. While Collins is careful not to label Ezek. 28 an alternate version of Gen. 2–3, he argues that the rhetorical effect of the prophet's message is meaningful only in light of the fall of Adam in Gen. 3.[79] Likewise, Tryggve Mettinger sees an Eden "myth" underlying both the Genesis and Ezekiel accounts.[80] Although it is difficult to argue dependence of Ezek. 28 on Gen. 3, it does not follow that Ezekiel demands an original Adamic sin to account for the king's downfall. Instead, by placing the King of Tyre in Eden, the prophet is likely suggesting that just as Adam rebelled, so too does every human who proclaims themselves to be "god." Such an attitude is tantamount to rebellion against God, incurring divine judgment, condemnation, and dismissal from the garden sanctuary.

Resuming his derision of Egypt, the prophet draws on the fall of Assyria as a warning against Pharaoh—even the greatest empires meet their inevitable demise when they think too highly of themselves. Assyria's stature was once like that of a cosmic tree whose crown reaches the heavens, whose roots extend into the subterranean waters, and whose boughs provide shelter and shade for all the inhabitants of the world.[81] This tree is unrivaled among the loftiest trees in Eden, a reference to Assyria's allies. As a metaphor for mighty Assyria, this haughty cedar would be cast down to Sheol along with its allies, who have already been buried, figuratively speaking. Fritz Stolz attempted to demonstrate that a prebiblical Edenic myth underlies the various strands of Edenic imagery throughout the biblical corpus. In the original Eden Myth, a primal man attempted to overthrow the god of Lebanon, the garden of the gods, and was subsequently condemned to Sheol for his failed coup d'état.[82] Despite Stolz's assiduous argument, it is unnecessary and ultimately amounts

79. Collins, "Adam and Eve," 24–25.

80. Tryggve N. D. Mettinger, *The Eden Narrative: A Literary and Religio-historical Study of Genesis 2–3* (Winona Lake, IN: Eisenbrauns, 2007), 85–98.

81. For more on the mytho-cosmic nature of this tree, see Walther Eichrodt, *Ezekiel: A Commentary*, OTL (Philadelphia: Westminster, 1970), 425–26.

82. Fritz Stolz, "Die Bäume des Gottesgartens auf dem Libanon," *ZAW* 84 (1972): 141–56.

SIDEBAR 1.2

Ezekiel 28:11–19

[11]Moreover the word of the Lord came to me: [12]Mortal, raise a lamentation over the king of Tyre, and say to him, Thus says the Lord God:

> You were the signet of perfection,
>> full of wisdom and perfect in beauty.
> [13]You were in Eden, the garden of God;
>> every precious stone was your covering,
> carnelian, chrysolite, and moonstone,
>> beryl, onyx, and jasper,
> sapphire, turquoise, and emerald;
>> and worked in gold were your settings and your engravings.
> On the day that you were created
>> they were prepared.
> [14]With an anointed cherub as guardian I placed you;
>> you were on the holy mountain of God;
>> you walked among the stones of fire.
> [15]You were blameless in your ways
>> from the day that you were created,
>> until iniquity was found in you.
> [16]In the abundance of your trade
>> you were filled with violence, and you sinned;
> so I cast you as a profane thing from the mountain of God,
>> and the guardian cherub drove you out from among the stones of fire.
> [17]Your heart was proud because of your beauty;
>> you corrupted your wisdom for the sake of your splendor.
> I cast you to the ground;
>> I exposed you before kings,
>> to feast their eyes on you.
> [18]By the multitude of your iniquities,
>> in the unrighteousness of your trade,
>> you profaned your sanctuaries.
> So I brought out fire from within you;
>> it consumed you,
> and I turned you to ashes on the earth
>> in the sight of all who saw you.
> [19]All who know you among the peoples
>> are appalled at you;
> you have come to a dreadful end
>> and shall be no more forever.

to speculation. Although the descent of Eden's trees to Sheol appears odd in light of Gen. 2–3, one must bear in mind that the prophet is pressing his analogy to extremes to underscore the downfall of Egypt. Once Ezekiel connects Assyria's allies to the trees of Eden, he has little choice but to carry the analogy to its logical conclusion, even if it leads to some confusing characterizations of Eden.

Conclusion

Although themes of Gen. 1–2 permeate the entire OT canon, biblical authors were not compelled to articulate the themes in a consistent manner. We have seen that despite the numerous allusions to the creation narrative of Gen. 1 in the OT, they do not share the same concern for the order or time frame of Gen. 1. While the character Adam plays prominently in Gen. 2 (through Gen. 5), he is all but missing in the rest of the OT. In fact, his counterpart Eve is never to be heard from again (after Gen. 4:1). However, while OT reverberations need not coincide with the opening chapters of the canon, it does not follow that there are no such corresponding echoes. The cosmic structure so eloquently detailed in Gen. 1 runs throughout the OT. Traces of Eden as God's garden, protected by cherubim and home to a cosmic tree, can be identified in more than a few passages. While at times it appears that the biblical authors consciously engaged the ideas and themes of Gen. 1 and 2, at other times they seem either to be unaware of these traditions or to have found other interpretations more in line with their rhetorical efforts.

For Further Reading

Brown, William P., and S. Dean McBride Jr., eds. *God Who Creates: Essays in Honor of W. Sibley Towner*. Grand Rapids: Eerdmans, 2000.

Clifford, Richard J., and John J. Collins, eds. *Creation in the Biblical Traditions*. CBQMS 24. Washington, DC: Catholic Biblical Association of America, 1992.

Greenwood, Kyle. *Scripture and Cosmology: Reading the Bible between the Ancient World and Modern Science*. Downers Grove, IL: IVP Academic, 2015.

Klingbeil, Gerald A., ed. *The Genesis Account and Its Reverberations in the Old Testament*. Berrien Springs, MI: Andrews University Press, 2015.

Lanfer, Peter T. *Remembering Eden: The Reception History of Genesis 3:22–24*. Oxford: Oxford University Press, 2012.

Mettinger, Tryggve N. D. *The Eden Narrative: A Literary and Religio-historical Study of Genesis 2–3*. Winona Lake, IN: Eisenbrauns, 2007.

Stordalen, Terje. *Echoes of Eden: Genesis 2–3 and Symbolism of the Eden Garden in Biblical Hebrew Literature*. Contributions to Biblical Exegesis and Theology 25. Leuven: Peeters, 2000.

Primary Texts

Job 38–39	Psalm 104	Ezekiel 28; 31
Psalm 8	Proverbs 8	Ezekiel 47
Psalm 19	Isaiah 65	

Primary Texts Online

1. Online searchable Bible with over 150 versions
   www.biblegateway.com
2. YouVersion Bible with English and foreign language versions (also available as an app)
   https://www.bible.com/bible/12/GEN.1.ASV

2

Interpretations of Genesis 1–2
in Second Temple Jewish Literature

Michael D. Matlock

Out of the overall pool of Second Temple Jewish interpreters, four larger groups emerged: the Septuagintal (LXX) interpreters, the authors of the works found in the Apocrypha and Pseudepigrapha, the sectarian Qumran (DSS) writers, and the Hellenistic Jewish interpretive texts by named individuals— the most prominent writers being Philo of Alexandria and Flavius Josephus. Within the interpretive spectrum there is great variance in how these many interpreters present their relationship to the biblical text they interpret. At one pole are writings from named individuals such as Philo and Josephus, which present manifest points of view at some historical, linguistic, and perspectival distance from the biblical texts. The opposite pole consists of translations, retellings, and even commentaries that efface the authors from clear view.

A primary source of information concerning the composition of the original LXX is the Jewish Letter of Aristeas written in the second century BCE. This epistle indicates that the Hebrew text of the Pentateuch was translated into Greek in the third century BCE by seventy-two men in Alexandria (Let. Arist. 32, 39, 46). The early date of some papyri of the Pentateuch makes this date

plausible.[1] Concerning the Greek translations of the remainder of the books
of the Hebrew Bible, Ben Sira's grandson was conscious of the books of the
Prophets and part of the Hagiographa in 132 or 116 BCE. Thus, this trajectory
points to a probable *terminus ad quem* for Greek translations of virtually all
of the books of the Hebrew Bible at around the end of the second century
or early first century BCE. A variety of translators with differing gifts and
backgrounds who worked in diverse places over several centuries translated
the nonpentateuchal books.[2] Accordingly, the Greek translations of the books
of the Hebrew Bible do not contain a unifying translation work as the term
Septuagint might suggest. Nevertheless, the LXX translations contain some
of the earliest witnesses to the history of biblical interpretation and have
the potential to improve our understanding of how the Hebrew Bible was
utilized at the time the books were translated into Greek. The books of the
LXX "reflect more *significant* variants than all other translations combined."[3]
The translators were concerned with conveying their contemporary religious,
social, and political understandings, traditions, and sensibilities within the
linguistic context of Hellenistic Greek. Thus the LXX books offer potential
access to the exegetical principles, theological trends, and sociopolitical concerns of strands of Judaism in the Hellenistic period.[4]

Both corpora of the so-called Apocrypha and Pseudepigrapha contribute
to a fuller, more diverse picture of Judaism between 200 BCE and 100 CE.
There is no qualitative difference between the books in the Apocrypha and
Pseudepigrapha at least regarding genre and dates of writing. Therefore, the
boundary between the two corpora is often unstable. Having no significance for
Judaism, the only distinction between the two corpora is the canonical status
ascribed to the Apocrypha by the Catholic and Orthodox Christian churches.
These religious communities refer to these books as deuterocanonical. The
writings located in the Apocrypha and Pseudepigrapha of the OT share in
common their treatment of persons, events, and topics derived from the Hebrew Bible. Generally these writings are either Jewish or Jewish-Christian and
bear testimony to the continued conversations with the God of Israel during
political, social, and religious upheaval.

1. Emanuel Tov, "The Septuagint," in *Mikra: Text, Translation, Reading and Interpretation of the Hebrew Bible in Ancient Judaism and Early Christianity*, ed. Martin Mulder and Harry Sysling (Peabody, MA: Hendrickson, 2004), 162.
2. Chaim Rabin, "The Translation Process and the Character of the Septuagint," *Textus* 6 (1968): 14.
3. Emanuel Tov, *The Text-Critical Use of the Septuagint in Biblical Research*, JBS 8 (Jerusalem: Simor, 1997), 204.
4. Karen H. Jobes and Moisés Silva, *Invitation to the Septuagint*, 2nd ed. (Grand Rapids: Baker Academic, 2015), 93–94.

The communities whose members deposited the scrolls in the Qumran caves were formed between about 140 BCE and 67 CE.[5] The Qumran sectarian texts were most likely written by and for rigid Essene members of Judaism in the late Second Temple period.[6] Over one hundred similarities connect what Josephus reports about the Essenes and the ideas, customs, and rules mentioned in the scrolls composed at Qumran. Beyond the sectarian texts, the Qumran covenanters possessed authoritative copies of virtually all the books of the Hebrew Bible as well as literature known and utilized by earlier Jewish groups (e.g., Jubilees, 1 Enoch). Although these scrolls are written in Aramaic, Greek, and Hebrew, the sectarian texts were all written in Hebrew. Two predominant features of the Qumran sectarian writings are their Torah and priestly foci—namely, priestly roles are preeminent and their lineage is Zadokite (i.e., the priestly line that overtook the high-priestly office during the postexilic times and remained in office until the early second century BCE). Moreover, the covenanters viewed atonement as symbolic because the priests who practiced at the Jerusalem temple were abhorred, and the covenanters maintained a strong focus on ritual bathing. These sectarian texts also describe the current and eschatological struggle between the Teacher of Righteousness and the sons of light against the Wicked Priest and the sons of darkness.

From another interpretive group, the two most prolific Jewish-Hellenistic writers in the first century CE were Philo Judaeus (ca. 15 BCE–45 CE) and Josephus Flavius (ca. 37–100 CE). An Alexandrian Jew, Philo wrote for the benefit of Jewish and Hellenistic readers.[7] For Philo, the LXX was authoritative; thus he tangentially employed insights from the Hebrew text. Of Philo's forty-eight surviving treatises, as many as thirty-nine of them explicate the biblical text, which equates to the Pentateuch for him. Philo's major achievement was the synthesis of philosophical insight, chiefly Middle Platonic philosophy, with the Jewish scriptural heritage.

Josephus, a military leader in Palestine during the Jewish revolt against Rome (66–70 CE), surrendered to the Romans and became a court historian and apologist, authoring *The Jewish War*. He also wrote *The Life of Josephus*, *Antiquities of the Jews*, and *Against Apion*—the latter two are defenses of Jewish culture written for a Greco-Roman readership. The *Antiquities* (93–94

5. Shemaryahu Talmon, "The Community of the Renewed Covenant: Between Judaism and Christianity," in *The Community of the Renewed Covenant: The Notre Dame Symposium on the Dead Sea Scrolls*, ed. Eugene Ulrich and James VanderKam, Christianity and Judaism in Antiquity 10 (Notre Dame, IN: University of Notre Dame Press, 1994), 3.
6. Talmon, "Community of the Renewed Covenant, " 3–4.
7. Peder Borgen, "Philo of Alexandria," in *Jewish Writings of the Second Temple Period: Apocrypha, Pseudepigrapha, Qumran Sectarian Writings, Philo, Josephus*, ed. Michael Stone (Philadelphia: Fortress, 1984), 233.

CE) also present a worthy and lofty Stoicized Jewish conception of God, free of mythology and idolatry. Josephus argues for the estimable nature of Jewish traditions and commends Jewish morality and the reasonableness of the Jewish conception of God.[8] His theology can be observed through his reinterpretation of traditional religious formulations in a historiographical medium.[9] Both Josephus's *Antiquities* and most of Philo's works present a justification for Judaism within Greco-Roman culture, which seeks to gain respect and esteem for the Jewish legacy.[10]

Within the space of this chapter, it is not feasible to indicate all interpretive nuances concerning Gen. 1–2 from these four groups of Second Temple Jewish interpreters. Thus I have selected representative and unique interpretive features from each of the four groups. My description of these interpretations will focus on the following topics: treatment of days, cosmology, Adam and Eve, the garden of Eden, and a few selected peculiarities from each group. From the ancient interpretations of Gen. 1–2, readers will discover the interpretive strategies employed by the exegetes during the Second Temple period and the milieu influencing these strategies.

Treatment of Days

In the LXX we discover a very interesting difference from the Hebrew text concerning the seventh-day description of creation in Gen. 2:2. The translators noted an ambiguity of the Creator God either working a little bit on the seventh day and then stopping or not working on the seventh day at all—tension created by the wording "on the seventh day God concluded his work" (my translation). This ambiguity is exegetically handled by substituting the wording that "on the sixth day God ended his work" in the LXX. The translator viewed the upholding of the Sabbath as vitally important, so much so that the reader of this translated text must clearly understand that God finished working on the sixth day, not at any time on the seventh day.

From the diverse works in the Apocrypha and Pseudepigrapha, we will accentuate features from Jubilees, 4 Ezra, and 2 Baruch. Jubilees (2nd c. BCE) is one of the earliest pseudepigraphical works, and much of the editorial activity regarding Gen. 1:1–Exod. 12:50 is a response to second-century (BCE)

8. Harold W. Attridge, "Josephus and His Works," in Stone, *Jewish Writings of the Second Temple Period*, 217–19.

9. Harold W. Attridge, *The Interpretation of Biblical History in the Antiquitates Judaicae of Flavius Josephus*, HDR 7 (Missoula, MT: Scholars Press, 1976), 181.

10. Mark Harding, "Josephus and Philo," in *Prayer from Alexander to Constantine: A Critical Anthology*, ed. Mark Kiley (New York: Routledge, 1997), 89.

SIDEBAR 2.1

Jubilees 2.2

For on the first day he created the heavens, which are above, and the earth, and the waters and all of the spirits which minister before him:

> the angels of the presence, and the angels of sanctification, and the angels of the spirit of fire, and the angels of the spirit of the winds, and the angels of the spirit of the clouds and darkness and snow and hail and frost, and the angels of resoundings and thunder and lightning, and the angels of the spirits of cold and heat and winter and springtime and harvest and summer, and all of the spirits of his creatures which are in heaven and on earth.

Note: O. S. Wintermute's translation in James Charlesworth, ed., *The Old Testament Pseudepigrapha*, vol. 2, *Expansions of the "Old Testament"* (New York: Doubleday, 1985).

---

external and internal threats to Judaism. This "rewritten" work contains significant differences from the Hebrew text of Gen. 1–2. As part of a growing treatment of angelology in the Second Temple Jewish literature, Jubilees indicates that all types of angels were created on day 1 of creation: angels of presence (standing before God), sanctification, spirits of fire, winds, clouds, darkness, snow, hail and frost, sounds, thunder, lightning, cold, heat, winter, springtime, harvest, and summer (Jub. 2.2). Two other works in the Pseudepigrapha (4 Ezra and 2 Baruch) contend that on the fifth day of creation, God created two legendary creatures, Leviathan and Behemoth (4 Ezra 6.49–52; 2 Bar. 29.3–4). These creatures will be discussed more fully in the next section.

Culling interpretations from the sectarian Dead Sea Scrolls (DSS) is challenging because little exists in the way of a running commentary on Gen. 1–2, and too often manuscripts that could provide assistance are disappointingly fragmentary. Although 4Q252 and 4Q253 provide commentary on sections in Genesis, there exists no extant commentary on the first two chapters. Nevertheless, by culling through DSS texts that briefly mention elements of creation, I can call attention to elements of creation selected for discussion in this volume.

From several of the twenty DSS calendrical texts (4Q320–30, 4Q335–37, 6Q17), we discover that Qumran's covenant community followed a solar year containing 364 days (fifty-two weeks) which was subdivided into four quarters of three months (thirteen weeks or ninety-one days each). Moreover, the community also stressed the importance of priestly watches from twenty-four priestly families who served cultic temple duty on a one-week rotation every half-year (see 1 Chron. 24:1–19).[11] And 4Q319 I, 11 indicates that the priestly watches can be traced back to the very beginning of the world, on the fourth day of creation (i.e., when God established the luminaries for marking seasons, days, and years).

Moreover, 4Q320 frag. 2 I, 2–7 seems to echo details from the fourth day of creation in Gen. 1:14–19, the foundational reference text for all calendrical texts among the DSS. These Qumran texts declare that God created the luminaries to divide the day from the night and placed them "for signs and for festivals and for years and for days." As a result, the luminaries began to pour out their light, which permits the measurement of time, days, years, and Jubilees. The moon, not the sun, seems to be the luminary that shines "from evening until morning" and is "the head of all the years."[12] The text of 4Q321 gives additional evidence of the importance of the moon by denoting one year of lunar observation dates followed by a six-year listing of lunar event dates and feast days.[13] The start of each month lined up with the week and priest cycle.

As with the book of Jubilees, several Qumran texts indicate that angels were present at the beginning of the creation days. Thus, in the Hymn to the Creator (11Q5 XXVI), angels are said to have witnessed the separating of light from deep darkness. These angels were also singing aloud because the Creator God showed them what they had previously not known. This same text from Qumran also declares that God created the world with Wisdom, as does Philo. From the War Scroll (1QM IX, 15–16), one observes the names of the principal angels: Michael, Gabriel, Sariel, and Raphael. Also, 11Q13 II, 8–13 declares that Melchizedek is the ruler of the lot of light and carries out the vengeance of God's judgments.

Philo focuses on God's order in creation and the length of time as a symbolic feature of the creation story (*Creat.* 13–14). Working within the parameters of Platonic dualism (e.g., world-soul), Philo's interpretation of creation contains both a set of days when an ideal incorporeal creation was made and then a set of days when God made the corporeal creation. God freely decreed the creation of the cosmos first in a purely intellectual manner and second through the agency of his Logos, which is a sum total of God's thoughts and then a hypostatization of these thoughts. Philo comments that it took God six days to complete creation because six is the first perfect number, indicating completion. Taking his cue from ancient Greek mathematicians, Philo

11. It is difficult to reconcile how the twenty-four weeks can account for a half year if the year contains fifty-two weeks.

12. Florentino García Martínez, "Creation in the Dead Sea Scrolls," in *The Creation of Heaven and Earth: Re-interpretations of Genesis 1 in the Context of Judaism, Ancient Philosophy, Christianity, and Modern Physics*, ed. Geurt Hendrik van Kooten, TBN (Leiden: Brill, 2005), 60–61.

13. For the moon phases, see 4Q317.

SIDEBAR 2.2

Philo, *On the Creation of the World* 13–14

[13]And he says that the world was made in six days, not because the Creator stood in need of a length of time (for it is natural that God should do everything at once, not merely by uttering a command, but by even thinking of it); but because the things created required arrangement; and number is akin to arrangement; and, of all numbers, six is, by the laws of nature, the most productive: for of all the numbers, from the unit upwards, it is the first perfect one, being made equal to its parts, and being made complete by them; the number three being half of it, and the number two a third of it, and the unit a sixth of it, and, so to say, it is formed so as to be both male and female, and is made up of the power of both natures; for in existing things the odd number is the male, and the even number is the female; accordingly, of odd numbers the first is the number three, and of even numbers the first is two, and the two numbers multiplied together make six. [14]It was fitting, therefore, that the world, being the most perfect of created things, should be made according to the perfect number, namely, six: and, as it was to have in it the causes of both, which arise from combination, that it should be formed according to a mixed number, the first combination of odd and even numbers, since it was to embrace the character both of the male who sows the seed, and of the female who receives it.

Note: C. D. Yonge, *The Works of Philo: Complete and Unabridged* (Peabody, MA: Hendrickson, 1993).

---

reasons that six is perfect because 1, 2, and 3 are the proper positive divisors of 6, and $1 + 2 + 3 = 6$. Within Pythagorean number symbolization, six is above all associated with the coupling of male and female functions.

Also, each day signifies some deeper meaning; thus, for example, day 1 contains prime importance because God created heaven the first day. Corresponding to Plato, Philo regards heaven as the purest, most excellent thing that was made. Concerning day 4, Philo remarks that four is significant because of its relation to the harmonious concords in music and is the number that first displays the nature of a solid cube (*Creat.* 48–49). Finding additional significance in the number six, Philo deduces that the motions of organic animals equals six—forward, backward, upward, downward, to the right, and to the left (*Alleg. Interp.* 1.4). Thus the complete number for a mortal is six, but the complete number for an immortal being is seven. God, therefore, on day 7 began the formation of more divine beings. In Philonic philosophy, God never ceases from making something because the property of God is to be creating at all times. Indeed, the dynamic infinitude of God allows God to be able to do everything and never cease from acting; God is the first cause of any action, the intellect of the universe on which all other beings depend for their existence.[14] Therefore Philo does not broach the topic of keeping the Sabbath in this portion of his writings. Regarding the phrase "God blessed and sanctified," Philo interprets it as God honored the seventh day as the birthday of the entire cosmos.

Of final note, Philo comments that to consider that the earth was created in six literal days (i.e., twenty-four-hour periods) would be a sure indication of great simplicity (*Alleg. Interp.* 1.2). Indeed, he goes on to argue that the world was not created in time because time equates to the space of days and nights. Thus all of creation was an instantaneous process, and time gained its existence as a consequence of the creation of the world.

Josephus's *Jewish Antiquities* contains his version of a rewritten Hebrew Bible in which he resolves apparent obscurities, contradictions, and theological questions, as well as the historicity of biblical events in order to make the Jewish people, their Scriptures, and their history more palatable to the Greek-speaking world. In *Jewish Antiquities* book 1, chapter 1, Josephus reinterprets the creation accounts of Gen. 1–2. Concerning his treatment of the days, Josephus indicates no concern with the length of days. He follows Philo in noting that the first day should be viewed as Moses so understood it as "one day." Unlike Philo, who argues that "one" is needed in order to indicate the uniqueness of the intelligible world (*Creat.* 35), Josephus defers to give his rationale in another work, which is not currently extant.

Finally, regarding the seventh day, Josephus, like Philo, argues that God never fully ceases from making something because the property of God is to be creating at all times. He states that God "ceased and took a rest from his activities," implying that the Creator had taken a respite but would later resume his work (*Ant.* 1.33). The Hebrew text states that God rested from all work without indication or implying that he would later recommence his activities.

Cosmology

The Septuagint denotes an incomplete character of the earth after the summary statement in Gen. 1:1.[15] Calling the earth "unformed" corresponds to the Hebrew text, but calling the earth "invisible" or "unseen" does not (Gen. 1:2). The Greek term used, *aoratos*, is the same term employed by Plato to designate the invisible preexisting world of ideas (e.g., *Tim.* 51a). Thus this Greek word

14. Roberto Radice, "Philo's Theology and Theory of Creation," in *The Cambridge Companion to Philo*, ed. Adam Kamesar (New York: Cambridge University Press, 2009), 130.

15. Susan Brayford, *Genesis*, Septuagint Commentary Series (Leiden: Brill, 2007), 207.

lends support to the Platonic philosophical cosmology of the translators to join Plato and Moses, as was common in Hellenistic Jewish writers.[16]

As we turn our focus to the works of the Apocrypha and Pseudepigrapha, we will survey the texts of 4 Ezra and 2 Baruch. Technically the date of both works, around 100 CE, falls just slightly beyond the Second Temple period. Nevertheless, it is worth noting elements of these two Jewish interpretations of Gen. 1–2 because the elementary theological beliefs in Leviathan and Behemoth stem from earlier years in the Second Temple period and the First Temple period (1 En. 60.24; Isa. 27:1; Job 3:8; 40:15; Ps. 74:14). Significant for our purposes is that both 4 Ezra and 2 Baruch denote how these mythological creatures materialize on the fifth day of creation, as mentioned above. In addition, the authors emphasize that these large semidivine monsters of chaos are indeed created by God. God separates the two creatures by placing Behemoth on land and leaving Leviathan in the water. Eventually the creatures will become the main entrée on the menu of the Messiah's banquet in the eschaton (2 Bar. 29.4).

Among the Dead Sea Scrolls, the text God the Creator (4Q392 frag. 1) considers a few of the details of the first day of creation. Concerning the creation of light and darkness, the author believes that God created these elements for himself, not simply as a foundational piece of the remaining portions of creation. The text asserts that light and darkness coexist simultaneously with God, "a paradox beyond human comprehension."[17] Because human beings would need light and darkness differentiated, the Creator uses the heavenly bodies to accomplish this necessity.

As for Philo, his view of an intelligible cosmos derives from his Middle Platonic and Stoic philosophies, worlds of thought often alien to the modern reader. The earth and heavens are the senses and mind being created during this period (*Alleg. Interp.* 1.19). In this schema, thinking, wisdom, and the mind are central to the incorporeal items; body takes a lower place and thus a lower value. Philo considers the earth first created in the mind of God as perfect, much like an architect would plan a building or a city. After God perfects the idea, the earth is created.

In Philonic thought, the physical world consists of eight concentric circles around the earth.[18] Directly above the earth is the sphere with the moon;

---

16. Ronald Hendel, *The Book of Genesis: A Biography*, Lives of Great Religious Books (Princeton: Princeton University Press, 2013), 89–90; Hendel, *The Text of Genesis 1–11: Textual Studies and Critical Edition* (New York: Oxford University Press, 1998), 19.

17. Michael Wise, Martin Abegg, and Edward Cook, *The Dead Sea Scrolls: A New Translation* (San Francisco: HarperSanFrancisco, 1996), 356.

18. R. K. McIver, "'Cosmology' as a Key to the Thought-World of Philo of Alexandria," *AUSS* 26 (1988): 271.

the air between the earth and moon contains souls and angels. In the outer-most sphere away from the earth, stars are located. Within the remain-ing six spheres between the outer- and innermost spheres, Saturn, Jupiter, Mars, Sun, Mercury, and Venus are positioned (*Cherubim* 21–22). As may be expected, these concentric circles are allegorical representations of the seven-branched candelabra, with the central position filled by the sun (*Heir* 221, 224). Thus, from an unchangeable perfect God extend heavenly bodies and beings—God, the Logos, creative and royal powers, stars, planets, sun, moon, angels, and finally humans. This is an often-overlooked element of Philo's cosmology.[19]

Josephus, like Philo (*Creat.* 29), follows the LXX's rendering of *tōhû wābōhû*, "formless and void" (Gen. 1:2), as *aoratos kai akataskeuastos*, "un-seen and unformed" (*Ant.* 1.27). The concept of God not having brought the earth into sight perhaps impinges on the notion of an incorporeal creation before the corporeal creation existed. Regarding the concept of God sweeping or brooding over the waters in Gen. 1:2, Josephus tries to alter the meaning by leaving out God as subject and stating "a breath from above sped rapidly over it." By removing the notion of brooding, Josephus seemingly attempts to avoid the Greek Orphic account of creation.[20] In this ancient creation myth, the cosmic egg comes into existence from void or fluid chaos.

Also, for the obscurity of the phrase, "Let there be a dome in the midst of the waters, and let it separate the waters from the waters" (Gen. 1:6), Josephus explains that what God did was to set the heavens above the universe and to congeal ice about it (*Ant.* 1.30). He thus explains the origin of rain, which in the biblical account is left unexplained, and endeavors to prevent the charge of obscurity regarding creation made by some Romans (e.g., Juvenal, *Sat.* 14.102).[21] Filling in another gap in the text (Gen. 1:9), namely, that the earth existed before the creation, Josephus comments that God established the earth on the third day and poured the sea around it (*Ant.* 1.31).

Creation and Nature of Humanity

In the second account of creation in Gen. 2, the LXX seems to shift focus into the material aspect of the ideal forms that God has made in the first account. This movement arises from a Platonic reading and translation of

19. McIver, "'Cosmology' as a Key," 272.
20. Louis Feldman, *Flavius Josephus: Translation and Commentary*, vol. 3, *Judean Antiqui-ties 1–4* (Leiden: Brill, 2000), 10.
21. Feldman, *Flavius Josephus*, 11.

Gen. 1–2.[22] The LXX text keeps in step by referring to the human placed in the garden by using a generic term (*anthrōpos*) in Gen. 2:15. However, the LXX translator takes a more interpretive route in Gen. 2:16 by not using the generic term for human but rather using the human's proper name, "Adam," and continues to do so in most of the remaining account. In contrast, the Hebrew text incorporates the generic word for humanity throughout the first three chapters of Genesis.[23] Of final note, in reference to God's making of Eve, the LXX translator uses a verb (*ōkodomēsen*) that can be translated as "to build" and is most often used when referring to altars and also to refer to building cities and the Tower of Babel. Therefore we might conclude that Eve's creation consists of great sophistication and sacredness.[24]

Regarding the works in the Apocrypha and Pseudepigrapha, we first examine one of the oldest (early second-century BCE) and longest books in the Apocrypha, Ben Sira. According to this Wisdom literature, the divine gift of wisdom for humans separates them from the rest of the creation (Sir. 17:6–17). Wisdom takes the specific form of Mosaic Torah, and thus the giving of the Torah to humanity constitutes the high-water mark of human creation. Moreover, Ben Sira comments that God has given humanity an eternal covenant, which allows humans to overcome their fragility and acquire immortality.[25] Tobit, another early book in the Apocrypha, anchors the concept of marriage within the Gen. 2 creation account and stresses that a man should not marry because of lust for a woman (Tob. 8:4–9).

As noted above, Jubilees contains significant differences from the Hebrew text of Gen. 1–2. Because God's work ends on the sixth day of the first account of creation, the second account of the creation of man, animals, and woman is merged with the first into one chronologically continuous account in Jubilees. Moreover, let us consider these other alterations: God grants dominion to Adam only (Jub. 2.14); Adam recognizes his loneliness when he observes the paired animals (3.3); Eve is created outside the garden (3.5–9); and Adam and Eve have sexual intercourse before setting foot into the garden of Eden because it is considered holy or a temple prototype (3.6).[26] Several items are

---

22. See Martin Rösel, *Übersetzung als Vollendung der Auslegung: Studien zur Genesis-Septuaginta* (Berlin: de Gruyter, 1994), 30.

23. Genesis 4:25 contains the first unmistakable use of the male human's proper name in the Hebrew text; even in Gen. 2:20, the MT reads anarthrous Adam.

24. Brayford, *Genesis*, 233.

25. Ari Mermelstein, *Creation, Covenant, and the Beginnings of Judaism: Reconceiving Historical Time in the Second Temple Period*, JSJSup 168 (Leiden: Brill, 2014), 26.

26. Kristen E. Kvam, Linda S. Schearing, and Valarie H. Ziegler, eds., *Eve and Adam: Jewish, Christian, and Muslim Readings on Genesis and Gender* (Bloomington, IN: Indiana University Press, 1999), 51.

curiously left out of the first creation account in Jubilees but included in later portions of the book. For example, the creation of humanity in the image of God is excluded in the details of Jub. 2. However, when discussing Gen. 9:6, the author does note that God has made humans in the image of God (Jub. 6.8). Thus the author does believe in the conception of the *imago Dei* but selects another place in Genesis to comment on it.

In another work in the Pseudepigrapha, the Sibylline Oracles,[27] the male human in the second account of creation is described as "youthful, beautiful, and wonderful" (Sib. Or. 1.23–24). This depiction of the man is influenced by a Hellenistic depiction of the male species that reveals the Jewish-Hellenistic character of this oracle. In Greek culture, if a man was gorgeous in appearance, he was a good person. As regards the creation of woman, she is needed because Adam is lonely and yearns for conversation (Sib. Or. 1.27). She is described as "a wonderful maidenly spouse," and the two of them enjoy conversation "with wise words which flowed spontaneously" (1.29–30, 33–34). God creates Eve to be an equal partner with Adam. Interestingly, the couple is created asexual and enjoys a Platonic relationship. They only experience sexual intercourse as a result of the divine curse that arises from eating from the tree of the knowledge of good and evil.

Within the pseudepigraphical work of 2 Enoch, the author offers many details regarding humanity on the sixth day of creation. First, a man is created with seven components: flesh from earth, blood from dew and the sun, eyes from the bottomless sea, bones from stone, reason from the mobility of angels and clouds, veins and hair from the grass of the earth, and his spirit from divine spirit and the wind (2 En. 30.10). To the seven components of man, God adds functionality by providing hearing to the flesh, sight to the eyes, smell to the spirit, touch to the veins, taste to the blood, endurance to the bones, and sweetness to reason (30.11). The woman is also created on the sixth day and before she enters the garden of Eden; Eve is not created as a result of Adam's loneliness, nor is she indicated as his helper or someone "like him," as is stated in the Hebrew text of Gen. 2. Finally, sexual intercourse is introduced when Eve has sex with Satan, who entered the garden of Eden as a demon (31.5–6).

As noted above, only a small amount of material exists encompassing interpretations and rereadings of, allusions to, or echoes from Gen. 2 among the Qumran literature. Even among the twenty copies of the book of Genesis found at Qumran, the residue of the Eden narrative is extremely scarce. As

27. The first two books in the Sibylline Oracles are Jewish with Christian redactions and date to about the turn of the era.

SIDEBAR 2.3

4QMiscellaneous Rules, 4Q265 frag. 7 II, 11–17

[11]In the fir[st] week [Adam was created . . . be-] [12]fore he was brought into the garden of Eden. [Blank] And bone [from his bones . . .] [13]was for her before she was brought to his side [in the second week . . .] [14][for] holy is the garden of Eden. And every shoot which is in its middle, is holy. Therefo[re *Leviticus 12:2–5* a woman who conceives and bears a male child] [15]shall be impure for seven days; as in the days of her menstrual impurity, she shall be impure. And th[irty-three days she shall remain in the blood of] [16]her purification. [Blank] But if she gives birth to a baby girl, she shall be impure [for two weeks, as in her menstruation, and sixty-six days] [17][she shall rem]ain in the blood of her purification. [No] holy thing [shall she touch . . .]

Note: Florentino García Martínez and E. J. C. Tigchelaar's translation in *The Dead Sea Scrolls*, Study Edition, vol. 1, *1Q1–4Q273* (Leiden: Brill, 1997).

---

for the Qumran sectarian or quasi-sectarian texts, the Damascus Document (CD) offers an interesting interpretation regarding Adam and Eve. Thus CD IV, 21 asserts that God made one male and one female for one another on the sixth day of creation because this is a "principle of creation." In other words, this DSS text is defending monogamy as a part of the inherent principle offered when God created them one male and one female (Gen. 1:27). God has created humankind sexed, which provides the rationale that a man cannot take two wives simultaneously; neither can he have two marriages at any time in his lifetime due to divorce or death of his wife.[28] Also, we observe from 4Q265 frag. 7 II, 11–17, as was the case in Jubilees, that both Adam and Eve were created outside of the garden of Eden.

Philo deems the first account of the creation of man as a heavenly creation that did not touch or interact with anything on the earth. This heavenly man is perfect and made in the image of God, in terms of the mind and reason (*Alleg. Interp.* 1.31); this human is asexual, and thus there are not separate sexes.[29]

28. Florentino García Martínez, "Man and Woman: Halakhah Based upon Eden in the Dead Sea Scrolls," in *Paradise Interpreted: Representations of Biblical Paradise in Judaism and Christianity*, ed. Gerard P. Luttikhuizen, Themes in Biblical Narrative: Jewish and Christian Traditions (Leiden: Brill, 1999), 109.

29. Some scholars (e.g., Jacob Jervell, *Imago Dei: Genesis 1, 26f. im Spätjudentum, in der Gnosis und in den paulinischen Briefen*, FRLANT [Göttingen: Vandenhoeck & Ruprecht, 1960], 64) have argued that Philo believes the perfect heavenly human is androgynous. I think this is less likely since Philo believes in a sharp contrast between rationality and passions or senses. See Richard A. Baer, *Philo's Use of the Categories Male and Female*, ALGHJ 3 (Leiden: Brill, 1970), 33–34.

Philo's verb to describe the mind in the body, *agalmatophoreō*, connotes a god in a sacred shrine (*Creat.* 69).[30] The second creation account delineates how God makes an earthly man who births all subsequent humans. The earthly man bears his image from the heavenly man who has been made in the image of God. The female human is brought forth from the sexed earthly man, not the heavenly human who is asexual. Therefore the male-female polarity is part of the mortal, corruptible world of body and senses.

Philo indicates his belief that man is made of two elements, the rational soul and the body/irrational soul (*Alleg. Interp.* 3.161). To argue this same type of distinction, but by using slightly different terms, Philo states that a human being has two parts, animal and man (*Worse* 82–84). The former part contains vital power (i.e., senses and passions) that causes us to exist with blood containing the essence of the power. The latter part consists of rational power that causes a rational being; the spirit or breath contains the essence of this power.

Finally, Philo offers some of the most derogatory comments for Eve arising out of this period. Eve arises only from the second corporeal creation and is thus two steps removed from the immortal image of God found in Gen. 1. According to Philo, woman initiates the trouble for man, which consists of mortality. The source of mortality is sexual desire that has arisen from the woman (*Creat.* 151–52).

Regarding Josephus, he omits commentary for Gen. 2:4–6 and begins commenting after the seventh day that Moses is simply giving the particulars of the Creator's formation of man in Gen. 2 (*Ant.* 1.34). Perhaps this omission is circumstantial evidence that Josephus was mindful of the dual accounts of creation in Gen. 1 and 2 but wanted to rewrite the two creation accounts in a more seamless single account. After he describes the origin of man as coming from red soil, Josephus alters the biblical text by having God, not Adam, name the animals. Nevertheless, in his account Josephus still includes that God brings the animals before Adam with the caveat that both male and female species of each animal appear before him (*Ant.* 1.35). This latter detail begs the question, Why does Josephus add that Adam viewed both sexes of each animal? Louis Feldman, an eminent scholar of Josephus, surmises that God was seeking to arouse in Adam the instinct for a female mate.[31]

---

30. David T. Runia, *Philo of Alexandria: On the Creation of the Cosmos according to Moses; Introduction, Translation and Commentary*, PACS 1 (Leiden: Brill, 2001), 227. Runia supports this idea by stating than "an excellent parallel is found at Cicero, *Rep.* 1.59: 'For the person who knows himself will recognize first that he has a divine element in himself and will regard his mind in himself as a kind of consecrated divine image (*simulacrum*).'"

31. Feldman, *Flavius Josephus*, 14.

As for the *imago Dei*, Josephus omits the phrase "Let us make humankind in our image" (Gen. 1:26) and other references to this topic elsewhere. For Josephus, God cannot be described, and images should be strictly avoided. He also leaves out of his account that God "breathed into his nostrils the breath of life" (Gen. 2:7) because Josephus greatly restricts anthropomorphic language in his interpretation of the biblical text. Thus, after the man was formed from dirt, God injected into him spirit and soul. An additional interesting feature from Josephus is that Eve is created almost immediately after Adam, in contrast to the biblical account, in order to link more closely Adam's failure to find a mate from the animals. Furthermore, Eve is created before the Creator forms the garden of Eden so that both Adam and Eve enter the garden together, not separately.

Garden of Eden

As noted under the Adam and Eve section above, the LXX seeks to show the material aspects in the second creation account; in doing so, the LXX tends to reconcile the second creation account with the first one. By using the word "again" (*eti*) in Gen. 2:9, the LXX indicates that the earth had already produced trees as indicated in chapter 1. The garden is translated as a *paradeisos*, from which we receive our English word "paradise." This Greek term is a Persian loanword and refers to a closed area such as a park, garden, or orchard. Finally, we note that the LXX translator updates the names of the latter two rivers that flow out from Eden by giving them the names Tigris and Euphrates.[32]

The works in the Apocrypha and Pseudepigrapha, Jubilees, the Sibylline Oracles, and 2 Enoch, incorporate noteworthy details regarding the garden of Eden. In Jubilees, the author emphasizes the Jewish Torah and calendar as well as the virtues of Israel's ancestors to counter unwanted Hellenistic influence. The garden of Eden is understood as holy ground or a prototype of the temple and the place where the Lev. 12 purity legislation is enacted. Jubilees declares that Adam's entrance into the garden is delayed forty days and Eve's entrance eighty days (Jub. 3.9–12). The rationale for Eve's additional delay of forty days may be because of purification regulations found in the case law of Lev. 12:1–5.

---

32. Theo van der Louw, *Transformations in the Septuagint: Towards an Interaction of Septuagint Studies and Translation Studies*, CBET 47 (Leuven: Peeters, 2007), 121–24. The Hebrew word *ḥiddeqel* was identified as Tigris by the Greek translator on geographical grounds, close to Assyria but distinct from the Euphrates. Since Herodotus, the name Tigris had been familiar for Greek readers.

In the Sibylline Oracles, the beautiful man is placed in an "ambrosial garden," and the words of Gen. 2:15 "to till it and keep it" are interpreted as "that he might be concerned with beautiful works." The text also indicates the garden as a "luxuriant plantation" (Sib. Or. 1.25–26). In 2 Enoch, the garden is created along with the trees and grass and enclosed on the third day of creation (30.1).

As for the Dead Sea Scrolls, one observes in 4Q265 frag. 7 II, 11–17 that the garden of Eden is sacred or holy as well as a place where the Lev. 12 purity legislation is binding (similar to the account in Jubilees). Thus the writer offers an explanation of the period of purification after birth as a result of the elapsed time between creation and Adam and Eve's move into the garden of Eden. The garden is the holy of holies, "for holy is the garden of Eden, and every shoot which is in its middle is holy" (4Q265 frag. 7 II, 14). Purity must be attained before entrance is gained.

Concerning the garden of Eden, Philo says, "I rather conceive that Moses was speaking in an allegorical spirit, intending by his paradise to intimate the dominant character of the soul, which is full of innumerable opinions as this figurative paradise was of trees" (Creat. 154). He imagines that because no tree

---

SIDEBAR 2.4

Jubilees 3.8–12

[8]In the first week Adam was created and also the rib, his wife. And in the second week he showed her to him. And therefore the commandment was given to observe seven days for a male, but for a female twice seven days in their impurity. [9]And after forty days were completed for Adam in the land where he was created, we brought him into the garden of Eden so that he might work it and guard it. And on the eighth day his wife was also brought in. And after this she entered the garden of Eden. [10]And therefore the command was written in the heavenly tablets for one who bears, "If she bears a male, she shall remain seven days in her impurity like the first seven days. And thirty-three days she shall remain in the blood of her purity. And she shall not touch anything holy. And she shall not enter the sanctuary until she has completed these days which are in accord with (the rule for) a male (child). [11]And that which is in accord with (the rule for) a female is two weeks—like the two first weeks—in her impurity. And sixty-six days she shall remain in the blood of her purity. And their total will be eighty days. [12]And when she finished those eighty days, we brought her into the garden of Eden because it is more holy than any land. And every tree which is planted in it is holy.

Note: Wintermute's translation in Charlesworth, *Old Testament Pseudepigrapha*, vol. 2.

of life or tree of knowledge have ever been found, Moses was speaking about the fruit of virtues or characteristics of good moral being. Thus the tree of life produces the fruit of piety, and the tree of knowledge the fruit of prudence, wisdom, and self-discipline. Philo does not directly comment on the divine prohibition against eating from the tree of knowledge. He concludes that the earthly man and woman are removed from the garden of Eden because God could already see that they were inclined toward vice or evil.

Josephus adopts many Greek notions in his presentation of the garden of Eden. For example, the Greek notion (attributed to Homer) of the spherical shape of the earth, with an outer stream flowing around the earth (called Okeanos) versus the inner seas, is adopted in his description of the river that flows out of Eden to water the garden (*Ant.* 1.38).[33] Following Herodotus and other Greek writers, he links the notion that India consists of the land of gold when he denotes that the first river, the Pishon, runs into India and is known to Greeks as the Ganges River.[34] Moreover, again like Herodotus, he seeks to identify exotic foreign place names with places familiar to the Greek people when he denotes that the River Gihon is the Nile.

Josephus also borrows from the Hesiod and Stoic visions of a golden age in describing and developing the idea of the original bliss of humankind in the garden of Eden (*Ant.* 1.46). His concept has no parallel in the Scriptures. Adam originally delighted to be in God's company and associating with him. The golden age is marked by the lack of evil, distress, and toil; the absence of cares about which to fret; the presence of all things working together for enjoyment with pleasure abounding; and the gift of humans living long lives. When Adam retreats from God after his sin, Moses has signaled the end of the golden age.

Interpretive Peculiarities

The major unusual features of the Septuagint have been noted in the previous sections. Thus, let us mention a couple of other peculiarities from a work in the Pseudepigrapha, 2 Enoch (late first-century CE). In 2 En. 24–36, the author describes precreation activities as well as eight days of creation. In chapters 24–27, God reveals to Enoch and Gabriel how God made the existent out of the nonexistent and the visible out of the nonvisible. The Creator God calls

33. Around 330 BCE, Aristotle provided empirical evidence for the spherical shape of the earth. He theorized that all bodies are made up of five elements: earth, water, air, fire, and aether. These elements naturally move up or down, fire being the lightest and earth the heaviest.

34. Louis Feldman, *Studies in Josephus' Rewritten Bible*, JSJSup 58 (Leiden: Brill, 1998), 1–2.

two beings out of the invisible things. From the primordial aeon or agent Adoil, the great light is born, and from the aeonic demiurgic Arukhas, darkness is produced. Water is created by solidifying a mixture of light and darkness. Interestingly, these elements take shape before the first week of creation has even begun, according to the author of 2 Enoch.

Beyond these atypical features prior to creation in 2 Enoch, I will mention a couple of unusual features of the days of creation (2 En. 28.1–33.2). On the first day, God creates the seas and the earth. On the second day, the Creator makes fire and angels, and the fall of Satan occurs. At this point, let us take note that much of present-day thinking about angels developed in many late Second Temple Jewish texts rather than directly from the biblical texts.

The garden of Eden is created on the third day. On the fourth day, seven planets and the zodiac are created. Adam and Eve are created, then fall from their original state and are expelled, all on the sixth day. Finally, the author includes an eighth day to provide a symbol of the beginning of a new era.[35]

Adding to the several remarkable features noted above, from one of the Qumran texts, Paraphrase of Genesis and Exodus (4Q422 1), more importance is attached to God's spirit being "holy" in the act of creation than does Gen. 1:2.[36] Moreover, the author of this text may be placing the word of God as God's mediator in the act of creation (see John 1:1, 3). We cannot be dogmatic on this point because the Hebrew word for "word" is in a reconstructed place in the scroll.

Another unfamiliar feature of Philo's understanding of creation pertains not only to his adoption of Platonic ideas but also to his modification of these ideas as well. The Logos consists of the shadow of God that was employed as a pattern and instrument of all creation (*Alleg. Interp.* 3.96). Moses anticipated Plato by instructing that before the world came into being, water, darkness, and chaos existed (*Creat.* 22). Being at the height of philosophical thought, Moses came to recognize the active and passive fundamental principles of being.[37] The intellect of the universe is the active cause, and the inanimate and motionless power of things is the passive cause (*Creat.* 8–9).

Philo continues in this philosophical line of thought by drawing an analogy between the creation of man in the image of God and the visible world in the

---

35. J. van Ruiten, "The Creation of Man and Woman in Early Jewish Literature," in *The Creation of Man and Woman: Interpretations of the Biblical Narratives in Jewish and Christian Traditions*, ed. Gerard Luttikhuizen, TBN 3 (Leiden: Brill, 2000), 55–56.

36. Torleif Elgvin, "The Genesis Section of 4Q422 (4QParaGenExod)," *DSD* 1, no. 2 (1994): 186.

37. Marian Hillar, *From Logos to Trinity: The Evolution of Religious Beliefs from Pythagoras to Tertullian* (New York: Cambridge University Press, 2011), 51–52.

image of its archetype in the mind of God (*Creat*. 25). Thus the Creator God is ceaselessly ordering matter by his thought. Because the ideas themselves were always in the mind of God, there has never been a time when God did not create. On this latter point, Philo offers a pivotal modification to the Platonic doctrine of the forms, namely, that the Creator God himself "eternally creates the intelligible world of ideas as his thoughts."[38]

Of final comment, Josephus adds to the biblical narrative that in the earliest period all the animals spoke a common language (*Ant*. 1.41). Such a detail, to be sure, is found in Jubilees (3.28) and in a few places in rabbinic literature. Interestingly, Philo attributes the notion of a common language of animals to mythologists. Also, by omitting the phrase "Let us make humankind in our image" (Gen. 1:26), as noted above, Josephus avoids a difficulty in the use of the plural and can simply report that God formed man.[39] On the other hand, Philo infers a plurality of creators (*Creat*. 72).

Conclusion

These Second Temple Jewish interpretations of Gen. 1–2 offer quite a diversity of thought in how one should comprehend the creation accounts. Apart from the sectarian writings in the Dead Sea Scrolls, Hellenization has played an essential ingredient in the mixture of thought in these Jewish writings. These authors adopted Hellenistic ideas and employed them in varying degrees to shape their understanding of the creation accounts. We mentioned how ideas from Greek philosophical schools such as Platonism and Stoicism and how Moses anticipated some of these Greek concepts, which have shaped Jewish interpretation from this period. The Septuagint initiates the notion of a two-tiered creation of incorporeal and corporeal elements, which is later developed by Philo and Josephus. The Sibylline Oracles interpret Adam through the common Hellenistic depiction of the male species, namely, beautiful in appearance.

On the other hand, the DSS texts examined in this chapter indicate concern for how the creation accounts relate to the priestly interests of the Qumran community, upholding monogamous relationships between a man and woman, and the creation and role of angels for the covenanters. The Qumran

---

38. Hillar, *From Logos to Trinity*, 53.

39. See Jacob Jervell, "Imagines und *Imago Dei*: Aus der Genesis-Exegese des Josephus," in *Josephus-Studien: Untersuchungen zu Josephus, dem antiken Judentum und dem Neuen Testament*, ed. Otto Betz, Klaus Haacker, and Martin Hengel (Göttingen: Vandenhoeck & Ruprecht, 1974), 197–204.

community viewed their understanding of the calendar as supremely important for the cultic functions of the priest. They offered an interpretation of
the fourth day of creation that linked their calendar to the creation and the
supreme importance of the function of the moon, created on this day. Also,
Qumran texts reveal an understanding that light and darkness were created
for God's own enjoyment; the separation of the two elements was only necessary because humans needed the two differentiated. When it comes to the
garden of Eden, DSS texts disclose it as the holy of holies (as does Jubilees).

Among the works in the Pseudepigrapha, the author of Jubilees offers
many unique interpretations of the creation accounts such as a highly developed understanding of angels and a merger of the two accounts into one
continuous account. As for Philo, his allegorizing of the biblical text leads
him to value the symbolic nature of the creation accounts. He scorns any
consideration of understanding creation in six literal days. Finally, Josephus
seeks to merge the two accounts into one more seamless account, as did the
writer of Jubilees, and his understanding of the garden of Eden corresponds
to the Greek notion of a golden age.

For Further Reading

Baer, Richard A. *Philo's Use of the Categories Male and Female.* ALGHJ 3. Leiden:
    Brill, 1970.

Kooten, Geurt Hendrik van, ed. *The Creation of Heaven and Earth: Re-interpretations
    of Genesis 1 in the Context of Judaism, Ancient Philosophy, Christianity, and
    Modern Physics.* TBN 8. Leiden: Brill, 2005.

Luttikhuizen, Gerard, ed. *The Creation of Man and Woman: Interpretations of the
    Biblical Narratives in Jewish and Christian Traditions.* TBN 3. Leiden: Brill, 2000.

Mermelstein, Ari. *Creation, Covenant, and the Beginnings of Judaism: Reconceiving
    Historical Time in the Second Temple Period.* JSJSup 168. Leiden: Brill, 2014.

Primary Texts in Print

Charlesworth, James, ed. *The Old Testament Pseudepigrapha.* Vol. 1, *Apocalyptic
    Literature and Testaments.* Garden City, NY: Doubleday, 1983.

————, ed. *The Old Testament Pseudepigrapha.* Vol. 2, *Expansions of the "Old Tes-
    tament" and Legends, Wisdom and Philosophical Literature, Prayers, Psalms and
    Odes, Fragments of Lost Judeo-Hellenistic Works.* New York: Doubleday, 1985.

Feldman, Louis. *Flavius Josephus: Translation and Commentary.* Vol. 3, *Judean An-
    tiquities: Books 1–4.* Leiden: Brill, 2000.

García Martínez, Florentino, and E. J. C. Tigchelaar. *The Dead Sea Scrolls*, Study Edition. Vol. 1, *1Q1–4Q273*. Leiden: Brill, 1997.

———. *The Dead Sea Scrolls*, Study Edition. Vol. 2, *4Q274–11Q31*. Leiden: Brill, 1998.

Muddiman, John, ed. *The Apocrypha*. Oxford Bible Commentary. Oxford: Oxford University Press, 2012.

Runia, David T. *Philo of Alexandria: On the Creation of the Cosmos according to Moses; Introduction, Translation and Commentary*. PACS 1. Leiden: Brill, 2001.

Vermès, Géza. *The Complete Dead Sea Scrolls in English*. Penguin Classics. London: Penguin, 2011.

Whiston, William, trans. *The Works of Josephus: Complete and Unabridged*. Peabody, MA: Hendrickson, 1987.

Wright, Benjamin G., and Albert Pietersma, eds. *A New English Translation of the Septuagint*. New York: Oxford University Press, 2007.

Yonge, C. D., trans. *The Works of Philo: Complete and Unabridged*. New updated edition. Peabody, MA: Hendrickson, 1993.

Primary Texts Online

1. Noncanonical Literature Documents to Aid Students and Scholars in Biblical Interpretation
   http://wesley.nnu.edu/sermons-essays-books/noncanonical-literature/
2. Early Jewish Writings
   http://www.earlyjewishwritings.com
3. Dead Sea Scrolls in English
   http://www.bibliotecapleyades.net/scrolls_deadsea/deadseascrolls_english/contents.htm
4. Online Critical Pseudepigrapha
   http://ocp.tyndale.ca
5. Josephus on Genesis
   https://sites.google.com/site/aquinasstudybible/home/genesis/josephus-on-genesis

3

New Testament Appropriations of Genesis 1–2

IRA BRENT DRIGGERS

The New Testament is a collection of twenty-seven ancient Christian documents composed by various authors throughout the Roman Empire.[1] All twenty-seven documents were written in Greek, which by the first century had become the common language of business and trade for most of the Mediterranean world. As *Christian* documents, they share a belief that Jesus of Nazareth was sent by God to be the Savior of the world, that he was crucified by Roman authorities, that he was raised from the dead soon after his death, and that he currently reigns as "Lord" of creation.

The NT consists of various kinds of documents:

1. The four Gospels (deriving from the Greek term for "good news") are narratives of Jesus's public ministry, each with an extended account of his arrest, trial, crucifixion, and resurrection appearances. The Gospels are attributed to early Christian leaders: Matthew, Mark, Luke, and

---

1. On NT content and background, see Mark Allan Powell, *Introducing the New Testament: A Historical, Literary, and Theological Survey*, 2nd ed. (Grand Rapids: Baker Academic, 2018).

John. The first three of these are known as the Synoptic Gospels because they share much content in contrast to John. Most mainstream scholars believe that Matthew and Luke used Mark as a core source and also shared a source of Jesus's sayings, now lost to history.[2]

2. The Acts of the Apostles narrates important events in the early years of the Christian movement, emphasizing its spread from Jerusalem to various cities across the Roman Empire. Acts was written by the same author as the Gospel of Luke.

3. Most of the remaining NT documents are epistles, or letters, written from Christian leaders (such as the apostle Paul) to either Christian communities or other Christian leaders within the Roman Empire. The traditional titles of these documents draw from either the alleged author or the intended audience: Romans, 1–2 Corinthians, Galatians, Ephesians, Philippians, Colossians, 1–2 Thessalonians, 1–2 Timothy, Titus, Philemon, Hebrews, James, 1–2 Peter, 1–3 John, and Jude.

4. The final NT document is Revelation. Also called the Apocalypse, it contains numerous symbolic visions intended to persuade persecuted Christians of God's sovereignty over history. It is attributed to a certain "John," who was probably different from the author of the Gospel and epistles of that name.

It bears mentioning that modern biblical scholarship has long questioned the traditional explanation of authorship for most of the NT documents. In other words, many of the documents may be either pseudonymous (e.g., certain Pauline letters) or identified with an oversimplified authorship tradition (e.g., John). While the present writer accepts many of these scholarly conclusions, this essay uses the traditional author names to avoid unnecessary tangents. The one exception will be the discussion of certain pseudonymous Pauline letters, which were likely written by Paul's associates.[3]

Date(s) and Circumstances

The NT documents date from around the middle of the first century CE to the first quarter of the second century CE. It is impossible, however, to address

2. Scholars refer to this sayings source as "Q," from the German *Quelle* ("source"). For an influential counterview, see Mark Goodacre, *The Case Against Q: Studies in Markan Priority and the Synoptic Problem* (Harrisburg, PA: Trinity Press International, 2002).
3. The standard arguments are well summarized by Patrick Gray, *Opening Paul's Letters: A Reader's Guide to Genre and Interpretation* (Grand Rapids: Baker Academic, 2012), 139–52.

here the distinctive historical circumstances that prompted the writing of each document. It will suffice to say that they were written to various kinds of Christian audiences. Thus none of the NT writers were attempting to convert people to Christianity, since conversion was already assumed. Rather, the writers were trying to shape Christians in their beliefs and actions and to edify Christian communities in various ways.

This is not to suggest, however, that the NT writers agree about everything. Beyond the commonalities already mentioned, one finds a spectrum of views on, for instance, the person of Jesus, the nature of the Christian life, and even the future of creation. These differences may stem from the distinctive perspective of each writer, the distinctive circumstances of each audience, or a combination of the two. As the topical approach of this essay lends itself to a degree of oversimplification, readers are advised to bear in mind that the NT collects a diversity of theological beliefs and that the commonalities expressed here come alongside numerous differences.

Theological Concerns and Interpretive Method

Christianity originated as a movement of Palestinian Jews, with Jesus's followers heralding him as the anointed king, or "Messiah," of Israel ("Christ" became the Greek translation of the Hebrew "Messiah"). Thus it is hardly surprising that the NT shows a strong indebtedness to the beliefs and traditions of ancient Judaism (e.g., monotheism, covenant, law, and the goodness of creation). The Gospels remember Jesus as teaching a largely Jewish vision of God and God's kingdom, while NT moral teachings draw largely (though not exclusively) from Jewish ethical precedents such as the Ten Commandments.

Given the Jewish origins of Christianity, the NT writers were naturally inclined to draw extensively from Jewish Scripture—what Christians eventually called the Old Testament—since these were the texts through which ancient Jews formulated and passed on their beliefs and traditions (Jesus himself discussed Scripture a lot).[4] With few exceptions, the NT writers drew from the ancient Greek translation of Jewish Scripture, known to modern scholars as the Septuagint (signified by LXX in biblical citations). By quoting the LXX directly or alluding to it indirectly, the NT writers asserted continuity between Jesus's Jewish milieu and the movement that later bore his name. Particularly as Christianity expanded to Gentiles, who were accustomed to polytheism and religious syncretism, it was crucial to maintain that Jesus did not reveal

---

4. For a fuller discussion, see Stanley E. Porter, ed., *Hearing the Old Testament in the New Testament* (Grand Rapids: Eerdmans, 2006).

just any God. Rather, he revealed the God of Israel, the one Creator of the universe, and claimed to teach and act in accordance with this God's will. There was no better way to forward these claims than through engagement with Jewish Scripture.

Introductory students are sometimes alarmed to discover that the NT's use of OT texts often does not conform to the intentions of the original OT writers. That is because the early Christians were concerned less with discerning the "original" textual meaning than with using Scripture to support and elaborate on existing beliefs about Jesus and the church. Readers trained in modern interpretive methods might consider this a matter of reading the OT "out of context." Yet before we accuse the early Christians of misinterpreting, it must be noted that this kind of liberal appropriation of Scripture was already commonplace in Second Temple Judaism. In the case of the NT writers, the goal was not simply to interpret Scripture (its potential to have multiple meanings) but to interpret *Jesus*, that is, to elaborate on his identity and significance using scriptural language and motifs.[5] Often this interpretive project extended to the question of how the members of Jesus's community, the church, were supposed to live out their shared faith in relation to each other and the surrounding culture.

Renewal of Creation

Turning now to Gen. 1–2, we begin by noting how the NT writers inherited from these chapters at least three fundamental beliefs: (1) the God of Israel brought all of creation into existence, (2) the entirety of God's creation is inherently good,[6] and (3) humans enjoy a privileged place within the created order, having been uniquely fashioned in the image of God and having been given the corresponding responsibility of caring for the good creation of which they are a part.[7] Due to the NT's exclusive focus on Jesus, these fundamental beliefs are implied more than explicitly stated. Even though largely implicit, however, they undergird one of the main theological concerns of the NT: the renewal of creation. Specifically, the NT writers believed that God's saving actions *in the person of Jesus* had brought about the renewal of creation. Indeed, in the NT "salvation" is largely a matter of restoring human creatures

5. This applies to the NT what John Behr has argued with respect to the earliest post–NT theologians in *The Mystery of Christ: Life in Death* (Crestwood, NY: St. Vladimir's Seminary Press, 2006), 52–55.
6. God declares the creation "good" in Gen. 1:4, 10, 12, 18, 21, 25, 31. See also 1 Tim. 4:4.
7. Gen. 1:26–30; see also Gen. 2:7–9, 15, 18–25.

to the original plan of God as first described in Gen. 1–2. This is very much in keeping with a popular Second Temple Jewish hope that God would, at the end of the ages, restore creation to its original sinless goodness and perhaps even transform creation into a blessed state surpassing that original goodness.

According to the Gospels this renewal originated with Jesus's public ministry, not only in his demonstrations of power over the natural order (calming stormy winds and seas), but also and especially in his healing of suffering and broken humans.[8] In healing the physically ill (e.g., the blind, deaf, lame, demon-possessed, hemorrhaging), he affirmed the inherent goodness of humanity's embodied creatureliness. By extending compassion to sinners and reaching out to the socially marginalized (tax collectors, women, the poor, foreigners, and the physically infirm), he sought to mend exclusionary and fragmented social structures—structures predicated on embodied interpersonal relationships. In other words, Jesus healed human creatures at virtually every level, drawing people "into the story of the creating and redeeming God of Israel" by "putting things back to the way they were supposed to be in the beginning."[9]

This restoration seems to be what Jesus envisioned when he announced the arrival of God's kingdom through his ministry (Mark 1:15). In fact, for scripturally minded Jews this kingdom announcement would have denoted the end of the ages, that is, God's impending and final victory over the forces of evil and thus the very climax of salvation history.[10] Thus in the NT one finds the consistent claim that the full consummation of creation's renewal will take place on Jesus's glorious return at the eschaton. The Messiah will finish what he started.

If Jesus's ministry fueled the conviction that creation's renewal was nearing realization, then the announcement of Jesus's bodily resurrection only reinforced that conviction. While not all first-century Jews anticipated a "resurrection of the dead" at the eschaton, those who did envisioned it in bodily terms, specifically as God "restoring to some kind of bodily life those who had already passed through [death]."[11] They also envisioned resurrection in collective terms, as the simultaneous raising of *all* the righteous to new life. Interestingly, the early Christians claimed that the *individual* Jesus experienced resurrection and that this event pointed beyond itself to the impending

8. See Sean M. McDonough, *Christ as Creator: Origins of a New Testament Doctrine* (Oxford: Oxford University Press, 2009), 16–45.

9. McDonough, *Christ as Creator*, 29–30.

10. See N. T. Wright, *The New Testament and the People of God*, vol. 1 of *Christian Origins and the Question of God* (Minneapolis: Fortress, 1992), 302–7.

11. N. T. Wright, *The Resurrection of the Son of God*, vol. 3 of *Christian Origins and the Question of God* (Minneapolis: Fortress, 1994), 201.

resurrection of those who belonged to Christ. This difference notwithstanding, the early Christians saw resurrection in an essentially Jewish way, as an affirmation of God's benevolence as Creator, the inherent goodness of creation, and humanity's privileged place within creation.[12]

Due chiefly to their belief in Jesus's bodily resurrection, the early Christians maintained that the new creation glimpsed in Jesus's public ministry continued into the life of the church. Paul refers to this community, manifest in various places, as "the body of Christ"[13] because it receives and extends Christ's own healing and reconciling ministry (2 Cor. 5:19). Paul even goes so far as to connect his own apostolic ministry to the creation of light in Gen. 1:3–4: "For it is the God who said, 'Let light shine out of darkness,' who has shone in our hearts to give the light of the knowledge of the glory of God in the face of Jesus Christ" (2 Cor. 4:6). For Paul, the baptized are members of Christ's body because they have participated in Christ's death, emerging as a "new creation" for whom worldly, conventional ways of thinking no longer apply (2 Cor. 5:17; Gal. 6:15; Eph. 4:24).[14]

While Paul is the only NT writer to use the phrase "new creation," numerous other writers express similar ideas. James, for instance, claims that the origin of the Christian life is "the Father of lights" (echoing Gen. 1:14–19) who "gave us birth by the word of truth, so that we would become a kind of first fruits of his creatures" (James 1:17–18). Similarly, the Johannine and Petrine literature speak of new "birth" from God made possible through the redemptive work of Christ and giving rise to new ways of acting in the world.[15] Even when the precise language of creation/birth is lacking, the NT's many references to the radical "newness" of the Christian life communicate a similar notion since it is precisely human creatures that God renews.[16]

It bears repeating that "creation renewed" is a major unifying theme of the NT. In fact it is the logical corollary to the claim that the Creator of the world saves the world through Christ. When it comes to the NT's treatment of Gen. 1–2, then, readers will do well to remember that the following topics are not substantially different from this unifying theme but more like subsets of it. Moreover, as I have demonstrated here, there are other ways of conveying the theme of "creation renewed" besides direct engagement with Gen. 1–2.

12. Other differences are noted by Wright, *Resurrection of the Son*, 476–79.
13. Rom. 12:4–5; 1 Cor. 10:16–17; 12:12–13, 27. See also Eph. 4:12; 5:29; Col. 1:18, 24.
14. See T. Ryan Jackson, *New Creation in Paul's Letters: A Study of the Historical and Social Setting of a Pauline Concept* (Tübingen: Mohr Siebeck, 2010).
15. John 1:13; 3:3–8; 1 Pet. 1:3, 23; 1 John 2:29; 3:9; 4:7; 5:1, 4, 18. See also Titus 3:5.
16. Rom. 7:6; 12:2; 1 Cor. 5:7; 2 Cor. 4:16; Eph. 2:15; 4:23; Col. 3:10–11; Heb. 10:20; Rev. 5:9; 14:3.

Treatment of Days

The NT does not make explicit reference to the seven-day sequence of creation in Gen. 1:1–2:3.[17] There are, however, numerous references to the Sabbath day, which ancient Judaism connected to the seventh day of creation, the day of God's rest (Gen. 2:1–3). Of those references, the most noteworthy occur in the Gospels and Hebrews, where the meaning of Sabbath derives from the significance of Jesus, who draws human creatures into God's kingdom.

Sabbath Healings in the Gospels

In the Gospels, Jesus creates controversy by prioritizing basic human need over a strict application of Sabbath law. In one instance the controversy centers on Jesus allowing his disciples to satiate their hunger by plucking heads of grain on the Sabbath.[18] In several other instances it centers on his healing physical infirmities on the Sabbath.[19] In every case Jesus's opponents perceive him to be violating (or endorsing the violation of) the scriptural commandment to refrain from work on the seventh day of the week.

While there was no uniform way of observing Sabbath among ancient Jews,[20] to be charged with Sabbath violation was no small matter. After all, the Sabbath commandment was part of the revered Decalogue and thus of paramount importance to ancient Jewish identity. Culturally speaking, Sabbath-keeping functioned to separate the covenant people from foreign cultural forces that threatened to undermine its singular allegiance to the one Creator God.[21]

In the Sabbath controversy stories, Jesus's opponents never take umbrage at his general emphasis on human need. Rather, they object to his timing. Healing on the Sabbath, they contend, violates God's Sabbath commandment. By contrast, simply waiting until sundown (the start of the new day by Jewish reckoning) would have allowed Jesus to meet human needs while also honoring the Sabbath.[22] After all, the infirmities in question were not life

---

17. See, however, the minority view of Thomas Barrosse, "The Seven Days of the New Creation in St. John's Gospel," *CBQ* 21 (1959): 507–16.

18. Mark 2:23–28 // Matt. 12:1–8 // Luke 6:1–5.

19. Mark 3:1–6 // Matt. 12:9–14 // Luke 6:6–11; Luke 13:10–17; 14:1–6; John 5:1–46 (cf. 7:22–23); 9:1–41. For Jesus's teaching on the Sabbath, see also Mark 1:21 // Luke 4:31; Mark 6:1–5 // Matt. 13:54–58; Luke 4:16–30.

20. Lutz Doering, "Sabbath and Festivals," in *The Oxford Handbook of Jewish Daily Life in Roman Palestine*, ed. Catherine Hezser (Oxford: Oxford University Press, 2010), 568.

21. See Andreas Schuele, "Sabbath," in *NIDB* 5:8.

22. See esp. Luke 13:14.

threatening (and legal caveats existed for life-threatening circumstances).[23] From the perspective of Jesus's opponents, this strict application of Sabbath law ensures the community's adherence to God's commandment without precluding the healing of the infirm.

In response to these objections, Jesus claims to be "lord even of the sabbath"[24] and thus the authoritative interpreter of the Sabbath law. As Lord of the Sabbath, he prioritizes human need to the fullest extent. Yet instead of prioritizing human need *over* the Sabbath, he contends that his healings *fulfill the purpose* of the Sabbath. Since "the sabbath was made for humankind, and not humankind for the sabbath" (Mark 2:27)," the Sabbath is the *most appropriate* day to deliver people of their infirmities. Consequently, people *receive rest* from the physical, emotional, and social labors that their maladies have forced on them. Freed from such burdens, the newly healed can finally and truly keep the Sabbath, celebrating the goodness of creation just as God did in the beginning (Gen. 2:1–3).[25]

It bears mentioning that John 5:1–18 approaches the issue of Sabbath healing from a somewhat different christological angle.[26] While the protest of his opponents is roughly the same, the response of the Johannine Jesus is distinctive: "My Father is still working, and I also am working" (5:17). In a clear allusion to the seventh day of creation, Jesus insinuates that the Creator's work has actually not yet reached completion. Indeed, many ancient Jews reasoned that Gen. 2:1–3 could not refer to the outright cessation of God's creative activity since God continued to sustain creation.[27] John takes this logic in a christological direction: God's creative activity continues in the person of Jesus, meaning the true Sabbath has yet to arrive. The Creator is still at work, bringing all things into being through the Word, who was in the beginning (John 1:1–4). For this Gospel it is not until the crucifixion that Jesus, now glorified and returning to the Father, definitively declares, "It is finished" (19:30).[28]

---

23. Donald A. Hagner, "Jesus and the Synoptic Sabbath Controversies," *BBR* 19 (2009): 234.

24. Mark 2:28 // Matt. 12:8 // Luke 6:5.

25. Barbara E. Reid, OP, "Sabbath, the Crown of Creation," in *Earth, Wind, and Fire: Biblical and Theological Perspectives on Creation*, ed. Carol J. Dempsey and Mary Margaret Pazdan (Collegeville, MN: Liturgical Press, 2004), 67–76, here 70.

26. On John's distinctive approach to Sabbath, see Harold Weiss, "The Sabbath in the Fourth Gospel," *JBL* 110 (1991): 311–21.

27. See Andrew T. Lincoln, "Sabbath, Rest, and Eschatology in the New Testament," in *From Sabbath to Lord's Day: A Biblical, Historical, and Theological Investigation* (Grand Rapids: Zondervan, 1982), 203.

28. On the cross as Jesus's glorification, see John 12:23, 28; 13:31; 17:1, 4.

Eschatological Rest in Hebrews

Whereas the Gospels refer to the Sabbath in the conventional Jewish way as a weekly and earthly rest, Heb. 3:7–4:11 interprets Sabbath figuratively as an eschatological rest awaiting persecuted Christians. It is a metaphor, in other words, for divine deliverance at the end of the age, a figuration of Christians' direct enjoyment of God's glory in the heavenly tabernacle (Heb. 2:1–18; 10:19–25) and even their own glorification in the kingdom that exists beyond the material cosmos.[29] In this way the promise of Sabbath rest functions to foster faithfulness among those who might otherwise be dissuaded by anti-Christian pressures.

The writer's argument is difficult to follow, as he draws on seemingly disparate scriptural verses by means of common linking terms (a preferred mode of interpretation among some ancient Jews). To simplify matters, I focus here on the term "rest," to which the writer attaches two correlative meanings.[30] First, there is the rest that God denied to the first generation of Israelites who left slavery in Egypt, when they were forbidden from entering the promised land (Heb. 3:7–11, quoting Ps. 95:7–11). Second, there is the rest described in Gen. 2:2, when "God rested on the seventh day from all his works" (Heb. 4:4). For Hebrews, this divine rest is an ongoing state into which God desires to draw human creatures. It is not a twenty-four-hour period, long since passed, but rather an eternal rest into which Christians may hope to enter.

In essence, the writer interprets the first of these "rests" in light of the second. In other words, the wilderness sojourn to the promised land, while historically real, was a figuration of the human sojourn to God's eternal Sabbath. While this argument comes largely at the expense of the rebellious Israelites, the point is not to disparage that group as much as it is to encourage the first-century audience to remain unswervingly loyal to God. According to Heb. 4:9–10, "a sabbath rest still remains for the people of God; for those who enter God's rest also cease from their labors as God did from his." Through faithful obedience, then, the audience of Hebrews can expect to enter God's own rest.

What does Christ have to do with this argument? While there is no explicit mention of him in the discussion of rest in Heb. 3:7–4:11,[31] preceding verses make clear that Christ is the means by which God brings human creatures to

---

29. On eschatology and cosmology in Hebrews, see David deSilva, "Entering God's Rest: Eschatology and the Socio-rhetorical Strategy of Hebrews," *TJ* 21 (2000): 26–29.

30. My interpretation is indebted especially to Harold Attridge, "'Let Us Strive to Enter That Rest': The Logic of Hebrews 4:1–11," *HTR* 73 (1980): 279–88.

31. See, however, Nicholas J. Moore, "Jesus as 'The One Who Entered His Rest': The Christological Reading of Hebrews 4:10," *JSNT* 36 (2014): 383–400.

SIDEBAR 3.1

Hebrews 4:9–11

[9]So then, a sabbath rest still remains for the people of God; [10]for those who enter God's rest also cease from their labors as God did from his. [11]Let us therefore make every effort to enter that rest, so that no one may fall through such disobedience as theirs.

glory, chiefly through his sharing in their suffering and death (Heb. 2:5–3:5). Indeed, Hebrews insists that Christ, as "pioneer and perfecter of our faith" (12:2), first accomplishes for himself what he bestows on believers. Furthermore, as a consequence of Christ's salvific accomplishment, there is a sense in which God's eternal rest is available—at least partially—to believers in the present (4:3).[32] Paradoxically, then, believers have some degree of access to the eschatological rest by virtue of Christ's atoning sacrifice in the heavenly tabernacle (Heb. 8:1–10:22), even as their difficult earthly sojourn continues in the present.

Cosmology

The NT draws on the cosmological themes and language of Gen. 1–2 (esp. Gen. 1) in ways that give a Christian perspective to the origin, structure, and destiny of the physical universe. With respect to origin, every NT writer assumes the truth of the claim of Gen. 1:1 that the God of Israel "created the heavens and the earth." In several places that truth is stated explicitly.[33] In four different documents the claim is given a distinctively christological thrust, with Jesus himself playing a decisive role in the work of creation.[34] Preeminent among these four is the prologue to John's Gospel (John 1:1–15).

John's prologue draws on Gen. 1 in multiple ways.[35] First, its opening phrase mirrors the opening phrase of Gen. 1:1: "In the beginning" (John 1:1). In addition, John's focus on the creative "Word" (*Logos*) of God echoes the way

32. Lincoln, "Sabbath, Rest, and Eschatology," 206.
33. For God as Creator or Lord of "heaven and earth," see Matt. 11:25 // Luke 10:21; Acts 4:24; 14:15–17; 17:24–27; 2 Pet. 3:5; Rev. 14:7. For other explicit acknowledgments of God as Creator, see Mark 10:6 // Matt. 19:4; Mark 13:19 // Matt. 24:21; Rom. 1:20; Eph. 3:9; 1 Tim. 4:3; Heb. 11:1–3; Rev. 4:11; 10:6.
34. John 1:1–3; 1 Cor. 8:6; Col. 1:15–20; Heb. 1:2, 10–12. For analysis see McDonough, *Christ as Creator*, 150–234.
35. For background see Masanobu Endo, *Creation and Christology: A Study on the Johannine Prologue in the Light of Early Jewish Creation Accounts* (Tübingen: Mohr Siebeck, 2002).

SIDEBAR 3.2

John 1:1–5

¹In the beginning was the Word, and the Word was with God, and the Word was God. ²He was in the beginning with God. ³All things came into being through him, and without him not one thing came into being. What has come into being ⁴in him was life, and the life was the light of all people. ⁵The light shines in the darkness, and the darkness did not overcome it.

---

in which the God of Gen. 1 speaks creation into existence. It was through this Word that all things came into being (John 1:3). Yet for John this Word is not only a divine utterance but also a kind of divine entity who "was with God . . . and was God" (v. 2). Echoing the creation of light and day in Gen. 1:3–5, John claims that this preexistent divine Word was and is "the light of all people" (v. 4).[36] Moreover, this same Word "became flesh" in the person of Jesus, dwelling among humans to reveal God's glory among them (v. 14). For the Gospel of John, then, the very God who creates the world is also the God who becomes incarnate in the world for its salvation.[37] Given this christological appropriation of Gen. 1, hearers are not surprised to find Jesus consistently linked with "life" throughout this Gospel.[38] Indeed, it is chiefly by invoking Gen. 1 that John's prologue "signals that the Jesus story will illuminate the ongoing story of God's creation and provide its culmination."[39]

In terms of cosmological structure, the NT writers usually adhere to the same three-tiered view of the cosmos that was common throughout the ANE.[40] The tier of human habitation was the earth, conceived as a round, disk-shaped mass of land with "depths" extending to an underworld reserved for the dead.[41] Above the earth existed a heavenly tier, the lower part of which

---

36. See also John 1:7–9; 3:19–21; 8:12; 9:5; 12:35–36, 46.

37. John 1:29; 3:16–17; 4:42; 12:47.

38. John 1:4; 5:26, 29, 40; 6:33, 35, 48, 51, 53, 63; 8:12; 10:10; 11:25; 14:6; 20:31. The Johannine refrain of "eternal life" is not unrelated to this creational theme. See Jeannine K. Brown, "Creation's Renewal in the Gospel of John," *CBQ* 72, no. 2 (2010): 276–90, here 278.

39. Brown, "Creation's Renewal," 277.

40. The following summary draws on Kyle Greenwood, *Scripture and Cosmology: Reading the Bible between the Ancient World and Modern Science* (Downers Grove, IL: IVP Academic, 2015), 33–118.

41. NT references to "the ends of the earth" evidence this view of a nonglobular landmass (Matt. 12:42; Mark 13:27; Luke 11:31; Acts 1:8; 13:47; Rom. 10:18 [quoting Ps. 19:4]). References to "Hell" (Gehenna) and "Hades" evidence belief in an underworld (Matt. 5:22 // Luke 12:5; Matt. 11:23 // Luke 10:15; Matt. 16:18; 23:15, 33; Mark 9:43 // Matt. 5:29 [see also Matt. 5:10, 28–30; 18:9]; Luke 16:23; Acts 2:27, 31; James 3:6; 2 Pet. 2:4; Rev. 1:18; 6:8).

was composed of celestial luminaries (sun, moon, and stars) affixed to a solid dome, or firmament. Above the firmament was imagined the upper heavens, the abode of the gods.[42] Finally, the third tier consisted of cosmic waters. Yet this was more extensive than a mere "tier," since the cosmic waters existed below and around the earth, as well as above the firmament, from which place the waters could descend on the earth in the form of precipitation.

Because Gen. 1 draws on common ANE cosmology, it is sometimes difficult to tell if a NT writer is deliberately alluding to the scriptural account of creation or simply drawing from the common ANE worldview. For instance, when the heavens are "opened" to allow for a divine revelation,[43] scripturally minded hearers may hear echoes of the creation of the firmament in Gen. 1:6–8. Of course ancient Jews and Christians did not believe God's heavenly abode *precluded* God's presence among earthbound humans. The opening of the heavens was simply a helpful way to express the paradox of divine transcendence and immanence. In the case of Jesus's baptism,[44] that paradox takes a decidedly christological shape since the opening of the heavens allows for God's Spirit to descend on Jesus, anointing him for his public ministry.

In a similar vein, when the Gospels describe Jesus's godlike authority over the stormy sea,[45] scripturally minded hearers may hear echoes of the primordial waters of Gen. 1 (vv. 1–2, 9). Since land waters were believed to be connected to the primordial "deep"—the dark and chaotic ocean to which God brought light and order (vv. 1–5)—sea storms were perceived as vestiges of that life-threatening chaos, even as manifestations of evil forces.[46] Thus, for Jesus to calm such storms by a mere word, or to exert his authority by walking on the chaotic waters,[47] evokes the story of God speaking the orderly creation into existence. The setting of these stories at a time of darkness reinforces the parallel, particularly with respect to the primordial darkness that "covered the face of the deep" (v. 2).

42. On God's heavenly abode, see Matt. 5:16, 34–35, 45; 6:1, 9; 7:11, 21; 10:32–33; 12:50; 16:17; 18:10, 14; 23:9, 20–22; Mark 11:25; Luke 2:14; 15:18, 21; John 6:32–33, 50–51; 12:28; Acts 7:56; Eph. 6:9; Col. 4:1; Heb. 12:25; Rev. 4:2; 5:13; 11:19. Appropriately, Christian belief in Jesus's divine status could be expressed in terms of his heavenly ascension and manifestation (e.g., Mark 13:24–27; Luke 24:51; John 3:13; Acts 1:2; 7:55; Rom. 10:6; Eph. 4:10; Heb. 4:14; 7:26; 8:1–2; 1 Pet. 3:22; 2 Pet. 1:18).

43. John 1:51; Acts 10:11; Rev. 19:11.

44. Matt. 3:16; Mark 1:10; Luke 3:21–22; John 1:32–33.

45. Mark 4:35–41 // Matt. 8:23–27 // Luke 8:22–25; Mark 6:45–52 // Matt. 14:22–33; John 6:16–21.

46. Greenwood, *Scripture and Cosmology*, 63–64, 97–101.

47. See also Job 9:8.

Also with regard to cosmological structure, one may notice the following echoes (or possible echoes) of Gen. 1:

- Any mention of "heaven and earth"[48] has the potential to remind hearers of the famous opening of Gen. 1:1, even if the phrase is not unique to that verse.
- The Synoptic description of darkness enveloping the earth during Jesus's crucifixion[49] likely alludes to the primordial darkness of Gen. 1:1–5. The echo may suggest that Jesus's death, and not just his public ministry, effects a renewal of creation.
- A few NT writers refer to the "abyss" (the earthly depths or underworld), using the same term that is found in the Greek version of Gen. 1:1 (*abyssos*; NRSV: "the deep"). Especially noteworthy is the repeated use of *abyssos* in Revelation to describe the origin and destiny of demonic forces that oppose God.[50]
- At least two NT writers evoke the creation of celestial luminaries in Gen. 1:14–19. Paul does this when he compares the glory of the resurrected body to the glory of the sun, moon, and stars (1 Cor. 15:41),[51] while James refers to God as "the Father of lights" (James 1:17). John may also echo Gen. 1:14–19 when he describes Jesus as "the light of the world" (John 8:12; 9:5; 11:9; 12:46).
- In its description of God's heavenly throne room, Revelation describes "in front of the throne . . . something like a sea of glass, like crystal" (Rev. 4:6). While the reference to crystal echoes Ezek. 1:22, John has applied this to a celestial sea, located in the upper heavens by virtue of the separation of the waters in Gen. 1:7. The peacefulness implied by this image suggests God's final victory over the destructive forces of chaos.[52]

When it comes to the final destiny of the cosmos, the NT provides intermittent references and no uniform perspective. Of course, there is a decidedly eschatological tenor to much of the NT due to the aforementioned belief that Jesus's life, death, and resurrection signaled the renewal of creation and

48. See Matt. 5:18; 11:25; 28:18; Mark 13:31 // Matt. 24:35 // Luke 21:33; Luke 10:21; 16:17. See also Matt. 6:10; 16:19; 18:18; 23:9; Luke 2:14; John 3:31; Acts 2:19; 7:49; Eph. 1:10; 3:15; Phil. 2:10; Col. 1:16, 20; Heb. 12:25; James 5:12; Rev. 5:3, 13; 20:11; 21:1.

49. Mark 15:33 // Matt. 27:45 // Luke 23:44.

50. Rev. 9:1, 11; 11:7; 17:8; 20:1, 3. See also Luke 8:31; Rom. 10:7.

51. See also 2 Cor. 4:6.

52. Brian K. Blount, *Revelation: A Commentary* (Louisville: Westminster John Knox, 2009), 92.

SIDEBAR 3.3

2 Peter 3:5–7

[5]They deliberately ignore this fact, that by the word of God heavens existed long ago and an earth was formed out of water and by means of water, [6]through which the world of that time was deluged with water and perished. [7]But by the same word the present heavens and earth have been reserved for fire, being kept until the day of judgment and destruction of the godless.

---

thus a transition into the final chapter of salvation history. References to the eschaton, however, tend to focus less on cosmological speculation and more on God's final judgment of humanity.[53] Beyond this, the NT gives "the general impression . . . that the kingdom will be realized not in some other world but on this earth made new—a revised, second edition with the earlier deficiencies corrected."[54] To take one well-known example, Paul contends that while creation "has been groaning in labor pains" (Rom. 8:22) due to the effects of sin, it will ultimately "be set free from its bondage to decay" (8:21) at the eschaton. For Paul, the redemption of humans is wrapped up in this larger cosmic redemption.[55]

Interestingly, the NT passages that invoke Gen. 1–2 in connection with the fate of the cosmos tend to envision some sort of cataclysm. For instance, 2 Peter borrows from a combination of Jewish and Stoic expectations in claiming that "the present heavens and earth have been reserved for fire, being kept until the day of judgment and destruction of the godless" (3:7).[56] How will this come about? By "the same word" (3:7) that spoke creation into existence in the beginning: "By the word of God heavens existed long ago and an earth was formed out of water and by means of water" (3:5). This clear allusion to Gen. 1 brings a kind of symmetry to the history of creation: God speaks creation into fiery destruction just as God speaks creation into existence out of water. The writer anticipates this destruction at Christ's return in judgment on the wicked (2 Pet. 3:7). Yet, in keeping with one Second Temple tradition,

---

53. E.g., Matt. 25:31–46; Mark 8:38 // Luke 9:26 (cf. Matt. 16:27); Mark 13:24–27 // Matt. 24:29–31 // Luke 21:25–28; John 6:40; 1 Cor. 15:12–34; 1 Thess. 4:13–18; James 5:7–12; 1 Pet. 4:12–19; 1 John 2:28; Rev. 20:11–15.

54. Dale Allison, "Eschatology of the NT," *NIDB* 2:298.

55. See also 1 Cor. 15:1–58.

56. See John Dennis, "Cosmology in the Petrine Literature and Jude," in *Cosmology and New Testament Theology*, ed. Jonathan T. Pennington and Sean M. McDonough (London: T&T Clark, 2008), 165–77.

he also anticipates a "new heavens and a new earth" (3:13) for the righteous, meaning that the benevolence of the Creator will not be nullified by human rebellion.[57] Thus the same divine word that creates also judges and re-creates.

The book of Revelation foresees cataclysmic destruction in the form of apocalyptic catastrophes such as earthquakes, plagues, wars, and persecutions.[58] Particularly noteworthy are several references to the darkening or falling of the celestial luminaries, thus signaling the reversal of Gen. 1:14–19.[59] Indebted to certain strands of Jewish apocalypticism, John foresees such cosmic destruction as the only viable solution to evil's pervasive hold on creation[60] (the specific image of falling stars likely derives from Isa. 34:4 LXX). Indeed, as I stated at the outset of this chapter, scholars believe that John's original audience consisted of victims of Roman anti-Christian persecution and was thus well acquainted with the pervasiveness of evil in the world. For these abused Christians, the undoing of Gen. 1:14–19 by means of cosmic cataclysm held promise that they would not suffer forever under the dominion of satanic forces. Evil so pervaded the fabric of the cosmos, in other words, that God's defeat of Satan would reverberate tumultuously throughout the cosmos.

While it can be argued that the cosmic catastrophes of Revelation were intended metaphorically rather than literally, even as metaphors they seem to convey the expectation of real cosmological destruction of some sort,[61] albeit not in the sense of wholesale cosmic annihilation.[62] In fact, Revelation parallels 2 Peter in its expectation of a *new creation*, recapitulating the creation of Gen. 1: "Then I saw a new heaven and a new earth; for the first heaven and the first earth had passed away, and the sea was no more" (Rev. 21:1). Within this new cosmos will reside a new Jerusalem, descended from heaven to earth for the habitation of God among humans (vv. 2–4). In another distant echo of Gen. 1:14–19, John claims that this new Jerusalem "has no need of sun or moon to shine on it" (v. 23), and that "there will be no more night, . . . for the Lord God will be their light" (22:5).

57. See Isa. 65:17; 66:22; 1 En. 91.16; LAB 3.10 (cited by Allison, "Eschatology of the NT," 298).

58. E.g., Rev. 6:8, 11–12, 16; 8:5; 9:1–21; 11:6–7, 13, 19; 12:17; 13:7; 15:1, 6–8; 16:9, 21; 17:14; 18:8; 19:11, 18–20; 21:9.

59. Rev. 6:12–13; 8:10, 12; 9:1–2; 12:4.

60. See Edward Adams, *The Stars Will Fall from Heaven: Cosmic Catastrophe in the New Testament and its World*, LNTS 347 (London: T&T Clark, 2007), 52–100, 240–41.

61. So Adams, *Stars Will Fall*, 236–51.

62. John T. Carroll, "Creation and Apocalypse," in *God Who Creates: Essays in Honor of W. Sibley Towner*, ed. William P. Brown and S. Dean McBride Jr. (Grand Rapids: Eerdmans, 2000), 254–56.

Finally, in the Gospel of Mark, Jesus expresses a similarly apocalyptic vision of the eschaton. In a speech that appears to convey Mark's own anticipation of the Roman destruction of Jerusalem (70 CE), Jesus warns the disciples of impending catastrophes: wars, earthquakes, famines, and persecutions (Mark 13:7–13). He then predicts the falling of the celestial luminaries on his glorious return:

> The sun will be darkened,
>   and the moon will not give its light,
> and the stars will be falling from heaven,
>   and the powers in the heavens will be shaken.
>   Mark 13:24–25

Like Revelation, these words anticipate the reversal of Gen. 1:14–19.[63] Yet the Markan Jesus goes further, saying that "heaven and earth will pass away" even though "my words will not pass away" (Mark 13:31).[64] While omitting explicit reference to a *new* cosmos, the Markan expectation of resurrection (12:18–27) strongly suggests some kind of renewal or re-creation. This is made more explicit by the Matthean Jesus, who speaks of a future "renewal of all things" (*palingenesia*, Matt. 19:28: lit., an "again genesis").[65]

It bears repeating that the sequence of cosmological cataclysm and re-creation, while rather well attested,[66] is not the only way that the NT envisions the destiny of the cosmos. Some would even consider it a marginal perspective, pointing instead to Jesus's own emphasis on the kingdom coming "on earth, as it is in heaven" (Matt. 6:10).[67] It happens to be the case, however, that the passages that come the closest to invoking Gen. 1 share a common expectation of cataclysm and re-creation. This makes sense given that such expectations naturally imply a reversal and reiteration of Gen. 1, in keeping with certain strands of Jewish apocalypticism. At the end of the day, then, NT readers must hold in tension these divergent views, remaining mindful of the common link of God's sovereignty and faithfulness.

63. See the analysis of Adams, *Stars Will Fall*, 133–81. OT echoes include Isa. 13:10; 24:21, 23; 34:4; Ezek. 32:7–8; Joel 2:10, 31; 3:15. See also Joel Marcus, *Mark 8–16: A New Translation with Introduction and Commentary*, AB 27A (New Haven: Yale University Press, 2009), 906–8.

64. See also Matt. 24:35 // Luke 21:33; cf. Matt. 5:18.

65. See David C. Sim, "The Meaning of παλιγγενεσία in Matthew 19:28," *JSNT* 50 (1993): 3–12.

66. See also Heb. 12:25–27 (discussed in Adams, *Stars Will Fall*, 182–99).

67. E.g., N. T. Wright, *Surprised by Hope: Rethinking Heaven, the Resurrection, and the Mission of the Church* (New York: HarperOne, 2008).

Creation and Nature of Humanity

New Testament allusions to Adam and Eve are numerous and seem to take for granted their historicity as the first created humans. However, in referring to Adam and Eve, the NT writers do not concern themselves with questions of historicity but rather with questions of theology, Christology, and ecclesiology. Besides two rather nondescript verses,[68] these allusions may be categorized as follows. First, there are Synoptic and Pauline passages that invoke the creation of Adam and Eve to make a point about marriage or human sexual union. Second, there are Pauline passages that invoke the creation of Adam and Eve to make a point about the status of women in the church. Finally, there are Pauline passages that explain the redeeming significance of Christ in juxtaposition to Adam. Across the spectrum of all these passages, the writers show affinities with an ancient interpretive tradition that extrapolated from the story of Adam and Eve universal truths about the human condition, the relationship between men and women, and the unique guilt of Eve in her primal disobedience.

Adam, Eve, and Marriage

In Mark 10:6–8, Jesus quotes directly from Gen. 1–2 to assert the indissolubility of marriage.[69] This comes in response to Pharisees who claim, by reference to Deut. 24:1–5, that "Moses allowed a man to write a certificate of dismissal and to divorce [his wife]" (Mark 10:4). At that time virtually all Jewish groups allowed for divorce under certain circumstances.[70] Jesus, however, contends that Moses allowed for divorce only as a concession to human hard-heartedness (Mark 10:5), yet the original will of the Creator, as stated in Gen. 1–2, precludes divorce. In bringing the kingdom of God, Jesus seeks to reclaim God's original plan.[71]

To make his case, Jesus appropriates two key verses from Genesis. First he quotes Gen. 1:27: "God made them male and female" (quoted in Mark 10:6). He then quotes Gen. 2:24: "The two shall become one flesh" (quoted in Mark 10:8). In its original scriptural context this verse explained the conjugal union as a natural outworking of Eve having been formed from Adam's rib (Gen.

---

68. Luke 3:38; Jude 14.

69. See also the parallel in Matt. 19:4–6.

70. Adela Yarbro Collins, *Mark* (Minneapolis: Fortress, 2007), 459–65.

71. The point is not to denigrate the Mosaic law. See Marcus, *Mark 8–16*, 702. See also Anthony E. Harvey, "Genesis versus Deuteronomy? Jesus on Marriage and Divorce," in *The Gospels and the Scriptures of Israel*, ed. Craig A. Evans and W. Richard Stegner (Sheffield: Sheffield Academic, 1994), 55–65.

SIDEBAR 3.4

Mark 10:6–9

⁶But from the beginning of creation, "God made them male and female." ⁷"For this reason a man shall leave his father and mother and be joined to his wife, ⁸and the two shall become one flesh." So they are no longer two, but one flesh. ⁹Therefore what God has joined together, let no one separate.

2:23–24). Jesus, however, cites the verse to suggest that the conjugal union follows logically from the complementarity asserted via Gen. 1:27: God created them male and female, and "for this reason" (Mark 10:7) the man leaves his parent's household to be joined to the woman.[72] Jesus clinches this argument by casting the conjugal union itself as a divine act: "Therefore what God has joined together, let no man separate" (v. 9). Since the union of man and woman is intrinsic to their very creation, that union is indissoluble. While the parallel passage in Matthew provides a caveat based on unchastity (Matt. 19:9), the main argument is the same.

Turning to the Pauline literature, one finds two references to Gen. 2:24 in connection with the issue of marriage: 1 Cor. 6:16 and Eph. 5:31. The first of these comes in the context of a discussion about sexual immorality (1 Cor. 6:1–20). Some men of the Corinthian church were apparently keeping sexual relations with prostitutes, which was a common practice in Greco-Roman antiquity. In response, Paul insists that nonconjugal sexual unions carry a kind of spiritual power that defiles one's membership in Christ's ecclesial body: "Do you not know that whoever is united to a prostitute becomes one body with her? For it is said, 'The two shall be one flesh'" (6:16). In so quoting Gen. 2:24, Paul contends that sexual union with a prostitute "creates an unholy bond between the Lord's members and the sinful world."[73]

Significantly, then, this appropriation of Gen. 2:24 does not contrast nonconjugal sexual union with *married* sexual union, as one might expect. Rather, it contrasts nonconjugal sexual union with the Corinthians' spiritual union with Christ. Sexual union with prostitutes violates both the believer's body, which is "a temple of the Holy Spirit" (1 Cor. 6:19) and the ecclesial body of Christ to which the believer belongs. Whereas the Corinthians in question

---

72. Other ancient Jewish sources invoke Gen. 2:24 in discussions about divorce. See Marcus, *Mark 8–16*, 704–5.

73. Richard B. Hays, *First Corinthians*, IBC (Louisville: Westminster John Knox, 1997), 105.

SIDEBAR 3.5

Ephesians 5:28–33

[28]In the same way, husbands should love their wives as they do their own bodies. He who loves his wife loves himself. [29]For no one ever hates his own body, but he nourishes and tenderly cares for it, just as Christ does for the church, [30]because we are members of his body. [31]"For this reason a man will leave his father and mother and be joined to his wife, and the two will become one flesh." [32]This is a great mystery, and I am applying it to Christ and the church. [33]Each of you, however, should love his wife as himself, and a wife should respect her husband.

---

take their spiritual union with Christ as a license to devalue their bodies, Paul insists that union with Christ encompasses and redeems their bodies. Indeed, their bodies have been reclaimed by God and thus should be used to glorify God (6:20).

The second Pauline reference to Gen. 2:24 occurs as part of a standard household code (Eph. 5:1–6:9) in which the writer instructs the various members of the household (wives and husbands, children and parents, slaves and masters) in their obligations toward one another. Such household codes were common in Greco-Roman ethical texts and typically reinforced strict hierarchical and patriarchal relationships among the parties concerned (although NT household codes show some distinctive concerns for the reciprocating care of the patriarch).[74] In the case of the Ephesians, the likely pseudonymous "Paul" compares the relationship of the husband and wife to that of Christ and his church (Eph. 5:25–33). The point of this comparison is to reinforce the husband's obligation toward his wife: the husband should love and sacrifice himself for his submissive wife just as Christ loved and sacrificed himself for his submissive church.

To conclude this argument, the writer cites Gen. 2:24: "'For this reason a man will leave his father and mother and be joined to his wife, and the two will become one flesh.' This is a great mystery, and I am applying it to Christ and the church" (Eph. 5:31–32). The second sentence is crucial since it shows that the union of Adam and Eve is being read analogically as a reference to the bond between the believer (the woman) and Christ (the man). This spiritual interpretation is similar to 1 Cor. 6:16. Paradoxically in this case, however,

---

74. See also Col. 3:18–4:1; 1 Pet. 2:13–3:7. On the basic differences between Christian and Hellenistic household codes, see Carolyn Osiek, "The Bride of Christ (Eph. 5:22–33): A Problematic Wedding," *BTB* 32 (2002): 30–31.

the underlying point of the analogy is precisely to explain a key element of Christian marriage, namely, the husband's love for his wife that reciprocates the wife's submission to the husband.

Adam, Eve, and the Status of Women

In his Letter to the Galatians, Paul makes an astounding claim about the liberating effects of Christ's redeeming work. He claims that within the Christian community "there is no longer Jew or Greek, there is no longer slave or free, there is no longer male and female; for all of you are one in Christ Jesus" (Gal. 3:28). Paul's basic point is that various cultural divisions no longer apply to those who belong to Christ by virtue of faith and baptism. In this respect the church is what J. Louis Martyn calls "the beachhead of God's new creation."[75]

While Paul's primary concern in this letter is the elimination of the Jew/Gentile distinction, the Genesis echo may be found in the elimination of the male/female distinction. Specifically, Paul alludes to Gen. 1:27: "Male and female he created them." But what does it mean to say that this distinction no longer applies to those who are "in Christ"? Most likely the apostle intends to make a point about the fundamental *unity of the church* rather than social equality between the sexes.[76] Still, the claim likely contained socially liberating potential for Christian women, as can be seen in Paul's commendations of women coworkers (Phil. 4:2–3; Rom. 16:1–16) and his reference to women's leadership in worshiping assemblies (1 Cor. 11:2–16). Paradoxically for Paul, the distinction of Gen. 1:27 does not apply to the underlying reality of the church—which is the one person Jesus Christ (1 Cor. 12:1–30)—even as it still applies to various forms of social interaction within the church.

Something of this paradox may be glimpsed from 1 Cor. 11:2–16, a passage that also invokes Gen. 1. In these verses Paul responds to a report that in the gathered assembly Corinthian women have been praying and prophesying with heads uncovered. While the actions themselves indicate a degree of social equality with men, the women's uncovered heads (allowing hair to fall loosely) defied a time-honored convention by which Greco-Roman and Jewish cultures recognized gender differences. Without criticizing their leadership in the assembly, Paul insists that women conform to this convention, most likely to prevent scandal and shame vis-à-vis the broader society.[77] To support his

---

75. J. Louis Martyn, *Galatians: A New Translation with Introduction and Commentary*, AB 33A (New York: Doubleday, 1997), 377.

76. Martyn, *Galatians*, 377.

77. See Hays, *First Corinthians*, 182–86; Benjamin A. Edsall, "Greco-Roman Costume and Paul's Fraught Argument in 1 Corinthians 11:2–16," *JGRChJ* 9 (2013): 132–46.

SIDEBAR 3.6

1 Corinthians 11:7–9

[7]For a man ought not to have his head veiled, since he is the image and reflection of God; but woman is the reflection of man. [8]Indeed, man was not made from woman, but woman from man. [9]Neither was man created for the sake of woman, but woman for the sake of man.

---

view, Paul forwards a notoriously convoluted and patriarchal argument, appealing not only to Scripture but also to the order of nature and social custom.

Focusing here on Paul's scriptural arguments, Paul ties together three details from Gen. 1–2 that show his patriarchal perspective. First, referring to Gen. 1:26–27, Paul claims that the man rather than the woman is the "image and glory of God," whereas the woman is the "image and glory of man" (1 Cor. 11:7, fn.). Of course the actual text of Gen. 1:26–27 claims that both "male and female" were created in the divine image, with no insinuation that the woman derives her glory through the man. It may be, however, that Paul has interpreted Gen. 1:26–27 through the lens of Gen. 2, in which Adam is created before Eve, since his subsequent scriptural points draw from that story. Alluding to Eve's creation from the rib of Adam (Gen. 2:22–23), he states that "man was not made from woman, but woman from man" (1 Cor. 11:8). He then adds, echoing Gen. 2:18, that man was not created "for the sake of woman" but rather "women for the sake of man" (1 Cor. 11:9), remembering that Eve was created to cure Adam's solitude and to provide him with a helper. Altogether, these verses from Genesis suggest to Paul a patriarchal order inherent in creation, an order that the church is obligated to recognize in its own worshiping assemblies. He concludes with an acknowledgment of mutual interdependence between men and women (1 Cor. 11:11–12), but this nuance does not change the gist of his argument: as leaders in the worshiping assembly, women may practice a degree of equality with men, but not in a way that eliminates the gender distinctions inherent to the underlying patriarchal order of creation.

Turning to 1 Tim. 2:8–15, we find the pseudonymous "Paul" pushing these arguments in a more suppressive direction, instructing women to remain altogether silent in the worshiping assembly. While it is not clear what prompted these instructions, the best clue resides in the letter's overarching concern with safeguarding the church from false teaching.[78] Specifically, the writer has

---

78. See 1 Tim. 1:3–7, 19b–20; 4:1–10.

come to associate false teaching, at least partly, with the "old wives' tales" of women members (1 Tim. 4:7).[79] For this reason, he opposes women's authority, insisting that they "learn in silence with full submission" and permitting "no woman to teach or to have authority over a man" (2:11–12). More so than 1 Cor. 11, these instructions align the church more firmly with Hellenistic patriarchal ideals.[80]

To justify his instructions, the writer follows Paul in appealing to details in the Adam and Eve story. First, like the apostle, he notes that "Adam was formed first, then Eve" (1 Tim. 2:13, citing Gen. 2:7). The audience is left to infer from this allusion the primacy of men over women, if not also the abiding authority of men over women. Next, the writer turns to Gen. 3, noting that "Adam was not deceived [in the garden], but the woman was deceived and became a transgressor" (1 Tim. 2:14, citing the "deception" language of Gen. 3:13).[81] From this allusion—which avoids reference to Adam's participation in the primal transgression (Gen. 3:6)—the audience is led to infer the relative imperviousness of men, as well as the susceptibility of women, to false teaching. As Jouette Bassler summarizes the argument, "women must not be permitted to exercise the crucial role of teacher lest their vulnerability to deception permit the spread of false teachings in the church."[82] Finally, in an attempt to affirm some positive role for women in the life of the church, the writer claims that women "will be saved through childbearing, provided they continue in faith and love and holiness, with modesty" (1 Tim. 2:15). Likely a combined allusion to Gen. 1:22 and 28 ("be fruitful and multiply"), as well as Gen. 3:16 ("I will greatly increase your pangs in childbearing"), this statement limits the leadership of women to the raising of Christian offspring, provided their vocation exhibits the proper Christian virtues.

It bears mentioning that the patriarchal arguments of these Pauline letters directly reflect the dominant patriarchal culture of the time. Strict literalist interpreters commonly apply these passages directly to the present day in such a way that upholds the natural (or at least vocational) inferiority of women (for example, by prohibiting their ordination as Christian ministers). But a

79. See Jouette M. Bassler, *1 Timothy, 2 Timothy, Titus* (Nashville: Abingdon, 1996), 56, 60, 62. See also 1 Tim. 5:13; 2 Tim. 3:6–7. The writer may also be reacting to what he considers inappropriate female attire in the assemblies (1 Tim. 2:9–10).
80. See Raymond F. Collins, *I and II Timothy and Titus: A Commentary*, NTL (Louisville: Westminster John Knox, 2002), 64–78.
81. Cf. 2 Cor. 11:3.
82. Bassler, *1 Timothy, 2 Timothy, Titus*, 60–61. On the pre-Christian history of interpretation emphasizing Eve's unique guilt, see Geert van Oyen, "The Character of Eve in the New Testament," in *Out of Paradise: Eve and Adam and Their Interpreters*, ed. Bob Becking and Susanne Hennecke (Sheffield: Sheffield Phoenix, 2011), 24–25.

more nuanced approach, exemplified in various mainline Christian churches, recognizes that patriarchy is not endemic to the Christian faith. It is rather a cultural evil—still present today—that the Christian biblical and theological tradition, when considered in its entirety, strongly opposes. Galatians 3:28 leans more in this egalitarian and liberating direction.

Adam, Christ, and Resurrection

One of the most interesting and hotly debated aspects of Paul's thought is his understanding of Christ in relation to Adam. This topic surfaces in two main places. First, in 1 Cor. 15:21–22 and 45–49, the apostle juxtaposes Adam and Christ as a way to affirm a future resurrection of the dead. Second, in Rom. 5:12–21 the apostle invokes the disobedience of Adam as a foil to Christ's redemptive obedience. Since only the first of these passages ties directly to Gen. 1–2, it will be the exclusive focus here.[83]

The entirety of 1 Cor. 15 is aimed at assuring the Corinthians of a future resurrection.[84] The christological heart of the argument begins with Paul reminding them that Christ himself was raised as "the first fruits of those who have died" (15:20). That is, Christ marks the beginning of the resurrection and thus serves as a kind of eschatological guarantee of the Corinthians' own fate. To further support this christological argument, Paul next invokes the figure of Adam: "For since death came through a human being [anthrōpos], the resurrection of the dead has also come through a human being [anthrōpos]; for as all die in Adam, so all will be made alive in Christ" (15:21–22). This statement reflects Paul's belief (shared by many of his Jewish contemporaries) that human mortality entered creation as the result of Adam's primal disobedience (Gen. 3:6–7, 17–19).[85] The apostle invokes this human dilemma to make a point about the divine solution: God does not circumvent the problem of bodily mortality through the provision of a purely spiritual salvation, like the soul escaping the body after its death. Rather, God defeats death itself though the bodily resurrection of Christ.

Paul also wants to clarify that the resurrected body will not be the same as the earthly body. It will be transformed into a glorious and imperishable state. To accentuate the extent of this transformation, the apostle returns to the Adam-Christ juxtaposition (1 Cor. 15:45–49). Whereas Adam was a "living

83. For an overview of the Adam/Christ typology in Paul, see L. J. Kreitzer, "Adam and Christ," *DPL*, 9–15.
84. Space does not permit discussion of the issues in Corinth that prompted Paul's argument. See Hays, *First Corinthians*, 252–77.
85. See also Rom. 5:12–21.

SIDEBAR 3.7

1 Corinthians 15:45–49

[45]Thus it is written, "The first man, Adam, became a living being"; the last Adam became a life-giving spirit. [46]But it is not the spiritual that is first, but the physical, and then the spiritual. [47]The first man was from the earth, a man of dust; the second man is from heaven. [48]As was the man of dust, so are those who are of the dust; and as is the man of heaven, so are those who are of heaven. [49]Just as we have borne the image of the man of dust, we will also bear the image of the man of heaven.

---

being," the "last Adam became a life-giving Spirit." Whereas Adam was "from the earth, a man of dust," Christ is "from heaven." So also Christians who "have borne the image of the man of dust" can look forward to bearing "the image of the man of heaven" by virtue of their resurrection at the eschaton.

At first glance the difference between the Adamic and resurrected bodies can seem to suggest the replacement of the former by the latter rather than the transformation of the former into the latter.[86] Some popular English translations reinforce this misreading by using the terms "natural" and "spiritual" to capture the juxtaposition. These English terms imply a dichotomy between the material and nonmaterial and thus an utter discontinuity between the two bodies. Paul, however, wishes to assert a more paradoxical continuity with discontinuity. While the transformation from perishable to imperishable is indeed radical, Paul's own terms do not juxtapose a physical body and a spiritual body. Rather, they juxtapose a "natural" or "soul-animated" body (*to psychikon*) on the one hand, and a "Spirit-animated" body (*to pneumatikon*) on the other hand. The Spirit-animated body is the mortal body having become fully animated by God's own Spirit (1 Cor. 15:44, 46). That is why Paul refers to the risen Christ as a "life-giving spirit" (15:45)— not because Jesus entered into a merely spiritual, bodiless state but because Christ's mortal body was spiritualized, made imperishable by God's own Spirit. This transformation, Paul believes, is prototypical of the resurrection of all believers.[87]

Paul ventures no details beyond this bald description of the resurrected body. He apparently knows enough from early apostolic testimony and his own

---

86. The question is hotly debated by scholars. In addition to Hays (*First Corinthians*, 269–77), I am indebted to James Ware, "Paul's Understanding of the Resurrection in 1 Corinthians 15:36–54," *JBL* 133 (2014): 809–35.

87. See Luke Timothy Johnson, "Life-Giving Spirit: The Ontological Implications of Resurrection," *SCJ* 15 (2012): 75–89.

encounter with the risen Christ (1 Cor. 15:1–11) to assert the basic paradox. But he refuses to elaborate beyond it. Rhetorically, this reserved approach helps to keep the focus squarely on the way in which Christ's resurrection prefigures the redemption of human bodies and all of creation (see also Rom. 8:22–23). Indeed, Paul's reference to the risen Christ as "life-giving" may allude to the Creator who, in the beginning, breathed the "breath of life" into Adam (Gen. 2:7).[88] Obviously, however, this is much more than the restoration of an Adamic state. For Paul, the "last Adam" ushers creation into an entirely new state, free from death and decay. The resurrected body encapsulates both the "newness" and the "createdness" of this new state.

Garden of Eden

References to Paradise

The word *paradise* (Greek *paradeisos*) derives from an Old Persian term denoting an enclosed garden.[89] In early Jewish literature it became associated with the primordial garden of Eden.[90] Over time, and perhaps initially in Christian circles, it became associated with the afterlife, denoting the renewed Eden of eternal rest for the deceased righteous.[91] This is clearly the meaning of at least one of the three NT references to paradise, when the Lukan Jesus assures a criminal crucified alongside him, "Today you will be with me in Paradise" (Luke 23:43).

However, the other two NT references are somewhat different. In 2 Cor. 12:1–20 Paul refers to paradise in conjunction with a mystical experience in which an unnamed person (likely Paul himself) "was caught up into Paradise and heard things that are not to be told, that no mortal is permitted to repeat" (2 Cor. 12:4). In this instance an experience of paradise is assumed possible for the living, albeit in a limited way. Second, in Rev. 2:7, John communicates the following promise from God: "To everyone who conquers [i.e., proves faithful to God in the face of persecution], I will give permission to eat from the tree of life that is in the paradise of God." In this instance paradise has more to do with eschatology, the final culmination of salvation history, than with the

---

88. Jan Lambrecht, "Paul's Christological Use of Scripture in 1 Corinthians 15:20–28," *NTS* 28 (1982): 513.

89. James H. Charlesworth, "Paradise," *NIDB* 4:377.

90. See LXX Gen. 2:8, 9, 10, 15, 16; 3:1, 2, 3, 8, 10, 23, 24; Isa. 51:3; Ezek. 28:13; 31:8–9; Joel 2:3.

91. Martin Goodman, "Paradise, Gardens, and the Afterlife in the First Century CE," in *Paradise in Antiquity: Jewish and Christian Views*, ed. Markus Bockmuehl and Guy G. Stroumsa (Cambridge: Cambridge University Press, 2010), 57–63.

afterlife per se.[92] In fact this motif of the eschatological garden recurs again in Rev. 22, and with enough elaboration to warrant separate discussion below.

The New Edenic Jerusalem in Revelation 22:1–5

As previously noted, Rev. 21–22 contains a climactic vision of "a new heaven and a new earth," at the center of which stands "the new Jerusalem," descended from the upper heavens.[93] The new Jerusalem symbolizes the Christian community within God's new creation. John likens it to "a bride adorned for her husband" (21:1–2), thus suggesting an intimate bond between the persecuted Christian audience, on the one hand, and Christ (the husband), on the other hand. To make this point clear, John records the following heavenly voice: "See, the home of God is among mortals. He will dwell with them" (21:3). The vision of the new Jerusalem thus clarifies that no amount of persecution will prevent God's salvific communion with the faithful.

Additionally, scripturally minded hearers would have understood the new Jerusalem as an "improved, urban Eden,"[94] with the divine-human communion reversing Adam and Eve's expulsion from the garden (Gen. 3:23–24).[95] Supporting this interpretation is the fact that, in the new Jerusalem, "death will be no more; mourning and crying and pain will be no more" (Rev. 21:4). It was in the garden of Eden, after all, that God warned Adam that death would result from their disobedience (Gen. 2:17).

Further supporting this interpretation are subsequent references to "the river of the water of life" (Rev. 22:1) and "the tree of life" (v. 2) situated within the new Jerusalem. The river calls to mind Gen. 2:10: "A river flows out of Eden to water the garden." Significantly, in John's vision the river flows "from the throne of God and of the Lamb through the middle of the street of the city" (vv. 1–2). This makes clear the perpetual, divine source of the river (improving on its primordial counterpart),[96] as well as the primacy of the new Jerusalem as home to God's life-giving presence.

"The tree of life" (first mentioned in Rev. 2:7) refers to the tree that God planted in the midst of the primordial garden alongside the "tree of the knowl-

92. See Grant Macaskill, "Paradise in the New Testament," in Bockmuehl and Stroumsa, *Paradise in Antiquity*, 64–81.

93. See above under the heading "Cosmology."

94. Blount, *Revelation*, 395.

95. On the precedent for associating Jerusalem with Eden, see Terje Stordalen, "Heaven on Earth—or Not? Jerusalem as Eden in Biblical Literature," in *Beyond Eden: The Biblical Story of Paradise (Gen. 2–3) and Its Reception History*, ed. Konrad Schmid and Christoph Riedweg (Tübingen: Mohr Siebeck, 2008), 28–50.

96. Blount, *Revelation*, 396.

> **SIDEBAR 3.8**
>
> ## Revelation 22:1–5
>
> [1]Then the angel showed me the river of the water of life, bright as crystal, flowing from the throne of God and of the Lamb [2]through the middle of the street of the city. On either side of the river is the tree of life with its twelve kinds of fruit, producing its fruit each month; and the leaves of the tree are for the healing of the nations. [3]Nothing accursed will be found there any more. But the throne of God and of the Lamb will be in it, and his servants will worship him; [4]they will see his face, and his name will be on their foreheads. [5]And there will be no more night; they need no light of lamp or sun, for the Lord God will be their light, and they will reign for ever and ever.

edge of good and evil" (Gen. 2:9). By eating from the latter, Adam and Eve violated God's commandment, thus meriting various curses as well as expulsion from the garden (2:16–17; 3:1–24). The tree of life does not factor in the story of primal rebellion except at the very end, when God casts Adam and Eve from the garden in order that they "might [not] reach out [their] hand and take also from the tree of life, and eat, and live forever" (3:22). Having expelled the two humans, God goes so far as to place cherubim and a flaming sword at the east of Eden "to guard the way to the tree of life" (3:24).

While the mixing of urban and garden imagery in Rev. 22 creates some conceptual awkwardness, the presence and prominence of the tree of life[97] allows John to identify the new Jerusalem as the eschatological locus of God's new creation. The aforementioned claim that "death will be no more" (Rev. 21:4) now finds scriptural grounding, since it is by eating from the tree of life that humans receive immortality (Gen. 3:22). Likewise, the fact that "nothing accursed will be found" (Rev. 22:3) in the new Jerusalem may suggest the final lifting of the curses leveled against Adam, Eve, and the serpent (Gen. 3:14–24).[98] In place of curses and alienation, John envisions divine presence and worship (Rev. 22:3–4).

Various details of the tree of life in Revelation derive from Ezek. 47:1–12, a sixth-century BCE vision of an Edenic-like garden centered on a life-giving river and bountiful fruit trees.[99] To an extent, then, John has appropriated

97. See also Rev. 22:14, 19.
98. Robert H. Mounce, *The Book of Revelation*, rev. ed. NICNT (Grand Rapids: Eerdmans, 1998), 398. The linguistic parallels are not precise in the Greek.
99. On the similarities and differences, see David Mathewson, *A New Heaven and a New Earth: The Meaning and Function of the Old Testament in Revelation 21:1–22:5* (Sheffield: Sheffield Academic, 2003), 187–90.

Gen. 2 by means of a third, intermediary text. Regardless of the precise origin
of John's imagery, however, it is clear that he has drawn on the story of Eden
to support his underlying claim that God is both "the Alpha and Omega, the
first and the last, the beginning and the end" (Rev. 22:13).[100] Just as creation
begins as a garden, so its final consummation is a garden. Again, the point
would not have been lost on a persecuted community: "The one who over-
comes is guaranteed participation in the paradise of God."[101]

Garden and New Creation in John 19–20

The Gospel of John is unique among the canonical Gospels in diffusing the
passion story with garden imagery. Jesus prays in a garden (John 18:1). Peter
disavows Jesus by denying his own presence in the garden (18:26–27). Moreover,
both the crucifixion and entombment of Jesus occur in a garden (19:41). It is no
coincidence, then, that in Mary Magdalene's confusion over the empty tomb,
she mistakes the risen Jesus for a gardener (20:15) who has carried the dead Jesus
away. In reality, however, Jesus has been raised to new life in that same garden.

Given John's propensity for rich symbolism, it is unlikely that these uniquely
Johannine garden references function simply as historical descriptors or as
mere literary decoration. They make better sense in terms of an Eden motif
employed by John to convey the theological significance of Jesus's death and
resurrection.[102] This is, after all, the same Gospel that opens with a christological appropriation of Gen. 1 (John 1:1–15) and that consistently associates
the incarnation of God's creative word with the gift of life.[103] It is also the
same Gospel that, according to some scholars at least, includes various other
echoes of Gen. 1–2 within the Passion Narrative.[104] For instance, Pilate's presentation of Jesus to the crowd, "Behold, the man!" (*anthrōpos*, John 19:5)
may allude to the primal "man" (*anthrōpos*) of Genesis.[105] Also, the flowing
of water and blood from Jesus's pierced side (John 19:34) may allude to the

100. See also Rev. 1:8; 21:6.
101. Mathewson, *New Heaven*, 214.
102. It does not matter that John (19:41; cf. 18:1) uses a different word for garden (*kēpos*)
than LXX Genesis (*paradeisos*) since both words can translate the original Hebrew term (*gan*,
Gen. 2:8, etc.), as can be seen even in certain alternative translations of Gen. 2–3. See Brown,
"Creation's Renewal," 280.
103. See above under the heading "Cosmology."
104. On the following, see Brown, "Creation's Renewal," 281–84; John Painter, "Earth Made
Whole: John's Rereading of Genesis," in *Word, Theology, and Community in John*, ed. John
Painter, R. Alan Culpepper, and Fernando F. Segovia (St. Louis: Chalice, 2002), 65–84. For an
opposing view, see Carlos Raul Sosa Siliezar, *Creation Imagery in the Gospel of John* (London:
Bloomsbury, 2015).
105. Gen. 1:26–27; 2:7–8, 15, 18, 24.

creation of Eve out of the rib extracted from Adam (Gen. 2:21–23).[106] Finally, and more certainly, John's description of the risen Jesus "breathing" the Holy Spirit onto his disciples invokes the moment that God "breathed" life into Adam (*emphysaō*, John 20:22; Gen. 2:7 LXX).[107] While some of these Genesis echoes may not persuade independently, their cumulative effect is difficult to dismiss. There are good reasons for detecting in John's Passion Narrative "the iconography of Genesis 2."[108]

As for the Eden motif, it is a critical literary means by which John depicts Jesus's death and resurrection as salvific—indeed, as a unified act of new creation. It was in the primal garden that human communion with God (Gen. 2) deteriorated into disloyalty, shame, and alienation (Gen. 3). Significantly, the Johannine Passion Narrative reverses this sequence: disloyalty, shame, and alienation—particularly in the character of Peter (John 18:15–18, 25–27)[109]— are followed by the restoration of human communion with the Son of God (John 20). What were once cherubim guarding human entrance to the garden (Gen. 3:24) are now angels welcoming humans into the garden tomb (John 20:11–13). Thus, while Mary Magdalene may be wrong to assume that Jesus is a literal gardener, her misunderstanding ironically communicates an affiliation between Jesus and the one divine Gardener,[110] the God who sets the once-derailed story of creation back on track through the restoration of divine-human fellowship, which is eternal life.[111] Significantly, the same Peter who betrayed the crucified Jesus is singled out by the risen Jesus for restoration and commissioning (John 21:15–19).

Conclusion

While more could be said about each of the above topics, this essay has at least given readers a basic sense of how the NT writers engage Gen. 1–2 for their own rhetorical and theological purposes. It has been shown that the NT writers do not engage Genesis (or any other OT document) as a way to preserve its "original" meaning, much less to verify the historicity of past people and events, but rather they draw out the implications of the central

---

106. See also the symbolic meaning of water and blood in John 3:5; 4:13–15; 6:53–56; 7:38.
107. See also Ezek. 37:9 (LXX).
108. Mary L. Coloe, "Creation in the Gospel of John," in *Creation Is Groaning: Biblical and Theological Perspectives*, ed. Mary L. Coloe (Collegeville, MN: Liturgical Press, 2013), 77.
109. See also Judas's betrayal in John 18:1–11.
110. Gen. 2:8; 13:10; Isa. 51:3; Ezek. 31:8.
111. See Mariusz Rosik, "Discovering the Secrets of God's Gardens: Resurrection as New Creation (Gen. 2:4b–3:24; John 20:1–18)," *Liber Annuus* 58 (2008): 84–87.

Christian claim that Jesus Christ is risen Lord. Thus the diverse ways in which the NT appropriates Gen. 1–2 are a function of the diversity inherent in the NT itself, in which certain core convictions about Jesus lead in various directions, depending on the writer in question and the circumstances of the audience being addressed. In the specific case of Gen. 1–2, scriptural language and themes have been used by the NT writers both to recall God's creation of the cosmos and to anticipate apocalyptic cataclysm, both to challenge gender-based differences and to reinforce them, both to direct readers toward a paradisiacal future and to ground them in a this-worldly redemption.

To the extent that there exists a unifying link to these claims, it is the conviction that Jesus's life, death, and resurrection bring about a renewal of creation. The Christian gospel affirms the benevolence of the Creator, the inherent goodness of creation, and the privileged place of human creatures within salvation history. In this respect, God's salvific actions in the present and future mirror God's creative actions in the beginning.

For Further Reading

Brown, Jeannine K. "Creation's Renewal in the Gospel of John." *CBQ* 72, no. 2 (2010): 275–90.

Brown, William P., S. Dean McBride Jr., eds. *God Who Creates: Essays in Honor of W. Sibley Towner*. Grand Rapids: Eerdmans, 2000.

Lincoln, Andrew T. "Sabbath, Rest, and Eschatology in the New Testament." In *From Sabbath to Lord's Day: A Biblical, Historical, and Theological Investigation*, edited by D. A. Carson, 197–220. Grand Rapids: Zondervan, 1982.

Mathewson, David. *A New Heaven and a New Earth: The Meaning and Function of the Old Testament in Revelation 21:1–22:5*. JSNTSup 238. Sheffield: Sheffield Academic, 2003.

McDonough, Sean M. *Christ as Creator: Origins of a New Testament Doctrine*. Oxford: Oxford University Press, 2009.

Menken, Maarten J. J., and Steve Moyise, eds. *Genesis in the New Testament*. LNTS 466. London: T&T Clark, 2014.

Pennington, Jonathan T., and Sean M. McDonough, eds. *Cosmology and New Testament Theology*. LNTS 355. London: T&T Clark, 2008.

Primary Texts

Matthew 11:28–12:37   John 18
Mark 10:1–12   Romans 5

1 Corinthians 11:2–16   2 Peter 3

1 Corinthians 15   Revelation 21–22

1 Timothy 2

Primary Texts Online

1. Online searchable Bible with over 150 versions
   www.biblegateway.com
2. YouVersion Bible with English and foreign language versions (also available as an app)
   https://www.bible.com/bible/12/JHN.1.ASV

4

Early Rabbinic Interpretations
of Genesis 1–2

JOEL S. ALLEN

After the destruction of Jerusalem's temple in 70 CE, the Jewish Sanhedrin sought to discover a new foundation for their faith. Without a temple, they were prevented from carrying out the biblical laws concerning sacrifice. They arrived at a concept called Talmud Torah (study of the Torah), which signified that since they were no longer able to actually fulfill many of the laws of the Torah (the first five books in the Hebrew Bible), God ordained that the law be kept through the study of it. Schools for the study of Torah became the new temple, rabbis/scholars the new priests, students the new attendants, and the study itself the new sacrificial offering. This revolutionary understanding became the spring from which a river of biblical interpretation flowed and shaped the contours of rabbinic literary landscape.

One of the primary sources for rabbinic interpretation on the creation texts is a collection called Genesis Rabbah. This commentary on Genesis examines almost every single verse, often word by word. Genesis Rabbah is the first section of a larger collection of biblical commentary called Midrash Rabbah.[1] The standard English translation of Midrash Rabbah is that of H. Freedman and Maurice Simon. Jacob Neusner has published both a new translation and a separate anthology of readings and commentary on Genesis Rabbah called *Confronting Creation*. Pertinent here are also two well-known collections of rabbinic legends related to the Bible. Louis Ginzberg edited countless midrashic stories into a single stream of narrative called *Legends of the Jews*, which has recently been republished in two volumes. The Israeli poet Hayim Bialik with Yehoshua Ravnitsky produced a lovely collection translated into English as *Book of Legends*. I have written a general introduction for Christians called *Jewish Biblical Legends: Rabbinic Wisdom for Christian Readers*.[2]

The exact compilation date of Genesis Rabbah is unknown, although it is likely to have been in the late fourth and early fifth centuries CE. This collection of midrash comes from the first two periods of rabbinic history, the Tannaitic and Amoraic periods. The Tannaitic period spans approximately 10–220 CE, when much of this literature remained in oral form. "Tannaim" actually means "repeaters," reflecting the repetition, memorization, and instruction of the oral Torah. The Amoraic period was named after the Amoraim, the rabbinic spokesmen who were teachers and compilers of Jewish Law from the critical period of 220–500 CE.

The primary language of the midrash is Mishnaic Hebrew, a form of Hebrew associated with the Mishnah and the Talmuds. Mishnaic Hebrew was a language of the study halls, with Aramaic as the language of the household. A shift toward Aramaic as the language of the academy is evidenced in the text of Genesis Rabbah itself since explanatory portions that date from a later time appear in Aramaic. After the publication of the Mishnah, Mishnaic Hebrew began to fall from academic use; hence much of the commentary that followed in the Talmud appears in Aramaic. Mishnaic Hebrew survived as an academic/liturgical language.

The original setting for the material we encounter in Genesis Rabbah arises from the public lectures of the beth midrash (rabbinic training centers) and the preaching of the synagogue. Rabbis expounded the depths of Scripture for their disciples and sought to outdo their fellow rabbis with feats of exegetical wonder.[3]

1. Midrash refers to all rabbinic biblical interpretation. The word *midrash* comes from the Hebrew verb *dārash*, meaning "to study" or more fundamentally "to inquire."
2. See For Further Reading at the end of this chapter for more information.
3. Jacob Neusner provides one possible interpretive background for Genesis Rabbah. See *Confronting Creation: How Judaism Reads Genesis; An Anthology of Genesis Rabbah* (Columbia: University of South Carolina Press, 1991), 9.

Midrash is sometimes serious, sometimes lighthearted, and often playful. Many times we should imagine rabbis playing games with Scripture with an eye to getting a chuckle from their students. Often, after hours of exhausting work studying and debating legal texts, rabbis turned to this nonlegal work for comedic relief. Over and over we find the rabbis making sport of Scripture—often by tweaking a feature of the Hebrew text. Rabbis also loved to create clever background stories to illuminate a well-known biblical story with a new coloration and application. Usually their new perspective invests a feature of the Hebrew text with a profound twist or insight. Typically we find rabbis ascribing mountains of meaning to mundane features of the Hebrew text. Because the words of Torah are the very words of God, even its incidental details were of vast significance.

Halakah comes from the verb "to walk" (*hālak*) and refers to all legal instruction for the walk of life. All the legal texts of the rabbinic world (namely, the Mishnah, Tosefta, and the Talmuds) concerned the daily living of a typical Jew. The great majority of what they debated and wrote about was legal. The rabbinic texts we will explore are called *haggadah*, meaning "what is told."[4] Haggadic literature includes anything the rabbis said that fell outside the bounds of halakah: simple sayings of wisdom, anecdotes about the lives of the rabbis, parables about kings and palaces, stories about characters in the Bible, and even fully developed sermons. In rabbinic literature, haggadah is engaging and entertaining, while halakah is complicated and often quite burdensome.

Rabbis wrote about haggadah as if it contained an almost seductive power. The phrase "delights of the flesh" (Eccles. 2:8) is said to refer to the haggadah, which gives delight to the study of Scripture. Haggadah is described as fragrant with aroma redolent of the lilies in the Song of Solomon. Whole episodes in the life of Abraham, Isaac, Jacob, and Moses seem to be spun out of thin air. They believed that what the Bible left unmentioned, a wise interpreter could fill in through careful reading of contextual clues. Countless stories, completely unmentioned in Scripture, were told about biblical characters. Who knew that Abraham as a young man destroyed the household gods of his idolatrous father? In telling these stories, rabbis sometimes shed light on the meaning of the biblical stories, and sometimes they created whole new frameworks of meaning. From the haggadah, we learn virtually everything the rabbis believed about God, creation, commandments,

---

4. While *midrash* explicitly refers to rabbinic biblical interpretation, *haggadah* is a broader term, including all nonlegal sayings and wisdom. The two words are closely related but distinct; all midrash is haggadah, but not all haggadah is midrash.

angels, demons, magic, superstition, folktales, folk medicine, charms, and so on.[5]

More importantly, for the rabbis the study of haggadah qualifies as a distinct and direct pathway to the worship and knowledge of God. If a person wants to know and understand God, the study of the haggadah is essential since it provides countless insights helpful for the interpretation of Scripture.[6] For the rabbis, the Bible was not only a source of Torah. The words of Torah became a lens through which the rabbis viewed every element of life. The Torah gave them the vocabulary by which they interpreted the tragedies and triumphs of life. The study of Torah became a sacred temple of divine presence that replaced the Jerusalem temple after its destruction in 70 CE. Seeking the meaning of particular verses, "they would search after it, first, in themselves, in their own experiences and in what they knew to be true. If Scripture could not lie, neither could it be false or contradictory to the rabbis' own selves and to their knowledge, their sense of the world and of their place in it."[7]

James Kugel identifies several basic assumptions that underlie all traditional biblical interpretation. The first assumption is that the Scriptures are fundamentally relevant to contemporary life and its challenges. Second, the Scriptures are perfect and perfectly harmonious. While there might appear to be discrepancies in the Bible, these apparent variances are not mistakes but opportunities to search for the deeper textual truths. Because there is perfect harmony within all parts of the Bible, any biblical text can be used to illustrate another. Third is the notion of "omnisignificance," which claims that nothing is said in vain or for rhetorical flourish. Every detail of Scripture is an access point to a never-ending world of interpretive possibilities to be explored. Finally, all Scripture is of divine provenance, or divinely inspired.[8]

There has been a long debate over the question, Does midrash seek to interpret Scripture or to manipulate Scripture to advance rabbinic ideology? Collections of midrash were seen to be interpretations that could be read in isolation from one another and that divine the deeper meaning of Scripture.[9]

---

5. David Stern, introduction to *The Book of Legends: Sefer Ha-Aggadah Legends from the Talmud and Midrash*, ed. Hayim N. Bialik and Yehoshua H. Ravnitzky, trans. William G. Braude (New York: Schocken, 1992), xvii.

6. Stern, introduction, xxi.

7. Stern, introduction, xx.

8. James Kugel, *The Bible as It Was* (Cambridge, MA: Belknap, 1999), 17–23.

9. For example, see Kugel, *Bible as It Was*, 17–23. Jay M. Harris is largely of the same opinion as Kugel. He writes, "The relentless insistence on the exegetical foundations of Jewish practice that dominate *halakhic* discussions of the various rabbinic documents leaves little doubt that,

The other scholarly position seeks to construe the midrashic texts as tightly constructed, with a broad theological purpose. Midrash generally and haggadic traditions specifically were not snippets of isolated rabbinic exegesis but sustained arguments on various topics in which Scripture plays only a secondary role. Neusner and Green argue that the rabbis' initial catalyst was not the canonization of Scripture but the destruction of the Second Temple in 70 CE and the theological transformation by which the study of Torah replaced the temple as that which mediated divine presence.[10]

Richard Sarason and Philip Alexander offer a median position. According to Sarason, what has led to such an intractable difference in perspective is the tendency to maximize emphasis of certain elements of midrash at the expense of others. One must bear in mind at least three factors that are always at play in rabbinic midrash: the eisegetical, the exegetical, and the performative.[11] The very opacity of Scripture provided a climate for eisegesis. The more arcane the text, the more interpretation is unchained from authorial intent and the greater freedom the interpreter has to import their own bias and agenda. Yet the rabbis are often careful readers of Scripture both in terms of its actual content and its textual details. This is the exegetical factor. Their commentary often serves "to deepen the biblical text through contemporizing paraphrase or dramatization."[12] The final impulse, the performative, involves the competitive spirit of the beth midrash, according to which each interpreter gained status and praise for his ability to discover new insights from well-known passages of Scripture.[13] According to Sarason, these three factors or impulses are in constant dialogue with each other, and the modern interpreter of the midrash must bear in mind all three components.[14]

---

in general, these documents are informed by the belief that many Jewish practices are to be derived from the Torah exegetically." *How Do We Know This?* (New York: State University of New York Press, 1995), 3.

10. Jacob Neusner and William Green, *Writing with Scripture* (Eugene, OR: Wipf & Stock, 2003), 10.

11. Richard Sarason, "Interpreting Rabbinic Biblical Interpretation: The Problem of Midrash, Again," in *Ḥesed ve-Emet: Studies in Honor of Ernest S. Frerichs*, ed. Jodi Magness and Seymore Gitin (Atlanta: Scholars Press, 1998), 133–54. See also P. Alexander, "Midrash," in *A Dictionary of Biblical Interpretation*, ed. R. J. Coogins and J. Houlden (Philadelphia: Trinity Press International, 1990), 455.

12. Sarason, "Rabbinic Biblical Interpretation," 138–39.

13. Sarason, "Rabbinic Biblical Interpretation," 140–41.

14. Rimon Kasher has argued similarly by using the language of *confirmatory midrashim*, which provide biblical backing for existing legal rulings, and *creative midrashim*, which deduce new laws from Scripture. "Scripture in Rabbinic Literature," in *Mikra: Text, Translation, Reading and Interpretation of the Hebrew Bible in Ancient Judaism and Early Christianity*, ed. Martin Mulder and Harry Sysling (Peabody, MA: Hendrickson, 2004), 581.

Treatment of Days

> In the beginning, when God created the heavens and the earth. (Gen. 1:1)

The rabbis were able to find depths of meaning in something as mundane as the first letter in the Torah. The Hebrew Bible begins with the word *bərē'šît*, so the first letter is the letter *B* (*bêt* in Hebrew). A *bêt* has this shape: ‏ב‎. Rabbis imagine many possible reasons why. One view is that the *bêt* has the numerical value of 2, which represents the two worlds of rabbinic interest (this present world and the coming messianic age). In another opinion, *bêt* is the first letter of Torah since the word "blessed" in Hebrew (*bāruk*) begins with a *bêt*. The first letter of the alphabet in Hebrew (*'aleph*) is also the first letter in the word "cursed" (*'ārûr*). Rabbis imagine an argument between the letters *A* and *B* as to which would be the first in Torah. When *A* claims that being the first letter in the alphabet, it should also be first in Torah, God counters by saying that when he reveals his commandments at Sinai, he will commence with none other than the letter *A*. Therefore, *B* gets to start the Torah.[15]

To understand the following interpretation, it is important to know that Hebrew is read from right to left rather than from left to right. That means that the open part of the *bêt* is facing forward. There must be deep significance to the fact that the very first letter of Holy Scripture takes this particular shape. "Why was the world created using the letter ‏ב‎? Just how the *bet* is closed on the sides and open to the front, so it isn't permitted to investigate what is above, what is below and what is before and what is behind. But from the day the world was created and thereafter (it is permitted)."[16]

The rabbis imagine themselves residing in the *bêt* of *bərē'šît* and thus looking forward toward the opening. There is a line behind them, under them, over them but not in front of them. However, the two arms of the letter only extend out a little way and stop. This is deeply instructive as the shape of the *bêt* indicates limitations of human knowledge and direction for our spiritual inquiry. We should not inquire too much about what came before the creation of the world (there is a boundary behind us), what is above the creation (there is a boundary above us), or what is below creation (there is a boundary below us). Our focus must be on the created world, and our inquiry must end when the world ends (where the arms of the *bêt* end). The letter *bêt*, shaped as it is, provides a clue about the limitations of theological inquiry; our focus

---

15. Gen. Rab. 1:10. The Ten Commandments were seen as beginning with the word "I" (Exod. 20:2), which in Hebrew begins with an *'aleph*. The letters *A* and *B* are used symbolically here, as *'aleph* is transliterated not with the letter *A* but with the symbol '.

16. Gen. Rab. 1:10.

must be on this created world and the challenges of the present. Excessive speculations, enthralling though they might be, distract the community from its primary task.[17]

Other texts further restricted study of the work of creation (*ma'ăseh bərē'šît*).

A. The biblical division on illicit sexual relations may not be expounded by three, nor the creation story (*ma'ăseh bərē'šît*) by two, nor the chariot by one alone, unless he was wise (a scholar) and understood on his own accord.

B. Anyone who gazes at four things, it would be merciful for him had he not come into the world: What is above and what is below, what is ahead and what is behind.

C. Anyone who has no concern for the honor of his owner, it would be merciful for him had he never come into the world.[18]

In point A, the restriction against study of *ma'ăseh bərē'šît* is placed alongside restrictions against expounding on texts dealing with explicit sexual content (Lev. 18 and 20) and texts that can be interpreted in excessively mystical ways (chariots were associated with mysticism; Ezek. 1 is in view). Our text restricts study on the creation texts (Gen. 1:1–2:3) by two, which the talmudic commentary explains to mean that one must never teach this topic to two persons at once. This must be one-on-one education between a trusted teacher and an advanced student. God, our true owner, has not provided this esoterica, so excessive seeking amounts to disrespect for the limitations God has set on human knowledge.[19]

God called the light Day. (Gen. 1:5)

Rabbis discuss in great detail God's creation of original light, which appears on the first day. Some claimed it was formed from the irradiated luster of the robes of divine majesty. Others claimed it was created from the place

---

17. The dangers of excessive philosophical speculation are echoed in Col. 2:8. Irenaeus also warned against gnostic-like speculations into the creation (*Haer.* 1.18.1), which he later calls rash suppositions by which one is tempted to replace God himself with speculative foolishness (*Haer.* 2.28.3). Irenaeus is likely aware of and influenced by rabbinic warnings against fascination with creation since both rabbis and early Christians struggled against similar gnostic tendencies.

18. See m. Ḥag. 2:1, trans. Yair Furstenberg, based on Codex Kaufmann, in "The Rabbinic Ban on *Ma'aseh Bereshit*: Sources, Contexts and Concerns," in *Jewish and Christian Cosmogony in Late Antiquity*, ed. Lance Jenott and Sarit Kattan Gribetz, Texts and Studies in Ancient Judaism 155 (Tübingen: Mohr Siebeck, 2013), 43.

19. Furstenberg, "Rabbinic Ban," 62.

of the temple. Why is light mentioned five times in Gen. 1? This is to remind
the reader of the five books of Moses, which compose the Torah.[20] Rabbis
understand the creation of the original light as different from the light that
comes from the sun, seeing that it was created before the sun. Some rabbis
point out that God's original light is not presently visible since it would completely eclipse the sun. So where is it? It is being stored up for the righteous
in the world to come.[21]

In Gen. 1:5, the rabbis noticed what might appear to be a very minor and
grammatically mundane feature of the biblical text. The word *God* only appears when God called the light "Day," yet the pronoun "he" occurs in the next
phrase when God called the darkness "Night." Why is the word *God* absent
from the phrase referring to night? According to one rabbi, this is because
God always refuses to link his name with evil.[22] Another rabbi notices that
in Gen. 1:5, the text does not say that God created evening and morning but
only that evening and morning existed. This led him to suppose that God
had created many worlds before he created this one. "This one pleases me,
but those did not please me," God said. When God surveyed everything he
made and proclaimed it "very good," he contrasted the present good world
to previously made but deficient worlds.[23]

When God considered the world he was about to create, he drew to mind
the actions of both the righteous and the wicked. When the creation story
says the earth was desolate, it alluded to the deeds of the wicked. In saying,
"Let there be light" and "God saw the light was good," the text refers to
deeds done by the righteous, which are seen beforehand by God. When it
says, "There was evening," it refers to the encroaching night of darkness of
evil deeds. The Hebrew text in Gen. 1:5 literally says, "There was evening,
and there was morning, one day." What is this "one day"? This refers to the
day of judgment, on which the wicked of the earth will suffer divine wrath.[24]

Another topic concerned the day on which angels were created. The biblical
account says nothing on the matter, yet they must have been created sometime
during the first week. One view is that angels must have been created on day 2,
when God separated the lower waters from the upper waters. Since God created the heavenly realms that day, this must have included angels. Another
view is that God created angels on day 5, when God created all other flying

20. Gen. Rab. 3:5.
21. Gen. Rab. 3:6. This messianic light finds biblical support in Isa. 30:26, which speaks of
a future light in a new age as seven times brighter than present light.
22. Gen. Rab. 3:6.
23. Gen. Rab. 3:7.
24. Gen. Rab. 3:8.

things. They agreed that angels were not created on the first day lest someone claim that angels were due some of the glory of creation. As is typical of rabbis, they here compare and contrast God to a human king. Both make use of royal dignitaries, but human kings share the burden of their rule with their dignitaries. God makes use of angels without sharing the actual burden of his reign with them. Angels therefore have no share in God's glory. God created the world alone and alone is truly God. To make this distinction absolute, God created no angels on day 1.[25]

Cosmology

> Let there be a dome in the midst of the waters. (Gen. 1:6)

In accord with ancient understandings, rabbis also believed the earthly sphere was suspended between lower and upper waters.[26] The firmament functioned as a spherical shield to hold back the upper waters and provide an air pocket for living things. Rabbis, discussing Gen. 1:6, contrasted God's creative power to that of an earthly monarch. While human monarchs roof their palaces with stones, timber, and earth, God is able to roof his world with water.[27] Other rabbis imagine this happening through the solidification of a middle layer of waters into a protective barrier. This solidification of the middle waters was produced by a fire proceeding from the heavens itself. Opinions on the thickness of the firmament vary between the thickness of the earth itself and the thickness of a plate. The firmament was created out of fire and water beaten together.[28]

Rabbis did not necessarily believe in creation ex nihilo ("out of nothing"). The Hebrew text of Gen. 1:1 allows that some original matter may have existed out of which God created the universe. This is reflected in the NRSV translation: "In the beginning when God created the heavens and the earth." The opening verse stands as an introduction to God's first act of creation, which here is the creation of original light (Gen. 1:3). The preexisting circumstances are that the earth was already formless and void (tōhû wābōhû). This poses a problem. Some claimed that God used inferior building materials (tōhû wābōhû) in creation so that the resulting world was equally defective.

25. Gen. Rab. 1:3.
26. An image search for "three-tiered universe" (e.g., via Google) will produce many depictions of this ancient worldview.
27. Gen. Rab. 4:1.
28. Gen. Rab. 4:5. As is almost always the case, biblical texts support each opinion.

SIDEBAR 4.1

Genesis Rabbah 4:3

R. Phinehas said in R. Oshaya's name: As there is a void between the earth and the firmament, so is there a void between the firmament and the upper waters, as it is written, LET THERE BE A FIRMAMENT IN THE MIDST OF THE WATERS, meaning, midway between them. R. Tanhuma said: I will state the proof. If it said, "And God made the firmament, and He divided between the waters ... which are upon the firmament," I would say that the water lies directly upon the firmament itself. Since, however, it is stated, "And between the waters which are above the firmament," it follows that the upper waters are suspended by the word [of God]. R. Aha said: It is like [the flame of] a lamp and their fruits are the rain.

Note: Maurice Simon, trans., *Midrash Rabbah: Genesis*, vol. 1 of *Midrash Rabbah* (London: Soncino, 1939; repr., San Bernardino, CA: Ulan Press, 2012).

Rabbis disagreed yet recognized that their own Scriptures seemed to allow for this possibility.[29]

The text that addresses this problem is Gen. Rab. 1:5, here quoted only in part.

Rab said, "Under ordinary circumstances, if a mortal king builds a palace in a place where there had been sewers, garbage, and junk, will not whoever may come and say, 'This palace is built on a place where there were sewers, garbage and junk,' give offense? So too, will not whoever comes and says, 'This world was created out of chaos, emptiness, and darkness' give offense?" R. Huna in the name of Bar Qappara: "Were the matter not explicitly written in scripture, it would not be possible to state it at all: 'God created the heavens and the earth' (Gen. 1:1). From what? From the following: 'And the earth was chaos'" (Gen. 1:2).[30]

In Rab's opinion, the Hebrew text does imply that God created the world from preexistent materials, but this does not mean that God created a faulty world. God, being perfect, created an absolutely perfect world even though it was built by using a chaotic mass. One cannot blame suffering on God's

29. Neusner, *Confronting Creation*, 27.
30. Gen. Rab. 1:5. I based this rendering on the translation of Neusner, primarily removing the outline system he followed as it was thrown off by my abridgement (*Confronting Creation*, 27). I also consulted the translation of Freedman where the Neusner translation was hard to follow. See H. Freedman and Maurice Simon, *Midrash Rabbah: Genesis*, vol. 2 of *Midrash Rabbah* (New York: Socino, 1983), 2.

defective creation since this pins on God the responsibility for our own sins. Even so, R. Huna claims that if it were not explicitly stated in Scripture, one would never be inclined to claim that God created the universe from an original chaotic state.

The notion of *creatio ex nihilo* is accepted more readily in other rabbinic texts. For instance, rabbis love to provide lists of things. In one list, they name things that existed before the creation of the world. They are as follows: Torah, throne of glory, patriarchs, Israel, temple, name of Messiah, and repentance.[31] The chaotic material is not on this list. Another rabbinic list defines six items required for a typical building project: water, earth, wood, stones, canes, iron. Yet God needed only Torah to create the world.[32] In another passage, rabbis list ten things that were created on day 1: heaven and earth, *tōhû wābōhû*, light and darkness, wind and water, and the measure of day and night.[33] Again, the *tōhû wābōhû* were created on day 1 and were not preexisting creation.

Creation and Nature of Humanity

This one shall be called *Woman*! (Gen. 2:23)

The *imago Dei* of Gen. 1:26–27 shapes rabbinic understanding of our humanity as the following rather humorous haggadah illuminates.

> When the Holy One, blessed be he, created the first man, the serving angels mistook him [for God Himself] and asked if they could proclaim him holy. What did the Holy One, blessed be he, do? He made him fall into a deep sleep so that everyone would know that he was a mere man. This can be compared to a king and a governor riding together in a state carriage. The people of the province were about to cry out, "*Domine!*" but did not know which one was king. What did the king do? He pushed the governor out of the carriage so that everyone would know that that one was no more than a governor.[34]

In the above interpretation, God put Adam to sleep, not only to take a rib to create Eve, but also to prove to the angels that Adam was a mere man and thus to discourage the angels from worshiping Adam! The idea that the angels would be tempted to worship Adam may stem from traditions in which Adam, when first created and before the entrance of sin, was of absolutely

---

31. Gen. Rab. 1:4.
32. Gen. Rab. 1:8.
33. See b. Ḥag. 2:12.
34. Gen. Rab. 8:10.

massive size and beauty. His body virtually reached from earth to heaven and spanned from east to west. After Adam's sin, God laid his hands on him and diminished him to his present size.[35]

Tremendous interpretive energy went into explaining the serpent, Eve, and the first sin. What is the relationship between Satan and the serpent? Why did Eve fall for the serpent's wiles? Why didn't Adam do something to stop Eve? The rabbis, from the beginning, appreciate Eve not only as the mother of the human race but also as a submissive wife. They speculated about the reason why two wives seem to have been created for Adam (one unnamed in Gen. 1:27 and Eve in 2:23) and decided that Adam must have been married twice. They ascribed the name Lilith to Adam's first wife. She insisted on having equal status with her husband and was thus dispelled from the garden. Genesis 1:27 implies that both she and Adam were equally made in God's image, and Lilith insisted on claiming her half.[36] In place of Lilith, God gave Adam the woman Eve, made from his own rib. While a little gullible, Eve knew her place and knew not to rise above it. It is this duality—liking Eve because she is not Lilith but finding her partly responsible for the fall—that shapes rabbinic thinking about her. In fact, in spite of how unsympathetic the rabbis are with Lilith, they, at least in this instance, give Eve every benefit of the doubt concerning her innocence and integrity.

> The Holy One, blessed be He, said, "For when you eat of it, you will certainly die" (Gen. 2:17). She, however, didn't say this [to the serpent when asked] but said, "God said, 'You should not eat of it *or even touch it* or you will die (Gen. 3:3).'" The serpent saw her speaking an untruth. He took her and threw her against the tree. "Did that kill you?" he asked. "Just as you were not killed by touching it, you won't be by eating it."[37]

The rabbis noticed that Eve, when she explained the prohibition against eating of the forbidden fruit, added the line "or touch it" (Gen. 3:3). God had initially only told Adam not to eat of the tree (2:17), so Adam must have added the prohibition "or touch it" when he relayed the information to Eve.

35. See b. Ḥag. 2:1. For the striking degree to which rabbis were free to think of God in thoroughly human terms, see Jacob Neusner and William Green, *Rabbinic Judaism: Structure and System* (Minneapolis: Fortress, 1994).

36. Louis Ginzberg, *Legends of the Jews*, trans. Henrietta Szold and Paul Radin (1909; repr. in 2 vols., London: Forgotten Books, 2008), 1:64. The Lilith tradition developed significantly in the eighth to tenth centuries (after the period discussed here). However, Lilith is mentioned several times in the Babylonian Talmud, a fact that underlies my assumption that these traditions had some prehistory in the earlier rabbinic period.

37. Gen. Rab. 19:4–5.

SIDEBAR 4.2

Genesis Rabbah 19:3–5

AND THE WOMAN SAID UNTO THE SERPENT: OF THE FRUIT OF THE TREES OF THE GARDEN WE MAY EAT (Gen. 3:2). Now where was Adam during this conversation? Abba Ilalfon b. Koriah said: He had engaged in his natural functions [sc. intercourse] and then fallen asleep. The Rabbis said: He [God] took him and led him all around the world, telling him: "Here is a place fit for planting [trees], here is a place fit for sowing [cereals]." Thus it is written, THROUGH A LAND THAT NO MAN PASSED THROUGH AND WHERE NO MAN (adam) DWELT (Jer. 2:6): i.e., Adam had not dwelt there. BUT OF THE FRUIT OF THE TREE WHICH IS IN THE MIDST OF THE GARDEN, GOD HATH SAID: YE SHALL NOT EAT OF IT, NEITHER SHALL YE TOUCH IT, LEST YE DIE (Gen. 3:3). ... Thus, the Holy One, blessed be He, had said, FOR IN THE DAY THAT THOU EATEST THEREOF THOU SHALL SURELY DIE (Gen. 2:17); whereas she did not say thus, but, God hath said: YE SHALL NOT EAT OF IT, NEITHER SHALL YE TOUCH IT. When he [the serpent] saw her thus lying, he took and thrust her against it. "Have you then died?" he said to her; "Just as you were not stricken through touching it, so will you not die when you eat it, but FOR GOD DOTH KNOW THAT IN THE DAY YE EAT THEREOF," etc. (Gen. 3:5).

Note: Simon, Midrash Rabbah: Genesis, vol. 1.

Rabbis speculate about why Adam included something God had not actually said. They supposed that Adam added the proscription against touching the forbidden tree out of zeal for God's law.

Yet the shrewd serpent is able to exploit this addition and execute his plan for their downfall. The serpent knows God never said that touching the tree would evoke death. Yet Eve believes this is what the Lord said. The serpent shoves Eve up into the tree. According to the fuller midrash elsewhere, this causes Eve to say to herself, "All that my master [as she referred to Adam] has said to me is but lies."[38]

Another midrash contains a conversation between the rabbis as to what Adam was doing during Eve's interlocutions with the serpent. One rabbi claimed that they had just had sexual intercourse and he had fallen asleep![39] This is based on the fact that the last verse in chapter 2 speaks of the two of them becoming one flesh, which of course refers to sexual intercourse. Genesis 3:6 says that when she ate, she gave some to her husband, who was with her, and he ate. Why did he not say anything to stop her if he had been there all along? The answer is that they had had sex and he had fallen asleep!

---

38. Ginzberg, *Legends*, 1:71.
39. Gen. Rab. 19:3.

Then he woke up and innocently ate the fruit Eve handed him, not knowing from whence it came.

Some sages question why God chose to create a single human as the progenitor of the entire human race rather than a group of people all at once.

> Man was created alone in order to teach that anyone who murders a single soul (from Israel), Scripture treats him as if he was guilty of the destruction of the entire world. And anyone who saves alive a single soul (in Israel), Scripture treats him as if he established the whole world. Again, [man was created alone] in the interest of peace among men, so that one man might not say to his companion, "My father was more glorious than yours," and that heretics cannot say, "There are many ruling forces in heaven." Another purpose is to proclaim the greatness of the Holy One, blessed be He. For if a man strikes many coins from one die, they all look like the others; in fact, they are all exactly the same. But though the King of kings, the Holy One, blessed be He, fashioned every man from the die of the first man, not a single one of them is exactly like his fellow. Hence, each and every person should say, "The world was created for my sake."[40]

Rabbis believed that destroying a single life was commensurate to the destruction of the whole world. By this, they mean that when we destroy a human life, we erase from the earth all the benefits and influence that person and their descendants might have had. Thus the potential world that would have resulted including that particular person is forever lost. God chose to create all people from one man, Adam, so that we would always have a clear lesson of the impact of a single life.

The second saying looks in the opposite direction. God chose to create all from one, not to glorify the individual, but to humble the individual. No one can claim a superior bloodline since all human ancestry goes back to the same person created by the same deity. The creation of all humans from one original human also speaks to the unity of God. We would expect different gods to create their own distinct prototypes of our race. The final opinion is strikingly clever. It notes the superiority of God's creative power in comparison to our human creative powers. When humans strike coins, each coin coming from the press has an identical image. While God created all humans from the same template, every human being has a unique appearance. God is not simply striking humans out of a die like one might find in a mint. The uniqueness of our humanity and the glory of God's creative power are extolled.

40. See b. Sanh. 38a.

Garden of Eden

And the Lᴏʀᴅ God planted a garden in Eden, in the east. (Gen. 2:8)

As we have seen, the interests of the rabbis are not primarily historical but practical. They were interested in what God wants from his *imago Dei* in the present reality. In their estimation, the situation of the first humans led to the current predicament of all humanity. Thus the rabbis read back into the Eden story legal principles that might not be evident to the casual reader, for the story was a harbinger of all God's expectations left unmet by our human sinfulness.

> Rabbis interpret the passage in this way: "'And the Lord God commanded' (Gen. 2:16). He said to him, 'What am I? I am God. I wish to be treated like God, so he may not curse me.' [That proves only that Adam was commanded not to blaspheme.] How do we know that he was commanded not to fornicate? 'And cleave to *his* wife' (Gen. 2:24), and not to the wife of his neighbor, to a male, or to an animal." [So rabbis find in the verse only two prohibitions, against blasphemy and fornication.][41]

This passage has as its context a discussion of how much of the later human condition can be creatively read back into the creation story. If we know that God has general moral requirements for all humans—that is, natural laws that gentiles are required to observe—how many of these can be gleaned through a careful reading of the original story of creation? In this passage, rabbis deduced several implied commandments lurking in the textual minutia. The text is interpreted so that Torah is foreshadowed in the beginning. God's laws are unchanging and apparent only to the trained reader. On the surface, there is only one law in the creation texts (Gen. 2:17), but a creative reading might find much more.

In the text above, the interpreter claims that the reason the full name "the Lᴏʀᴅ God" appears in Gen. 2:16 is because God wanted to remind humans of who he is and that his name is not to be blasphemed. He is not just God but "the Lᴏʀᴅ God." This implies the commandment not to take the name of "the Lᴏʀᴅ God" in vain. A reader is reminded to cleave to *his* wife because he is not to commit adultery. In this way, rabbis claimed that God's laws are eternal and in force even before they were enumerated to Moses on Mount Sinai.

While rabbinic reading often seems out of sync with modern readings, at times these match quite well. With the increasing alarm concerning

---

41. Gen. Rab. 16:6. The translation is Neusner's in *Confronting Creation*, 91.

environmental degradation due to human activity, the following haggadah speaks more potently than when the rabbis first proclaimed it.

> At the time the Holy One, blessed be He, created the first human, he took him for a walk and showed him all the trees of the Garden of Eden. He said to him, "Take a close look at all the things I have created. How beautiful and splendid they all are. Everything I have made, I made for your sake. Now take care lest you become corrupt and destroy my world. For if you become corrupt, there is no one else who will repair it after you."[42]

God is thrilled with the beauty of his creation and consequently calls on Adam to share in this pleasure as if to say, "Come, enjoy this lovely place I created!" But then comes the warning: You had better not become corrupt and damage this lovely garden! The implication here is that personal corruption precedes and precipitates environmental corruption. Responsibility for creation's care is given over to Adam and his descendants. The saying thus encourages a kind of creation care that flows from both self-interest and obligation for what the Creator himself loves.

Rabbis also pondered several questions about the garden: Where is the garden of Eden? Does it still have relevance as a location? Why does Genesis claim that God protected the garden with cherubim after expelling Adam and Eve (3:24)? Why not simply destroy it altogether? Some readers assumed that the garden continued to be a location on earth reserved as a final resting place for the righteous. Others believed that the garden had been transported into heaven and was the abode of God and his angels. As a repository of all delights, this heavenly garden continued to be the final resting place for all those who act in righteousness on earth. In any case, whether in earth or in heaven, the garden of Eden came to be understood as being protected by God as the final resting place for the righteous.[43]

Interpretive Peculiarities

Right at the start of Genesis Rabbah, we encounter one of the strangest features of rabbinic midrash. This feature, called *petikhta*, interprets a base verse (here Gen. 1:1) by immediate juxtaposition to some other verse that seems completely unrelated to the base verse (sometimes called a "dissecting" verse). After this second verse is presented, we encounter a series of possible

42. Eccles. Rab. 7:13.
43. For specific texts, see Kugel, *Bible as It Was*, 78–82.

understandings until, finally, some interpretive connection is made that provides a fresh perspective on the base verse.

The whole of Genesis Rabbah begins with Gen. 1:1 as the base verse, after
which the teacher cites Prov. 8:30 (our dissecting verse). Proverbs 8 describes
wisdom's directive role in the creation of the world. Rabbis had long interpreted this wisdom as the Torah itself, which participated with God in the
act of creation. In other words, God created wisdom/Torah first and then by
Torah's wisdom created all else. The rabbi utilizes Prov. 8:30 as the dissecting verse to make this point: "Then I was beside him, like a master worker,
and I was daily his delight." He provides a list of possible meanings of the
Hebrew word 'āmôn ("master worker"). 'Āmôn is a perplexing Hebrew word
with many possible meanings: nursing child, master worker, or teacher. The
various meanings for 'āmôn are explored, but the interpreter seems to settle
on the meaning "teacher." The midrash here compares the role of the 'āmôn
to the blueprints that provide instruction to a builder during a construction
project. Proverbs 8:30–31 therefore indicates that the Torah stood beside God
as a blueprint/teacher and was daily God's delight. He explains with a parable
based on the observation that human kings build palaces not by their own
skill but by the plan of an architect.

> The architect moreover does not build it out of his head, but employs plans and
> diagrams to know how to arrange the chambers and the wicket doors. Thus,
> God consulted the Torah and created the world, while the Torah declares, "In
> the beginning, God created" (Gen. 1:1), "beginning" referring to the Torah, as
> in the verse, "The Lord made me as the beginning of His way" (Prov. 8:22).[44]

If God had used wisdom/Torah as a blueprint to create the whole world,
why does Gen. 1 not mention this fact? Why do we not read in Gen. 1:1 that
God created the blueprint, or Torah, and then God created the whole universe
based on that blueprint? His answer is that Gen. 1 does mention the blueprint
in a subtle manner. Our teacher observes that in Prov. 8:22 we read, "The Lord
created me the *beginning* of his work." The word *beginning* in Gen. 1:1 is
meant to be an allusion to this same blueprint/Torah made at the *beginning*
of all God's work. Thus he understands Gen. 1:1 to mean, "By means of the
'āmôn [that is, the blueprint/Torah], God created the heavens and the earth."
In other words, God created the Torah as the first of his creations and then
created everything else, following the plan spelled out in the Torah.[45] So by

44. Gen. Rab. 1:1, Simon, *Midrash Rabbah: Genesis*, vol. 1.
45. Since the Hebrew preposition translated "in" ("*In* the beginning") can easily be translated
"by means of," the interpretation is feasible provided we allow that "beginning" alludes to the

this creative reading, rabbis prove that God created the universe by consulting his own Torah.[46]

This interpretation ties into both cosmology and current conditions. In this passage our rabbi (R. Oshaya) believes, as do most rabbis of his day, that God consulted Torah, which he had previously created in the same way a builder might consult an architectural plan that he had previously approved. If God designed the world in the pattern of the Torah, then Torah has an eternal role in shaping faith and life because it corresponds to the blueprint for all of creation. How should Jews respond to the desperations of their time? By consulting the document by which the whole cosmos was shaped and designed. It alone should be the blueprint of their lives. Here cosmology and ethics intersect.

Conclusion

Rabbinic interpretation engaged biblical texts in both serious and playful ways to both inform and entertain their communities. Typically, a particular biblical text was in view, and their interpretive method sought discovery of creative new ways of explaining texts in order to find a deeper and untapped reservoir of meaning. Imagine someone who finds a treasure in a mountain cavern. The explorer could take each golden nugget, polish it, and bring it out for others to see. But the cavern is massive, and its treasure cannot be exhausted. Since texts had unending layers of meaning as a result of their divine provenance, no one could exhaust these resources. The very opacity of many biblical passages provided material for the interpreters. The treasure may need to be dusted and polished, but meaning can always be discovered, not only one meaning but also a hundred million possible meanings awaiting the eager explorer.

Although early rabbis and the literature they produced engage Scripture from a radically different set of assumptions and interests than those that drive modern Christian hermeneutics, they provide an important link to the Jewish roots of the Christian faith. Certainly some of these readings arose later than the formation of the NT, yet Jesus and Paul, both Jews, were influenced by similar rabbinic patterns of thought and interpretation. It is an interesting fact of history that Jesus and John the Baptist are the first persons known to have been called "Rabbi."[47] In the rabbinic world, that title only became

---

blueprint/Torah. The text now reads, "By means of the blueprint [or Torah], God created the heavens and the earth."

46. See Kugel, *Bible as It Was*, 55–57.

47. Matt. 26:25, 49; Mark 9:5; 11:21; 14:45; John 1:38, 49; 3:2, 26 (John the Baptist), 4:31; 6:25; 9:2; 11:8.

officially ascribed to teachers after the destruction of the Second Temple in 70 CE. Early Christian thinkers were not only disputing with rabbis but also engaging with them and learning from them as a child learns from its elders. A student of the Christian faith can hardly ignore this world of interpretive insight and theological reflection; it is the very soil from which the tree of Christian faith has sprung.

For Further Reading

Allen, Joel. *Jewish Biblical Legends: Rabbinic Wisdom for Christian Readers*. Eugene, OR: Cascade Books, 2013.

Kugel, James. *The Bible as It Was*. Cambridge, MA: Belknap, 1999.

Neusner, Jacob. *Confronting Creation: How Judaism Reads Genesis; An Anthology of Genesis Rabbah*. Columbia: University of South Carolina Press, 1991.

Primary Texts in Print

Bialik, Hayim N., and Yehoshua Ravnitzky, eds. *The Book of Legends = Sefer Ha-Aggadah: Legends from the Talmud and Midrash*. Translated by William G. Braude. New York: Schocken, 1992.

Freedman, H., and Maurice Simon. *Midrash Rabbah: Genesis*. Vol. 2 of *Midrash Rabbah*. New York: Soncino, 1983.

Ginzberg, Louis. *Legends of the Jews*. Translated by Henrietta Szold and Paul Radin. 1909. Repr. in 2 vols. London: Forgotten Books, 2008.

Neusner, Jacob. *Genesis Rabbah: The Judaic Commentary to the Book of Genesis; A New American Translation*. Vol. 1, *Parashiyyot One through Thirty-Three on Genesis 1:1 to 8:14*. BJS. Atlanta: Scholars Press, 1985.

Simon, Maurice, trans. *Midrash Rabbah: Genesis*. Vol. 1 of *Midrash Rabbah*. London: Soncino, 1939. Repr., San Bernardino, CA: Ulan Press, 2012.

Primary Texts Online

1. Genesis Rabbah
   https://www.sefaria.org/Bereishit_Rabbah?lang=bi
2. Legends of the Jews
   http://www.sacred-texts.com/jud/loj/loj103.htm

5

Interpretations of Genesis 1–2 among the Ante-Nicene Fathers

Stephen O. Presley

The interpretation of Gen. 1–2 has been woven into the fabric of Christian discourse throughout the history of Christian exegesis. It is no exaggeration to say that in comparison to other books of the Bible the patristic reflection on Genesis is "quite extraordinary."[1] In many cases Christian thinkers are simply responding in counterpoint to the prevailing philosophical views on cosmology in the Greco-Roman world. At other times, they apply their own exegetical acumen and extend key points of the apostolic testimony they inherited. As a result, their applied exegesis offers highly involved theological interpretations of Gen. 1–2 that integrate the language and imagery of these creation accounts within their philosophical, apologetic, or ecclesiastical discussions.[2]

1. Andrew Louth, "The Fathers on Genesis," in *The Book of Genesis: Composition, Reception, and Interpretation*, ed. David L. Petersen, Joel N. Evans, and Craig A. Evans (Leiden: Brill, 2012), 561–78, here 561.

2. For quotations of the writings of the church fathers on creation, see William A. Dembski, Wayne J. Downs, and Fr. Justin B. A. Frederick, *The Patristic Understanding of Creation: An Anthology of Writings from the Church Fathers on Creation and Design* (Riesel, TX: Erasmus, 2008); Andrew Louth, ed., *Genesis 1–11*, ACCS 1 (Downers Grove, IL: IVP Academic, 2016).

While there are very few formal commentaries on Genesis prior to the fourth century, an extensive number of allusions and citations to Gen. 1–2 remain, and they saturate the letters, sermons, catechetical texts, apologetic dialogues, and polemical writings of early Christianity.[3] This chapter will consider the early Christian interpretation of Gen. 1–2 in the pre-Nicene context (before 325 CE), from the earliest days of the postapostolic period to the end of the third century. This analysis is by no means exhaustive but instead uses broad strokes to paint the reception of the creation accounts in the writings of these early church fathers. The chapter begins with a brief introduction to the interpreters of this period and a few hermeneutical assumptions that guided their reading of Gen. 1–2. This essay continues with a survey of some common threads that knit together their interpretations of specific aspects of Gen. 1–2, including the days of creation, the cosmological language, the formations of Adam and Eve, and the nature of the garden of Eden. Together, these features in the writings of the earliest Christian interpreters portray both the diversity and the unity of their interpretations.

Introduction to the Interpreters

The early church was born into a complex intellectual world composed of deep-rooted streams of Greco-Roman philosophical inquiry and Jewish thought. Debates with these competing theological systems tested and refined the early Christian readings of Gen. 1–2. At times, the patristic writers reflect on Genesis in conversation and debate with various interlocutors including Platonists, gnostics, or Marcionites. On other occasions they find themselves engaged in theological disputes with diasporic Jews or Jewish-Christian sects such as the Ebionites. Paul Blowers summarizes a few of the crucial philosophical questions that frequently intersect in these dialogues, including debates over teleology and creationism, as well as discussions of the "cosmic *archai* [ruling powers]." These points all raise questions about design, causation, and origins.[4] All in all, the early Christian relationship to

3. For a brief summary of patristic commentaries on Genesis, see Charles Kannengiesser, *Handbook of Patristic Exegesis* (Leiden: Brill, 2004), 1:278–81. Eusebius mentions several fathers, including Clement of Alexandria and Origen, who either wrote or promised to write a commentary on Genesis. See Eusebius, *Hist. eccl.* 3.1.1; 6.13.9; 6.24.2. For a good introduction to theology of creation in the fathers, see Peter C. Bouteneff, *Beginnings: Ancient Christian Readings of the Biblical Creation Narratives* (Grand Rapids: Baker Academic, 2008).
4. Paul Blowers, *Drama of the Divine Economy: Creator and Creation in Early Christian Theology and Piety* (Oxford: Oxford University Press, 2012), 34–38. For a discussion of cosmological models in the Greco-Roman context, see David Sedley, *Creationism and Its Critics in Antiquity* (Berkeley: University of California Press, 2007); David Furley, *The Formation of*

Greco-Roman philosophy was a mixed bag of appropriation and rejection of philosophical concepts and idioms.[5] At the same time, Christian thinkers also drew from the well of Hellenistic Jewish sources including especially Philo and the Wisdom of Solomon.[6] These sources challenged and confirmed Christian interpretation on some important intellectual questions mentioned above.[7] In the end, though, early Christian theologians also claimed that the apostles received new revelation through Christ that reinterpreted various theologies of creation inherited from Judaism.

The sources for this analysis of Gen. 1–2 come from three separate phases of theological development in the pre-Nicene period, including the Apostolic Fathers, early Christian apologists, and later patristic heresiologists and theologians.[8] The writings of the Apostolic Fathers comprise the earliest Christian interpretation of the postapostolic age and include works such as the Didache, an early Christian manual for worship, and 1 Clement, a letter written to the church at Corinth purportedly from Clement, the bishop of Rome. This period provides the initial rudimentary reflection on creation with a loose collection of allusions and citations of Gen. 1–2 scattered throughout these works.

The next phase of writers that arose in the mid-second century includes a group of thinkers who are considered Christian apologists. As their name suggests, these defenders of the faith actively debated various authorities in the wider Greco-Roman culture. These early Christian apologists include such thinkers as Athenagoras, Theophilus, Justin Martyr, and Tatian. Their apologetic writings are a unique type of literature that addresses common misconceptions of Christianity prevalent in the broader culture and at the same time explains features of basic Christian belief and practice. For several of these apologists, their debates often turn on cosmological and teleological arguments that involve the interpretation of Gen. 1–2.

---

the Atomic Theory and Its Earliest Critics, vol. 1 of The Greek Cosmologists (Cambridge: Cambridge University Press, 1987). For a discussion of the relationship between Scripture and cosmology, see Kyle Greenwood, Scripture and Cosmology: Reading the Bible between the Ancient World and Modern Science (Downers Grove, IL: IVP Academic, 2015).

5. Blowers, Drama of the Divine Economy, 34.

6. Eusebius singles out Philo's works on Genesis as important for the church's theological reflection. Eusebius, Hist. eccl. 2.18.1–4.

7. Blowers, Drama of the Divine Economy, 63–66.

8. For a few good introductions to the writings, theology, and writers of these periods, see Clayton N. Jefford, Reading the Apostolic Fathers: A Student's Introduction, 2nd ed. (Grand Rapids: Baker Academic, 2012); Robert M. Grant, Greek Apologists of the Second Century (Philadelphia: Westminster John Knox, 1988); Claudio Moreschini and Enrico Norelli, Early Christian Greek and Latin Literature: A Literary History, trans. Matthew O'Connell, vol. 1 (Grand Rapids: Baker Academic, 2005); D. Jeffrey Bingham, ed., The Routledge Companion to Early Christian Thought (London: Routledge, 2010).

Finally, the remaining years of the second and third centuries include the works of a number of prominent heresiologists and theologians, including Irenaeus, Clement of Alexandria, Tertullian, Origen, and Lactantius. The works of these theologians represent some of the most sophisticated theological reflection prior to the flowering of patristic thought in the fourth and fifth centuries. Much of their writings were engaged in shaping early Christian faith and practice or debating various heterodox sects that challenged the ecclesiastical establishment. Origen was the towering figure of this period and is essential for understanding the early Christian reception of Gen. 1–2. His work *On First Principles* details a cosmological system, and his homilies on Genesis are the earliest extant sermons on the book. His spiritual readings of Gen. 1–2 set an interpretative trajectory that echoes throughout the rest of the patristic period.

Amid these writings, several are noteworthy for their concentrated interest on the opening chapters of Genesis. While there is no extant commentary, there are a few texts that contain some measure of verse-by-verse analysis of Gen. 1–2. These include the second book of Theophilus's *To Autolycus*, Irenaeus's *Demonstration of the Apostolic Preaching*, and Origen's *Homilies on Genesis*. Other polemical or ecclesiological writings that contain significant citations of and allusions to Gen. 1–2 include Irenaeus's *Against Heresies*, Tertullian's *Against Hermogenes* and *Against Marcion*, and Lactantius's *Divine Institutes*. These early Christian writers typically prefer the Greek translation of the Septuagint, though there is evidence that some appeal to the Hebrew when it supports their theological agenda.[9]

These ancient writers also approach the exegesis of the creation accounts with several prevailing hermeneutical assumptions that provide a theological canopy under which they apply the particular features of their exegesis. First, early patristic writers often call for a measure of hermeneutical humility when approaching questions of cosmology or interpretation of Gen. 1–2. This posture of humility acknowledges the transcendence and omniscience of God and the inability of human facilities to grasp all the mysteries of creation. Gnostics and others who fully absorbed the Platonist cosmology were known for their intricate primordial narratives, which informed their interpretation of the creation accounts. Irenaeus in particular argues against this speculation and suggests that it is better to know nothing about the creation of the world and "to believe in God and continue in his love, than by knowledge of this kind to be puffed up and fall away from love."[10] This same kind of piety

9. Irenaeus, *Epid.* 43.
10. Irenaeus, *Haer.* 2.26.1. See also Lactantius, *Inst.* 2.9.

SIDEBAR 5.1

Theophilus of Antioch, *Ad Autolycum* 2.12

No man can adequately set forth the whole exegesis and plan of the Hexaemeron (six days' work), even if he were to have ten thousand mouths and ten thousand tongues. Not even if he were to live ten thousand years, continuing in this life, would he be competent to say anything adequately in regard to these matters, because of the surpassing greatness and riches of the Wisdom of God to be found in this Hexaemeron quoted above. To be sure, many writers have imitated it and have desired to compose a narrative about these matters, but, although they derived their starting-point from it in dealing with the creation of the world or the nature of man, what they said did not contain even a slight spark worthy of the truth. What has been said by philosophers, historians, and poets is thought to be trustworthy because of its embellished style, but what they say is proved foolish and pointless by the abundance of their nonsense and the absence of even the slightest measure of the truth in their writings.

Note: Text and trans. Robert M. Grant, Oxford Early Christian Texts (Oxford: Clarendon, 1970).

---

toward cosmological questions led other fathers, such as Theophilus, to take the argument even further and claim that the Greco-Roman philosophical tradition contributed little to the Christian understanding of creation. In his view, the sacred writers of the prophets and apostles alone provide enough revelation to craft a coherent theology of creation, and there is no way to grasp the depth of all the divine mysteries outside of what has been revealed. Theophilus introduces his commentary on the days of creation with this sentiment: "No man can adequately set forth the whole exegesis and plan of the Hexaemeron (six days' work), even if he were to have ten thousand mouths and ten thousand tongues."[11] Certainly the fathers, especially Origen, speculate about what God was doing before creating the world, but their speculation is often tempered with a posture of humility.

Second, as the gnostics and philosophers dissect the creation accounts and excise the imagery to substantiate their own cosmology systems, the early Christians defend the antiquity and authority of the Mosaic account. In classic apologetic fashion, Justin argues for the antiquity of the Mosaic tradition and suggests that Plato actually borrowed from the creation accounts in Gen. 1–2 when he crafted his cosmology.[12] But Justin is not alone in this

---

11. Theophilus, *Ad Autolycum*, text and trans. Robert M. Grant, Oxford Early Christian Texts (Oxford: Clarendon, 1970), 2.12.

12. See Justin, *1 Apol.* 50–54.

argument, as the defense of the antiquity of Moses was a common theme in patristic writings.[13] The fathers also couple this argument from antiquity with a defense of the authority of his account based on its divine origin.[14] Irenaeus, for example, grounds his polemic against gnostics and his exegesis of the creation accounts in an argument for the integrity of Gen. 1–2 over and against any of their testimony of creation.[15]

Finally, these fathers approach their exegesis of Genesis with an applied hermeneutic that balances both literal and spiritual senses of Scripture. Even a cursory reading of Theophilus's letter *To Autolycus* or Origen's *Homilies on Genesis* reveals this basic hermeneutic strategy.[16] Theophilus regularly argues that the material creation in Genesis signified spiritual realities.[17] Origen more clearly defends this hermeneutic when, after commenting on most of Gen. 1:1–25, he writes, "There is certainly no question about the literal meaning. For they [the created animals of Gen. 1:24–25] are clearly said to have been created by God, whether animals or four-footed creatures or beasts or serpents on the earth. But it is not unprofitable to relate these words to those which we explained about in a spiritual sense."[18] Like Origen, Irenaeus also describes these two senses plainly in his interpretation of the seventh day of creation in Gen. 2:1–2. He pauses his exegesis of this passage to explain his interpretative method: "This is a narrative of things formerly created, as also it is a prophecy of what is to come."[19] These spiritual readings of the fathers are often described with various labels—including allegorical, typological, figurative, tropological, or eschatological—depending on the context and the way the Genesis imagery was read intertextually alongside other Scriptures or interpreted in light of the revelation of Christ.

The criterion for authentic interpretations of Gen. 1–2, then, is the church's rule of faith, or the summary of the apostolic teaching. The doctrine of creation is an essential part of this statement.[20] The introductory clause for

13. See, e.g., Clement of Alexandria, *Misc.* 5.14; Tertullian, *Herm.* 19.

14. Theophilus, *Autol.* 2.12; Irenaeus, *Haer.* 2.2.5.

15. Irenaeus, *Haer.* 2.2.5.

16. Peter Martens, "Origen's Doctrine of Pre-existence and the Opening Chapters of Genesis," *ZAC* 16 (2013): 516–49, 520–21.

17. For example, he believed that the fecundity of the vegetation signified the resurrection and the eminence of the sun signified God's omnipotence. Theophilus, *Autol.* 2.14.

18. Origen, *Hom. Gen.* 1.11.

19. Irenaeus, *Haer.* 5.28.3.

20. The literature on the rule of faith is extensive. For a few recent articles that help set the historical and hermeneutical context of this discussion, see Tomas Bokedal, "The Rule of Faith: Tracing Its Origins," *JTI* 7, no. 2 (2013): 233–55; Paul Hartog, "The 'Rule of Faith' and Patristic Biblical Exegesis," *TJ* 28 (2007): 65–86.

many summaries of the rule of faith (or rule of truth) is often a reference to the creative activity of the Father through the Son. For example, Irenaeus begins one summary of the rule of faith thus: "The rule of truth which we hold, is, that there is one God Almighty, who made all things by His Word, and fashioned and formed, out of that which had no existence, all things which exist."[21] For these fathers, the interpreter of Genesis is on safe ground as long as the interpretation, either literal or spiritual, harmonizes theologically with what the apostles confessed about the work of God in Christ and God's proper relationship to creation. A general hermeneutical framework for the interpretation of Gen. 1–2 having been established, what follows summarizes a few of the specific interpretations of the pre-Nicene fathers as they engaged the particular literary features of the creation accounts.

Treatment of Days

The reception of the interpretation of the days of creation in the early church is far from uniform. Some such as Theophilus, Origen, or Lactantius comment, more or less, on even the most subtle imagery of each day of creation. Theophilus's work even quotes the whole of Gen. 1:3–2:3, presumably to introduce the section of Scripture to his pagan reader before he begins walking through it carefully.[22] On the other hand, several Apostolic Fathers, Justin Martyr, and Irenaeus only rarely cite any of the verses from the days of creation.[23] Nevertheless, taking into account these extremes, there are several important streams of interpreting the days of creation in general amid all the fathers, along with the particular commentary found in Theophilus, Origen, and Lactantius.

First, these fathers regularly summarize the creation accounts with simple and succinct descriptions of the creative activity in Gen. 1. Melito, for example, laces together allusions to the events of creation in a unified narrative.[24] He presents the imagery of the creation account in a literal fashion that is filtered through a doctrine of preexistence of the Son to heighten the theological connections between the Creator and the crucified Lord. He writes that the one who was crucified was the same one "who caused the light to shine forth, the

---

21. Irenaeus, *Haer.* 1.22.1. See also Irenaeus, *Epid.* 5–6; Melito of Sardis, *Pasc.* 47.

22. Theophilus, *Autol.* 2.11.

23. Justin never explicitly comments on the days of creation and, apart from *Haer.* 1.18.2 and an implicit echo in *Haer.* 5.30.4, Irenaeus rarely alludes to any passage from Gen. 1:6–25. See also Jack P. Lewis, "The Days of Creation: An Historical Survey of Interpretation," *JETS* 34, no. 2 (1989): 435.

24. Melito, *Pasc.* 104.

one who made bright the day, the one who parted the darkness."[25] Likewise, Clement of Rome interprets the imagery of Gen. 1 in a literal, coherent, straightforward fashion as a simple account of the creation of the world that is attentive to a theology of divine goodness characterized in Gen. 1:5–2:8.[26] Tertullian also emphasizes this literal interpretation of the days when he distinguishes the formation of the heavens and earth out of previously formed matter in the days of creation with creation ex nihilo articulated in Gen. 1:1–2. He observes that the earth brought forth vegetation in Gen. 1:11–12 and the waters brought forth creatures of all kinds in 1:20–21.[27] This was material creation being formed from material creation. This kind of literal interpretation accepts the creation accounts as a coherent narrative description of God's formation of the world and humankind.

This literal interpretation, however, is not always emphasized in the same way. Origen, for example, is skeptical of the historicity of some of the language and assumes that much of it was intended to be figurative. He writes, "Now what man of intelligence will believe that the first and the second and the third day, and the evening and the morning existed without the sun and moon and stars? . . . I do not think anyone will doubt that these are figurative expressions which indicate certain mysteries through a semblance of history and not through actual events."[28] Thus, while many fathers accept the descriptions of Gen. 1 as reflecting the narrative of creation, they debate the way the literal interpretations correspond to the historical events of creation.

There is little discussion about the length of the days of creation, though most assume that the references to "evening and morning" refer to twenty-four-hour solar days.[29] However, several pre-Nicene fathers, including Irenaeus and Origen, make a theological judgment based on the distinction between the ordinal number on "the first day" or "one day" (*hēmera mia*) of creation (Gen. 1:5) and the cardinal numbers used in the subsequent days of creation ("a second day," *hēmera deutera*, 1:8), "a third day" (v. 13), "a fourth day" (v. 19), "a fifth day" (v. 23), "a sixth day" (v. 31), and "the seventh day" (2:2). Origen believes that time did not begin until the second day, when evening and

25. Melito, *Pasc.* 82–83.

26. 1 Clem. 33.

27. Tertullian, *Herm.* 22.

28. Origen, *Princ.* 4.3.1. For a recent introduction to the discussion of the nature of "history" in Origen's use of allegory, see Paul C. Boles, "Allegory as Embodiment: The Function of History in Origen's Genesis Homily," *JTI* 10, no. 1 (2016): 87–101.

29. For example, Lactantius, *Inst.* 2.10. See also Emmanouela Grypeou and Helen Spurling, *The Book of Genesis in Late Antiquity: Encounters between Jewish and Christian Exegesis* (Leiden: Brill, 2013), 59–61.

morning are first mentioned. Referring to Gen. 1:1, Origen writes, "Scripture is not speaking here of any temporal beginning, but it says that the heaven and the earth and all things which were made were made 'in the beginning,' that is, in the Savior."[30]

In his work *Against Heresies* (*Haer.* 5.23.2), Irenaeus summarizes five different interpretations of the term "day" (*hēmera*) in God's divine prohibition in Gen. 2:16–17 in order to explain why Adam and Eve did not immediately die when they ate from the tree.[31] One possible interpretation is that "day" in Gen. 2:16–17 refers back to the "one day" of creation in Gen. 1:5, which is understood as the great universal "day" of creation's perpetual existence that is distinct from the cycle of days mentioned later. In this interpretation, anyone who ate from the tree of the knowledge of good and evil (2:9, 17) would die not in twenty-four hours but at some point during the great day of creation before the consummation of the cosmos.

For other fathers, especially Theophilus and Origen, there were not only literal but also spiritual meanings to be found amid the specific elements of each day of creation. We'll examine just a sampling of their spiritual readings of the days of creation. To begin with, Theophilus interprets the freshwater spring that brings sweet water to the earth (Gen. 2:6) as the Scriptures, and the islands scattered among the seas (1:9–10) as the church, which either is a safe harbor for the faithful or contains rough edges that harm the ships when they try to dock.[32] In another instance he interprets the sun as representing God, who always remains full and bright with power, wisdom, and intelligence. The moon, on the other hand, is a reflection of humankind, which waxes and wanes throughout life.[33] In the subsequent days, Theophilus also reads the creation imagery in correspondence to the faithful or the ungodly. The stars that remain steadfast are the prophets who keep the law unswervingly, while the planets that come and go are those who depart from the law.[34] The blessing of the water on the fifth day symbolizes the coming repentance and remission of sin through the waters of baptism.[35] Some of the beasts created on the fifth day live in harmony with creation and eat only seed-bearing plants; these are like the righteous. The sinners, on the

30. Origen, *Hom. Gen.* 1.1.
31. For a discussion of these interpretations, see Antonio Orbe, "Cinco exegesis Ireneanas de Genesis 2:17b: *Adv. haer.* V 23, 1–2," *Greg* (1981): 75–113; and Matthew Steenberg, "To Test or Preserve? The Prohibition of Genesis 2:16–17 in the Thought of Two Second-Century Exegetes," *Greg* 86 (2005): 723–41.
32. Theophilus, *Autol.* 2.14.
33. Theophilus, *Autol.* 2.15.
34. Theophilus, *Autol.* 2.15.
35. Theophilus, *Autol.* 2.16.

SIDEBAR 5.2

Origen, *On First Principles* 3.5.1

In regard, then, to the creation of the world, what other book of scripture is more able to enlighten us than that which was written by Moses concerning its origin? This account may well enshrine certain deeper truths than the mere record of the history seems to reveal and may contain a spiritual meaning in many passages, using the letter as a kind of veil for profound and mystical doctrines; nevertheless the language of the narrator certainly indicates this, that all visible things were created at a definite time. And as for the consummation of the world, Jacob is the first to refer to this when, in giving his testament to his sons he says, "Gather to me, ye sons of Jacob, that I may tell you what shall be in the last days," or, "after the last days." If then there are "last days," or a time "after the last days," it follows of necessity that the days which had a beginning also come to an end. David also says: "The heavens shall perish, but thou shalt remain; and they all shall grow old as a garment, and as a vesture shalt thou change them, and they shall be changed; but thou art the same, and thy years shall not fail." And when our Lord and Savior says, "He who created in the beginning made them male and female," he himself bears witness that the world was made; whereas when he says that "heaven and earth shall pass away, but my words shall not pass away," he shows that it is corruptible and destined to come to an end.

Note: Trans. G. W. Butterworth (Gloucester, MA: Peter Smith, 1973).

---

other hand, are the carnivores that break God's law. Finally, the quadrupeds and the various wild animals are types of those people think only of earthly things and sin against God.[36]

Origen's interpretation in his homily is similar, though much more anthropologically nuanced. To be sure, Origen's reading of Gen. 1–3 is notoriously debated. It seems that for heresiological purposes Origen maps his doctrine of the preexistence of the souls and their subsequent fall into a corporeal world onto the opening chapters of Genesis.[37] This anthropological reading yields several interesting interpretations. After citing the reference to the creation of the firmament in Gen. 1:6–7, Origen ascribes the spiritual sense to the unseen heavens above and the literal sense to the firmament that is observable to the senses. He writes, "For since everything which God was to make would consist of spirit and body, . . . therefore, that first heaven indeed, which we said is spiritual, is our mind, which is also itself spirit, that is

---

36. Theophilus, *Autol.* 2.17.
37. Martens, "Origen's Doctrine," 520–21, 542.

our spiritual man which sees and perceives God. But that corporeal heaven, which is called the firmament, is our outer man which looks at things in a corporeal way."[38] Contrary to gnostic or Platonic anthropological dualism, Origen believes that the distinctions among creatures was not predetermined but a consequence of their free moral actions in the cultivation of the spiritual perception of the human person.[39] As he preaches through the creation accounts in his homilies, he applies the elements created in each of the days to the spiritual lives of the congregation and their struggle with virtues and vices in pursuit of the holy life.

Finally, Origen and several fathers give serious consideration to the final Sabbath day of creation. Just as the days of creation build to Sabbath, so also will creation progress toward the culmination of an eschatological Sabbath rest.[40] When Barnabas of Alexandria describes the eschatological thrust of the seventh day, he depicts God as granting "rest" to all creation and establishing the "beginning of an eighth day, which is the beginning of another world."[41] Papias, Barnabas, Justin, and Irenaeus began the chiliastic tradition that links the days of creation (six days) with the extent of the life of the earth (six thousand years), based on their reading of Ps. 90:4 and 2 Pet. 3:8.[42] This chiliastic vision builds toward a Sabbath rest as the culmination of God's creative activity in a new creation.

Cosmology

The cosmology of the early fathers is theologically oriented and predicated on their reading of Scripture and interaction with the prevailing systems of their Greco-Roman interlocutors. They certainly borrow from Aristotelian and Platonic cosmologies, but at the same time they reject the ways that gnostics used the Genesis material to explain their myth.[43] The first nine chapters of Irenaeus's major work against gnostics detail and refute an early version of Valentinianism that drew from Ptolemaic thought.[44] As Irenaeus shows, the gnostic reading purges the imagery of creation and especially the opening verses of Gen. 1:1–2 of any literal meaning and in these verses

38. Origen, *Hom. Gen.* 1.2.
39. Origen, *Princ.* 2.9.5–6.
40. Irenaeus, *Haer.* 4.16.1; 5.30.4; 5.33.1–4; 5.36.3.
41. Barn. 15.8.
42. Barn. 15.3–5.
43. For a discussion of the gnostic myth, see Gerard P. Luttikhuizen, *Gnostic Revisions of Genesis Stories and Early Jesus Traditions* (Leiden: Brill, 2006).
44. Irenaeus, *Haer.* 1.1–8.

instead identifies emanations that ordained the pleromic world, which is the spiritual realm containing all divine powers and emanations.[45] As a result, the description of creation in Gen. 1:1–2 features prominently in the writings of the church fathers, and they read this pericope through several prominent lines of interpretation.[46]

First, by the end of the second century the works of Justin Martyr, Tatian, Theophilus, and Irenaeus had fashioned a highly developed doctrine of *creatio ex nihilo*, creation out of nothing.[47] Over against the gnostic myth, these early fathers of the church appealed to the omnipotence and unity of God, as expressed in the Scriptures (esp. Genesis), which required all matter to be created ex nihilo (out of nothing). For example, Tatian, borrowing from the Logos theology of his teacher Justin, argues that only God is unoriginate, so all matter necessarily comes from God.[48] Commenting on Gen. 1:2, Theophilus also remarks, "Matter from which God made and fashioned the world was in a way created, having been made by God."[49] For Theophilus, God becomes known through his works, and Theophilus links Gen. 1:1 and 1:2 to indicate that the matter from which God fashioned the earth was formed first. Likewise, Irenaeus argues that God creates all things "Himself within himself" and through "his hands," that is, the Son and the Spirit.[50] For his part, Tertullian is also very interested in the interpretation of Gen. 1:1–2. He devotes no less than seven chapters of his work *Against Hermogenes* (*Herm.*) to critique Hermogenes's assumption that Gen. 1:2 expresses the eternality of matter.[51] Lactantius also takes up this topic, arguing, "It follows that He who made the things which are composed of matter, made matter also. For it was neither possible nor befitting that anything should exist without the exercise of God's power, or against His will."[52]

---

45. Among the Nag Hammadi Codices, e.g., see Codex XIII 2, 98–103, On the Origin of the World; Codex II 4, 86–94, Hypostasis of the Archons; Codex I 5, 75–112, Tripartite Tractate.

46. For a good summary of the history of interpretation of Gen. 1:1–5, see S. D. Giere, *A New Glimpse of Day One: Intertextuality, History of Interpretation, and Genesis 1:1–5* (Berlin: de Gruyter, 2009).

47. For a discussion of creation ex nihilo in the early church, see Gerhard May, *Creatio ex Nihilo: The Doctrine of "Creation out of Nothing" in Early Christian Thought*, trans. A. S. Worrall (Edinburgh: T&T Clark, 1994).

48. Tatian, *Or. Graec.* 4.

49. Theophilus, *Autol.* 2.10.

50. Irenaeus, *Haer.* 2.2.5. For a discussion of this theological concept, see D. Jeffrey Bingham, "Christianizing Divine Aseity: Irenaeus Reads John," in *The Gospel of John in Christian Theology*, ed. Richard Bauckham and Carl Mosser (Grand Rapids: Eerdmans, 2008), 53–67.

51. Tertullian, *Herm.* 23–29.

52. Lactantius, *Inst.* 2.9.

SIDEBAR 5.3

Irenaeus, *Against Heresies* 2.2.4–5

On the contrary, he predetermined in himself all things in advance according to his nature, which to us is ineffable and inscrutable, and he made them as he willed, bestowing on all things their form and order, and the principle of their creation—giving to spiritual beings a spiritual and invisible substance; to supercelestial, a supercelestial; to Angels, an angel; to animals, an animal; to swimming creatures, an aquatic; to land creatures, one fitted for land; that is, giving to all a suitable substance. But all beings that have been made he made through his indefatigable Word. It is proper to God's preeminence not to be in need of other instruments for creating things to be made. His own Word is sufficient for the formation of all things. Thus John, the Lord's disciple, says of him: All things were made by him and without him was made nothing. Now in "all" is contained also this world of ours. It too was made by his Word, as Scripture tells us in Genesis; he made all things around us by his Word. David in like manner says: For he spoke and they were made, he commanded and they were created. Whom, then, will we believe more in regard to the making of the world—the heretics we mentioned above, who babble about foolish and incoherent things, or the disciples of the Lord, and Moses, God's faithful servant and prophet? He it was who first narrated the origin of the world when he said: In the beginning God created the heavens and the earth, and after that all the rest. But Gods and Angels did not create.

Note: Irenaeus of Lyons: Against the Heresies Book 2, trans. Dominic J. Unger, intro. Michael Slusser, Ancient Christian Writers 65 (New York: Newman, 2012).

Second, they often interpret "beginning" (*archē*) in Gen. 1:1 LXX in a personal, or christological, sense rather than a temporal sense.[53] In other words, the fathers' reading of creation does not begin with the question of "when" but "who," pointing to the personal agent through whom all things were created. The "Beginning" in Gen. 1:1, then, is seen as a title for the Son of God, who began creating, and the revelation of the Son of God in Christ was the means by which they reimagine the Son's preexistence in the creation accounts. This also explains the regular conflation of Gen. 1:1–2 with John 1:1–3. For example, Irenaeus mentions Gen. 1:1–2 on only three occasions, and in every instance he also cites John 1:1–3.[54] Matthew Steenberg goes so far as to claim that "no single verse of NT writings is of stronger influence

53. Martens, "Origen's Doctrine," 524.
54. Irenaeus, *Haer.* 1.22.1; 2.2.5; and *Epid.* 43. See also Origen, *Hom. Gen.* 1.1; Theophilus, *Autol.* 2.10; Clement of Alexandria, *Misc.* 6.7; Tertullian, *Herm.* 20–22.

on Irenaeus's cosmological considerations than John 1:3."[55] In one instance he also appeals to an older midrashic reading of Gen. 1:1 that interprets this passage along the lines of the preexistence of the Son. He argues that even Moses prophesied the Son's preexistence and translated the midrashic reading from the Hebrew as, "A Son [in] the beginning God established then heaven and earth" [Gen. 1:1].[56] In his commentary on Gen. 1:1–2, Theophilus describes God as dwelling with his Logos and Wisdom in Gen. 1:1–2 with a sophisticated intertextual reading that is attentive to various divine titles. He states that all things were made through "the Spirit of God" (Gen. 1:2) and the "Beginning" (Gen. 1:1), that is, "Wisdom" (Prov. 8:22) and the "Power of the Most High" (Luke 1:35).[57] Tertullian, on the other hand, represents how some fathers walked a fine line between interpreting it personally and temporally. In his debate with Hermogenes, Tertullian argues against Hermogenes's perspective on the eternality of matter by claiming that the term "beginning" is a "term of inception, not the name of a substance," and yet in the same paragraph he acknowledges that *archē* can be interpreted as the principal authority through which God created all things.[58]

At the same time, other important terms—such as "heaven," "earth," "spirit," "abyss," and "firmament"—caught their interpretive imagination as well. Origen sometimes interprets "heaven" and "earth" literally as the visible cosmos, but at other times he interprets this imagery allegorically as the creation of preexistent souls and the matter that God used to form all things.[59] Theophilus interprets the earth in Gen. 1:1 as the foundation, and the abyss as the waters that the darkness pervaded because heaven covered the earth like a lid.[60] Theophilus distinguishes between the "heaven" in Gen. 1:1, which is the unseen heaven, and the firmament in Gen. 1:6, which is the visible heavens that shower the earth in season. Theophilus notes the subtle ordering of creation and contrasts the way humans construct a building—beginning with a foundation and only afterward installing the roof—with the way God builds by constructing the roof first, which is the heaven and the firmament,

55. Matthew Steenberg, *Irenaeus on Creation* (Leiden: Brill, 2008), 69.
56. Irenaeus, *Epid.* 43. This text is preserved only in Armenian, and the transliteration of the Hebrew has been the point of debate. See J. P. Smith, "Hebrew Christian Midrash in Irenaeus Epid. 43," *Biblica* 38 (1957): 31–34; Adelin Rousseau, "La doctrine de Saint Irénée sur la préexistence du Fils de Dieu dans *Dém.* 43," *Le Muséon* 84 (1971): 14–15; Dominique Cerbelaud, "La citation 'Hébraïque' de la *Démonstration* d'Irénée (*Dém.* 43): Une proposition," *Le Muséon* 104 (1991): 228–29.
57. Theophilus, *Autol.* 2.10; see also *Autol.* 2.13.
58. Tertullian, *Herm.* 19.
59. Origen, *Princ.* 3.5.1; *Hom. Gen.* 1.2. See also Martens, "Origen's Doctrine," 526–27.
60. Theophilus, *Autol.* 2.13.

and then filling in what is below. He also identifies the Spirit of God hovering over the water as a participant along with the Son in God's creative activity. For Theophilus, the Spirit of God hovering over the water gives life to creation, like the soul in humans. He reads this in continuity with the illumination in Gen. 1:5 as the Logos shining forth in creation, illuminating everything under the heaven, like a lamp in a dark room.[61] Origen gives attention to the language of "abyss" and reads it eschatologically in connection with Rev. 12:9; 20:3; and Matt. 25:41 as the "place . . . where 'the devil and his angels' will be."[62] This kind of eschatological continuity between Gen. 1–2 and the future eternal state is common among the fathers, who frequently tie these theological points at the end of salvation history with the beginning of creation.[63]

Creation and Nature of Humanity

The discussion of their theological accounting of cosmology frames the particular interpretation of the creation of Adam and Eve depicted in Gen. 1–2. The fathers' interpretation of Gen. 1–2 is undoubtedly anthropologically oriented, which was common among the prevailing cosmological systems in the wider culture.[64] While the comments on the days of creation are limited, the sheer number of allusions to Gen. 1:26–27 and Gen. 2:7 is vast.[65] Referring to Gen. 1:26, Louth writes, "One verse, or rather half a verse, assumed immense significance in the thought of the fathers."[66] Turning to their readings of these anthropological texts, the pre-Nicene fathers first of all envision the formation of Adam and Eve as the centerpiece of the creation accounts where God in anthropomorphic fashion reaches down and molds humankind. The imagery of God's "hands" in connection with the formation of

61. Theophilus, *Autol.* 2.13.

62. Origen, *Hom. Gen.* 1.1.

63. Origen, *Princ.* 3.5.1. See also Peter Martens, *Origen and Scripture: The Contours of the Exegetical Life* (Oxford: Oxford University Press, 2012), 227–42.

64. Greenwood, *Scripture and Cosmology*, 154–56.

65. For example, consult the list of citations of Gen. 1–2 in Irenaeus in Stephen O. Presley, *The Intertextual Reception of Genesis 1–3 in Irenaeus of Lyons* (Leiden: Brill, 2015), 263–67. See also Mathew Steenberg, *Of God and Man: Theology as Anthropology from Irenaeus to Athanasius* (New York: T&T Clark, 2009), 9–10; Steenberg, *Irenaeus on Creation*, 69. See also Holsinger-Friesen's analysis of the hermeneutical performance of Gen. 1:26 and Gen. 2:7 in Thomas Holsinger-Friesen, *Irenaeus and Genesis: A Study of Competition in Early Christian Hermeneutics* (Winona Lake, IN: Eisenbrauns, 2009).

66. Louth, "Fathers on Genesis," 572. See also Steenberg, *Irenaeus on Creation*, 6. For an introduction to Irenaeus's and Origen's views on the image of God, see Jacques Fantino, *L'homme, image de Dieu, chez saint Irénée de Lyon* (Paris: Cerf, 1986); and Henri Crouzel, *Théologie de l'image de Dieu chez Origène* (Paris: Aubier, 1956).

Adam and Eve pervades the early patristic writers. In contrast to the rest of creation that was only spoken into existence, the formation of humankind was a "hands-on affair."[67] Clement of Rome writes, "Above all, as the most excellent and by far the greatest work of his intelligence, with his holy and faultless hands he formed man as representation of his own image."[68] This same imagery is also found in Theophilus, who regards Gen. 2:7 as a further explanation of the creation of humankind in Gen. 1:26.[69] He argues that the language of Gen. 1:26 reveals the "dignity" of humankind in comparison to all other created things. It was only the creation of humankind that required the "hands" of God.[70]

Second, by and large these fathers also read the creation of humankind in Gen. 1 and Gen. 2 as two accounts of the same event, even though they are aware of the differences.[71] Origen, like Philo, reads these passages as two stages of the single creative process.[72] He distinguishes between the creation of the soul or mind in Gen. 1:26 and the formation of the body in Gen. 2:7, saying, "The form of the body does not contain the image of God, nor is the corporeal man said to be 'made,' but 'formed.'"[73] For Origen, the image of God is located in the mind or soul, which has the capacity to contemplate God.[74] Irenaeus, though, rejects the notion of locating the image in the immaterial and instead connects it with the human form. He writes that it was "the flesh that was molded according to the image of God."[75] Some have also argued that Irenaeus distinguishes between the "image" and "likeness" of God, but Steenberg shows that this distinction should be understood as "the ontological formation of the human person (image) and the actualization of the human nature in an individual's lived life (likeness)."[76]

The preexistence of the Son, who for the fathers is the true image of God, is another important aspect of this discussion on the image of God. An appeal to the preexistence of the Son appears early in the work of Barnabas, who, after citing the language of image of God in Gen. 1:26–28, remarks that

67. John Behr, *Asceticism and Anthropology in Irenaeus and Clement* (Oxford: Oxford University Press, 2000), 38.

68. See 1 Clem. 33.

69. Theophilus, *Autol.* 2.19.

70. Theophilus, *Autol.* 2.18.

71. Lactantius, *Inst.* 2.11.

72. Anders L. Jacobsen, "The Importance of Genesis 1–3 in the Theology of Irenaeus," *VC* 62 (2008): 214.

73. Origen, *Hom. Gen.* 1.13.

74. Martens, "Origen's Doctrine," 528.

75. Irenaeus, *Haer.* 5.6.1.

76. Steenberg, *Irenaeus on Creation*, 138.

"these things he said to the Son."[77] Likewise, in Gen. 1:26–27, Justin reads the cohortative "let us make humankind in our image and as our likeness" as a divine conversation between the Father and the Son.[78] Similarly, Theophilus writes, "But he said 'Let us make' to no other than his own Logos and his own Wisdom."[79] These accounts envision an intertextual theological reading of the formation of humankind that integrates other biblical passages into their anthropology and cosmology.

Third, not only do the fathers interpret the preexistence of the Son, but also the whole scene of the formation and nature of Adam informs their Christology and participates in a highly developed (and developing) Adam-Christ typology. Melito, for example, uses rhetorical skill to blend the imagery of the crucified Jesus with the preexistence of the Son in the creation of Adam in Gen. 2:7. He evokes corresponding creation and crucifixion imagery and challenges his audience directly, saying, "You bound those beautiful hands of his, which had formed you from the earth. And that beautiful mouth of his, which had nourished you with life, you filled with gall."[80] Melito draws on the imagery of the "hands" and "mouth" that formed Adam from the dust and breathed into him the breath of life in the creation account, which are then tortured in the crucifixion. Barnabas also interprets Gen. 2:7 theologically: "For man is earth suffering, for Adam was formed out of the face of the earth."[81] He uses this "earth" imagery to describe the christological refashioning of humanity in the way that the Lord "made a second creation in the last days."[82] Irenaeus, however, provides the most extensive and consistent analysis of the typological relationship between Adam and Christ.[83] Throughout the course of his work *Against Heresies (Haer.)*, every phase of Christ's life, from his birth to his resurrection, is woven together with intertextual references back to Adam. For example, in *Haer.* 3.18.1 Irenaeus argues that when the Word became incarnate and was made man, he recapitulated humanity in himself, thereby recovering the image and likeness of God that was lost in Adam.[84] A

---

77. Barn. 6.12.

78. Justin, *Dial.* 62. See also Origen, *Cels.* 2.9. Interestingly, the fathers gave particular attention to these passages that contained divine discourse. See Charles Kannengiesser, "The 'Speaking God' and Irenaeus' Interpretative Pattern: The Reception of Genesis," *Annali di storia dell'esegesi* 15, no. 2 (1998): 337–52.

79. Theophilus, *Autol.* 2.18.

80. Melito, *Pasc.* 79.

81. Barn. 6.12.

82. Barn. 6.13.

83. For an introduction to this conversation, see J. T. Nielson, *Adam and Christ in the Theology of Irenaeus of Lyons* (Assen: Van Gorcum, 1968).

84. See Gen. 1:26; John 1:14; Eph. 1:10.

few chapters later Irenaeus argues that Gen. 2:5 points to Adam as fashioned from the "virgin earth," the untilled soil, just as Christ was born of the virgin.[85] These typological associations (and others) were derived from various symmetrical and asymmetrical scriptural connections between Adam and Christ in the thought of Irenaeus.

Fourth, the pre-Nicene fathers tease out the mystery of the paradisiacal relationship between Adam and Eve. Some choose to focus on the literal interpretation of the marriage relationship itself and its pastoral implications. Tertullian, for example, reflects on the ideal nature of the first marriage and its practical implications for the Christian community. He examines the imagery of Gen. 2:21–25 with great care and from this union discerns several attributes of marriage, such as monogamy.[86] Tertullian also reasons that the language of Gen. 2:24, "Man will leave his father and mother," cannot refer to Adam and Eve since neither had a father or a mother.[87] The passage instead refers to all future husbands and wives who will leave their parents and be united in matrimony. Theophilus, on the other hand, has a similar view but takes it in a more theological direction. He believes that God made the woman from Adam's side so that no one would assume that a separate god created her and so that the man might love her even more than his own family.[88]

Other fathers, such as Irenaeus, emphasize the typological and soteriological senses that interpret the Eve-Mary typology in continuity with the Adam-Christ typology.[89] This imagery clearly participates in a broader typological perspective that reads the whole atmosphere of Gen. 1–3 in relation to the person and work of Christ. Like the Adam-Christ typology, the Eve-Mary typology depends on several corresponding (or contrasting) characteristics recorded in their respective narratives and expressed through reflection on a network of texts. For example, Irenaeus points to the fact that both were virgins. While Mary's virginity is plainly recorded in the Gospels (Matt. 1:23–25; Luke 1:27–34), Irenaeus cites Gen. 2:25, "And the man and his wife were both naked, and were not ashamed," to prove Eve's virginity.[90] Their virginal correspondence is complemented by their respective betrothals, and Irenaeus points to the legal nature of betrothal in Deut. 22:23–24 to argue that a betrothed virgin is actually considered a wife under Mosaic law. For Irenaeus, this logical set of conceptual and textual interconnections (among others)

85. Irenaeus, *Haer*. 3.18.7.
86. Tertullian, *Exh. cast.* 5.
87. Tertullian, *Virg.* 5.
88. Theophilus, *Autol.* 2.28.
89. Irenaeus, *Epid*. 13–4. Cf. Irenaeus, *Haer*. 3.23.5.
90. Irenaeus, *Epid*. 14.

within the Eve-Mary typology reinforces the social and aesthetic stability of the Adam-Christ typology. Tertullian also draws out the Eve-Mary typology, though not nearly with the same precision as Irenaeus. Like Irenaeus, he connects the formation of the woman to Gal. 4:4, "God sent his Son, born of a woman," who was also a virgin.[91]

These literal and typological readings of the formation of the woman lay the groundwork for the spiritual understanding of their relationship as a model for the relationship between Christ and the church.[92] In a general sense, Origen interprets the formation of the woman allegorically in continuity with Eph. 5:31–32.[93] He reads the language "two will become one flesh" allegorically as the union of Christ and the church. Christ is the male and the preexistent church is the female.[94] He argues that Christ does not put away his former wife from the synagogue, but she bears responsibility for the divorce when she rejects and kills him. So then, in the words of Matt. 19:6, no one should be separated from the church and divorce that which God has brought together. For those in the church, there is also a "spiritual" union between the people of God that supersedes the bodily familial relation.[95]

Garden of Eden

The interpretation of the relationship of Adam and Eve has other implications for the early fathers' reading of the garden of Eden. Most of their interpretive energy is spent on the nature and quality of the paradise that God fashioned for Adam and Eve. The fathers go to great lengths to emphasize the beauty and fecundity of paradise as a place of rest, luxury, and, most importantly, the presence of God. For example, Melito writes that after God formed the man, God "placed him in paradise, which was eastward in Eden, and there they lived most luxuriously." The present fallen world by comparison is a mere "prison."[96] Theophilus gives even more detail when he writes that the garden was "in the eastern regions, excellent for its light, brilliant with brighter air, most beautiful with its plants."[97] Theophilus also regards paradise as a

---

91. Tertullian, *Virg.* 6. See *Haer.* 3.22.1; 4.40.3; 5.21.1–3.
92. Tertullian, *Res.* 61.
93. Origen, *Princ.* 4.3.7. See also Origen, *Comm. Song* 2.3.13–14; and Origen, *Comm. Rom.* 5.1. See also Tertullian, *Marc.* 5.18; Tertullian, *An.* 11.
94. Origen, *Comm. Matt.* 14.17. See also Origen, *Comm. Song* 2.8.4; Origen, *Princ.* 1.3.6; Clement of Alexandria, *Misc.* 1.135.3.
95. Origen, *Hom. Exod.* 1.3.
96. Melito, *Pasc.* 48.
97. Theophilus, *Autol.* 2.19.

"plantation planted by God" with plants similar to those previously created, with the exception of the tree of life and the tree of knowledge. But this paradise offers an "intermediate state" between the rest of the world and heaven, so God transferred Adam and Eve out of the world he created into paradise, to keep it and guard it.[98]

For the fathers, the place of Eden was also a divine space where God's presence dwelt freely.[99] Several fathers also suggest that if Adam and Eve were obedient to God in paradise, they would have remained in the presence of God and ascended toward immortality.[100] Theophilus, for example, regards the command of Gen. 2:16–17 as a "test" to see if Adam and Eve would learn to be obedient to God just as a parent might lay down a rule for a child living in their home.[101] He points out that the tree of knowledge is good and does not itself contain death, but death is the result of disobedience. In this place, Theophilus reasons, the Logos appeared at the command of God and conversed with Adam. So Theophilus writes, "For the divine scripture itself teaches us that Adam said that he 'heard the voice.' What is the 'voice' but the Logos of God, who is also his Son?"[102] Since God cannot be contained, it is the Logos who appears and is present in a place. For Irenaeus, the language of "paradise" is a catchword that links the experiences of Enoch, Elijah, and Paul, who were all caught up to "paradise."[103] In his reading, paradise is an intermediate place where God dwells, a place separate from the present world. Yet eventually the present world will be renewed and all the faithful make their way back into paradise to dwell in the presence of God. The presence of God and the luxury of paradise connect the beginning of the divine narrative of salvation history with and provide an illustration of that eternal state at the end, a renewed earthly kingdom of God.[104]

Interpretive Peculiarities

A number of interpretative peculiarities surround the early Christian reading of Gen. 1–2. I have already mentioned a few of these, including Origen's

98. Theophilus, *Autol.* 2.24.

99. For a discussion of paradise in the early church, see Gerald P. Luttikhuizen, ed., *Paradise Interpreted: Representations of Biblical Paradise in Judaism and Christianity* (Leiden: Brill, 1999); Markus Bockmuehl and Guy G. Stroumsa, eds., *Paradise in Antiquity: Jewish and Christian Views* (Cambridge: Cambridge University Press, 2010).

100. Theophilus, *Autol.* 2.24, 27.

101. Theophilus, *Autol.* 2.25.

102. Theophilus, *Autol.* 2.22.

103. Irenaeus, *Haer.* 5.5.1–2. See Gen. 5:24; 2 Kings 2:11; 2 Cor. 12:4.

104. See Origen, *Princ.* 3.6.3; Irenaeus, *Haer.* 5.33.1–4.

doctrine of preexistence (of the Son and of souls) and the spiritual readings of the days of creation. However, two features that demarcate these early centuries and have implications for later theological discussions include the early fathers' chiliastic eschatology and the interpretation of Adam and Eve as prepubescent children in paradise. Beginning with the former, the roots of chiliasm are well attested in the second century and distinctive from an amillennialism that would develop later in the tradition.[105] Early Christian millennialism, or what Daniélou calls "paradisal millennialism," is explicit in the writings of the Apostolic Fathers, Justin, Irenaeus, and Tertullian; it focuses on the fecundity and blessing of the future earthly kingdom in a way that resembles the beauty and goodness of the original creation.[106] In this sense, they interpret the days of creation in Genesis eschatologically as a week of ages through an intertextual connection with Ps. 90:4 and 2 Pet. 3:8, "With the Lord one day is like a thousand years," and prophetic texts such as Isa. 65:17–25, which depict the nature of the restored earth and Jerusalem in a millennial kingdom.[107] As mentioned above, the millennial kingdom is also read in continuity with the inauguration of the eschatological Sabbath.[108] In this final day of Sabbath rest, the righteous "shall not be engaged in any earthly occupation; but shall have a table at hand prepared for them by God, supplying them with all sorts of dishes."[109] In this way the chiliasm of the early church uses Gen. 1–2 as a framework for the history of salvation.[110]

A second interpretive peculiarity is Theophilus's and Irenaeus's view that Adam and Eve were created as prepubescent children in paradise.[111] In Irenaeus's work *Demonstration of the Apostolic Preaching* (*Epid.*), he interprets the narrative of the formation of the woman in a straightforward literal sense, culminating in the final verse of Gen. 2 that Adam and Eve were naked and not ashamed.[112] Irenaeus interprets this passage to mean that Adam and Eve were innocent children, running and playing in all holiness in paradise. They felt no shame in their nakedness because they had no knowledge of procreation. He imagines this state of childhood innocence as the initial stage in the course

105. Eusebius, e.g., explicitly rejects chiliastic views. Eusebius, *Hist. eccl.* 3.39.11–12.

106. Jean Daniélou, *The Theology of Jewish Christianity*, trans. John A. Baker (Philadelphia: Westminster, 1977), 393, 399.

107. Irenaeus, *Haer.* 5.33.4.

108. Irenaeus, *Haer.* 5.28.3.

109. Irenaeus, *Haer.* 5.33.2.

110. For an introduction to this discussion in Irenaeus, see C. R. Smith, "Chiliasm and Recapitulation in the Theology of Irenaeus," *VC* 48 (1994): 313–31.

111. For a good analysis of this discussion, see Matthew C. Steenberg, "Children in Paradise: Adam and Eve as 'Infants' in Irenaeus of Lyons," *JECS* 12, no. 1 (2004): 1–22.

112. Irenaeus, *Epid.* 14.

of human growth and maturity, which includes procreation. Theophilus takes a similar position, claiming that Adam was created as a child in an "intermediate state, neither entirely mortal nor entirely immortal, but capable of either state."[113] Their immature state, which lacked the wisdom gained from experiencing life with God, contributed to their failure to remain obedient to God's command.

Conclusion

The Christians of the pre-Nicene context find in Gen. 1–2 decisive imagery to support the theological vision of God and the world they inherited from the apostolic teaching. They formulate their readings in conversation with Greco-Roman cosmologies and Jewish interpretations, at times borrowing and other times critiquing their philosophical and theological perspectives. When these fathers of the church interpret Gen. 1–2, they bring with them several hermeneutical assumptions, including a posture of humility toward cosmological questions, a defense of the antiquity and authority of the Mosaic account of creation, and a balance of literal and spiritual senses of Scripture. Their applied exegesis moves seamlessly between these literal and spiritual interpretations as they read creation in continuity with the rest of the scriptural testimony. Their interpretation of the days of creation anticipates the formation of Adam and Eve, who are seen as the crowning achievement of God's creative work. The unity and diversity of these interpretations of Gen. 1–2 in the early church set a trajectory of interpretation that continues to influence the rest of the Christian tradition.

For Further Reading

Blowers, Paul. *Drama of the Divine Economy: Creator and Creation in Early Christian Theology and Piety*. Oxford: Oxford University Press, 2012.

Bouteneff, Peter C. *Beginnings: Ancient Christian Readings of the Biblical Creation Narratives*. Grand Rapids: Baker Academic, 2008.

Dembski, William A., Wayne J. Downs, and Fr. Justin B. A. Frederick. *The Patristic Understanding of Creation: An Anthology of Writings from the Church Fathers on Creation and Design*. Riesel, TX: Erasmus, 2008.

Martens, Peter. "Origen's Doctrine of Pre-existence and the Opening Chapters of Genesis." *ZAC* 16 (2013): 516–49.

113. Theophilus, *Autol.* 2.24.

Presley, Stephen O. *The Intertextual Reception of Genesis 1–3 in Irenaeus of Lyons.* Leiden: Brill, 2015.

Steenberg, Matthew C. *Irenaeus on Creation.* Leiden: Brill, 2008.

———. *Of God and Man: Theology as Anthropology from Irenaeus to Athanasius.* New York: T&T Clark, 2009.

Primary Texts in Print

Irenaeus of Lyons. *Against Heresies.* In *Ante-Nicene Fathers: The Writings of the Fathers down to AD 325*, edited by Alexander Roberts and James Donaldson, 1:309–567. Peabody, MA: Hendrickson, 2004.

———. *On the Apostolic Preaching.* Translated by John Behr. Crestwood, NY: St. Vladimir's Seminary Press, 1997.

Lactantius. *The Divine Institutes: Books I–VII.* Translated by Mary Francis Mac-Donald. Washington, DC: Catholic University of America Press, 2008.

Origen. *Homilies on Genesis and Exodus.* Translated by Ronald Heine. Washington DC: Catholic University of America Press, 1982.

———. *On First Principles.* Translated by G. W. Butterworth. Gloucester, MA: Peter Smith, 1973.

Tertullian. *The Treatise against Hermogenes.* Translated by J. H. Waszink. Ancient Christian Writers 24. New York: Newman, 1956.

Theophilus. *Ad Autolycum.* Translated by Robert M. Grant. Oxford Early Christian Texts (Oxford: Clarendon, 1970).

———. *To Autolycus.* Translated by Marcus Dods. In *Ante-Nicene Fathers: The Writings of the Fathers down to AD 325*, edited by Alexander Roberts and James Donaldson, 2:85–122. Peabody, MA: Hendrickson, 2004.

Primary Texts Online

1. Theophilus of Antioch, *To Autolycus* (trans. *ANF*)
   http://www.earlychristianwritings.com/theophilus.html
   http://www.newadvent.org/fathers/0204.htm
2. Irenaeus of Lyons, *Demonstration of the Apostolic Preaching* (trans. J. Armitage Robinson)
   https://www.ccel.org/ccel/irenaeus/demonstr.iv.html
   http://www.tertullian.org/fathers/irenaeus_02_proof.htm
3. Irenaeus of Lyons, *Against Heresies* (trans. *ANF*)
   http://www.newadvent.org/fathers/0103.htm
   http://www.earlychristianwritings.com/irenaeus.html

4. Tertullian of Carthage, *Against Hermogenes* (trans. *ANF*)
   http://www.tertullian.org/works/adversus_hermogenem.htm
   http://www.earlychristianwritings.com/text/tertullian13.html

5. Tertullian of Carthage, *Against Marcion* (trans. *ANF* and Ernest Evans)
   http://www.newadvent.org/fathers/0312.htm
   http://www.tertullian.org/articles/evans_marc/evans_marc_00index
   .html

6. Origen of Alexandria, *On First Principles* (trans. *ANF*)
   http://www.ccel.org/ccel/schaff/anf04.toc.html
   http://www.newadvent.org/fathers/0412.htm

7. Origen of Alexandria, *Homilies on Genesis* (not in *ANF*)
   https://muse.jhu.edu/book/21468

8. Lactantius, *The Divine Institutes* (trans. *ANF*)
   https://www.ccel.org/ccel/schaff/anf07.toc.html
   http://www.newadvent.org/fathers/0701.htm

6

Interpretations of Genesis 1–2 among the Nicene and Post-Nicene Fathers

C. Rebecca Rine

Patristic interpretations of Gen. 1–2 are as imaginative and varied as the individuals and communities who fashioned them. Nicene and post-Nicene Christians returned to the opening words of Scripture time and again, and many of their reflections have been preserved through the labor of countless publishers, translators, and scribes. Yet even the substantial literary record does not tell the whole story; it is only the surface of a vast sea of exegetical, philosophical, theological, rhetorical, spiritual, scientific, and pastoral endeavors undertaken by the church between 300 and 700 CE.

To inquire into patristic approaches to the beginning of the Bible and creation is to do more than simply recapitulate what the fathers say about this verse or that; it is to acquire a specific set of navigational skills that enables both breadth and depth of analysis. To begin, one must envision Gen. 1–2 as more than a source of information about humanity's origins or the divine fiat. The fathers understand Scripture as a pathway to *transformation*, and thus they attend to both its reference (what the words might teach about creation or the garden, for instance) and its capacity to shape its hearers (how the same words might bring about spiritual maturation, for example).[1] In addition, one must become attuned to the many resonances between Gen. 1–2 and other portions of the Bible, resonances that may not be immediately discernible to the modern ear. The fathers often elucidate one word, image, or passage of Scripture by connecting it with others, such that the full significance of their insight extends beyond the realm of exegesis to the poetic. Furthermore, one must heighten one's appreciation for the precise linguistic details of Gen. 1–2, including not only diction, word order, and event sequencing, but also the contrast between what is written and what only might have been. The fathers regard these details as indicators of God's divine purposes in speaking (through Moses), and even the most minute aspect of Scripture's language may yield significant insight into those purposes. These expectations—that the words of Gen. 1–2 are formative, speak in concert with other Scriptures, and are the outworking of purposeful divine action—undergird the patterns and complexities of patristic ruminations on the beginning.

Introduction to the Interpreters

During the period known as late antiquity,[2] the expanding church was engaged in a massive educative effort. At the forefront of this effort were the individuals whose preaching and teaching reached beyond the sound of their voice by means of the written word. The line between oral delivery and written composition was not sharp—authors often composed by giving dictation, and many surviving lectures, sermons, and commentaries are transcriptions of instruction first given in person. Likewise, as Christian writings circulated beyond their place of original composition, they were frequently read aloud to auditors rather than merely viewed on parchment or papyrus.

Those individuals whose works were published had gained access to the ancient church's expansive literary network. This network was concentrated around centers of learning such as Jerusalem, Alexandria, Antioch, and Rome, where libraries and catechetical schools had long been established, but it also extended into ecclesial outposts and several emerging forms of Christian monasticism. Most prominent figures in this network had been ordained, and they carried out a number of responsibilities that spanned, in today's parlance,

1. For instance, as Kathryn Greene-McCreight has noted, "For Augustine, the act of reading scripture and Christian formation cannot be split apart." *Ad Litteram: How Augustine, Calvin, and Barth Read the "Plain Sense" of Genesis 1–3* (New York: Peter Lang, 1999), 32.
2. Late antiquity has been variously defined but roughly spans the fourth through the eighth centuries, marking the transition between the classical and medieval periods.

the political, academic, and religious spheres. Though some appear to have been more gifted preachers, while others preferred the ancient equivalent of a classroom, their various compositions defy easy categorization into "church" and "school" genres. The same person frequently composed in multiple genres, perhaps offering a homily, a commentary, an apologetic treatise, or an encyclical letter, depending on the occasion. Additionally, works of the same genre sometimes originated in divergent social contexts: a series of homilies, for instance, might have been delivered to a local congregation, an elite group of preachers-in-training, or one's traveling companions, who might be persons of mixed spiritual and intellectual training. Thus one cannot identify the original audience of a work simply by considering its genre, nor should one make a strong distinction between the fathers' scholarly and pastoral pursuits.

Patristic discussions of Gen. 1–2 appear in a variety of instructional genres, many of which derive their structure from the sequence of the biblical narrative. Chief among these is a form of literature uniquely tied to Gen. 1:1–2:3: the Hexaemeron, or "Six Days." These books proceed through the days of creation verse by verse, and prime examples survive from Basil of Caesarea (ca. 329–79) as well as Ambrose of Milan (ca. 340–97).[3]

The Hexaemera of Basil and Ambrose are presented as collections of homilies, and the homily is also the form in which John Chrysostom's expert preaching on the whole of Genesis is preserved. Chrysostom (ca. 349–407) likely delivered these homilies to the church at Antioch in 385, during worship on the weekdays of the Lenten season, and Robert Hill surmises, based on internal evidence, that the Antiochenes were "presumed to be readers of scripture at home," "a typical group of lay people, from family situations, preoccupied with secular affairs, and yet prepared to assemble daily for a lengthy scriptural homily on a fairly empty stomach in Lent."[4] Chrysostom's listeners usually heard a three-part homily after the appointed Scripture was read: an introduction and transition from the previous sermon, the primary exposition, and a closing exhortation.[5] Additional homilies on creation can be found in the corpora of Narsai (ca. 399–502) and Jacob of Serug (ca. 449–521),

---

3. Gregory of Nyssa (ca. 335–95) also wrote a sequel of sorts to his brother Basil's hexaemeral work titled *On the Making of Man*. For an investigation of Gregory's theological anthropology in this and other discourses, see Elizabeth Agnew Cochran, "The *Imago Dei* and Human Perfection: The Significance of Christology for Gregory of Nyssa's Understanding of the Human Person," *HeyJ* 50 (2009): 402–15. Doru Costache analyzes Gregory's lesser-known *Apology for the Hexaemeron* in "Approaching *An Apology for the Hexaemeron*: Its Aims, Method, and Discourse," *Phronema* 27, no. 2 (2012): 53–81.

4. Robert C. Hill, introduction to *St. John Chrysostom: Homilies on Genesis 1–17*, trans. Robert C. Hill (Washington, DC: Catholic University of America Press, 1986), 8.

5. R. Hill, introduction to *Homilies on Genesis 1-17*, 10.

who preached *memre*, or verse homilies, to their Syriac-speaking listeners. *Memre* are notable for their cadence as well as their content, which is arranged in couplets with the same number of syllables in each line.[6]

Another noteworthy mode of consecutive explication of Scripture is the commentary. For Bede (ca. 672–735), the commentary was a means of anthologizing former interpretations of Genesis.[7] For Augustine (354–430), however, the commentary took on more investigative overtones. As translator Edmund Hill observes, in Augustine's final commentary on Genesis, *The Literal Meaning of Genesis*, the bishop of Hippo "instructs his readers by letting them share in his own search for the meaning" rather than drawing clear-cut conclusions about the meaning of each and every verse.[8] Augustine himself caricatures his comments as "a heap of questions," finding in Genesis "a vast array of true meanings . . . extracted from a few words."[9] Augustine never seemed to tire of Gen. 1–2: if sections of his *Confessions* and *The City of God* are included, he undertook extensive commentary on the creation narratives on at least five separate occasions.[10]

The fathers' teaching on creation also emerges in many works that do not strictly follow the narrative progression of Gen. 1–2. For instance, Theodoret of Cyrus (ca. 393–460) adopts the conventions of the *questio*, a technique first applied to Homeric literature. In his *Questions on the Octateuch*, Theodoret addresses thirty questions about the first two chapters of Genesis alone.[11] Theodoret's expositions are much more elaborate than those of Jerome (ca. 347–420), whose *Hebrew Questions on Genesis* contains only a few brief textual notes on the relevant passages.

---

6. Ephrem popularized couplets of fourteen (7 + 7) syllables, while Jacob of Serug favored twenty-four (12 + 12) syllables per couplet in his *memre*. Thus Edward G. Mathews Jr. and Joseph P. Amar, general introduction to *St. Ephrem the Syrian: Selected Prose Works*, trans. Mathews and Amar (Washington, DC: Catholic University of America Press, 1994), 41–42. On Syriac verse homilies and poetics, see also Sebastian Brock, introduction to *St. Ephrem the Syrian: Hymns on Paradise* (Crestwood, NY: St. Vladimir's Seminary Press, 1990), 33–39.

7. Bede presents himself as a compiler of others' teachings, but Roger Ray queries Bede's perceptions of his own authority in "Who Did Bede Think He Was?," in *Innovation and Tradition in the Writings of the Venerable Bede*, ed. Scott DeGregorio (Morgantown: West Virginia University Press, 2006), 11–35.

8. Edmund P. Hill, introduction to *The Literal Meaning of Genesis*, in *On Genesis*, Works of Saint Augustine: A Translation for the 21st Century (Hyde Park, NY: New City, 2002), 155.

9. Quoted in E. Hill, *Literal Meaning of Genesis*, 188.

10. Roland J. Teske, introduction to *St. Augustine: On Genesis* (Washington, DC: Catholic University of America Press, 1991), 3–4.

11. Theodoret of Cyrus, *The Questions on the Octateuch*, vol. 1, *On Genesis and Exodus*, trans., introduction, and comm. Robert C. Hill (Washington, DC: Catholic University of America Press, 2007). The source of these questions, Theodoret says, is both those who "irreverently" find Scripture inconsistent or erroneous and those who sincerely desire to learn (5).

For churchmen such as Basil, Aphrahat (ca. 280–345), and Gregory of Nazianzus (ca. 329–90), a personal letter or isolated homily may become an occasion to expound on creational theology. Creation is a featured theme in Nazianzus's celebrated *Five Theological Orations* and in numerous theological, catechetical, and apologetic orations composed by Athanasius (ca. 297–373),[12] Hilary (ca. 310–67), Cyril of Jerusalem (ca. 313–86), and Gregory of Nyssa (ca. 335–95), among others. Ephrem the Syrian favors the hymnlike teaching poem, or *madrashe*, as an entrée to scriptural study, and his *Hymns on Paradise* remains one of the most vibrant examples of ancient retellings of Genesis. Ephrem, who also authored a commentary on Genesis, is one of several fathers whose teachings on creation have survived in more than one genre.

A patristic author's choice of instructional genre is significant, in part, because its literary conventions condition his interpretive options and mode of expression. Furthermore, each interpreter's expositions are influenced by the form and language in which he encounters the biblical text. The interpreters above (except Jerome, a student of Hebrew) all read Gen. 1–2 in translation—in Greek, Latin, or Syriac.[13] Sometimes they read multiple translations. In his discussion of Gen. 1:2, Gregory of Nyssa cites four Greek versions of Scripture, and none of them agree about the wording of "a formless void." Was the earth "invisible and unstructured, idle/fruitless and unspecified, deserted and nothing, or utter nothingness"?[14] Gregory's determination on this point affects the exegetical possibilities available to him as well as the potential of verse 2 to resonate with biblical and extra-biblical literature.[15]

Even if only one translation is in play, the semantic range of biblical words changes from language to language. For instance, Hebrew *'ādām* may be either a proper name or a term for all humankind. This ambiguity cannot be maintained in Greek or Latin, which also lose the lexical link between Hebrew "Adam/humankind" and *'ǎdāmâ*, "earth" or "ground." At times, translations introduce substantive changes as well. In the Latin Vulgate and the Hebrew of Gen. 2:2, according to Jerome, God completes creative action

12. See esp. Athanasius's *Incarnation of the Word*, which expounds on the theological import of creation as it relates to the incarnation.

13. For in-depth exposition concerning the Hebrew and Septuagintal Greek of Gen. 1–2, see William Loader, "Creation Stories," in *The Septuagint, Sexuality, and the New Testament: Case Studies on the Impact of the LXX in Philo and the New Testament* (Grand Rapids: Eerdmans, 2004), 27–52.

14. Costache, "Approaching *An Apology*," 65.

15. For instance, Gregory rejects the fourth translation cited above because it sounds too similar to Epicurean ways of speaking (Costache, "Approaching *An Apology*," 65–66).

on the seventh day of creation,[16] but in some versions of the Greek Septuagint and Syriac Peshitta, God's action ceases on the *sixth* day.[17] Every linguistic detail, from basic vocabulary to the grammatical number of a word, opens and closes interpretive avenues.[18]

Beyond the intricacies of genre, textual transmission, and translation, many contemporary readers of the fathers are interested in patristic interpretive and theological methods more broadly: How do the fathers move from reading Gen. 1–2 in their language of choice to the articulation of various teachings on these chapters? What is the relationship between what Scripture says and what the fathers say?

In past scholarly discussions, patristic exegesis has often been evaluated with respect to how "literal" or "allegorical" it is. As a case in point, the organizing question of Peter Bouteneff's *Beginnings: Ancient Christian Readings of the Biblical Creation Narratives* is "how literally did [each father under consideration] read the creation narratives?" Bouteneff acknowledges the limitations of analytical categories such as "allegory, typology, myth, literal sense, and so on," but maintains that "it is scarcely possible to describe the early church's reading of Scripture without them."[19] Indeed, these categories are widely used, but they are not as widely understood. Modern scholars as well as the fathers themselves disagree about the definition and relative value of literal and allegorical interpretation, and the terms of this ongoing debate are notoriously difficult to pin down.

Also at issue is the connotation of these terms: the classification of patristic interpretations as either "literal" or "allegorical" is sometimes shorthand for their wholesale approval or dismissal. For instance, literal readings may be derided as necessarily naive: one may expect the fathers' literal (and therefore simplistic) exposition of Gen. 1–2 to bypass post-Enlightenment concerns about the relation of faith to science. Alternatively, the literal sense may be exalted: one may believe that, in order to read Scripture faithfully, one must necessarily read it literally. Similarly, the fathers' association with *allegorēsis* may render them suspect in some circles and irrelevant in others. To allegorize is, most basically, to speak of "other" (Gk. *allos*) meanings of a given word or

16. *Saint Jerome's "Hebrew Questions on Genesis,"* trans. C. T. R. Hayward (Oxford: Clarendon, 1995), 31.

17. *Saint Jerome's "Hebrew Questions,"* 106.

18. If the language of a translation conscribes interpretive choices, so too does the expositor's attitude toward that translation. For instance, to the extent that the translation itself is regarded as divinely inspired, patristic interpreters may be reluctant to resolve apparent difficulties by proposing alternative wordings or martialing the tools of textual criticism.

19. Peter C. Bouteneff, *Beginnings: Ancient Christian Readings of the Biblical Creation Narratives* (Grand Rapids: Baker Academic, 2008), xi, xiii.

passage, and this practice has often been critiqued as a form of *eisēgēsis*, or reading one's own interests "into" (Gk. *eis*) the biblical text. Patristic allegory may also be dismissed simply because it is unfamiliar, difficult to follow, and no longer taught as a staple of biblical or literary scholarship.

Thus, while the descriptors "literal" and "allegorical" can illuminate basic aspects of patristic exegesis, such as the fathers' penchant for discovering more than one meaning in a particular word or verse, they can also obscure important features of the very literature they are intended to clarify, especially if one accepts or rejects an interpretation purely based on its status as either literal or allegorical. The same is true of two additional labels frequently employed in discussions of patristic theology: "orthodox" and "heretical." These terms are useful for establishing the value of a work within a confessional context, for just as the perceived boundary line between orthodoxy and heresy affected which patristic works were preserved in antiquity, the same line affects which works are studied and with what aims they are read today. However, these labels are not always helpful guides in the reading of patristic literature, because many of the fathers' interpretations do not fit neatly into either category.

This can be demonstrated via analysis of a short section of Ambrose's *Paradise*, the sequel to his *Hexaemeron*. In his reflections on Gen. 2:10, Ambrose identifies the "river [that] flows out of Eden to water the garden" as "our Lord Jesus Christ, the Fount as well as the Father of eternal life." He accomplishes this, first, by pairing Gen. 2:10 with Ps. 36:9 (35:10 LXX), "For with thee is the fountain of life," and John 7:38, "from within [the one who believes on Christ] there shall flow living waters."[20] Ambrose here applies the insight that Scripture interprets Scripture to his reading of Gen. 2:10, concluding, based on shared keywords and themes, that the fount of Eden is the fount of life. There is nothing *unorthodox* (in the theological sense) about Ambrose's claim that Jesus is a fountain of life. Yet few contemporary readers would find his conclusions theologically satisfying *as interpretations of Genesis*. They may thus appear orthodox, but irrelevant.

At the same time, it seems likely that Ambrose would maintain that he has interpreted Gen. 2:10 *literally*, insofar as "by the letter" of these words the Holy Spirit intended to communicate a truth about Jesus for the purpose of forming the Christian soul. Ambrose later discusses the four rivers that spring from the fount, which he identifies as the Ganges (Pishon), the Nile (Gihon), the Tigris, and the Euphrates. On the one hand, he speaks of the

---

20. Ambrose, *Paradise*, in *St. Ambrose: Hexameron, Paradise, and Cain and Abel*, trans. John J. Savage (Washington, DC: Catholic University of America Press, 1961), 294–95.

rivers in what might be construed as a literal, or at least geographical, way: the Nile was the site of Israel's "sojourn in Egypt," and the Tigris, "which flows by the Assyrian land," was the place to which "Israel was dragged as a prisoner." But he then associates the rivers with two of the four classical virtues: Prudence, Temperance, Fortitude, and Justice.[21] Specifically, Ambrose notes that the Nile signifies Temperance or chastity: the river's name indicates its capacity to wash away impurities, and one's body must be purified from sin in order to "partake of a lamb" as the Israelites did in Egypt. The Tigris is "the swiftest of all rivers" and therefore signifies Fortitude: "Fortitude in its rapid course tosses aside everything standing in its path and like this river is not hindered by any material object."[22]

Classifying these interpretations as literal or allegorical does little to clarify their function within Ambrose's wider pedagogical project. Ambrose's aim is to demonstrate how the words of Genesis can serve as tutors of the soul, and any interpretation that serves that purpose is a plausible one. However, this does not mean that "anything goes" for Ambrose, or that he lacks a methodological compass.

Generally speaking, a patristic teacher must steer an exegetical course through at least three guideposts that constrain his proclamations. First, a proper Christian interpretation must pass a hermeneutical test. It must accord with the intention of Scripture's author—the Holy Spirit, who speaks through the human author. Second, a proffered interpretation must pass a theological test. This test, known as the rule of faith, ensures that an interpretation accords with the church's fundamental teachings and other portions of Scripture. A third patristic requirement for Christian exegesis is a performative, or effectual, test: an authentic interpretation must result in the sanctification of the interpreter, the hearers, or both. Augustine, for instance, maintains that successful interpretations always increase one's love for both God and neighbor.[23]

This trivium of concerns establishes the ground rules for patristic exegesis, and it also helps to explain why *allegorēsis* was commonly practiced within the ancient church. First, it aligned well with patristic conceptions of divine speech. The fathers expected that the language of God would overflow with meaning, and therefore they were not surprised to find more than one level

21. According to translator Roland J. Teske, "The interpretation of the four rivers as signifying the cardinal virtues . . . goes back to Philo (*Quaestiones in Genesim* 1.12)." See also Teske, *Two Books on Genesis against the Manichees*, in *Augustine: On Genesis*, 109n63.

22. Ambrose, *Paradise*, 296–98.

23. Augustine, *On Christian Teaching*, trans. R. P. H. Green (Oxford: Oxford University Press, 1997), 27.

SIDEBAR 6.1

Chrysostom, Homily 8 in *Homilies on Genesis*

Come now, let us see what it is today also Moses is teaching us through the text we've read, or rather what the grace of the Spirit has to say to us all through his tongue. "God said," the text goes on, "Let us make a human being in our image and likeness." Let us not rush idly by what is said, dearly beloved; instead, let us investigate each expression, get right to the depth of its meaning, and divine the force concealed in these brief phrases. I mean, although the words may be few, immense is the treasure concealed in them; we must remain alert and vigilant and not stop short at the surface.

Note: Chrysostom, *Hom. Gen.* 8, p. 106.

---

of signification in the pages of Scripture. Second, *allegorēsis* smoothed the exegetical pathway from the words of Scripture to the teachings of the church, facilitating the connection of obscure passages with clearer ones and with fundamental Christian doctrines. Third, it was regarded as a reliable pathway toward spiritual formation, for in the act of allegorizing, Scripture becomes an apparatus for advanced theological discernment. Although ancient allegorizing is often evaluated as though it were an *interpretive strategy*, concerned primarily with a text and its meaning, it is best thought of instead as a *spiritual and theological practice* in which identifying the meaning of a text is only one part of a broader process of spiritual and intellectual maturation, or sanctification.

In sum, the fathers' interpretive and theological methods are ultimately tied to their educative aims. The interpretation of Scripture is central to these aims, as is the formation of their hearers. Thus patristic teachings on Gen. 1–2 are always *more than* explanations of what these opening chapters of the Bible might mean. They are also attempts to lead listeners into a life of faith, and to do so within a crowded pedagogical space inhabited by competing scientific norms, philosophical schools, regional and theological loyalties, and methodological standards. To read patristic literature is to listen in on an ancient ecclesial classroom, and making sense of what is heard there requires sensitivity to multiple dimensions of patristic pedagogy.

Treatment of Days

One technique for comprehending the fathers' lessons on Genesis is to consider the questions they ask as well as the answers they propose. These questions reveal their theological and literary sensibilities as well as their perspectives on the natural world. For instance, a significant feature of Gen. 1:1–2:3 is its description of creation in seven "days." But what do these days signify? The fathers do not simply list possible denotations of the term "day," as though scriptural interpretation were a matter of compiling dictionary definitions. Instead, they establish a robust culture of inquiry in which Scripture is put to the test, and it, in turn, puts human wisdom to the test.

For instance, the Nicene and post-Nicene fathers pose a recurring question about the reason "days" appear in the narrative at all: why should God create over a period of days rather than in a moment, which it is clearly within his power to do? Behind this question is a characteristic patristic preoccupation with, and resistance to, anthropomorphism, or the association of humanlike qualities (Gk. *anthrōpos* = human) with God. Viewed from this angle, the fact that God should take as many as six days to create the world is something of a scandal. As Chrysostom preaches, "God's all-powerful hand and boundless wisdom were not at a loss even to create everything in one day. Why say 'one day'? Even in a brief moment."[24]

However, in this feature of Gen. 1:1–2:3, Chrysostom also finds a fitting response to a belief prevalent in his day: the assertion that matter (Gk. *hylē*) was self-creating or preexistent, and that God was only responsible for reshaping it. He thus proposes that God deliberately spelled out what happened on each day in order to correct those who think the world was created by chance, without the action of a divine being.[25] Ambrose attributes similarly errant views to students of the Greek philosophers: "Plato and his pupils" assume that the fundamental principles of being are "uncreated, incorruptible, and without a beginning," and Aristotle teaches that "the world always was and always will be."[26] Genesis 1–2 rebuts these claims.

Jacob of Serug, in his *memra* on day 1 of creation, similarly emphasizes that nothing existed before God spoke,[27] but he proposes a different reason why six days were required: "It was not because the power of God lacked anything that he was patient / And [only] after six days was all creation entirely completed; / But creation needed ordering / . . . Patience was necessary for the establishment of each [creation] / So that they might make way for their

24. Chrysostom, *Hom. Gen.* 3, p. 44.
25. Chrysostom, *Hom. Gen.* 3, pp. 44–45.
26. Ambrose, *Hexameron*, in *St. Ambrose*, 3–4.
27. Jacob of Serug, "On the Establishment of Creation, Memra One, The First Day," trans. Robin Darling Young, in Joseph W. Trigg, *Biblical Interpretation* (Wilmington, DE: Michael Glazier, 1988), 184–202, here 187.

fellow-creations as they were made."[28] In other words, due to the limitations of the created, the Creator delayed his actions.

Augustine is troubled over the related question of how long it took God to speak: it is "astonishing," he says, "when God said, *Let light be made*, . . . why should it take such a long time to make light, until the space of a whole day had passed, and evening could be made."[29] Through a number of sophisticated proofs, Augustine maintains that these words were not spoken audibly but "in the Word co-eternal with himself, . . . in a timeless manner."[30] In antiquity, debates over the nature of "days" tend to center not on whether they lasted twenty-four hours or longer but on whether the term "day" indicates a set period of time or is only a figure of speech that describes a *timeless* event.[31]

Another question articulated by the fathers concerns an apparent contradiction between their experience of the natural world and the syntax of Scripture. Six times in Gen. 1, the phrase "evening and morning" appears, and in each instance, evening *precedes* morning. Basil, in his *Hexaemeron*, wonders why evening is mentioned first, when daytime clearly precedes night.[32] This question is particularly acute with respect to days 1 and 4, when God creates light(s): how could up to twelve hours of "evening," which is presumably dark, follow the creation of something luminous? Augustine and others also note the absence of the term "evening" with respect to the seventh day, asking what this teaches readers about the nature of God's rest.[33]

Curiosity about the sequence of events in Scripture and the observed attributes of the natural world also engenders questions such as "How could plants created on day 3 thrive without the lights created on day 4?" or "How could plants created on day 3 be ready for consumption by animals on day 5?" Ephrem correlates his knowledge of Scripture and of the natural world while commenting on Gen. 1:16, which describes God as making "two great lights" on day 4; he surmises that the newly created moon must have been full, in the fifteenth day of its cycle, even though it was only one day old. The sun, he believes, was created on day 4 of its cycle, accounting for the eleven-day gap, discovered by the "Chaldeans," between a solar and a lunar year.[34] As Ephrem comments on the verse, he simultaneously answers several questions: "Why is

28. Jacob of Serug, "Establishment of Creation," 198.

29. Quoted in E. Hill, *Literal Meaning of Genesis*, 176.

30. Quoted in E. Hill, *Literal Meaning of Genesis*, 174.

31. See J. C. M. van Winden, "In the Beginning: Some Observations on the Patristic Interpretation of Genesis 1:1," *VC* 17 (1963): 105–21.

32. Basil, *Exegetic Homilies*, trans. Sister Agnes Clare Way (Washington, DC: Catholic University of America Press, 1963), 33–34.

33. Quoted in E. Hill, *Literal Meaning of Genesis*, 250–58.

34. Ephrem, quoted in Mathews and Amar, *St. Ephrem the Syrian*, 92.

there a gap between the solar and the lunar year?" "What is the relationship between Scripture's words and the findings of leading astrologers?" "How could God have created two lights at once while still preserving the currently observed rotation of the moon and sun?"

This brief sampling of patristic questions about the days of Gen. 1:1–2:3 highlights a few of the fathers' theological, literary, and scientific concerns as they engage with the Genesis narratives. Behind their specific questions about select phrases lie broader questions about how God speaks in Scripture, how language itself works, and the origins and reliability of human knowledge. Convinced that every word of Scripture has been placed there purposefully, the fathers consider the details of each passage and seek to correlate the words of Scripture with prevalent assertions of their day. As teachers, they demonstrate that scriptural interpretation is a demanding task requiring mastery of both divine and human canons of knowledge, and that Scripture, properly studied, both stands up under questioning and calls other viewpoints into question.

Cosmology

In addition to teaching their students how to ask and answer questions about Genesis, the fathers also mentor their listeners in appropriate conversational demeanor, or how to conduct themselves while dialoging about Genesis with others. As noted above, the Nicene and post-Nicene fathers carry out their pedagogical activities on contested ground. Their voices compete with those outside the fold of Christendom (such as Jewish rabbis or professional philosophers) as well as those within (such as members of various sects or other teachers in the church) and those of dubious or unknown status. This is particularly evident in patristic teachings on the Christian view of cosmology, or the arrangement of the universe, because the fathers often cite alternative viewpoints while expounding their own. These passages reveal how the fathers distinguish their teaching from others' and how they interact with students, colleagues, and opponents.

One such passage appears in Augustine's first foray into sustained interpretation of Genesis, his apologetic *Two Books on Genesis against the Manichaeans*. Though the title of this work suggests that it is addressed to Augustine's interlocutors, as his translator Roland Teske observes, "Like any apologetic work, [*Against the Manichaeans*] is aimed to a large extent at the defense of those who already believe, or at the protection of those who are wavering." Teske distinguishes between the Manichaeans "against whom Augustine wrote," on the one hand, and "the uneducated Catholic for whom

[he] wrote," on the other.[35] Augustine's pastoral concern is to win listeners over from the school of the Manichaeans to the teaching of the church.[36]

In refuting the Manichaeans and guiding his students, Augustine places a premium on holding the right view of Scripture and persevering in faith.[37] The Manichaeans, he says, challenge the claim of Gen. 1:1 that God made heaven and earth, on the basis of Gen. 1:2, which describes the earth as invisible and without form. At issue here is the doctrine of creation ex nihilo, for the Manichaeans maintained, like many ancient thinkers cited above, that God merely arranged preexistent matter rather than creating it from nothing.[38] Augustine accuses the Manichaeans of insufficient study of Scripture ("They want to attack the divine Scriptures before they know them") and points out that Gen. 1:2 "clearly" speaks of God's initial creation of all things before he ordered them by means of subsequent commands. Augustine also describes how a faithful reader of Scripture, who has discerned its "great mysteries," should regard dissenting interpreters: with pity or lament, because those interpreters have revealed their limitations, or with derision, because they are persisting in unwarranted pride.[39] Augustine's commentary not only contrasts two potential interpretations of Gen. 1:1–2 and proposes a *reason* for the divergent views but also specifies an appropriate affective *response* to one who holds such a view.

Like Augustine, Basil situates his preaching on Genesis as a rejoinder to prevailing opinions and an invitation to orient oneself to God, keeping in view both the claims of competing authorities and his own hearers' purposes for listening. The third homily of his *Hexaemeron* addresses the cosmological implications of Gen. 1:6–8 and its description of the firmament.

Basil first asks whether the firmament of 1:6–8 is the same as the heavens of 1:1, for 1:8 calls the firmament "heavens." He attributes numerous views to "the philosophers," including the assertions that there is only one heaven and that there is an infinite number of heavens. He next turns to opinions within the church, such as the proposal that Gen. 1:1–2 is a summary statement of the verses that follow. Basil acknowledges this view but postulates instead that, because this second "heavens" also has a different name, "firmament," and because its purpose, "to divide the waters," is recorded, that it is, in fact, a second creation.[40]

---

35. Teske, introduction to *Augustine: On Genesis*, 7.
36. On Augustine's pastoral attitude, see Teske, introduction to *Augustine: On Genesis*, 13.
37. Teske, introduction to *Augustine: On Genesis*, 47–48.
38. Teske, introduction to *Augustine: On Genesis*, 52n20.
39. Teske, introduction to *Augustine: On Genesis*, 52–53.
40. Basil, *Exegetic Homilies*, 39–41.

SIDEBAR 6.2

Basil, Homily 3 in *Exegetic Homilies*

Let our explanations concerning the second day, however, be brought to a close here, so as to afford time to our industrious hearers for a review of what they have heard. Thus, if there is anything useful in it, they may keep it in their memory, and by their diligent rehearsal, as if by a sort of ripening, they may expect an assimilation of the benefits. Thus also, it may give to those busy about their livelihood opportunity to dispose of their business in the intervening time, so that they may present themselves for the evening banquet of words with a soul free from anxieties. May God, who created such mighty things and ordained that these petty words be spoken, grant to you an understanding of His truth in its entirety, in order that from visible objects you may comprehend the invisible Being, and from the greatness and beauty of creatures you may conceive the proper idea concerning our Creator. "For since the creation of the world his invisible attributes are clearly seen—his everlasting power also and divinity" [Rom. 1:20]. Therefore, in the earth, in the air, and in the heavens, in water, in night and in day, and in all things visible, clear reminders of the Benefactor grip us. We shall not give any opportunity for sins, nor shall we leave any place in our hearts for the enemy, if we have God as a dweller in us by our constant remembrance of Him, to whom be all glory and adoration, now and always, and for all ages of ages.

Note: Basil, *Exegetic Homilies*, pp. 53–54.

As Basil proceeds with his inquiry, he continues to bring up opposing viewpoints and to persuade his congregants concerning the physical properties of the firmament and the waters. In taking on "the futile questioning of philosophers about the heavens," he suggests that the best argumentative technique is to leave the philosophers to undermine each other, for "why trouble ourselves to refute their falsehood, since it suffices for us to set out their books in opposition to each other and sit in all silence as spectators of their war?" Though Basil does, in fact, frequently attempt refutation, he also reminds his listeners of guiding concepts concerning the purposes of creation, teaching them to read Genesis, and contemplate creation, as a means of knowing God. Basil further quibbles with certain teachers *within* the church who understand the divided waters as signifying two kinds of "spiritual and incorporeal powers," with the waters above signifying "excellent" powers and the waters below signifying those that are "malignant." Basil dismisses this interpretation because it is not required by reason; as he says, "Let us consider water as water."[41] Throughout this homily,

---

41. Basil, *Exegetic Homilies*, 51–52.

Basil adopts a more critical, derisive tone when discussing opinions originating outside the church, and even though he appears to be respectful of diverse viewpoints within the church, he defends his own perspective with confidence.[42]

Augustine and Basil, like all Nicene and post-Nicene fathers, articulate their claims about cosmology in dialogue with others. Their comments on Genesis are exchanges in an ongoing conversation, and they seek to initiate their hearers into the rules of this conversation. As they explicate Scripture, they exemplify various attitudes toward their interlocutors and show their listeners how to engage with alternative points of view. Their remarks are valuable not only for what they indicate about the influence of Platonism, Aristotelianism, and/or Scripture on Christian conceptions of the cosmos but also for their teaching on the interpersonal dimensions of exegesis.

Creation and Nature of Humanity

The Nicene and post-Nicene fathers approach Gen. 1–2 with a keen interest in the creation and nature of humanity.[43] In seeking to discern what Genesis teaches on this topic, they invite their listeners to develop the skill of detecting the fine verbal distinctions that appear in Scripture. These distinctions are regarded as important indicators of how and why God created humankind and as avenues to understanding his communicative intent. While instructing listeners in the theological anthropology of Genesis, then, the fathers also instill habits of scriptural analysis.

For example, a first distinction frequently cited by the fathers concerns the linguistic form of God's creative command, which changes when he prepares to create humans. Whereas previously God had said, "Let there be," and there was, on day 6 God says, "Let us make." Theodoret observes two shifts that have occurred here, one from third person to first and the other from singular ("God") to plural ("us").[44] As he notes, some people account for the shift to first person by imagining that "Let us make" was spoken to the angels and demons. Theodoret, however, concludes that these people have failed to read Scripture well, because the verse goes on to say, "Let us make the human being in *our* image and likeness," and certainly God did not create humans

42. For analysis of Basil's perceptions of his audience and the effect of these perceptions on his interpretations of Genesis, see Richard Lim, "The Politics of Interpretation in Basil of Caesarea's *Hexaemeron*," VC 44 (1990): 351–70.

43. As Wynand Vladimir de Beer notes, "In the patristic understanding, the human being is the climax of God's creation." See "Being Human, Becoming Like God: Patristic Perspectives on Humankind," *JTSA* 148 (March 2014): 65–82, here 68.

44. The following analysis is based on Theodoret, *Questions*, 44–49.

in the image and likeness of angels and demons. Theodoret also dismisses an explanation of "Let us make" that he attributes to the Jews, namely, the claim that God is using the "royal we" here, or the literary convention of speaking in the plural in formal, official situations. Theodoret emphasizes that these Jews have failed to understand not only the significance of this particular verse but also God's way of speaking in general. To prove his point, Theodoret adduces as evidence several verses from other portions of Scripture where God says "I" rather than "we." The astute reader of Scripture, Theodoret implies, is familiar with God's typical patterns of speech and will analyze any apparent departures from those patterns in light of their theological import. In this case, as at the tower of Babel, where God said "let us go down," the use of the plural pronoun and verb points the observant reader to the Trinity. Theodoret confirms this proposal by noting that the contrast of singular "God" and plural "us" as well as singular "image" and plural "our" points to both "the identity of substance" and the "numerical distinction of persons" of the Trinity.

A second significant distinction appears, according to many fathers, between the terms "image" and "likeness" in Gen. 1:26. These are not mere synonyms but point to separate aspects of God's creation, and discerning their meaning requires close reading of Scripture. Chrysostom combats those who interpret "image" as bodily form by referring readers to the words that follow: "Let them have control." He concludes that being created in God's image means being created to rule, and in God's likeness, with the capacity to grow in virtue.[45] Gregory of Nyssa, in *On the Making of Man*, sees a further distinction between humans made "in the image and likeness of God" and the "male and female" mentioned in Gen. 1:27. Frances Young summarizes as follows: "[Gregory] argues that the Bible contains two accounts of man's creation: man-in-the-image is different from man in his present state. The intellectual element in man, man like to God, preceded the irrational, which is characterized by its polarization into male and female."[46] Gregory thus reads Gen. 1:27 as referring to two separate points in time, one before and one after the fall.

Another distinction highlighted by several patristic authors concerns the verb "formed" or "fashioned" that appears in Gen. 2:7, "The LORD God formed man from the dust of the ground."[47] Chrysostom recites a litany of

45. Chrysostom, *Hom. Gen. 9*, pp. 110, 120. See also de Beer, "Being Human," 68–71, for a list of several standard patristic distinctions between "image" and "likeness."
46. Frances M. Young, "Adam and Anthropos: A Study of the Interaction of Science and the Bible in Two Anthropological Treatises of the Fourth Century," *VC* 37 (1983): 112.
47. Cf. Gen. 2:8, "There he put the man whom he had formed."

God's previous commands, such as "Let there be light" and "Let the stars be made," and then asks:

> Do you see how they were all created by a word? Let us notice instead what it says in the case of the creation of human beings. "God formed the human being." Do you see how, by the considerateness shown in the words he uses on account of our limitations, it teaches us both the manner of the creation and the difference [between the creation of humans and the creation of other things], and all but shows us . . . man being shaped by God's hands—as another author says, "Your hands made me, and formed me" [Job 10:8]?[48]

Christians must, Chrysostom continues, "understand the whole narrative in a manner appropriate to God," and he aids them in this by connecting the words of Genesis with the words of a Psalm.[49] For Chrysostom, the shift in Genesis from recording God's commands to depicting a scene in which the reader sees God working reveals how God "displays such marks of regard . . . right from the outset" for the creature he forms.[50] The literary shift has theological significance.

A fourth distinction that captures patristic attention occurs in Gen. 2:15, where God "puts the man in the garden of Eden to till and keep it." This phrasing poses a number of problems for Ephrem, such as "With what did Adam till the garden since he had no tools for tilling?" and "From what did he guard it since there were no thieves to enter it?"[51] Adam's responsibility to "till and keep," according to Ephrem, was to obey the one command that God had given him. Similarly, Ambrose interprets "till and keep" as denoting moral and spiritual responsibilities, though, in contrast with Ephrem, Ambrose defines tilling and keeping as the pursuit and maintenance of virtue, not as adherence to the law.[52] Chrysostom envisions "tilling and keeping" as physical activities prescribed by God in order to prevent Adam from becoming slothful, a "stabilizing influence . . . to prevent him from overstepping the limit" in the midst of "delights, relaxation, and freedom."[53] Chrysostom derives his

48. Chrysostom, *Hom. Gen.* 13, p. 171.
49. Chrysostom, *Hom. Gen.* 13, p. 173.
50. Though Chrysostom focuses on the distinction between "God said" and "God formed," the same verb "formed" that appears in 2:7 also occurs in 2:19. Ephrem addresses this in his *Commentary on Genesis* by distinguishing between two uses of the same word. Commenting on 2:19, he states that the beasts and birds "were not really *formed* [by God in the same sense that humans were], for the earth brought forth the animals and the water the birds." Mathews and Amar, *St. Ephrem the Syrian*, 103.
51. Quoted in Mathews and Amar, *St. Ephrem the Syrian*, 101–2.
52. Ambrose, *Paradise*, 302–3.
53. Chrysostom, *Hom. Gen.* 14, p. 185.

interpretation with reference to God's considerateness (Gk. *synkatabasis*) in caring for humans; understanding God's characteristic ways of interacting with humans is crucial for interpreting the wording of Scripture.[54]

In each of these examples, the fathers observe how shifts in the narrative or paired terms introduce key distinctions that offer insight into the creation and vocation of humans. Guiding their students through these lessons, the fathers exhibit expert interpretation in the same way that an accomplished musician might lead a master class. The purpose of their instruction is not just to play the musical score well but also to introduce multiple ways of *approaching* that score. The fathers do the same, taking Genesis as their score and verbal instruction as their instrument.

Garden of Eden

If, for the fathers, one essential element of biblical interpretation is careful analysis of scriptural language, another is the ability to connect words and images that recur in the canon. This is not only an exegetical technique but also a rhetorical one, for homilies such as Aphrahat's *Demonstrations* 17 are organized around two verses that, when juxtaposed, appear to contradict one another. Aphrahat goes on to examine how it can be true both that Adam was in God (Ps. 90:1)[55] and that God was in Adam (Lev. 26:11),[56] a conundrum that he resolves by proposing that Adam was first created in the mind of God and then, after he was created in bodily form, God came to dwell in him. This argument is part of a larger analogy Aphrahat draws between the figure of Adam and the figure of Christ.

While exploring the links between various sections of Scripture, the fathers cultivate the literary and theological imaginations of their listeners. The descriptions of creation in Gen. 1–2, and particularly the vivid natural imagery of 2:8–17, offer rich possibilities for imaginative retelling. Some fathers, such as Chrysostom, urge their hearers to envision the garden as a physical locale,

54. For further investigation of these themes in Chrysostom's works, see Robert C. Hill, "On Looking Again at *Synkatabasis*," *Prudentia* 13 (1981): 3–11; and "*Akribeia*: A Principle of Chrysostom's Exegesis," *Australian and New Zealand Theological Review* 14, no. 1 (1981): 32–36.

55. "Lord, you were a habitation for us generations before the mountains were conceived." The translation here and for the following note are Loepp's and are based on the Syriac. See Dale Loepp, "The Adamic Creation Tradition in the Seventeenth *Demonstration* of Aphrahat," in *Exegesis and Hermeneutics in the Churches of the East*, ed. Vahan S. Hovhanessian (New York: Peter Lang, 2009), 15.

56. "I [God] will dwell in you"; Aphrahat also quotes 1 Cor. 3:16, "The temple of God are you."

created somewhere on earth, and not in heaven.[57] Augustine determines that the tree of life is both real and figurative, in the same way that Hagar and Sarah were living women and also "signified the two covenants."[58] The tree of life "was created in the bodily paradise," and "Wisdom—which is the same as Christ himself—is also the tree of life in the spiritual paradise, where he sent the thief from the cross."[59] Here, Augustine establishes a double bridge between Genesis and the Gospels, equating Christ with the tree of life and paradise with the garden.

In the poetic imagination of Ephrem, author of the *Hymns on Paradise*, the garden of Gen. 2 gestures toward spiritual rather than physical realities. He seeks a transcendent experience through the reading of the narrative, "a tale that is short to read / but rich to explore." By reading the "outward narrative," Ephrem's "intellect [takes] wing . . . and perceive[s] the splendor of Paradise."[60] The garden, he says, is "described by things visible, / but glorious for what lies hidden."[61]

Ephrem visualizes the garden in connection with several later passages of Scripture. First, he understands the garden as a tabernacle.[62] Ephrem locates Eden on a mountain higher than any other mountains, and the boundaries of Eden conscribe the outer court, where Adam and Eve live and the priests were ordinarily allowed. According to Ephrem, the boundary between the outer and inner courts of the garden is marked by the tree of knowledge, and because of their transgression, Adam and Eve are denied access to the inner court, or holy of holies, where the tree of life grows. The tree of knowledge was a gate to the inner court, and its fruit, a veil.[63]

Ephrem also connects both the tree of life and the tree of knowledge with the cross. In his *Hymn on Virginity* 16, Ephrem depicts a "saddened" tree of life that "[sinks] down into the virgin ground" once Adam was banished from Eden, only to "burst forth and reappear on Golgotha" so that humans, like birds, may perch in it.[64] He also contrasts Adam's experience of touching the tree of knowledge, which resulted in his banishment from paradise, with Adam's approach to the tree of the cross, which resulted in his entry

57. Chrysostom, *Hom. Gen.* 13, pp. 174–76.
58. Quoted in E. Hill, *Literal Meaning of Genesis*, 351; see Gal. 4:21–31.
59. Quoted in E. Hill, *Literal Meaning of Genesis*, 352; see Luke 23:43.
60. See Ephrem, *Hymns* 1.3, p. 78.
61. See Ephrem, *Hymns* 1.1, p. 77.
62. Gary A. Anderson, *The Genesis of Perfection: Adam and Eve in Jewish and Christian Imagination* (Louisville: Westminster John Knox, 2001), 56–58. Anderson points to Jewish precedents for this conceptualization in Jubilees (see 8.19), where the garden is a temple.
63. See Ephrem, *Hymns* 3, pp. 90–96.
64. See Ephrem, *Hymn on Virginity* 16.10, pp. 60–61.

SIDEBAR 6.3

Ephrem, Hymn 12 in *Hymns on Paradise*

> Because Adam touched the Tree
>   he had to run to the fig;
> he became like the fig tree,
>   being clothed in its vesture:
> Adam, like some tree,
>   blossomed with leaves.
> Then he came to that glorious
>   tree of the Cross,
> put on glory from it
>   acquired radiance from it,
> heard from it the truth
>   that he would return to Eden once more.

Note: Ephrem, *Hymns* 12.10, p. 164.

---

to paradise. The boundary, or fence,[65] that God places around Eden to keep Adam out is guarded with a sword, and Ephrem associates this sword with Jesus's piercing on the cross, the Christian's entryway to paradise: "Through the side pierced with the sword I entered the Garden fenced in with the sword. Let us enter in through that side which was pierced."[66]

Ephrem's call to enter paradise reveals his fundamental orientation toward a present and future paradise rather than one of the past. The coming of the Spirit at Pentecost entailed the advent of paradise.[67] The breezes of paradise waft through the incense of worship, and the rivers of paradise feed the baptismal font.[68] "The assembly of saints / bears resemblance to Paradise,"[69] and paradise personified welcomes those who are righteous into its womb but casts out those who are not, in the same way that Jesus, as the gate, welcomes the sheep and repels the thief.[70] For Ephrem, the story of paradise in Gen. 2 possesses its own agency; when he reads the passage, "its verses and lines / spread

---

65. For discussion of this term as well as other examples cited here, see Brock, introduction to *St. Ephrem the Syrian: Hymns on Paradise*, 57–66.

66. Ephrem, *Commentary on the Diatesseron* 21.10, in Brock, introduction to *St. Ephrem the Syrian*.

67. See Ephrem, *Hymns* 11.14, p. 159.

68. See Ephrem, *Hymns* 11.12, p. 158; translator Sebastian Brock specifies that Ephrem is likely referring to the rite of baptism here.

69. See Ephrem, *Hymns* 6.8, p. 111.

70. See Ephrem, *Hymns* 2.1, p. 85; John 10:7.

SIDEBAR 6.4

Ephrem, Hymn 6 in *Hymns on Paradise*

The keys of doctrine
   which unlock all of Scripture's books,
have opened up before my eyes
   the book of creation,
the treasure house of the Ark,
   the crown of the Law.
This is a book which, above its companions,
   has in its narrative
made the Creator perceptible
   and transmitted His actions;
It has envisioned all His craftsmanship,
   made manifest His works of art.

Scripture brought me
   to the gate of Paradise,
and the mind, which is spiritual,
   stood in amazement and wonder as it entered,
the intellect grew dizzy and weak
   as the senses were no longer able
to contain its treasures—
   so magnificent they were—
or to discern its savors
   and find any comparison for its colors,
or take in its beauties
   so as to describe them in words.

Note: Ephrem, *Hymns* 6.1–2, pp. 108–9.

---

out their arms to welcome me" and "when I reached that verse / wherein is written the story of Paradise / it lifted me up and transported me / from the bosom of the book / to the very bosom of Paradise."[71] One need not wait for an eschatological paradise: through Scripture's words, one may enter it now.

Fathers such as Ephrem, Augustine, and Chrysostom differ with respect to their conceptions of the garden, but they share a desire to induct their students into the language of Gen. 2 and its relationship to other portions of Scripture. Augustine is more restrained and precise in the connections he makes, while

---

71. See Ephrem, *Hymns* 5.3, p. 103.

Ephrem seems to see paradise everywhere he looks. In either case, and for other fathers who comment on the garden, a key aspect of Christian teaching is the crafting of theological vision, often accomplished by collocating several passages of Scripture that share an image, word, or theme.

Interpretive Peculiarity: The Creation of Genesis

Although the fathers often praise Gen. 1–2 for its beauty, lofty subject matter, and revelatory value, they also acknowledge that some of its features are difficult to explain. Many comment on the fact that, contrary to their expectations, Gen. 1 does not mention all four of the elements—earth, wind, fire, water—or the creation of angels and spiritual beings. Basil remarks on the absence of technical details about the shape or circumference of the earth,[72] and Theodoret wonders why Genesis begins with a narrative rather than a theological discourse on the eternality of God.[73]

When offering an account of why Genesis begins the way that it does, several patristic authors speculate about Moses, the human author of Scripture, and his own purposes in writing the book of Genesis. They are first of all concerned to establish his authority. Basil and Ambrose, for instance, recite Moses's credentials as the chosen prophet of God, one whose prior training and experiences have prepared him to author the Pentateuch. For instance, only Moses has spoken with God face to face (Exod. 33:11).

Several fathers tell the "origin story" of Genesis. Moses is sometimes depicted as a model teacher who chose the words of Gen. 1–2 because he thoroughly understood the people to whom and for whom he was writing. Chrysostom says that, during the generations that preceded Israel's relocation to Egypt, God spoke to people in more personal and direct ways. But while the Israelites lived in Egypt, they took on Egyptian customs such as the worship of creation rather than Creator. When people lost the capacity to hear God's voice, he decided to send them "letters," that is, the Pentateuch, to teach them the truth.[74] Chrysostom goes on to compare Moses's teaching in Genesis with that of Paul before the Athenians, asserting that Moses's language is milk for newborns, whereas the NT authors can speak more plainly and in more detail. Similarly, Theodoret points out that Moses did not need to begin with a discourse on the eternal nature of God, because Moses's original audience already knew "I am who I am" (Exod. 3:14). Moses also declined to mention

---

72. Basil, *Exegetic Homilies*, 136.
73. Theodoret, *Questions*, 6–9.
74. Chrysostom, *Hom. Gen.* 2, pp. 31–34.

SIDEBAR 6.5

Chrysostom, Homily 2 in *Homilies on Genesis*

When God formed human beings in the beginning, he used to speak to them personally, in a way that was possible for human beings to understand him. This was the way, for example, that he came to Adam, the way he upbraided Cain, the way he conversed with Noah, the way he accepted Abraham's hospitality. And even when all humankind fell into evil ways, the Creator of all did not abandon the human race. Instead, when they then proved unworthy of his converse with them, he wanted to renew his love for them; he sent them letters as you do to people far away from you, and this drew all humankind back again to him. It was God who sent them letters, Moses who delivered them. What do the letters say? "In the beginning God made heaven and earth."

Note: Chrysostom, *Hom. on Gen.* 2, p. 31.

---

the creation of angels because the Israelites were tempted to idolatry by the mere presence of a golden calf. How much more would they have been tempted to idolatry if Moses had reminded them of superior, invisible powers that could also be improperly worshiped?[75] Jacob of Serug demonstrates that, where Genesis is silent, other prophets such as David, Isaiah, and Ezekiel "fill in the blanks," for not every aspect of creation is mentioned in Gen. 1–2.[76]

Thus everything that Moses wrote or did not write was an outworking of his pedagogical purposes. Moses is a consummate teacher, as is the Spirit, who guided him. The fathers' recourse to the figure of Moses, his relationship with God, and his skill as a teacher is another patristic strategy for defending and expositing the creation accounts.

Conclusion

For the Nicene and post-Nicene fathers, the beginning of Genesis holds great promise—and great peril. The promise of these chapters lies in their weighty subject matter, their depictions of divine action, their surprising turns of phrase, and their intimations regarding human origins. Their peril, however, lies in their susceptibility to critique from a number of quarters, due to either what they say or fail to say. For the fathers, the difference between a profitable

---

75. Theodoret, *Questions*, 7–9.
76. Jacob of Serug, "Establishment of Creation," 194–97.

and a perilous interpretation of Genesis lies not in the words of Scripture, which remain the same, but in the life and exegetical-rhetorical skill of the one who approaches Genesis to receive or give instruction.

As part of an established yet variable literary and theological culture, the fathers privilege certain approaches to Genesis while rejecting others. Through lectures and sermons, commentaries and poems, intensive analysis and inventive allusions, they exhibit the many ways Gen. 1–2 may inspire an interpretive community. Later readers of the fathers, when comparing patristic and nonpatristic engagements with the stories of creation, will come to their own conclusions about the value of specific interpretations or commonplace approaches. Like the fathers, these students of patristic teaching must sift through multiple perspectives, evaluate conflicting claims, consider the import of wording and context, and discern underlying relationships that may or may not appear on the surface. In doing so, they may find that the Nicene and post-Nicene fathers are not only a source of intriguing interpretations but also a resource for acquiring aptitude in the act of interpretation.

For Further Reading

Blowers, Paul. *Drama of the Divine Economy: Creator and Creation in Early Christian Theology and Piety*. Oxford: Oxford University Press, 2012.

Bockmuehl, Marcus, and Guy G. Stroumsa, eds. *Paradise in Antiquity: Jewish and Christian Views*. Cambridge: Cambridge University Press, 2010.

Bouteneff, Peter C. *Beginnings: Ancient Christian Readings of the Biblical Creation Narratives*. Grand Rapids: Baker Academic, 2008.

Champion, Michael. *Explaining the Cosmos: Creation and Cultural Interaction in Late-Antique Gaza*. Oxford: Oxford University Press, 2014.

Marmodoro, Anna, and Brian D. Prince, eds. *Causation and Creation in Late Antiquity*. Cambridge: Cambridge University Press, 2015.

Sheridan, Mark. *Language for God in Patristic Tradition: Wrestling with Biblical Anthropomorphism*. Downers Grove, IL: IVP Academic, 2014.

Primary Texts in Print

Anthologies

Louth, Andrew, ed. *Genesis 1–11*. ACCS 1. Downers Grove, IL: IVP Academic, 2001.

McFarland, Ian A., ed. *Creation and Humanity: The Sources of Christian Theology*. Louisville: Westminster John Knox, 2009.

Complete Works

Ambrose. *Hexameron, Paradise, and Cain and Abel*. Translated by John J. Savage. Washington, DC: Catholic University of America Press, 2003.

Athanasius. *On the Incarnation*. Translated by John Behr. Crestwood, NY: St. Vladimir's Seminary Press, 2012.

Ephrem the Syrian. *Hymns on Paradise*. Translated by Sebastian Brock. Crestwood, NY: St. Vladimir's Seminary Press, 1990.

John Chrysostom. *Homilies on Genesis 1–17*. Translated by Robert C. Hill. Washington, DC: Catholic University of America Press, 1986.

Primary Texts Online

1. Ambrose, *Hexameron* and *Paradise*
   https://archive.org/stream/fathersofthechur027571mbp/fathersofthechur027571mbp_djvu.txt

2. Athanasius, *On the Incarnation of the Word*
   http://www.newadvent.org/fathers/2802.htm

3. Basil, *Nine Homilies of Hexaemeron*
   http://www.newadvent.org/fathers/3201.htm

4. Ephrem, *Hymns on Paradise*, Hymns 11 and 15
   http://www.syriacstudies.com/AFSS/Syriac_Articles_in_English/Entries/2007/10/19_St._Ephrem_the_Syrian_Hymns_on_Paradise_-_Introduction_and_Translation_by_Dr._Sebastian_Brock.html

5. Gregory of Nyssa, *On the Making of Man*
   http://www.newadvent.org/fathers/2914.htm

6. John Chrysostom, *Homilies on Genesis*, Homilies 12–18 on Genesis 2 and 3
   http://www2.iath.virginia.edu/anderson/commentaries/ChrGen.html

7

Medieval Jewish Interpretations
of Genesis 1–2

Jason Kalman

Writing about recent Jewish-community debates on conversion to Orthodox Judaism, Marc Angel, a prominent American rabbi, challenged new demands made concerning beliefs held by candidates for conversion and the members of religious courts supervising them. Angel noted reports that an Orthodox rabbi, Sholom Eliyashiv (1910–2012), held "that any rabbi who believes the world is more than approximately 6,000 years old should not serve on the rabbinic courts that perform conversions" and that a group advocating more stringent rules for conversion included a question for potential converts on "the Torah view of the age of the universe." Angel asked his readers, "Knowing that we have perfectly legitimate traditions in Torah Judaism that allow for belief in a universe billions of years old, should we allow the obscurantists to disqualify all rabbis who dare to accept the clear findings of science? Do we want such people as the gatekeepers of Jewish identity?"[1]

1. Marc D. Angel, "Return Conversion to the Rabbis," *Forward* (January 6, 2010; updated April 14, 2015), http://forward.com/opinion/122774/return-conversion-to-the-rabbis/#ixzz3ojutRxx9.

Despite Eliyashiv's position, the view that Gen. 1–2 should be taken as an accurate historical account of the world's creation is rare in Jewish sources and in the Jewish imagination. An exploration of midrash and Talmud shows numerous creative strategies for interpreting the Bible but rarely an effort to read the text "literally."

To complicate matters, medieval Jewish readers inherited a tradition banning the public dissemination of the deeper meaning of the creation narrative. The Mishnah (Ḥag. 2:1, 2nd c. CE) forbids expounding the creation and warns, "Anyone who examines four things, it would be better if he had not come into this world—what is above, what is below, what is before, and what is after. And anyone who does not honor the glory of his Creator, it would be better if he had not come into this world."[2] For the sages, expounding creation was an unwelcome investigation of the nature of God, but the ban went largely unheeded.

Medieval Jewish commentators devoted much attention to the question of time in Gen. 1. Did time exist before the creation? When was the earth created and in what sequence?[3] Answering these questions from the sacred text proved difficult. Reading the Bible literally was a new activity in the Middle Ages since the necessary tools of grammar and linguistics had only recently been introduced to Jewish communities. Reading literally from a translation is easier than from texts in their original languages. Translators make choices about the meaning of ambiguous words, and the reader rarely knows that the original text was unclear. Jewish Bible commentators who read the Bible in Hebrew could identify ambiguities where the text legitimately could have more than one meaning. Their interpretations were shaped by the peculiarities of the Hebrew, commitment to the authority of earlier rabbinic traditions, and, like their Christian and Muslim counterparts, the encounter with philosophy and mysticism.

Medieval Jews studied the Bible as a source of law and inspiration for the community and as a guide to individual practice. From the birth of Christianity

2. On the rabbinic ban on expounding the story of creation, see Yair Furstenberg, "The Rabbinic Ban on Ma'aseh Bereshit: Sources, Contexts and Concerns," in *Jewish and Christian Cosmogony in Late Antiquity*, ed. Lance Jenott and Sarit Kattan Gribetz, Texts and Studies in Ancient Judaism 155 (Tübingen: Mohr Siebeck, 2013), 39–63; and Annette Reed, "From 'Pre-Emptive Exegesis' to 'Pre-Emptive Speculation'? *Ma'aseh Bereshit* in *Genesis Rabbah* and *Pirqei de-Rabbi Eliezer*," in *With Letters of Light: Studies in the Dead Sea Scrolls, Early Jewish Apocalypticism, Magic, and Mysticism in Honor of Rachel Elior*, ed. Daphna Z. Arbel and Andrei A. Orlov, Ekstasis 2 (Berlin: de Gruyter, 2011).

3. For an overview of Jewish philosophical approaches to the questions of creation from antiquity to modernity, see Norbert Samuelson, *Judaism and the Doctrine of Creation* (New York: Cambridge University Press, 1994).

until the rise of Islam, most Jewish biblical interpretations were preserved in anthologies of midrash, a rabbinic approach to Scripture that expands and elucidates the material, often using fanciful or creative readings. Individual Jewish scholars did not begin to write commentaries on an entire biblical book until the ninth century under Islamic influence, although the practice was popular in Christian circles much earlier.[4] Jews in lands under Muslim rule appropriated the tools of qur'anic scholarship and applied them to the Bible. This advanced the study of Hebrew grammar and the compilation of sophisticated dictionaries. In contrast to midrash, which interpreted individual words or phrases out of context, the new approaches relied on the assumption that language has specific rules by which it conveys meaning and that meaning relies on context. Eventually some of these new works on grammar and language were translated from Arabic into Hebrew and became accessible to Jews in Christian Europe who then used them to develop new ways to interpret Scripture.

Introducing the Commentators and Their Works

Before discussing how medieval Jews interpreted Gen. 1 and 2, a brief introduction to the major intellectual trends and the figures who exemplified them is necessary. In the eleventh and twelfth centuries, northern French rabbis participated in a revolutionary change in biblical studies termed *peshat* exegesis. Generally, *peshat* (often, but mistakenly, called the *literal meaning*) refers to a contextual reading of the biblical text. French Jewish scholars did not reject midrash but, keeping with rabbinic tradition concerning polysemy, allowed it and *peshat* to stand as simultaneously correct readings of the text.

The standout figure of the *peshat* school is Solomon ben Isaac (Rashi, 1040–1105), whose Bible commentary continues to be regularly studied. Although Rashi wrote commentaries on almost every biblical book, he nowhere provides a systematic description of his method. On occasion, as in his comment on Gen. 3:8, he notes his intention to explain the *peshat* even while he

---

4. For a more extensive survey of medieval Jewish Bible commentary, see Barry Walfish, "Medieval Jewish Interpretation," in *The Oxford Jewish Study Bible*, ed. Adele Berlin and Marc Zvi Brettler (Oxford: Oxford University Press, 2005), 1876–1900; Robert A. Harris, "Medieval Jewish Biblical Exegesis," in *A History of Biblical Interpretation: The Medieval through the Reformation Periods*, ed. Alan J. Hauser and Duane F. Watson (Grand Rapids: Eerdmans, 2009), 141–71; Jason Kalman, "Rabbinic Exegesis," in *The Oxford Encyclopedia of Biblical Interpretation*, ed. Steven L. McKenzie (New York: Oxford University Press, 2014), 2:177–89; and Magne Sæbø, *Hebrew Bible / Old Testament*, vol. 1, *From the Beginnings to the Middle Ages (until 1300)*, part 2, *The Middle Ages* (Göttingen: Vandenhoeck & Ruprecht, 2000).

uses midrash to clarify a biblical word or phrase. As a result he frequently provides midrashic and *peshat* interpretations for a single verse.

Peshat exegesis was largely the product of Rashi's students. Rashi's grandson, Samuel ben Meir (Rashbam, 1085–1158), like his grandfather, was a biblical interpreter, Talmudist, and legal authority. He devoted his commentaries to literary-contextual interpretations, but because he occasionally explains verses in opposition to rabbinic tradition, his defense of their complementary nature is important. Rashbam was remarkably consistent in distinguishing between *peshat* and midrash. His comments often challenge Rashi's explanations, and according to Rashbam, his grandfather told him he would have corrected his commentary if he had had more time (commentary to Gen. 37:2).

While the *peshat* school was developing in France, vibrant approaches to biblical interpretation were likewise evolving among the Jews of Spain. The preeminent representative of the twelfth-century Spanish school is Abraham ibn Ezra (1089–1164), who, although he lived in Spain for more than fifty years, spent his last twenty-five wandering Rome, France, and England. Ibn Ezra is famed as a Neoplatonic thinker, liturgical and secular poet, grammarian, and astrologer. He composed commentaries on the Torah, Isaiah, the Book of the Twelve, Psalms, Job, the Five Scrolls, and Daniel. Ibn Ezra was commissioned by patrons to compose his biblical commentaries. For some books he wrote more than one commentary, and often long and short versions are extant (e.g., Exodus, Esther).

Ibn Ezra knew the work of the Hebrew grammarians, earlier commentators including Rashi, and the Karaites (a Jewish community that rejected rabbinic authority). His approach was primarily shaped by grammar and linguistics, and in contrast to some in the French *peshat* school, he would not allow his readings to undermine rabbinic legal traditions.

In addition to linguistic studies, Jewish scholars appropriated and contributed to philosophy and mysticism. In approximately 1191, Moses ben Maimon (also known by the latinized form, Maimonides, and by the acronym Rambam, 1138–1204), the Cordoba-born head of the Cairo Jewish community, completed his philosophical work *The Guide of the Perplexed* (*GP*). Although he never produced a systematic commentary on the Bible, the *Guide* is, in effect, a biblical commentary, arranged by theme. Maimonides composed it for students who had thoroughly studied Judaism (i.e., Torah) and philosophy and were troubled by apparent contradictions between revelation and reason. To resolve these contradictions, Maimonides argues that the Torah communicates on multiple levels according to the reader's intellectual ability. Simple people could read the narratives in a straightforward manner, while the intellectuals would read them as parables intended to reveal philosophical truths. Apparent contradictions between Torah and science or philosophy could be resolved by recognizing that biblical language operated simultaneously on different levels.

Maimonides's work had a substantial influence on David Kimhi (also known by the acronym Radak, 1160–1235). Born to a family of biblical commentators, his father, Joseph (1105–70), moved with David's older brother, Moses (1127–90), from Spain to Provence in about 1150. David's father died when he was ten. His brother, Moses, took responsibility for teaching him. By this period Provencal Jewry had largely rejected *peshat* interpretation like that of Rashi's students and preferred midrash. However, as the son of an educated Spanish family dwelling in France, David was heir to multiple interpretive traditions. He was renowned for his biblical commentaries (Genesis, the Prophets, Psalms, Proverbs, and Chronicles), a grammar (*Sefer Mikhlol*), and a dictionary (*Sefer Shorashim*). Although steeped in the knowledge of grammar and philology, Radak also studied the Talmudic-midrashic tradition and was influenced significantly by the rationalism of Abraham ibn Ezra and Maimonides. He distinguishes clearly between *peshat* and midrash, and both are significant in his works. Although sometimes he dismisses midrash as merely homiletical, its creativity is synthesized in his commentary (e.g., reading passages as if prophetically referring to the events of his day).

Although Maimonides's attempt to synthesize philosophy and traditional Torah study faced backlash from Jews who thought it undermined tradition, many commentators throughout Europe from the thirteenth to the fifteenth century appropriated his approach. The outstanding exemplar is Levi ben Gershom (also known as Gersonides and by the acronym Ralbag, 1288–1344), a polymath who produced works on Talmud and Jewish law, philosophy and logic, astronomy and mathematics. He wrote commentaries on the Torah, Early Prophets, the Five Scrolls, Proverbs, and Job. In organizing his commentaries, Gersonides first explains key words according to the rules of grammar and lexical knowledge, then paraphrases the text with explanatory glosses, and finally offers ethical and philosophical lessons. Influenced by Maimonides, Gersonides presents the Torah as revealing both religious and philosophical truths intended to direct the learned reader to philosophical and moral perfection.

Maimonides and Gersonides presented the Torah as containing hidden secrets only accessible if studied alongside science and philosophy. However, the philosophically minded interpreters were not the only commentators who believed deeper truths were hidden in the Bible. Simultaneously Jewish mysticism was developing primarily among Jews in Christian lands.

Moses ben Nahman (also identified as Nahmanides and by the acronym Ramban, 1194–1270) was born in Gerona in Christian Spain. He contributed to Talmudic studies, mysticism, biblical commentary, and poetry. A medical doctor, he was also among the leading Talmudists of the Middle Ages. So great was his reputation that in 1263 King James I of Aragon drew him into a public disputation with the apostate Pablo Christiani. Although victorious, after the publication of the disputation, Nahmanides was forced to flee Spain; he arrived in Acre (Israel) in 1267.

Nahmanides composed commentaries on the Torah and Job. As a product of Christian Spain, he was heir to the Jewish interpretative traditions of Muslim Spain, France, and Germany. He frequently cites rabbinic material and often tries to explain the connection between midrash and the biblical verse. He regularly quotes earlier interpreters, including Rashi, ibn Ezra, and Maimonides, and he often challenges their interpretations. He shows much interest in the literary structure of biblical narratives. He often uses a typological reading, a method generally rejected by Jews because of its use by Christians, and sees the events of Israelite history foreshadowed in the actions of the patriarchs. Nahmanides was among the earliest commentators to apply kabbalistic (mystical) methods to interpret the Bible. He was committed to the idea that even the most minute details in the Torah had to be more than mere literary features and must be appropriately interpreted for religious meaning. For Nahmanides, the Torah contains a hidden esoteric meaning, transmitted from teacher to student since antiquity, which complements rather than trumps literary-contextual and midrashic interpretations. This type of approach is perhaps most clear in the Zohar (Book of Radiance, or Splendor). A mystical midrash on the Torah traditionally attributed to the second-century sage Simeon bar Yochai, its composition was begun by Moses de León in Castile in the mid-thirteenth century. The Zohar's exegesis relies on decoding the biblical text as an allegory about the interaction of the *sefirot* (the ten emanations of God), which are symbolized by characters or elements in the narratives.

This quick review should make clear that medieval Jewish Bible interpreters had numerous acceptable ways of interpreting the text. Although some preferred the *peshat* or contextual meaning and others preferred distilling philosophical or mystical secrets, all recognized the need to negotiate with the teachings of previous generations of rabbis. To allow for these variances, these interpreters modeled the rabbinic dictum that the Torah has seventy faces. When rabbinic Bibles began to be printed in the sixteenth century (and as they continue to be published today), many of these commentaries were placed side by side, sharing the page with the sacred text. There they competed for the attention of the reader who came to understand the commentaries as a multigenerational dialogue about the meaning of the biblical text, which offered a variety of legitimate alternatives.

Treatment of Days and Cosmology

Arguing that medieval Jewish interpreters understood the six days of creation literally would only be a half-truth. Although they accepted that the narrative speaks of real twenty-four-hour days, they largely rejected its historicity. Concerning the nature of the days, Rashi begins by challenging the idea that the first days were really days at all since without the sun and the moon (created only on day 4), counting time accurately is impossible. Acknowledging this problem, he argues based on midrashic sources that *everything* was created on the first day. When the biblical account reports the creation of luminaries on the fourth day, it means they were put in their proper place. Since everything was created on day 1, the mechanisms for counting time were already established. Rashi's grandson Rashbam accepts that the days should be understood in the regular sense of the word "day" but raises a textual issue.[5] Genesis 1:5 records, "And it was evening and it was morning" instead of the expected "it was night and it was day." According to rabbinic tradition, a Jewish day is counted from sundown to sundown. Rashbam argues that the verse means day 1 started in the morning. He insists, not that Jews should change their practice, only that the days of creation started in the morning while all others start in the evening. His interpretation caused some turmoil when it became known. In the introduction to his *Sabbath Epistle*, Abraham ibn Ezra, an equally radical interpreter, pleads that God punish anyone who tries to disseminate Rashbam's explanation of Gen. 1:5 because it would undermine Sabbath observance. According to ibn Ezra, if a scribe tries to copy it, his arm should whither and his eye should go blind. Despite his concern about the sanctity of the Sabbath, ibn Ezra also wants to ensure a correct understanding of Scripture. His comment to Gen. 1:5 on the nature of the day provides a window into medieval cosmology. He argues that a day refers to "the movement of the sphere." A reader might be inclined to see ibn Ezra as ahead of his time in understanding the earth as revolving, but he was describing a geocentric universe in which the stars and planets are fixed in a series of concentric spheres surrounding the earth like the layers of an onion. Each planet, the collection of stars, the sun, and the moon were attached to their own sphere. A rotating external sphere caused the others to turn, and this accounted for the length of a day. Further, in this rationalist presentation of the universe, the firmament and heavens become part of the atmosphere within the sublunary sphere, while medieval mystics understand

---

5. For an overview of Rashbam's approach to creation, see Sarah Kamin, "Rashbam's Conception of the Creation in Light of the Intellectual Currents of His Time," *Scripta Hierosolymitana* 31 (1986): 91–132.

SIDEBAR 7.1

Maimonides, *Guide of the Perplexed* 2.29

Not everything in the *Torah* concerning the *Account of Creation* is to be taken in its external sense as the vulgar imagine. For if it were such ... the *Sages* would not have expatiated on its being kept secret and from preventing the talk about it in the presence of the vulgar. For the external sense of these texts leads either to a grave corruption of the imagination and to giving vent to evil opinions with regard to the deity, or to an absolute denial of the action of the deity and to disbelief in the foundations of the Law. The correct thing to do is to refrain, if one lacks all knowledge of the sciences, from considering these texts merely with the imagination. ... It is obligatory to consider them with what is truly the intellect after one has acquired perfection in the demonstrative sciences and knowledge of the secrets of the prophets.

Note: Moses Maimonides, *The Guide of the Perplexed*, trans. Shlomo Pines (Chicago: University of Chicago Press, 1963), 2:346–47.

---

the firmament as a metaphor for the boundary between the revealed world and the divine, or hidden, realm (e.g., Zohar 2.210a).

The medieval mystical commentator Nahmanides writes concerning Gen. 1:3, "Know that the term 'day' as used in the story of the creation was in the case of the creation of heaven and earth, a real day, composed of hours and seconds, and there were six days like the six days of the workweek, as in the plain meaning of the verse."[6] This appears to be a literal interpretation, but he also alludes to a deeper meaning: "In the profounder sense, the Emanations issuing from the Most High are called 'days.'" By arguing for a hidden meaning, Nahmanides shared an approach to reading with medieval Jewish philosophers like Maimonides. Maimonides may have been committed to the idea that Genesis discusses typical twenty-four-hour days as he hints in *Guide of the Perplexed* (GP 2.30). However, for Maimonides the story cannot be literally true, particularly if the sciences or philosophy have already demonstrated that the universe functions in ways that differ from biblical depictions.

Within this same chapter, Maimonides chastises interpreters who rely only on knowledge of linguistics and grammar. These, he argues, are necessary but insufficient for understanding Gen. 1–2. Although these chapters may explicitly describe God's creation of the world, they are not a detailed historical account of it. To maintain consistency with scientific knowledge, the text must be read as an allegory.

6. Charles Ber Chavel, *Ramban: Commentary on the Torah*, vol. 1 (New York: Shilo, 1971).

SIDEBAR 7.2

Maimonides, *Guide of the Perplexed* 2.25

Know that our shunning the affirmation of the eternity of the world is not due to a text figuring in the *Torah* according to which the world has been produced in time. For the texts indicating that the world has been produced in time are not more numerous than those indicating that the deity is a body. Nor are the gates of figurative interpretation shut in our faces or impossible of access to us regarding the subject of the creation of the world in time. For we could interpret them as figurative, as we have done when denying His [God's] corporeality. Perhaps this would be even much easier to do: we should be very well able to give a figurative interpretation of those texts and to affirm as true the eternity of the world, just as we have given a figurative interpretation of those other texts and have denied that He, may He be exalted, is a body. . . .

If, however, one believed in eternity according to . . . the opinion of Plato—according to which the heavens too are subject to generation and corruption, this opinion would not destroy the foundation of the Law and would be followed not by the lie being given to miracles, but by their becoming admissible. It would also be possible to interpret figuratively the [biblical] texts in accordance with this opinion. And many obscure passages can be found in the text of the Torah and others with which this opinion could be connected or rather by means which it could be proved. However, no necessity could impel us to do this unless the opinion were demonstrated. In view of the fact that it has not been demonstrated, we shall not favor this opinion, nor shall we at all heed that other opinion, but rather shall take the texts according to their external sense.

Note: Maimonides, *Guide of the Perplexed*, 2:327–29.

For medieval thinkers two intertwined issues are at the fore when exploring the creation: (1) Was the world eternal or created? If the latter, (2) was it created from nothing (ex nihilo)? These are religiously significant since God's ability to create ex nihilo is a demonstration of divine omnipotence. To accept that God did not create the world from nothing calls into question all biblical depictions of miracles. Maimonides appears to have rejected the position of the Greek philosophers that the world is eternal.[7] He notes that the Bible describes God as creating the world, so it appears to have a beginning.

---

7. Maimonides writes in a dense esoteric style, which has led to much disagreement about his precise views on the mechanics of creation. See Kenneth Seeskin, *Maimonides on the Origin of the World* (New York: Cambridge University Press, 2005); Sara Klein-Braslavy, *Maimonides as Biblical Interpreter* (Boston: Academic Studies Press, 2011), 19–86.

However, he *does not* rely on the Bible for proof of this point since only science and philosophy provide sufficient proofs (see sidebar 7.2).

Maimonides argues that the biblical text can be taken literally concerning the idea that the world came into being at a particular point in time and is therefore not eternal. However, Maimonides takes it literally not because the Bible claims it to be true but because neither the science nor the philosophy of his day could refute the point. If science could prove the eternality of the world, he would accept it and read the Bible figuratively instead to resolve conflicts between the text and science. Because Maimonides does not understand the Genesis story as a historical account, he has the flexibility to read some parts of the story literally and others as allegory to preserve the reliability of Scripture when confronted by the truths of science and philosophy.

Maimonides is far from the only medieval Jewish scholar to adopt this approach to Scripture. Gersonides likewise allegorizes the creation narrative. Although he accepts that the term "day" may really be a day, he is clear that the story is not about the chronology of creation. Rather, the sequence reflects issues of priority of some things over others. The rabbinic tradition concerning the creation of all things simultaneously on the first day allows him to think about the arrangement in terms of causal priority.[8] In contrast to Maimonides, who denied that the process of creation could be demonstrated rationally, Gersonides aligns with the Greek philosopher Plato by arguing that God willingly created the world outside of time from primordial matter, symbolized by the primeval waters at the beginning of Genesis.[9]

Although many medieval commentators might have accepted that Genesis intended the term "day" to literally mean a twenty-four-hour period, none accepted that the biblical text had to be taken as a literal account of the creation. Returning to Rashi, the difficulty in reading the text literally arose not only from a conflict with science but also from linguistic and grammatical problems specific to Gen. 1.[10]

The difficulty with the word *bərē'šît* (often translated as "In the beginning") for some medieval commentators rises from a grammatical problem. The word appears in the construct grammatical state, meaning that the following word

8. For a discussion of Gersonides's interpretation of this narrative, see T. M. Rudavsky, *Time Matters: Time, Creation, and Cosmology in Medieval Jewish Philosophy* (Albany: State University of New York Press, 2012), 54–55.

9. Seymour Feldman, "Gersonides' Proofs for the Creation of the Universe," *PAAJR* 35 (1967): 113–37; Jacob J. Staub, *The Creation of the World according to Gersonides*, BJS 24 (Chico, CA: Scholars Press, 1982).

10. An annotated translation of and commentary on Rashi's interpretation of creation is found in Pinchas Doron, trans., *The Mystery of Creation according to Rashi: A New Translation and Interpretation of Rashi on Genesis I–VII* (New York: Moznaim, 1982).

should be a noun rather than a verb (created). It cannot mean "In the beginning God created" because *barē'šît* describes the beginning of something, but the verse does not provide that something. For these readers the verse should be translated as "In the Beginning of X, God created the heavens and the earth." Rashi notes that we find *barē'šît* used this way elsewhere in the Bible, as in Jer. 26:1, "At the beginning [*barē'šît*] of the reign of King Jehoiakim." Rashi wonders whether the noun is implied, "In the beginning of [everything], God created the heavens and the earth," but he dismisses this because verse 2 reports that the waters had already been created when God created light, even though the Bible never explains when the water was created or where it came from. He concludes that despite providing a description of creation, Gen. 1 actually *reveals nothing at all about the order in which things were created*. Rashi was also troubled by verse 5, wherein evening and morning constituted day 1. Rashi notes that days 2 through 7 are described with ordinal numbers (second day, third day, etc.), but day 1 is exceptionally called by a cardinal number. This Rashi takes to mean "the Day of the One," since only God existed. Rashi highlights a problem in verse 6, where God creates the heavens by splitting the waters with a solid expanse. Since Gen. 2:4 reports that heaven and earth were created on the same day, and the earth was created on day 1, the heavens must have already come into existence. Therefore day 2 has to be accounting for some other act of creation, not the heavens, since they had to be created the previous day. Rashi was convinced that Gen. 1 was not for the purpose of explaining creation at all. He opened his commentary on Genesis by asking why the Torah begins with creation when, as a book of divine law, it really should begin with a commandment to the people. Rashi suggests that the purpose of including the creation narrative in the Torah is to show God's sovereignty and not to explain the specific construction of the heavens and the earth.

Rashbam takes a more radical view. His grandfather Rashi argued that understanding verse 1 relied on reading it in conjunction with verse 3; verse 2 should be understood as an aside: "In the beginning of the creation of heaven and earth (when the earth was void and dark), God said, 'Let there be light.'" Rashbam later argues that understanding verse 1 relies solely on verse 2. When Moses gave the Torah to Israel the account says, "Remember the Sabbath day, . . . for in six days did God make the heavens and the earth, the sea and all that is in it, and He rested on the seventh day." According to Rashbam, Moses actually said,

> Do you think that this world has forever existed in the way that you now see it, filled with all good things? That is not the case. Rather, *bereshit bara' 'elohim*—i.e., at the beginning of the creation of the heaven and the earth,

when the uppermost heavens and the earth *had already been created* for some
undetermined length of time—then, "THE EARTH" which already existed, "WAS
UNFORMED AND VOID"—i.e., there was nothing in it.[11]

The description of the earth as void indicates it had already been created
before the light on day 1; how long before remains an open question.

For Rashbam, Genesis's narrative could not be a full account of creation. He
understands its purpose as anticipating later issues in the Bible. The account
in Gen. 1 establishes the truth of God's claims in Exodus when God gave the
Torah to Israel: "Remember the Sabbath day, and keep it holy. . . . For in six
days the LORD made heaven and earth, . . . but rested the seventh day" (Exod.
20:8, 11). Rashbam argues that the six days are about the nature of God's
organization of the visible universe. This account does not explain how the
earth came to be, but it does describe a sequence of events to be symbolically
reenacted when the people of Israel rest on the Sabbath. The story in Genesis
is not about cosmogony; rather, it promotes the observance of the Sabbath
and God's commandments. When Moses gave the Torah to Israel, he told
the people the story of creation to inform them that what God said was true.

Abraham ibn Ezra uses a similar approach, arguing that the Bible was written in language the masses could understand. In so doing, God could not
provide a complete account of creation because the target audience would not
have understood the complex processes involved. Commenting on Gen. 1:1, he
writes: "I will state a principle: Know that Moses our master did not give the
Torah (Law) only to the wise of heart (the philosophers) but to everyone. . . .
Thus, in discussing the wonders of creation he spoke only of the lower world,
created for man's sake, and did not mention the sacred angels."[12] For ibn Ezra,
like Maimonides, an appropriate reading strategy allows the Bible's truths to
be understood as consistent with the findings of science. Concerning Gen.
1:16, "God made the two great lights," he notes that "great" must refer to the
amount of light the celestial bodies appear to give off because of their proxim-
ity to earth: "Do not the astronomers teach that Jupiter and all the stars, with
the exception of Mercury and Venus, are larger than the moon? Why, then, is
it written *the great lights?*" If the Bible really intended that the moon was a
"great one" with respect to size, the Bible would, by definition, be literally false.[13]

11. Samuel ben Meir, *Rabbi Samuel ben Meir's Commentary on Genesis: An Annotated
Translation*, trans. Martin I. Lockshin, Jewish Studies 5 (Lewiston, NY: Edwin Mellen, 1989), 32.
12. H. Norman Strickman and Arthur M. Silver, *Ibn Ezra's Commentary on the Pentateuch*
(New York: Menorah, 1988), 1:40.
13. On ibn Ezra's efforts to accommodate the Bible and science, see Amos Funkenstein,
Theology and the Scientific Imagination from the Middle Ages to the Seventeenth Century
(Princeton: Princeton University Press, 1986), 215–19.

Turning from the *peshat* school and medieval Jewish philosophy to the interpretations of Gen. 1–2 offered by Jewish mysticism, exploring how Nahmanides begins his commentary is worthwhile. He starts by refuting Rashi's assertion that the story of creation is included in the Bible only to establish the source of divine sovereignty (i.e., because God created the world, he also rules over it). For Nahmanides, the story is designed to establish that the world was created. With this comment he entered the medieval debate about the eternality of the world. In contrast to Maimonides, who allows for the possibility that the world is eternal, Nahmanides in his comment to Gen. 1:3 insists that accepting the world as created at a particular point in time is a key Jewish dogma: "He who does not believe in this and thinks the world was eternal denies the essential principle of the [Judaic] religion and has no Torah at all."[14] Nahmanides also asserts that God created ex nihilo one substance to make everything in the heavens and another for the earth and everything in it. "The Holy One . . . created these two substances from nothing, and they alone were created, and everything else was constructed from them."[15] Although he strongly proclaims this position, he continues by noting that the remainder of the story cannot be taken literally or as a complete picture of creation:

> The answer is that the process of creation is a deep mystery not to be understood from the verses, and it cannot truly be known except through the tradition going back to Moses our teacher who received it from the mouth of the Almighty, and those who know it are obligated to conceal it. It was for this reason that Rabbi Yitzhak [Rashi] insisted that it was not necessary for the Torah to begin with *In the beginning God created* and the narration . . . [through to] the story of the Garden of Eden and the expulsion of Adam from it, because all this cannot be understood completely from the verses.[16]

The creation narrative functions on multiple levels. First, as a basic narrative for common people. Second (offered in his comment to Gen. 2:3), the seven days of creation allude to the seven ages of the world, relying on the midrashic teaching (Gen. Rab. 19:14) that one of God's days is like a thousand years. The first two days represent two thousand years from Adam to Abraham. The water covering the world was fluid, like God's relationship with people. On the third day dry land appeared, which was solid like the covenant God made with Abraham. This third period ended with the covenant at Sinai.

14. Chavel, *Ramban*, 1:17.
15. Chavel, *Ramban*, 1:23.
16. Chavel, *Ramban*, 1:18.

The fourth day, the day of the establishment of the two great luminaries in the sky, corresponded to the thousand years, which included the two temples in Jerusalem. The sixth day, ending with the creation of man and woman, demarcated a period of foreign rulers, ending with redemption. The seventh day, then, marked the world to come.[17] This type of day-age interpretation, a typological reading of Scripture, was very much the result of the interplay between Jewish and Christian biblical scholarship in the Middle Ages.[18]

For Nahmanides, that the masses generally believe the creation story as depicted in the Ten Commandments (in similar fashion to Rashbam) is acceptable because a small group of individuals continued the chain of transmission of the deeper meaning handed down orally from God to Moses, to later generations of sages. This idea about an ancient parallel mystical interpretation is at the core of Nahmanides's approach to Scripture.[19] In this deeper level of understanding depicted by Nahmanides and other mystics, the biblical account of creation is an allegory about the interaction of the *Ten Sefirot* (attributes or emanations through which God continuously causes the heavens and earth to be), which Scripture also calls "days." In its opening passages, the Zohar explains that creation was a transition from primordial nothingness. All aspects of existence were bound up in God until he withdrew to create space in which the world could be established through transformations within and among the various emanations of God. Creation starts from a single point. All things eventually created are caused by the penetration of a spark through the surface of this point, like an eggshell cracking open to allow the universe to expand out of it.[20] Needless to say, this narrative is not the literal expression of the biblical text, but this complex understanding of the nature of the heavens and the universe explains why the medieval mystical interpreters could not take the Genesis account at face value.

Collectively, then, the exploration of medieval Jewish interpretations of Gen. 1 reveals that these readers inherited a long tradition of nonliteral readings

17. For a thorough discussion of Nahmanides's interpretation of the creation narrative and its place in medieval Jewish thought, see Nina Caputo, *Nahmanides in Medieval Catalonia: History, Community, and Messianism* (Notre Dame, IN: University of Notre Dame Press, 2007), 53–89.

18. On Nahmanides's typological reading of Scripture and the Christian influence thereon, see Amos Funkenstein, *Perceptions of Jewish History* (Berkeley: University of California Press, 1993), 105–21; Funkenstein, *Theology and the Scientific Imagination*, 263–64.

19. Moshe Idel, "We Have No Kabbalistic Tradition on This," in *Rabbi Moses Nahmanides (Ramban): Explorations in His Religious and Literary Virtuosity*, ed. Isadore Twersky (Cambridge, MA: Harvard University Press, 1983), 63–73.

20. On the Zohar's interpretation of creation, see chap. 3 of Pinchas Giller, *Reading the Zohar: The Sacred Text of the Kabbalah* (Oxford: Oxford University Press, 2000). On myths concerning the breaking open of a sphere to create the universe, see chap. 2 of Yehuda Liebes, *Studies in Jewish Myth and Messianism* (Albany: SUNY Press, 1993).

of Scripture that freed them from any obligation to read these texts according to their "plain sense." Even when they acquired grammatical and linguistic studies that promoted literal reading, they tended to choose other reading strategies so as to avoid conflicts with science, philosophy, and mystical teachings. Similar patterns are evident in their interpretations of the garden of Eden.

Creation and Nature of Humanity

God's decree, "Let us make man ['ādām] in our image," led most medieval Jewish interpreters to read the creation of man and woman as a unique act. The first question is why God used the plural form "let us," and the second is the significance of being created in the divine image. Rashi and Rashbam's answer to the first question is that God is addressing the angels. Ibn Ezra argues that the Hebrew is actually in the passive form, rendering it "Let man be made." While God may be addressing the angels, they are certainly not participants in creating man. Radak offers an interpretation he attributes to his father, in which God addresses the material elements. Ramban offers an expanded version of this interpretation. Since in Gen. 1 God created only two elements ex nihilo, and these were used to create the heavens and the earth, all other creations were created from the previously available elements. Thus in the plural form "Let us make . . . ," God is addressing the land, the material from which Adam was to be fashioned.

Maimonides opens the *Guide of the Perplexed* with a discussion of this verse. His goal was to contribute to a medieval debate about the corporeality of God—does God have a body? Both Maimonides and ibn Ezra deny the possibility. Maimonides expounds Gen. 1:26, and although he appears to suggest "us" is the angels, he is more concerned by the question of what it means to be created in the image and likeness of God. Mistaken readers, he suggests, have used this verse to argue that humans are a reflection of God's image, thus indicating that God has a body. Medieval philosophers could not have accepted this, and Maimonides devoted significant attention to explaining how to read anthropomorphic depictions of God in the Bible as metaphors. He argues "in the image" means reflecting something godlike. In this case what separates human beings from the animals is a full intellectual capacity (*GP* 2.30). For Maimonides, God is an intellect whose knowledge overflows to humans who have the capacity provided by God to use the knowledge for their common well-being. A similar view runs through many of the medieval commentaries, although some disagreement arises concerning whether image and likeness are one thing or two distinct qualities. Rashi distinguishes

between them, noting that image suggests humans were molded in the image
God planned for them (i.e., spiritual beings) and likeness refers to humans'
intellectual discernment and wisdom. Ramban (and similarly Radak) argues
that image means humans are like the earth from which they are made—that
is, temporary—while likeness refers to the soul, which is eternal. Ibn Ezra
likewise states that the soul provides humans with the divine image.

The question of whether this verse means that both men and women are
made in the image of God is also significant for some commentators. Many
claim that Gen. 1:26 refers to man alone, only afterward referring to man
and woman in verse 27. Maimonides's son, Abraham, also a distinguished
commentator, notes that the word 'ādām can refer both to an individual male
person and to the human species. He states that these biblical passages refer
to the species and not the individual. That he had to make the statement
confirms the prevalence of the alternate view.[21] Part of the reason that this
distinction could be reinforced was precisely because the creation of man and
woman appears in two different ways in the biblical text. Although Gen. 1:26
refers to their simultaneous creation, Gen. 2 describes the fashioning of Eve
from Adam, a second act of creation. This distinction in Gen. 1:27 between
man and woman provides the opportunity for reconciliation between the
two biblical texts. Although some late midrashic traditions (e.g., *Alphabet
of ben Sira*) suggest that the stories produce two Eves—the first identified
as the demoness Lilith who was Adam's first wife—this solution was largely
ignored by medieval Jewish commentators, and only the Zohar takes up this
mythic tale (Zohar 1.19b and 1.34b).[22]

In his comment to Gen. 1:27, Rashi shows he was well aware of another
midrashic tradition that Adam was originally created as a single being with a
male side and a female side, which were later split to create man and woman
(Lev. Rab. on Gen. 12:2). However, he rejects this teaching and argues that
Gen. 1:26 correctly reports that both man and woman were created on the
sixth day. The account is a general statement. The account in Gen. 2 provides
the details. Rashbam follows his grandfather's lead and relies on a technique
of biblical interpretation identified as "anticipation" to show that this verse
is present in Gen. 1 so the reader can contextualize the unfolding detailed
narrative that follows in chapter 2. By contrast, ibn Ezra explicitly accepts the
midrashic tradition rejected by Rashi that Adam was originally born as male
and female and later split in two to create Eve (commentary to 1:26 and 2:21).

21. For discussion, see Chaim Navon, *Genesis and Jewish Thought* (Jersey City, NJ: KTAV,
2008), 147–59.
22. Joseph Dan, "Samael, Lilith, and the Concept of Evil in Early Kabbalah," *AJSR* 5 (1980):
17–40.

The Zohar 2.55a provides the same explanation. Nahmanides, like Rashi and Rashbam, argues that Gen. 1 makes a general statement and Gen. 2 delineates specifics. He explains the creation of Eve in a rather unique way, arguing that Adam's task of naming the animals was simultaneously a way for God to encourage him to seek out his own partner. Only when Adam had seen every creature could he truly yearn for his own helper, at which point God created her out of him (end of comment to 2:20).[23]

Maimonides also adopts the tradition of the two-gendered Adam to reconcile the two narratives. However, he reads the story as a parable where Adam represents the intellect (Plato's form) and Eve the body (Plato's substance). In so doing he describes a power play in which bodily hungers constantly tempt people and drive their mistaken decisions by overpowering the intellect. For Maimonides, the purpose of the midrashic teaching concerning Adam's two halves is to explain how human beings must tend the constant struggle between the male and female parts of themselves, between body and mind.[24] However, Maimonides's interpretation also belies a medieval understanding of a divinely ordained imbalance between men and women. Thus Rashi argues that the command in Gen. 1:28 to multiply and fill the earth and to subdue it should be taken to mean "and subdue her," to teach that males exert control over females.[25] The various commentaries take up these issues more extensively in discussing the nature of the sins and punishments received by Adam and Eve for eating from the tree of knowledge in the garden of Eden.

Garden of Eden

There can be little doubt that Rashi took the presentation of the garden quite literally since he points to its location east (*qedem*) of Israel, and he identifies

23. On Nahmanides's interpretation of the significance of "naming" in biblical narratives, and in this story in particular, see Michelle J. Levine, *Nahmanides on Genesis: The Art of Biblical Portraiture*, BJS 350 (Atlanta: SBL Press, 2009), 69–124.

24. For a useful summary of Maimonides's explanation of the story of Adam and Eve, see Jonathan Jacobs, "Maimonides, 1138–1204," in *The Internet Encyclopedia of Philosophy*, http://www.iep.utm.edu/maimonid/.

25. On these interpretations concerning the hierarchy for men and women and its implications for medieval women, see Kristen E. Kvam, Linda S. Schearing, and Valarie H. Ziegler, eds., *Eve and Adam: Jewish, Christian, and Muslim Readings on Genesis and Gender* (Bloomington, IN: Indiana University Press, 1999), 163–69; Avraham Grossman, *Pious and Rebellious: Jewish Women in Medieval Europe* (Waltham, MA: Brandeis University Press, 2004), 10–20. On the history of the interpretation of the command to be fruitful and multiply, see Jeremy Cohen, *"Be Fertile and Increase, Fill the Earth and Master It": The Ancient and Medieval Career of a Biblical Text* (Ithaca, NY: Cornell University Press, 1992).

the *Pishon* river flowing from the garden as the Egyptian Nile. Nahmanides locates the garden in Israel, with the future site of the temple at its center. He commits to the historicity of the story of Adam and Eve, but the garden is primarily significant for him as part of a mystical system. After bodily death, for a period of twelve months, souls of the righteous return to the garden while they wait for their desire for physicality to wane. During this period souls are nourished not by the garden but by an overflow of heavenly delights, which emanate into the garden for them.[26] According to his commentary on Gen. 3:22, the earthly garden is matched by a heavenly garden, which shares its contours and details, and the four earthly rivers are paralleled with four bands of angels. Most significantly, Nahmanides argues that at the time of the final redemption the treasures of the celestial garden will be opened to the people of Israel.

The Zohar provides a more detailed version of Nahmanides's gardens. According to the Zohar, the cave of Machpelah, where Abraham buried Sarah, is the opening to the terrestrial (but subterranean) garden of Eden. It is matched by a heavenly garden where the divine throne stands. Souls are formed above but are embodied when placed in the terrestrial garden. They then live their lives and, if righteous, return to the terrestrial garden like the patriarchs and matriarchs of Israel who were buried at its entrance. There they are greeted by the new souls awaiting their embodiment so that they can begin their terrestrial lives.[27]

A preliminary reading of ibn Ezra's commentary on this chapter of Genesis suggests that he, too, understands the garden has a terrestrial location. In his comment to Gen. 2:11, he also identifies the Pishon as the Nile. He argues that since it flows from south to north with the delta in Egypt, the garden of Eden must have been located south of the equator. However, although he accepts that the garden existed and that the story happened as described (with a real snake who could speak and walk upright, thus denying Christian interpretations that the snake was an embodiment of Satan), ibn Ezra concludes his commentary to Gen. 3 with a rather remarkable statement:

> The story of the Garden of Eden is to be interpreted literally. There is no doubt that it happened exactly as described in Scripture. Nevertheless, it also has a secret meaning. It alludes to the following: Intellect (the Garden of Eden) gave

26. Nahmanides treats this topic most extensively in his essay "The Gates of Reward." For summary and discussion, see David Novak, *The Theology of Nahmanides Systematically Presented*, BJS 271 (Atlanta: SBL Press, 1992), 130–32.
27. Isaiah Tishby, *The Wisdom of the Zohar: An Anthology of Texts*, trans. David Goldstein (Oxford: Littman Library and Oxford University Press, 1989), 2:745–47.

birth to desire (the tree of knowledge). Desire gave birth to man's actions. It is via his actions that man can elevate himself. . . . There is also an allusion in all of this to man's potential immortality (the tree of life). The intelligent will understand that this is the ultimate purpose of man's life on earth.[28]

Ibn Ezra takes the position of the philosophers that immortality is achieved only when a person's actions are guided by the intellect, which is, after all, living in the image of God.

In *GP* 2.30 Maimonides explains that the tree of knowledge was never revealed to a real person. It is a figurative tree, the source of wisdom, and dominates a figurative garden that represents the perfected state of the human intellect. Human beings' desire to return here is fulfilled by perfecting their intellect and thus achieving immortality akin to that described by ibn Ezra. If one eats from the tree (i.e., acquires a perfect intellect), they surely will live forever (immortality not of the body but of the soul or intellect, which for Maimonides are synonymous). In contrast to Maimonides, Gersonides agrees with ibn Ezra that the story of the garden is historically true and also a parable. However, his historical truth only extends so far. He accepts that the garden was real but, unlike ibn Ezra, insists the snake is an allegory since God would never create a rational being (i.e., a snake who can think and speak) and then "reduce it to an inferior state" (see his comment on Gen. 3:1).[29] Similarly, Radak, who largely avoided allegorizing the biblical text, quite freely appropriated Maimonides's interpretation, arguing that the garden represents the active intellect (knowledge emanating from God), the tree of life represents the human (rational) intellect, and the tree of knowledge the material intellect. For Radak, "The virtuous human intellect strives toward the active intellect by pursuing the divine sciences, while material intellect languishes because of its material lusts."[30]

Conclusion

Was Rabbi Angel correct to be concerned about a test for would-be converts that required them to adopt the view of a young world? Does Judaism have

---

28. Strickman and Silver, *Ibn Ezra's Commentary*, 1:78–79.

29. Charles H. Manekin, "Conservative Tendencies in Gersonides' Religious Philosophy," in *The Cambridge Companion to Medieval Jewish Philosophy*, ed. Daniel H. Frank and Oliver Leaman (Cambridge: Cambridge University Press, 2003), 304–42, here 315.

30. Frank Talmage, "Apples of Gold: The Inner Meaning of Sacred Texts in Medieval Judaism," in *Apples of Gold in Settings of Silver: Studies in Medieval Jewish Exegesis and Polemics*, ed. Barry Walfish (Toronto: Pontifical Institute of Medieval Studies, 1999), 108–50, here 121.

authoritative teaching that might allow for commitment to a world as old as science suggests it is? Without hesitation the answer is yes. These views dominate medieval Jewish interpretations of the creation narrative. At Rosh Hashanah (the New Year celebration) in September 2017, the Jewish calendar read 5778 years from the creation of Adam. In other words, the world was 5778 years and 6 days old. What should now be clear from surveying medieval Jewish interpretations of Gen. 1–2 is that precisely how long those six days lasted remains an open question because the term "day" was rarely taken literally. Rashbam points out that the earth may have existed a long or short time before God created light. Maimonides is clear that the story cannot be taken literally (*GP* 2.7) and that natural laws did not function during the "six days of creation" (*GP* 2.30). Gersonides notes that God's creation of the world did not take place in time since his creation of something from nothing precedes time (*Wars of the Lord* 6.8). Nahmanides counts his seven eras from the creation of Adam, opening the days before his creation for broader interpretation. His student Bachya ben Asher (Spain, 1255–1340) explains that the time period between "In the beginning" and "Let there be light" cannot be counted: "For those days were not human days, but rather a day from those years was of the days about which there is no comprehension. This is as is it is written [in Job 36:26], 'Are Your years as those of men?' (*Wars of the Lord* 10.5), and 'Your years are not finished' (Ps. 102: 27 [102:28 MT])."[31] Ultimately, medieval Jewish interpreters were in agreement that Gen. 1 and 2 were included in the Torah to teach religious truths and not to provide a detailed historical narrative about creation or how long ago it occurred.

For Further Reading

Harris, Robert A. "Medieval Jewish Biblical Exegesis." In *A History of Biblical Interpretation: The Medieval through the Reformation Periods*, edited by Alan J. Hauser and Duane F. Watson, 141–71. Grand Rapids: Eerdmans, 2009.

Kalman, Jason. "Rabbinic Exegesis." In *The Oxford Encyclopedia of Biblical Interpretation*, edited by Steven L. McKenzie, 2:177–89. New York: Oxford University Press, 2014.

Sæbø, Magne, ed. *Hebrew Bible / Old Testament*. Vol. 1, *From the Beginnings to the Middle Ages (Until 1300)*. Part 2, *The Middle Ages*. Göttingen: Vandenhoeck & Ruprecht, 2000.

31. Translation of Bachya's *Commentary on Genesis*, at Gen. 1:3, found in Natan Slifkin, *The Challenge of Creation: Judaism's Encounter with Science, Cosmology, and Evolution* (Brooklyn, NY: Zoo Torah and Yashar Books, 2006), 170.

Walfish, Barry. "Medieval Jewish Interpretation." In *The Oxford Jewish Study Bible*, edited by Adele Berlin and Marc Zvi Brettler, 1876–1900. Oxford: Oxford University Press, 2005.

Primary Texts in Print

Chavel, Charles Ber. *Ramban: Commentary on the Torah*. 5 vols. New York: Shilo, 1971.

Doron, Pinchas. *Rashi: The Mystery of Creation according to Rashi; A New Translation and Interpretation*. New York: Moznaim, 1982.

Maimonides, Moses. *The Guide of the Perplexed*. Translated and with an Introduction and Notes by Shlomo Pines. 2 vols. Chicago: University of Chicago Press, 1963.

Samuel ben Meir. *Rabbi Samuel ben Meir's Commentary on Genesis*. Edited by Martin I. Lockshin. Jewish Studies 5. Lewiston, NY: Edwin Mellen, 1989.

Strickman, H. Norman, and Arthur M. Silver. *Ibn Ezra's Commentary on the Pentateuch*. 5 vols. New York: Menorah, 1988.

Tishby, Isaiah. *The Wisdom of the Zohar: An Anthology of Texts*. Translated by David Goldstein. 3 vols. Oxford: Oxford University Press, 1989.

Primary Texts Online

1. Commentaries of Rashi, Rashbam, ibn Ezra, and Nahmanides on the early chapters of Genesis, with discussion by David Blumenthal of Emory University
   http://www.js.emory.edu/BLUMENTHAL/GenIntro.html
2. Rashi on Genesis in English with link to Hebrew
   http://www.sefaria.org/Rashi_on_Genesis?lang=en
3. Rashbam on Genesis in English with link to Hebrew
   http://www.sefaria.org/Rashbam_on_Genesis?lang=en
4. Ibn Ezra on Genesis in English with link to Hebrew
   http://www.sefaria.org/Ibn_Ezra_on_Genesis?lang=en
5. Nahmanides on Genesis in English with link to Hebrew
   http://www.sefaria.org/Ramban_on_Genesis?lang=en

8

Medieval Christian Interpretations of Genesis 1–2

Timothy Bellamah, OP

Throughout the Middle Ages, here understood as the interval of more than a millennium extending from the fall of the Western Roman Empire to the Protestant Reformation, Genesis remained among the Bible's most frequently expounded books. Taking for granted that the creation narratives of Gen. 1–2 were in some sense historical, interpreters of the medieval Latin West set for themselves the task of explaining them by assimilating the insights of the commentarial tradition in which they stood. As matters of Christian doctrine, they left unquestioned the understandings that creation was from nothing, that it resulted from God's gratuitous action, that it was immediate (i.e., that it involved no mediation on the part of angels or other creatures), that angelic and human persons were gifted with freedom for the sake of enjoying communion with God, and correlatively, that they occupied the highest places among creatures.

Chief among the sources from which medieval commentators drew were the fathers, Greek and Latin. Few traits of medieval interpretation were as enduring and pervasive as the practice of compiling and synthesizing earlier commentaries on a given book of the Bible. To each book belonged its own commentarial tradition, with the consequence that the particular sources employed by interpreters varied from one book to the next. With respect to the tradition of commentary on the creation narratives of Genesis, the most important Greek patristic contributors were Origen, Athanasius, Basil of Caesarea, John Chrysostom, Theodoret of Cyrus, and John Damascene. Conspicuous among the Latin patristic sources were Hilary of Poitiers, Ambrose of Milan, and Augustine.

Introduction to the Interpreters

The commentarial tradition on the creation narratives came to include the works of early medieval writers, such as Isidore of Seville (ca. 560–636) and the Venerable Bede (672/673–735), and then Carolingian ones, especially Alcuin of York (730–804) and Rabanus Maurus (780–856). By the late twelfth century the treatments of Rupert of Deutz (ca. 1075–1129), Hugh of Saint Victor (ca. 1096–1141), Peter Lombard (ca. 1096–1160), and Peter Comestor († ca. 1178) had also become standard references. During the thirteenth century the diffusion of Latin translations of Arabic Neoplatonic works (esp. those of Avicenna, Averroes, and the anonymous *Liber de Causis*), in addition to Aristotle's works on natural philosophy (*Physics, Metaphysics, On the Soul, Meteors*), had dramatic effects on the interpretation of Gen. 1–2, notably in the commentaries of Robert Grosseteste (ca. 1175–1253), Alexander of Hales (ca. 1185–1245), Albert the Great (ca. 1200–1290), Bonaventure (1221–74), and Thomas Aquinas (ca. 1225–74).[1] In the early fourteenth century, Meister Eckhart (ca. 1260–ca. 1328) produced a commentary displaying a remarkable command of the entire preceding exegetical and philosophical tradition, going beyond earlier Christian writers in drawing from the speculations of the notable Sephardic Jewish philosopher Moses Maimonides (ca. 1138–1204). A later contemporary, Nicholas of Lyra (ca. 1270–1349), employed the Hebrew biblical text as well as Jewish commentary (esp. that of Rashi)[2] to an extent unprecedented among Christian commentators.

---

1. Study of the *Libri naturales* (*Physics, Metaphysics, De anima, Meteora*), public or private, was prohibited in Paris in 1210, according to the *Chartularium Universitatis Parisiensis*, ed. Heinrich Denifle (Paris: Ex typis fratrum Delalain, 1889), fn. 11, and again in 1215 (fn. 20). These measures failed to have lasting effect, and by 1255 the Arts faculty at the University of Paris mandated lecturing on them (fn. 247).

2. Rashi is an acronym for Rabbi Shlomo Itzhaki (1040–1105), a rabbi born and buried in Troyes, France. He left remarkably influential commentaries on the Talmud and on the Tanakh.

Language

Christian commentators of the medieval West were united by a common language, Latin, despite regional and periodic differences, and despite the early medieval emergence of the Romance languages. Throughout Western Europe this shared language facilitated the free and rapid circulation of texts, old and new, between the libraries of monasteries, cathedral schools, and from the thirteenth century onward, the houses of the emerging mendicant religious orders (mainly Franciscans, Dominicans, Augustinians, and Carmelites). And yet, commentators generally had little, if any, direct contact with original writings in Hebrew, Greek, or Arabic. Put another way, Hebrew, Greek, and eventually Arabic works exercised influence on them only to the extent that they became available in Latin translations.

The Biblical Text

Also uniting medieval interpreters was a common biblical text, the Vulgate, notwithstanding the variations that inevitably arose with frequent manuscript copying over many centuries.[3] To be sure, in the early Middle Ages the Bible was translated into several Romance languages, and eventually into Old English and German, but none of these versions threatened the Vulgate's authority. More important was the enduring influence of Old Latin versions, first because they continued to be copied and remained in circulation throughout the Middle Ages, then because they had served as the basis for the commentaries of the Latin fathers, including several of Jerome's, which were constantly consulted and quoted by medieval writers.[4] It was not until well into the Middle Ages that the Vulgate won broad acceptance as the standard Latin Bible, with the result that Latin patristic commentaries were generally based on Old Latin translations.

The frequency with which medieval commentators excerpted Old Latin versions is conspicuous in their quotations of the Bible's opening verse, which in the Vulgate appears as follows: *In principio creavit Deus caelum et terram,*

---

3. For a concise account of the production of the Vulgate and Jerome's role in it, see *Biblia Sacra Vulgata*, ed. R. Weber (Stuttgart: Deutsche Bibelgesellschaft, 2007), xxxiii–xxxvii.

4. The term "Old Latin" (Vetus Latina) designates any of the Latin biblical texts that preceded the Vulgate. Some of them may have preceded Christianity. Whereas the Vulgate of the OT was translated from the Hebrew, the Old Latin followed the Septuagint. For this reason, medieval commentators often used "LXX" to designate passages drawn from Old Latin versions. Another important respect in which it differed from the Vulgate was that it was never a unified text but a collection of them. On the Old Latin biblical texts, see http://www.vetuslatina .org/.

and in Old Latin versions is most often rendered: *In principio fecit Deus caelum et terram.*[5] The only difference, significant enough, is between the Vulgate's *creavit*, "created," and the Old Latin's *fecit*, "made."[6] To be sure, the Vulgate version appeared in Bede's commentaries in the early eighth century and thereafter remained the predominant text. But this did not prevent the Old Latin wording from appearing with some frequency throughout the Middle Ages.[7]

A significant instance in which the Old Latin exercised lasting influence on medieval interpretation appears at Gen. 2:1: "Thus the heavens and the earth were finished, and all their multitude." The scribes of the Septuagint had translated the Hebrew *kol-ṣəbāʾām*, "all their multitude," as *pas ho kosmos autōn*, which the Old Latin translators took in an aesthetic sense, rendering it *et omnis ornatus eorum*, "and all their ornamentation" (my translation). In producing the Vulgate, rather than following the Hebrew, Jerome retained an Old Latin rendering. As a result, it became commonplace among medieval interpreters to divide the work of creation into two, the work of division (*opus distinctionis*) and the work of ornamentation (*opus ornatus*).[8]

Medieval commentators remained well aware that their biblical text was a translation, and a faulty one at that. For this reason they often adverted to Hebrew texts, often under the heading of "Hebrew truth" (*Hebraica veritas*), an expression they had learned from Jerome.[9] In the early eighth century

5. *Bibliorum Sacrorum Latinae Versiones Antiquae seu uetus Italica*, ed. Pierre Sabatier, vol. 1/3 (Paris: Didot, 1751).

6. In his *Hebraice Quaestiones in Libro Geneseos* [Questions about the Hebrew Book of Genesis], Jerome made use of an Old Latin text: *In principio fecit Deus coelum et terram* (ed. P. de Lagarde, CCSL 72 [Turnhout: Brepols, 1959], 3), but in his *Liber Bresith, quae* [qui] *Graece dicitur Genesis*, he followed his own more recent translation: *In principio creavit Deus coelum et terram. Terra autem erat inanis et vacua, et tenebrae* [Vulg. addit erant] *super faciem abyssi, et Spiritus Dei ferebatur super aquas* (PL 28, col. 163).

7. What follows are a few examples of works presenting an Old Latin translation of Gen. 1:1: Bede, *De ratione temporum* (PL 90, cols. 308, 309); Alcuin, *De fide Sanctae Trinitatis* (PL 101, col. 32); Alcuin, *De cursu et saltu lunae* (PG 101, col. 995); Sedulius Scotus, *Collectanea in omnes Beati Paulus epistolas* (PL 103, col. 252); Rabanus Maurus, *Commentariorum in Genesim* (PL 107, col. 443); John Scot Eriugena, *De divisione naturae* (PL 122, col. 554); Rupert of Deutz, *De divinis officiis* (PL 170, col. 183); Peter Lombard, *Collectanea in epistolas Pauli* (PL 192, col. 31). As late as the second half of the thirteenth century, Thomas Aquinas made use of the Old Latin rendering on two occasions: *De substantiis separatis*, chap. 18; and *Catana aurea in Ioannem*, chap. 1, lectio 1. In all his works, Aquinas quoted the Vulgate version on no fewer than fifty-seven occasions.

8. Stanley Jaki views this development as a shift away from an essential point in the original, "the total dependence of all on the Maker of all," to something time conditioned, "a specific procedure of production, which could not be salvaged as man learned more and more about the physical world," in *Genesis 1 through the Ages*, 2nd rev. ed. (Edinburgh: Scottish Academic Press, 1992), 4–5.

9. Jerome, *Hebraice Quaestiones in Libro Geneseos*, 2.

the Venerable Bede referred to it repeatedly in his *Hexaemeron*,[10] and as late as the sixteenth century, Thomas de Vio (Cajetan) stated, in the title of his commentary on the Psalms, that his biblical text had been corrected according to the "Hebrew truth."[11] A typical example of the concept's exegetical functioning appears in Peter Abelard's twelfth-century exposition of Gen. 1:2. Beginning with a wording of the Vulgate current at the time, "And the Spirit of the Lord was carried over the waters" (*et Spiritus Domini ferebatur super aquas*), Abelard then presented an alternative translation, very likely drawn from Ambrose's *Six Days of Creation* (*Hex.*): "and the Spirit of the Lord fomented the waters" (*et Spiritus Domini fovebat aquas*).[12] Not long afterward, he presented a transliteration and explanation of the Hebrew counterpart of *spiritus*, *rûaḥ*, pointing out that it designates both spirit and wind (*pro spiritu Hebraicum habet ruauh, quod tam spiritum quam ventum figurat*).[13] The Hebraizing of Abelard's contemporary Hugh of Saint Victor (ca. 1096–1141) went further. In the prologue to his work *On the Sacraments* (*De sacramentis*), a work containing a lengthy exposition of the creation narratives, he presents several Hebrew terms, first in Hebrew script, then in transliterations followed by explanations.[14] From this it is clear enough that as a rule medieval Latin interpreters considered the Hebrew the normative text. But neither Bede, Abelard, Hugh of Saint Victor, Cajetan, nor medieval Latin commentators generally left clear evidence of competence in Hebrew.[15] In all likelihood, their contact with the language was fragmentary and derivative

10. The Venerable Bede, *Hexaemeron* I (PL 91, cols. 9–190). A more recent edition was produced by C. W. Jones, *Libri quattuor in principium Genesis usque ad natiuitatem Isaac et eiectionem Ishmaelis adnotationem (siue Hexaemeron)*, CCSL 118A (Turnhout: Brepols, 1967). Bede presents an interesting example in connection with Gen. 1:10, in his *Hexaemeron*: "*And God saw that it was good. Let us understand:* 'In the goodness of his Spirit.' . . . It is to be noted that the addition of this word here does not appear in the Hebrew truth" (*Notandum enim quod huius uerbi adiectio hoc in loco in Hebraica ueritate non habetur*, ed. Jones, 12). In Jones's edition, for other references to "Hebrew truth" see pp. 32, 46, 94, 95, 101, 163, 164, and 167.

11. Thomas de Vio, *Psalmi Dauidici ad hebraicum veritatem castigati et iuxta sensum quem literalem dicunt enarrati* (Venice, 1530).

12. Ambrose, *Exameron* I, in *Qua continentur libri*, ed. C. Schenkl CSEL 32.1 (Prague: Tempsky, 1897), 29: "*Et spiritus Dei fouebat aquas, id est uiuificabat, ut in nouas cogeret creaturas et fotu suo animaret ad uitam.*"

13. Peter Abelard, *Expositio in Hexameron* (PL 178, cols. 735–36).

14. Hugh of Saint Victor, *De sacramentis* (PL 176, col. 186).

15. Pointing to the mentioning of Hebrew terms in the Genesis commentaries of Peter Abelard and Hugh of Saint Victor, Stanley Jaki suggests, questionably, that they had direct knowledge of the Hebrew text (*Genesis 1 through the Ages*, 113–14). On the knowledge of Hebrew on the part of medieval Latin commentators, with specific reference to Abelard's exposition of Gen. 1:2, see Gilbert Dahan, *Les intellectuels chrétiens et les juifs au moyen âge* (Paris: Cerf, 2007), 263–70.

either from earlier writings or from personal contact with Jewish scholars.[16] We shall see that in the perspectives of medieval interpreters generally, the six days and cosmology were virtually inseparable. In their view questions concerning either one necessarily involved the other. For this reason, in the following section we have combined the two.

Treatment of Days and Cosmology

In reading Genesis with Christian doctrines in view, medieval commentators had in mind several antithetical worldviews, two of which merit discussion here. The first was Neoplatonism: in its pagan forms the world was considered to have resulted from a necessary emanation from an impersonal One, generally by way of intermediaries, and not from a gratuitous act of creation on the part of a benevolent God. But Neoplatonism was at odds with Christian doctrine in another significant respect. It viewed the human body as extraneous to human identity, united only accidentally and temporarily to the human spirit. Such an anthropology is not easily squared with the Christian doctrines on Jesus Christ's incarnation, death, and resurrection, as well as those on the general resurrection, the church, and the sacraments. Medieval Christian interpreters found it necessary to refute a few of Neoplatonism's core tenets, not because it posed a direct threat to the church of their time, but because it required differentiation from the Christian Neoplatonism to which they themselves were committed.

The second worldview medieval interpreters found themselves obliged to oppose was Manichaeism. They remained aware of the significance of Augustine's explicit dedication of one of his commentaries on Genesis to the refutation of their doctrines. Widespread in late antiquity in both the Latin- and Greek-speaking worlds, this form of gnosticism had for nine years claimed Augustine's allegiance; later it became the object of no small part of his apologetic writings, as well as those of other fathers, notably John Chrysostom. But toward the late twelfth century their opposition found another motive in the emergence and flourishing of the Cathars, a dualist sect also known as Albigensians. There is no evidence to indicate that this movement had any historical connection

16. A medieval exegete who had exceptional knowledge of Hebrew was the fourteenth-century Franciscan Nicolas de Lyre (Nicholas of Lyra). But for the understanding of several of his source texts, even he probably relied on scholars of Jewish background, most likely converts. See Ari Geiger, "Nicholas and His Jewish Sources," in *Nicolas de Lyre, franciscain du XIVe siècle, exégète et théologien*, ed. G. Dahan (Paris: Institut d'Études Augustiniennes, 2011), 167–203. See also A. Graboïs, "The *Hebraica Veritas* and Jewish-Christian Intellectual Relations in the Twelfth Century," *Spec* 50 (1975): 613–34.

with the Manichaeans known to Augustine and Chrysostom, and the available evidence concerning their beliefs remains fragmentary, but we do know that medieval writers considered them sufficiently similar to the Manichaeans of old that they referred to them by that name.[17] For the Manichaeans, all visible reality, including the human body, resulted from the agency of a primordial god of evil and darkness, who revealed himself in the OT, and was in unending conflict with the god of goodness and light, who revealed himself in the NT. By denying that creation is gratuitous, Neoplatonism had cast doubt on the world's goodness. But by calling the world the work of an evil deity, Manichaeism asserted that the world was positively evil. The Manichaeans also denied biblical monotheism and bifurcated revelation. Within the Manichaean cosmological dualism lay an anthropological dualism more radical than that of the Neoplatonists. Whereas Plato's ancient and medieval followers tended to consider the body a shell or dwelling for the human spirit, the Manichaeans deemed it a punishment and a source of suffering. Salvation, on their account, consisted of escaping it to enter the realm of light. This is understandable in view of the Manichaean belief that the human spirit is of the same essence or nature as the god of light. Rendered unintelligible in this perspective are several of Christianity's central doctrines: the gratuitousness of creation; the incarnation, death, and resurrection of the Word, as well as the bodily resurrection of the just.

In the writings of the fathers, medieval commentators found no common understanding of the "days" of creation. Among the Greek fathers, those from Alexandria, such as Clement,[18] Origen,[19] and Athanasius,[20] generally held that all things were created simultaneously, and they took the days not as actual intervals of time but as allegories of all the creatures' various levels of dignity. Cyril was a notable exception, taking at face value the Genesis narrative's succession of creative actions, without committing himself to an account of the days' duration.[21] On the other hand, those associated with the Antiochene school of thought, such as John Chrysostom[22] and Theodoret of

17. On the medieval identification of the Cathars with the Manichaeans, see my *The Biblical Interpretation of William of Alton* (New York: Oxford University Press, 2011), 113–15, here 155. Within the extensive literature on the Cathars, a good overview in English remains M. Lambert, *The Cathars* (Oxford: Oxford University Press, 1998).

18. Clement of Alexandria, *Misc.* 6.16 (PG 9, cols. 368–72).

19. Origen, *Princ.* 4.16 (PG 11, cols. 376–77); ET, *On First Principles* 4.1, 16, in *ANF*, ed. A. Coxe (Buffalo: Christian Literature, 1895), 4:707–8.

20. Athanasius, *C. Ar.* 2 (PG 26, col. 276).

21. Cyril of Alexandria, *Glaphyrorum in Genesim* [Elegant Comments in Genesis] 1.2 (PG 69, cols. 18, 20).

22. John Chrysostom, *Hom. Gen.* 3 (PG 53, cols. 34–35).

Cyrus,[23] were less sympathetic to allegorical interpretation and discarded the simultaneous creation of all things. Among the Cappadocian fathers, Basil of Caesarea held that the elements of matter (earth, air, fire, and water) were created simultaneously, and that the elements were organized during the six days, each of which lasted twenty-four hours. It is true that Basil also described the sequence of days as a sign of eternity, but in doing so he refrained from reducing them to an allegory.[24]

In the Latin fathers, medieval interpreters found little more consensus. Having read Basil's homilies on Genesis, Ambrose had likewise held for an initial creation of matter in its four elements, out of which the species of things were subsequently formed.[25] But in the most important of all their patristic sources, Augustine, they found an account of simultaneous creation.[26] His several expositions of the creation narratives are in basic agreement on the symbolic character of the days, even if they are less than unanimous on their signification. Most medieval commentators rejected his view on the matter, leaving us a salutary reminder of the limits of Augustine's authority over medieval thought.

The medieval Latin West's commentarial tradition on the creation narratives began with two works of the Venerable Bede. In the first, his *Hexaemeron*, he advanced a view similar to those of Basil and Ambrose, wherein heaven and earth were created with the four elements, and subsequently organized into the species of things.[27] In his treatment of the formation of Adam and Eve, Bede put forward a prescient exegetical principle, admonishing his readers to avoid the weakness of the text's carnal sense, lest we suppose that God used bodily hands to form Adam out of the earth's mud, or that he used a throat and lips to breathe life into him. Noting that these ways of speaking

23. Theodoret of Cyrus, *Quaestiones in Genesim* [Questions in Genesis], interr. vi–xvii (PG 80, cols. 88–97).

24. Basil of Caesarea, *Homiliae IX in Hexaemeron* [Nine homilies on the *Hexaemeron*] (PG 19, cols. 16–208). Basil's account of the sequence of days signifying eternity (homily 2.8, col. 49) need not be read as casting doubt on the days' actual twenty-four-hour duration. It is better understood as an example of *theōria* (θεωρία), common in the exegesis of the Cappadocian and Antiochene fathers, wherein mundane biblical events or realities are contemplated as signs of transtemporal or divine realities. By contrast with the allegorical interpretations characteristic of Alexandrian thinkers, *theōria* so understood does not cast doubt on the actuality of the mundane biblical events and realities signifying other realities. In any case, medieval commentators read Basil as understanding the days as periods of temporal succession. See, e.g., Thomas Aquinas, *Summa Theologiae* I, q. 66, art. 1, response: "Others, however, such as Basil, Ambrose and Chrysostom, hold that formlessness of matter temporally preceded its formation."

25. Ambrose, *Hex.* 1 (PL 14, cols. 135–40).

26. Augustine, *Conf.* 13.33; *Gen. litt.*, ed. J. Zycha, CSEL 28 (Vienna: de Gruyter, 1894), 49; *Gen. Man.* 2 (PL 34, col. 198).

27. Bede, *Hexaemeron* 1 (PL 91, cols. 9–55, here 18–34). In the preface, Bede acknowledges Basil, Eustathius (Basil's Latin translator), Ambrose, and Augustine (cols. 9–10).

are tropes rather than proper locutions, Bede was thus equipped to make two further points. One is that only the unlearned would believe that God, who as pure spirit is simple in his substance, is composed of bodily members. The other is that the souls of Adam and Eve, and by implication all other humans, were created not from the elements, nor from the divine substance, but from nothing. It is true that Bede was not the first to hold this view. Isidore of Seville had said as much.[28] But earlier writers had not been unanimous on the subject, whereas subsequent commentators were, despite their many differences on other matters.

Later, in his *Commentaries on the Pentateuch* (*In pentateuchum commentarii*),[29] Bede drew on Isidore's account to propose that God created unformed matter from nothing before the first day, and that during the six days he created the species of things from matter. Not created from matter were the angels and human souls. As he put it, God created the world, angels, and souls from nothing, whereas the species of things, including the human body (*hominem*) he made out of matter during six twenty-four-hour days. But the soul's creation from nothing is not the only key element common to both of Bede's commentaries. In both he endeavored to do justice to the sequence of the Genesis narrative, without doing violence to an indication of simultaneous creation in the Vulgate wording of Sir. 18:1, which we will render as follows: "He who lives eternally created all things at once" (*Qui vivit in aeternum creavit omnia simul*).[30] And in both commentaries, Bede followed no small number of earlier writers in taking the "beginning" of Gen. 1:1 to be the eternal Son. This allusion to the opening line of John's Gospel went on to become a stock interpretation, offering commentators the opportunity to explore the parallels and differences between the eternal procession of God's Word by God's act of self-knowledge, and the temporal procession of creatures by that same divine self-knowledge. Further, in both works Bede was concerned to exclude any notion of fatigue on God's part, so he presented God's rest on the seventh day as indicating the cessation only of his work of creation, not of his work of governance. Finally, in both accounts Bede took God's rest to prefigure the rest of the Sabbath and of heaven.

Interpretations dependent on and similar to Bede's *Commentaries on the Pentateuch* were produced by a long list of commentators over the next four

28. Isidore of Seville, *Liber differentiarum* [Book of Differences] 2.11 (PL 83, cols. 74–75); ed. Andrés Sanz, CCSL 111A (Turnhout: Brepols, 2006), 21–23.

29. The Venerable Bede, *In Pentateuchum commentarii* [Commentaries on the Pentateuch] I–II (PL 91, cols. 189–210).

30. Equivalents to the Vulgate's *simul* ("at once"), which lies at the heart of the matter, do not appear in modern translations, such Sir. 18:1, "He who lives forever created the whole universe."

and a half centuries, notable among whom were Alcuin of York (ca. 735–804),[31] Rabanus Maurus (ca. 780–856),[32] Haimo of Auxerre († ca. 878),[33] Remi of Auxerre (ca. 841–908),[34] the anonymous compiler of the *Glossa ordinaria* on Genesis,[35] Bruno of Segni (ca. 1047–1123),[36] Honorius Augustodunensis (ca. 1180–1254),[37] and Hugh of Amiens († 1164).[38]

But during the twelfth century several important commentators retrieved the account of Bede's earlier *Hexaemeron*, wherein heaven and the earth were created with the four elements, not entirely without form, but unformed by comparison with their subsequent beauty and order. As time and matter began simultaneously, this creation was before the first day. The forming, ordering, and distinguishing of things occurred over the course of the six days. Espousing this interpretation were Rupert of Deutz,[39] Hugh of Saint Victor,[40] Peter Lombard,[41] and Peter Comestor.[42]

Over the course of the thirteenth century, biblical interpretation and theology underwent dramatic development as they were practiced in the more cosmopolitan environments of the newly emergent universities. Especially at the Universities of Paris and Oxford, commentators were compelled to come to terms with new philosophical currents engendered by newly available Latin translations of Aristotle's works on natural philosophy (*Physics, Metaphysics, On the Soul, Meteors*), as well as the writings of his Arabic commentators, especially those of Avicenna and Averroes. Toward the end of synthesizing

31. Alcuin of York, *Interrogationes et responsiones in Genesin* [Questions and Responses on Genesis] (PL 100, col. 519).

32. Rabanus Maurus, *Commentariorum in Genesim* [Commentary on Genesis] 1.1–9 (PL 107, cols. 443–66).

33. Haimo of Auxerre (Ps. Haimo of Halberstadt), *Expositio in Epistolam ad Hebreos* [Exposition on the Epistle to the Hebrews] 11 (PL 117, col. 901).

34. Remigius of Auxerre, *Commentarius in Genesim* [Commentary on Genesis] 1 (PL 131, cols. 53–59).

35. *Biblia Latina cum Glossa Ordinaria*, ed. A. Rusch (Strasbourg, 1480/81; repr., vol. 1 of 4, Turnhout: Brepols, 1992). For a long time erroneously ascribed to Walafrid Strabo, the *Glossa ordinaria* on Genesis is the work of an unknown early twelfth-century scholar who made use of the former's writing. See Beryl Smalley, *The Study of the Bible in the Middle Ages* (Notre Dame, IN: University of Notre Dame Press, 1978), 55–66.

36. Bruno of Segni, *Expositio in Genesim* 1 (PL 164, cols. 147–59).

37. Honorius Augustodunensis, *Hexaemeron* 1–3 (PL 172, cols. 253–60).

38. Hugh of Amiens, *Tractatus in Hexaemeron* I (PL 192, cols. 1249–56, here 1253–54).

39. Rupert of Deutz, *De Trinitate et operibus eius, Commentariorum in Genesim* 1.1–14 (PL 167, cols. 199–211).

40. Hugh of Saint Victor, *Adnotationes elucidaoriae in Pentateuchum* 1.1–7 (PL 175, cols. 33–38); *De sacramentis christianae fidei* 1.1 (PL 176, cols. 187–206).

41. Peter Lombard, *Sententiae* 2, dist. 13–16 (PL 192, cols. 675–85; Grottaferrata: Collegii S. Bonaventurae, vol. 1 of 2 vols., 1971–81, pp. 384–409).

42. Peter Comestor, *Historia scholastica, Genesis I*, 1–11 (PL 198, cols. 1055–66).

these currents with Christian doctrine, university commentators employed more highly refined methods of language analysis and dialectic than had their predecessors. In addressing a given question they normally mentioned the views of a broad array of sources and engaged them dialectically, taking elements from each of the various perspectives and integrating them into a coherent synthesis. When this was not possible without doing violence to the texts, they often presented multiple interpretations as alternatives, without adjudicating between them. It was also typical of them to follow their literal interpretations with allegorical (mystical) and tropological (moral) ones. These, respectively, explored the text's lessons for the church and the soul.

The first thinker to produce a major exposition of the creation narratives in a university setting was a key proponent of all the aforementioned developments, Robert Grosseteste, chancellor of Oxford and future bishop of Lincoln, the diocese that included the university.[43] An important translator of Greek works, notable among which was Aristotle's *On the Heavens*, Grosseteste cites some thirty-six separate authors and ninety-eight separate titles in his *Hexaemeron*.[44] Offering several interpretations for the Vulgate's opening line, *In principio creavit Deus caelum et terram*, he draws on each to make key points. The literal sense is the temporal and successive creation of everything corporeal and visible in heaven and earth, and their subsequent ornamentation (*ornatus*). Then there is the imaginable sense, which in turn points to five other realities accessible only to the intellect. First, it signifies the archetypical uncreated world, that is, the immutable reasons of the created world in the divine mind. Second, it signifies the fashioning of the angels and their knowledge of the world to be created. Third, it signifies the creation from nothing of primordial matter and form, and from these the ordered conditioning of the sensible world. Fourth, it signifies allegorically the ordering (*ordinacio*) of the church. And fifth, it signifies tropologically the information (*informacio*) of the soul by faith and morals. These six modes of understanding and explaining Scripture's first line—the literal sense along with the five realities of the imaginable sense—correspond to the six days of creation. The first day is the archetypical world, which is none other than the begotten Wisdom of the Father. The second is the created angelic intelligences. The third is the drawing forth of matter and form from nothing into existence. The fourth is the constitution and ordering of the church. The fifth is the formation of

43. For the Latin text with a critical introduction, see *Robert Grosseteste: Hexaemeron*, ed. Richard Dales and Servus Geiben (London: British Academy, 1982). An ET has been produced by C. F. J. Martin, *Robert Grosseteste: On the Six Days of Creation; A Translation of the Hexaemeron* (Oxford: Oxford University Press, 1996).

44. Grosseteste, introduction to *Hexaemeron*, xix.

the wavering soul by the waters of baptism and by saving wisdom. And the sixth is the temporal formation of the visible world, in which God completed heaven and earth and all its ornamentation, and created man to his image and likeness.[45] To be sure, Grosseteste's discussions of an archetypical world of forms shows Plato's influence, and his account of primordial matter bears the marks of Aristotle's. But he does not hesitate to point out where, in his view, their thought is incompatible with Christian doctrine. Soon after the aforementioned interpretations of *In principio* (in Gen. 1:1), Grosseteste offers another, wherein the phrase indicates the beginning of time. This allows him to point out that Moses overthrew the errors of the philosophers, specifically Plato and Aristotle, as well as the latter's Greek and Arab commentators, according to all of whom the world and time had no beginning.[46]

University masters often expounded the creation narratives within two emergent genres of theological literature, namely, commentaries on Peter Lombard's *Sentences*, and the great syntheses of theology called *summae*. Alexander of Hales (ca. 1185–1245), a renowned secular master who on his entrance into the Franciscans became the first of that order's great theologians, left an account in each genre.[47] Another important Franciscan, Bonaventure (1221–74), also left two treatments. The first, appearing in his commentary on the *Sentences*, is a systematic exposition dating to his teaching at the University of Paris.[48] The second, his *Collationes in Hexaemeron*, is a more discursive account, replete with allegorical and tropological interpretations, which he produced toward the end of his life.[49] The Dominicans Albert the Great (ca. 1200–1290)[50] and Thomas Aquinas (ca. 1225–74)[51] both treated

45. Grosseteste, *Hexaemeron*, 52–53; Grosseteste, *On the Six Days*, 50–51.

46. Grosseteste, *Hexaemeron*, 58–59; Grosseteste, *On the Six Days*, 56–57.

47. Alexander of Hales, *Glossa in quatuor libros sententiarum Petri Lombardi, in II Librum*, dist. XII–XVIII, ed. Quaracchi, t. 13 (Grottaferrata: Collegii S. Bonaventurae, 1952), 116–65; *Summa theologica* (*Summa Halensis*) II, inq. III, ed. Quaracchi (Grottaferrata: Collegii S. Bonaventurae, 1928), 305–82. Questions surround the authorship of the latter work. Though attributed to Alexander from an early date, the *Summa*'s first and third books are known to have involved the efforts of collaborators, particularly those of John of La Rochelle. Its fourth book was produced after Alexander's death, under the guidance of William of Middleton.

48. Bonaventure, *Commentaria in IV Libros Sententiarum: In II Librum*, 12–15, ed. Quaracchi, t. 2 (Grottaferrata: Collegii S. Bonaventurae, 1885), 290–390.

49. Bonaventure, *Collationes in Hexaemeron*, ed. Quaracchi, t. 5 (Grottaferrata: Collegii S. Bonaventurae, 1891), 327–449. An ET of the latter has been produced by J. de Vinck, *Collations on the Six Days* (Paterson, NJ: St. Anthony Guild Press, 1970).

50. Albert the Great, in II *Sententiae*, dist. 12–28, *Opera omnia*, ed. Augustus Borgnet, t. 27 (Paris: L. Vivès, 1894), 229–325; Albert the Great, *Summa Theologiae*, *Opera omnia*, tractate 11, q. 43–67, ed. Augustus Borgnet, t. 32 (Paris: L. Vivès, 1895), 508–625.

51. Thomas Aquinas, *Scriptum in super libros Sententiarum* II, dist. 12–23, ed. P. Mandonnet, t. 2 (Paris: P. Lethielleux, 1929), 296–580; *Summa Theologiae* I, q. 65–74. For a Latin text of the

the creation narratives in their commentaries on the *Sentences* as well as in their *summae*. Aquinas also left an account in his disputed questions *De potentia*,[52] but among his properly exegetical works he left no commentary specifically on Genesis.[53]

Figuring largely in all the aforementioned expositions are the interpretations of Augustine, though not to the exclusion of the writings of the other important patristic commentators, Latin and Greek. But they also show the influence of Arabic Neoplatonist thinkers, especially the anonymous compiler of the *Book of Causes* (*Liber de causis*, 9th c.), Avicenna (Ibn Sina, 980–1037) and Averroes (Ibn Rusd, 1126–98), as well as Jewish ones, notably Avicebron (Ibn Gabirol, 1021–ca. 1065) and Moses Maimonides (ca. 1135–1204). Alexander of Hales, Albert the Great, and Bonaventure parted company with Augustine on several points, particularly on his account of simultaneous creation and ideal days. In their perspective, the world's elements were created simultaneously before the first day, from which the various kinds of things were made during the following six twenty-four-hour days. By contrast with commentators of earlier generations, they found it necessary to entertain—and reject—the notion that the unformed earth of Gen. 1:1 (*inanis et vacua* in the Vulgate) was prime matter. The idea had been engendered by Aristotle's natural philosophy, and its refutation found its origin in the same source. The aforementioned commentators pointed out that matter, as understood by Aristotle, cannot exist without form. This left them the task of explaining the existence of matter in some form before the creation of particular kinds of things. To this end they spoke of a common form lacking in splendor.

When Thomas Aquinas first takes up the question in his commentary on the *Sentences* (1254–55), he begins with a few methodological considerations for biblical interpretation. The first is that no sound interpretation can contradict any matter essential to Christian faith, such as God's unity of nature and Trinity of persons. The second is that no such constraint applies

---

latter, with facing ET, notes, and appendices by William Wallace, see *Thomas Aquinas: Summa Theologiae, Cosmogony*, vol. 10 (Cambridge: Cambridge University Press, 1967).

52. Thomas Aquinas, *Quaestiones disputatae de potentia dei* IV, art. 2, [Disputed Question on the Power of God], ed. P. Bazzi et al., t. 2 (Paris: Marietti, 1965), 102–29.

53. A commentary on Genesis, *In principio creavit*, was printed under Thomas's name several times between the sixteenth and nineteenth centuries. But the falsity of this work's attribution to Aquinas has long been widely recognized. Among the candidates for its authorship are two English Dominicans of the late thirteenth and early fourteenth centuries, respectively, Thomas Jorz and Thomas Waleys; cf. F. Stegmüller, *Repertorium Biblicum Medii Aevi*, t. 5 (Madrid-Barcelona: Matriti, 1955), fn. 8025, fn. 8133, fn. 8235. None of this prevented Stanley Jaki from employing the work as a substantial part of his basis for a sharply unfavorable evaluation of Aquinas's interpretation of the creation narratives, *Genesis 1 through the Ages*, 121–23.

SIDEBAR 8.1

Thomas Aquinas, *Commentary on the Sentences*

Whether all things were created simultaneously in distinct species.

It must be said that those (matters) which belong to the faith are to be distinguished in a twofold manner. Some are of the faith in and of themselves, such as that God is triune and one, and so forth, in which no one may opine otherwise. Hence the Apostle says to the *Galatians* 1 (8), that if an angel of God should evangelize otherwise than he had taught, let him be anathema. Some, however, (are of the faith) only accidentally, inasmuch as they are related by Scripture, which faith takes to be promulgated by the dictation of the Holy Spirit. These without danger may be unknown to those who are not bound to know Scripture. Many historical narratives are of this kind, and in these even the saints took diverse views, variously expounding divine Scripture. So, therefore, concerning the beginning of the world there is something belonging to the substance of the faith, namely that the world began at creation, and in this all the saints speak in concord. By what mode and order it was made, however, belongs to the faith only accidentally, inasmuch as it is related by Scripture, saving the truth of which, the saints related diverse things by diverse expositions.

Note: Scriptum in Sent. II, dist. 12, q. 1, art. 2, solution, ed. Mandonnet, t. 2, 305–6.

---

to interpretations contradicting matters belonging only accidentally to the faith. To illustrate, he states that whereas the world's creation in time is essential to the faith, the mode of its beginning is not. Adding the further exegetical principle that no sound interpretation can patently contradict the findings of reason, he observes that neither the position of Ambrose and others with respect to a sequential creation, nor that of Augustine with respect to a simultaneous one, runs up against either faith or reason. Acknowledging that the former account is more commonly held and more in keeping with a superficial reading of Scripture's letter, he describes Augustine's interpretation as more reasonable and better suited to defend Scripture from the derision of infidels, and on this basis he expresses a preference for it. The main difficulty with Ambrose's account, Aquinas suggests, is the questionable coherence of the aforementioned explanation of preexistent quasi-formed matter, out of which all other things were made. All the same, Aquinas declines to exclude the interpretation, and proceeds to defend both it and Augustine's account against several objections.[54] About a decade later, when revisiting the question

---

54. Aquinas, *Scriptum in Sent. II*, dist. 12, q. 1, art. 2, ed. Mandonnet, t. 2, 305–6.

Meister Eckhart, Comments on Genesis 2:7

Then the LORD God formed man from the dust of the ground, and breathed into his nostrils the breath of life; and the man became a living being.

Here it should be noted that in the lowest level of living things, such as herbs and plants, no mention is made of life or of the spirit, but only of germination and generation. Thus: "Let the earth put forth vegetation" (Gen. 1:11). But in the second level mention is made of life and the soul, albeit indirectly and in passing: "Let the waters bring forth swarms of living creatures (*reptile animae viventis*)" (Gen. 1:20). In the third level, mention is made of the soul and of life in a more perfect way, not merely of a soul of a living thing (*animae viventis*), but even of a living soul (*animam viventem*): "Let the earth bring forth living creatures" (Gen. 1:24). But in the fourth and highest level it is said that God himself, and nothing less, "breath[ed]" (*inspiravit*), indeed "into his [face]," indeed "the breath of life" (*spiraculum vitae*), not merely life, but "the breath of life" (Gen. 2:7). This is why it was said above, "Then God said, 'Let us make humankind in our image, according to our likeness'" (Gen. 1:26).

Note: L'Oeuvre latine de Maître Eckhart, vol. 1, Le commentaire de la Genèse (Paris: Cerf, 1984), 480. The ET here is my own. Brackets represent my adaptations of the NRSV.

in his *De potentia* (1265–66), Aquinas restates the aforementioned exegetical principles and employs them to the same effect, namely, to show the legitimacy of either interpretation and thus to relativize the differences between them.[55] Soon afterward he takes up the question a third time, in the first part of his *Summa theologiae* (1265–67), and similarly defends the plausibility of both interpretations. In neither of the later works, however, does he express a preference for either view.

During the early fourteenth century, Augustine's account of simultaneous creation found an adherent in the thought of the prominent and controversial Dominican Meister Eckhart.[56] As for Bede's accounts, both were largely supplanted by the innovations of the thirteenth-century university masters, but they enjoyed renewed influence in the fourteenth century and long afterward by way of their inclusion in the *Postilla in totam Bibliam* by the Franciscan Nicolas de Lyre (Nicholas of Lyra). This line-by-line commentary on the

55. Aquinas, *Quaestiones disputatae de potentia dei* IV, ed. P. Bazzi et al., t. 2, 113–16.

56. The Latin text cited in sidebar 8.2 includes facing French translation, introduction, and notes by Fernand Brunner, Alain de Libera, Edouard Wéber, et al., *L'Oeuvre latine de Maître Eckhart*, 1:240, 256–62.

entire Bible became a standard reference during the fourteenth century and eventually accompanied the *Glossa ordinaria* in most of that work's numerous printings from the late fifteenth to the seventeenth centuries. At the outset, Nicolas presented both of the aforementioned accounts with the stated purpose of allowing his readers to choose between them.[57]

Creation and Nature of Humanity; Garden of Eden

As a general rule, medieval commentators followed Bede's admonition against carnal understandings of the creation of Adam and Eve. They knew that the young Augustine's rejection of Scripture had resulted from his exposure to literalistic interpretations of Genesis. His *Confessions* had acquainted them with the problems, particularly anthropomorphism, inherent in failing to take biblical metaphor as such.[58] But if they avoided supposing that God made use of hands and other bodily organs to form the first couple, they did not doubt the historicity of Adam's creation from the earth and of Eve's creation from one of his ribs. Nor did they doubt that Eden was a historical location. Among their main concerns in discussing this earthly paradise (*paradisus terrestris*) was to differentiate it from the heavenly one (*paradisus caelestis*).

Not surprisingly, commentators saw the need to address a variety of questions suggested by the narrative. Several concerned the making of Adam. Among those Thomas Aquinas addresses in his *Summa* is whether it was fitting for Adam to be formed from the mire of the earth. A naysayer had urged that such matter would have been beneath Adam's dignity. Aquinas's reply draws attention to humanity's place in the hierarchy of creatures. Placed above subrational creatures, Adam was capable of knowledge, and so he must have been endowed with a soul. And yet, placed as he was below purely spiritual creatures, angels, he was not naturally endowed with knowledge but had to acquire it by the use of his bodily senses. For this he must have had a body made of the elements, and this for the sake of having kinship with corporeal creatures, and so stand as a medium between creation's spiritual and corporeal realms.[59]

Similarly, among the questions Aquinas takes up in connection with the making of Eve is whether her body was fittingly made from Adam's rib. An objector had pointed out that the rib could not have provided enough matter

---

57. Nicolas of Lyra, *Postilla in totam Bibliam*, on Gen. 1. Here I have consulted the edition of F. Fevardentius, et al., *Bibliorum sacrorum Glossa ordinaria*, t. 1 (Venice, 1603), 3–4.

58. Augustine, *Conf.* 3.5; 7.1–2, 19–21.

59. Aquinas, *Summa Theologiae* I, q. 91, art. 1, reply to objection 1.

for the making of her body. In response, Aquinas considers a solution advanced more than century earlier by Hugh of Saint Victor, according to which God multiplied the matter at hand without adding any other matter, as he later did in multiplying the five loaves.[60] Aquinas declares that any such multiplication is unintelligible since it would involve an inherent contradiction, specifically, that the matter in question would be expanded in its dimensions without a loss of its density and without the addition of any other material. He determines that in the making of Eve's body, as in the multiplication of the loaves, God supplied additional matter, either by creating it or by converting other matter into it. Aquinas concludes by pointing out that this solution does no violence to the biblical text's letter, because God may be truly said to have made the woman from Adam's rib and to have fed the crowds from five loaves, since the additions were made to the preexisting matter of the rib and the loaves.[61]

In the late medieval perspective, the very fact of Eve's creation before the fall gave rise to several questions. One of them was presented by the thought of Aristotle, according to whom the female is a misbegotten male. Since nothing misbegotten should appear in the original order of things, it would seem that the woman was out of place in Eden. Aquinas concedes that the female is misbegotten in the sense that her generation happens not by necessity but by accident, as it were. But he goes on to point out that this is so only with respect to the individual. With respect to the species considered as a whole, she is indeed intended by human nature, which itself is intended by nature's author, God. Aquinas is thus in a position to show that Eve's presence in Eden involved no contradiction.[62]

Another question he takes up has arisen from the lesser social stature and physical strength of the woman. A naysayer pointed out that her subjection and inferiority resulted from sin, as indicated by Gen. 3:16: "And he shall rule over you." On the objector's view, this development is at odds with the evident fact that the woman's lesser social stature and strength are natural, with the implication that they preceded the fall. Taken for granted here is Aquinas's previously established position that sin destroys only the life of grace, leaving intact nature's basic attributes. The naysayer thus concludes that Eve should not have had a place in Eden. By implication, the biblical narrative is implausible. Thomas resolves the difficulty by differentiating between two sorts of subjection, one slavish, the other civil. Slavish subjection has the purpose of benefiting superiors. This had no place in Eden but was introduced after sin.

60. Hugh of Saint Victor, *De sacramentis christianae fidei* 1.1 (PL 176, col. 284).
61. Aquinas, *Summa Theologiae* I, q. 92, art. 3, reply to objection 1.
62. Aquinas, *Summa Theologiae* I, q. 92, art. 1, reply to objection 1.

Civil subjection, by contrast, has the purpose of benefiting subjects. Aquinas notes that subjection of this sort is inherently good and necessary for family life and that, as such, it existed before sin. He is thus able to show that the natural inequality between Adam and Eve was by no means incompatible with Eden's idyllic character.[63]

Here something should be said about the methodology at work in the preceding discussions. Neither Thomas nor his contemporaries endeavored to prove by argument any of the biblical data, such as Eve's place in Eden. They took the biblical narrative as given. Nor did their methods involve placing the biblical evidence in the service of their own speculations, introducing verses as prooftexts for the validation of their own conclusions. Exegesis of that sort belonged to future generations. The procedure in evidence above, rather, involves speculation about what must be true of the persons, divine and human, appearing in the biblical narrative in view of that narrative's truth. In the foregoing inquiries, Aquinas's primary purpose was to save the biblical narrative's plausibility in the face of apparent contradictions. An added benefit, of no small consequence, is the clarification of the interpreter's understandings of the personal traits and motives of the narrative's various persons in the passage at hand: God, Adam, and Eve.

Conclusion

Though inherently traditional, medieval biblical commentary on Genesis was by no means static. To the contrary, it remained capable of incorporating the works of successive generations of interpreters, even non-Christian ones. Equally important, despite periodic resistance to scientific and philosophical developments, it was never immune to them. The commentators considered here were uncritical neither with respect to the biblical text they had at their disposal, nor with respect to its literary forms. Despite their limited knowledge of Hebrew, they remained aware of the Vulgate's derivative character, and they realized that the modes of speaking of Scripture's various authors, in this case presumably Moses, differed from their own. In the absence of the ANE cosmologies, they could not have known the extent to which the worldview of Genesis's first readers differed from theirs, and as a consequence they did not doubt that the creation narratives could be brought into agreement with the philosophy and science of their own times. But their concordism was motivated less by philosophical or scientific concerns than by historical ones.

63. Aquinas, *Summa Theologiae* I, q. 92, art. 1, reply to objection 2.

By contrast with modern exegetes generally, they took for granted that the creation narratives provided a historical record of some sort, and they took it as part of their task to ascertain the chronology of the events on which they commented, doing this for the sake of establishing a comprehensive history of the world.

Finally, it should be noted that medieval interpretations of Gen. 1–2 are far more varied than this chapter's groupings may suggest. If they may be accurately divided into two kinds, one espousing simultaneous creation, the other successive, the distinction should not be pressed too far. Their commitment to creation's simultaneity, or lack thereof, is a starting point, not a terminus, for the appreciation of their thought.

For Further Reading

Dahan, Gilbert. *Les intellectuels chrétiens et les juifs au moyen âge.* Paris: Cerf, 2007.

Geiger, Ari. "Nicholas and His Jewish Sources." In *Nicolas de Lyre, franciscain du XIVe siècle, exégète et théologien,* edited by G. Dahan, 167–203. Paris: Institut d'Études Augustiniennes, 2011.

Graboïs, Aryeh. "*The Hebraica Veritas* and Jewish-Christian Intellectual Relations in the Twelfth Century." *Speculum* 50 (1975): 613–34.

Jaki, Stanley. *Genesis 1 through the Ages.* 2nd rev. ed. Edinburgh: Scottish Academic Press, 1998.

Lambert, Malcolm. *The Cathars.* Oxford: Oxford University Press, 1998.

Mangenot, E. "Hexaméron." In *Dictionnaire de Théologie Catholique,* 6:2325–54. Paris: Letouzey & Ané, 1947.

Smalley, Beryl. *The Study of the Bible in the Middle Ages.* Notre Dame, IN: University of Notre Dame Press, 1978.

Stegmüller, Friedrich. *Repertorium Biblicum Medii Aevi.* Vol. 5. Madrid-Barcelona: Matriti, 1955.

Wallace, William. *Thomas Aquinas: Summa Theologiae; Cosmogony.* Vol. 10. Appendixes 1–11. Cambridge: Cambridge University Press, 1967.

Primary Texts in Print

Abelard, Peter. *Expositio in Hexaemeron.* Translated by Wanda Zemler-Cizewski as *An Exposition on the Six-Day Work.* CCT 8. Turnhout: Brepols, 2011.

Aquinas, Thomas. *Summa Theologiae I.* Vol. 10. Translation of qq. 65–74 by William Wallace. Cambridge: Cambridge University Press, 1967. Vol. 11. Translation of qq. 75–83 by Timothy Suttor. Cambridge: Cambridge University Press, 1970.

Bonaventure. *Collationes in Hexaemeron*. Translated by Jose de Vinck as *Collations on the Six Days*. Paterson, NJ: St. Anthony Guild, 1970.

Grosseteste, Robert. *Hexaemeron*. Translated by C. F. J. Martin as *Robert Grosseteste: On the Six Days of Creation*. Oxford: Oxford University Press, 1996.

Primary Texts Online

1. Works of Abelard
     http://onlinebooks.library.upenn.edu/webbin/book/lookupname?key
     =Abelard%2C%20Peter%2C%201079-1142
2. Works of Thomas Aquinas
     http://dhspriory.org/thomas/
3. Works of Bonaventure
     https://franciscan-archive.org/bonaventura/
4. Works of Albertus Magnus
     http://albertusmagnus.uwaterloo.ca/Downloading.html

9

Interpretations of Genesis 1–2
among the Protestant Reformers

JENNIFER POWELL MCNUTT

In his 1535 lectures on Genesis, German Reformer Martin Luther declared that church commentators had made such a muddle of Moses's first book that only one undeniable truth shone through: "God has reserved His exalted wisdom and the correct understanding of this chapter for Himself alone."[1] Interpreting Genesis was indeed a complex undertaking for sixteenth-century commentators, particularly during a period in which hermeneutical approaches were in flux, but such complexity was no deterrent. Considerable time and meticulous care were spent by Reformation-era scholars in interpreting Genesis. Copious numbers of manuscripts and published sixteenth-century commentaries are preserved to this day from a variety of early modern voices.[2]

1. Martin Luther, *Lectures on Genesis: Chapters 1–5*, in LW 1:3.
2. John Thompson should be consulted for a sense of the broad range of views on specific Genesis passages: Thompson, ed. *Genesis 1–11*, RCS: OT 1 (Downers Grove, IL: IVP Academic, 2012). For an inventory of commentaries on Genesis including unfinished commentaries from the period, see Mickey Mattox's *"Defender of the Most Holy Matriarchs": Martin Luther's Interpretation of the Women of Genesis in the "Enarrationes in Genesin," 1535–1545* (Leiden: Brill, 2003), 277–99. For a detailed survey of the commentaries, see Arnold Williams, *The*

For the Reformers, Genesis was more than the first book of Scripture; it also encompassed the entire metanarrative of human salvation.

The book of Genesis was particularly valued for providing the historical and theological framework for the salvation story from creation and the fall of humanity all the way to Jesus Christ. This understanding spurred Lutheran Reformer Philip Melanchthon to comment that Genesis established the two focal points on which all of Scripture pivoted: the origins of sin and the promise of grace.[3] Likewise, Wolfgang Musculus, Reformer in Strasbourg and later Bern, highlighted the way in which Genesis revealed the corruption of humanity and "the first promises of heavenly grace."[4] For Musculus as with others, Genesis established the "foundations of our faith."[5] Lutheran Reformer Johannes Brenz believed that Genesis powerfully convicted hearts toward repentance more than "scarcely any book in all of the sacred Scriptures."[6] Genesis also testified to the power and providence of God in a way that revealed his paternal goodness. To Italian Reformer Peter Martyr Vermigli, Genesis revealed God as a "beneficent father, a merciful guardian and a defender" of his church.[7] Overall, Genesis was appreciated by the Reformers for teaching the truths of human origins and the human moral struggle as well as the actions and character of the trinitarian God.

Furthermore, during an era of biblical hermeneutics that stressed the primacy of literal interpretation to combat an overreliance on allegorical readings, the hermeneutical lens of historicity dominated Reformation interpretations of Genesis.[8] This approach is well illustrated by the prefatory materials of Protestant vernacular Bibles from the time. François Estienne's *La Bible* (Geneva, 1567) offers an example. After describing the nature of Scripture and before the scriptural text began, he included a chart titled, "Descriptions of the Years since the Creation of the World until the Current Year of 1567."[9]

Common Expositor: An Account of the Commentaries on Genesis, 1527–1633 (Chapel Hill: University of North Carolina Press, 1948).

3. RCS: OT 1:3.
4. RCS: OT 1:4.
5. RCS: OT 1:4.
6. RCS: OT 1:5.
7. RCS: OT 1:3.
8. Protestant interpreters of Scripture did not completely reject allegorical readings in practice, though criticism of the approach by Luther certainly set the hermeneutical trend for Protestant biblical scholars. Timothy George and Scott Manetsch's RCS series (Downers Grove, IL: IVP Academic, 2011–) reveals the persistence of the allegorical approach among Protestants, though it is far from dominant.
9. *La Bible, qui est toute la Saincte Escriture: Contenant le Vieil & le Nouueau Testament. Autrement, La Vieille & Nouuelle Alliance; Auec argumens sur chacun liure, figures, cartes tant chorographiques qu'autres* (Geneva: François Estienne, 1567): University of St. Andrews' Special

Here the number of years between Adam's creation and the flood is detailed with supporting citations from Genesis. Exact calculations are provided for the number of years passed from Abraham to Isaac to Jacob to Joseph to Moses and so on until the birth and death of Jesus Christ, with specific passages from Scripture to substantiate calculations. The chart concludes with a tone of certainty that since the creation of the world until its publication date, 5,586 years had passed thereby didactically communicating to the reader the clear historicity of the Genesis account. This serves as one example of how Genesis functioned in the sixteenth century: as providing the primary framework for understanding human life and salvation history.

In order to understand this dynamic more fully, this chapter will explore the interpretation of Gen. 1–2 during the Reformation era by highlighting the perspective of first- and second-generation Reformers Martin Luther and John Calvin to give insight into the exegetical conversations, themes, and conclusions of the period. This analysis is in no way exhaustive since the Reformers never interpreted the Bible in isolation from contemporary discussions or the historical tradition. Because engagement with the larger tradition of Christian interpretation was faithfully practiced, Reformation commentaries on Genesis consistently echo the interpretations of patristic and medieval views.[10] Nonetheless, certain elements of the Reformation voice do stand out as Reformers sought to uncover the literal historical facets of Scripture (such as authorial intent) and as Christian Hebraism emerged during the sixteenth century. Most importantly, Reformers engaged with Genesis in anticipation that the meaning elucidated there could be potentially transformative for the reader or listener according to the work of the Holy Spirit in salvific and sanctifying ways. Genesis, along with the rest of Scripture, could both form faith and transform lives in enduring ways.

Introduction to the Interpreters

From May 1535, after completing his lectures on the Psalms at the University of Wittenberg, and over the next ten years, Luther intermittently lectured on Genesis. These lectures were then published by his students,[11] with Luther's

Collections, Bib BS230.B67. This chart is found in many other French Bibles, particularly those printed in Geneva including François Perrin's 1563 *La Bible*, L'Olivier de Henri Estienne's 1565 *La Bible*, and Pierre Bernard and Claude du Mont's 1565 *La Bible*.

10. Thompson, "Introduction to Genesis 1–11," in RCS: OT 1:liv–lv.

11. Peter Meinhold claimed that Luther's sixteenth-century editors took liberties in preparing the lectures for publication: Jaroslav Pelikan, "Introduction to Volume 1," in LW 1:ix–xii. See also John A. Maxfield's "Martin Luther's Swan Song: Luther's Students, Melanchthon,

appreciation.[12] To aid the reader better, he provided notes to the first four published volumes, and his preface to the first volume approved the edits of Caspar Cruciger, Viet Dietrich, and Georg Rörer. Luther's subsequent volumes on his Genesis exposition were published posthumously (1550, 1552, and 1554) just as John Calvin joined the exegetical conversation.

Following his forced departure from Geneva in 1538, Calvin began writing Bible commentaries soon after settling into his pastoral role in the city of Strasbourg.[13] Beginning with the book of Romans, Calvin wrote commentaries on nearly every book of the Bible during his lifetime. Ever the intentional scholar, Calvin formulated his exposition of Scripture in his commentaries according to the standard of "lucid brevity," a hermeneutical principle that relayed his method of focusing on salient elements of the text without either overindulging or underrepresenting critical theological explanation.[14] The goal was to strike a balance with an unwavering eye toward the text, and the purpose was to unveil the authorial intention of the text in service to the church. The seeds of Calvin's commentaries began with his Bible lectures delivered to students, ministers, and laity, and in 1550 Calvin began lecturing on Genesis. Near the end of his life, in 1563, he revised and republished his Genesis commentary, which he included with the rest of his commentary on the Pentateuch. Reflecting the new hope for the future of Reformed Protestantism in France, Calvin dedicated the volume to the ten-year-old Henri of Navarre, who would become Henri IV of France.[15]

The effort that Luther and Calvin put into interpreting Genesis was just a microcosm of the larger mission in which they were engaged. Both Reformers spent countless hours teaching, preaching, interpreting, and translating Scripture in its fullness, out of the conviction that the gospel message must be proclaimed unfettered to all people. As Calvin describes in his 1546 preface to the French Geneva Bible, Scripture offers the keys to the kingdom and is the true pasture of the people.[16] At the same time, both Luther and Calvin

---

and the Publication of the Lectures on Genesis," in *Lutherjahrbuch: Organ der internationalen Lutherforschung* 81 (2014): 224–48.

12. Robert Kolb, *Martin Luther and the Enduring Word of God: The Wittenberg School and Its Scripture-Centered Proclamation* (Grand Rapids: Baker Academic, 2016), 172–73.

13. See Randall Zachman's useful summary: "Calvin as Commentator on Genesis," in *Calvin and the Bible*, ed. Donald McKim (Cambridge: Cambridge University Press, 2006), 1–29.

14. John Calvin, "The Epistle Dedicatory to Simon Grynaeus," in *Commentaries on the Epistle of Paul the Apostle to the Romans* (repr., Grand Rapids: Baker Books, 2009), xxiii–xxviii.

15. See Raymond Blacketer, "The Old Testament Commentaries and Lectures," in *The Calvin Handbook*, ed. Herman J. Selderhuis (Grand Rapids: Eerdmans, 2009), 188–91.

16. John Calvin, "Epistle to the Readers concerning the Utility of the Holy Scripture" in *La Bible* (Geneva: Jehan Girard, 1546).

believed that Scripture should be approached and interpreted with care and in a methodologically sound way. As one shaped by the medieval scholastic tradition as well as Renaissance humanism, Luther gave primacy to a grammatical-historical engagement in opposition to Scholasticism's fourfold interpretation of Scripture (the *quadriga*), which too often prioritized an allegorical reading. Luther outlined his hermeneutical approach in his 1521 critique of Jerome Emser of Leipzig for pitting the letter of the text against the spirit of the text, thereby equivocating the meaning and ensuring that nothing in Scripture could be understood with certainty.[17] From the outset of his Genesis commentary, Luther puts principle into practice by claiming that Moses intended to "teach us, not about allegorical creatures and an allegorical world but about real creatures and a visible world apprehended by the senses."[18] And yet, as noted above, Luther does not deny the richness and complexity of Scripture or even the use of metaphor. The fact that the Holy Spirit is for him the "simplest writer"[19] or that Gen. 1 is "written in the simplest language"[20] does not mean for Luther that interpretation is *easy* or meaning attainable in every respect.[21] At the same time, Luther teaches that the gospel message is accessibly proclaimed in Scripture because of the Holy Spirit at work. Luther also does not ignore interpretive voices from church tradition or even the philosophers, though he finds Moses to be "the better teacher" by comparison.[22]

In many regards Calvin resonates with Luther's interpretive method. Like his predecessor, Calvin seeks to uncover the intentions of the biblical author and uses grammatical and historical insight to arrive at reasoned interpretations. Calvin's hermeneutical approach to Scripture emphasizes the accommodated nature of scriptural truth since God's purpose through the biblical authors was to communicate the gospel to the common person. This is famously illustrated in his *Institutes of the Christian Religion*, where Calvin describes the sovereign God as a nurse who speaks in baby talk to a child.[23] Here the ontological distinction between Creator and creature is affirmed,

17. See Martin Luther, "'Concerning the Letter and the Spirit' from Answer to the Hyperchristian, Hyperspiritual, and Hyperlearned Book by Goat Emser in Leipzig" (1521), in *Martin Luther's Basic Theological Writings*, ed. Timothy E. Lull and William R. Russell, 3rd ed. (Minneapolis: Fortress, 2012), 53–70.

18. LW 1:5.

19. Luther describes the Holy Spirit in this regard in his critique of Emser: Lull and Russell, *Luther's Basic Theological Writings*, 79.

20. LW 1:3.

21. Luther characterizes Gen. 1 as "very difficult to understand." LW 1:3.

22. LW 1:6.

23. John Calvin, *Institutes of the Christian Religion*, ed. John T. McNeil (London: SCM, 1961), 1.13.1.

and yet, by God's action and condescending initiative, revelation made possible human understanding. Scriptural truth, therefore, is accommodated to human capacity, and this orienting approach is readily evident in Calvin's commentary on Genesis, where he addresses current criticism of Moses for explaining the visible rather than the inner workings of creation.[24] Calvin contends that Moses sought to capture the ordinary experience of the world accessible to the human senses rather than to elevated philosophical inquiry.[25] Moses, he explains, "relates those things which are everywhere observed, even by the uncultivated, and which are in common use."[26] Turning Gregory the Great's famous quote—"Images are the books of the unlearned"—on its head, Calvin points to Genesis as "the book of the unlearned" instead,[27] a point that Luther stressed in his lectures before Calvin.[28]

In these ways, Genesis offers a critical example of how Reformers such as Luther and Calvin believed that Scripture could proclaim God's truth to all people with sufficient simplicity while also recognizing the depths of scriptural complexity. That complexity is attested to in the facets of their exposition of Genesis as they explore the meaning of the days, cosmology, creation, and the nature of humanity as well as the Trinity, clerical marriage, and Satan and demons.

Treatment of Days

From the start, Luther and Calvin give preference to a literal reading of the days in the Genesis account instead of past "mystical" and allegorical interpretations. In good Aristotelian fashion, Luther defines a natural day as the twenty-four-hour cycle of the sun's rotation around the earth.[29] He challenges any who could not grasp the concept of day or God's reason for a six-day creation to acknowledge their "lack of understanding rather than distort the words, contrary to their context, into a foreign meaning; . . . let us remain pupils and leave the job of teacher to the Holy Spirit."[30] He points out that

24. Calvin wrote, "For he does not call us up into heaven, he only proposes things which lie open before our eyes." Calvin, *Commentaries on the First Book of Moses, Called Genesis*, trans. John King, Calvin's Commentaries (repr., Grand Rapids: Baker Books, 2003), 1:87. Subsequent citations refer to this work as Calvin, *Genesis*.

25. Moses talking about God as "seeing" was regarded by Calvin as an example of accommodation. See Calvin, *Genesis*, 1:100.

26. Calvin, *Genesis*, 1:84.

27. Calvin, *Genesis*, 1:80.

28. "Moses was writing for an unlearned people." LW 1:43.

29. LW 1:44.

30. LW 1:5.

SIDEBAR 9.1

Martin Luther, Introduction to Genesis 1

For apart from the general knowledge that the world had its beginning from nothing there is hardly anything about which there is common agreement among all theologians. . . . Augustine resorts to extraordinary trifling in his treatment of the six days, which he makes out to be mystical days of knowledge among the angels, not natural ones. Hence debates are customary in schools and churches concerning evening and morning knowledge, subjects brought up by Augustine and scrupulously propounded by Lyra. Whoever wants to gain a knowledge of them, let him get it from Lyra.

Although these subjects are debated with keen reasoning, the result is no real contribution. For what . . . does it serve any useful purpose to make Moses at the outset so mystical and allegorical? His purpose is to teach us, not about allegorical creatures and an allegorical world but about real creatures and a visible world apprehended by the senses. . . . He employs the terms "day" and "evening" without allegory, just as we customarily do. The evangelist Matthew, in his last chapter, preserves this method of expression when he writes that Christ rose on the evening of the Sabbath which began to dawn into the first day of the week (Matt. 28:1). If, then, we do not understand the nature of the days or have no insight into why God wanted to make sure of these intervals of time, let us confess our lack of understanding rather than distort the words, contrary to their context, into a foreign meaning.

Therefore so far as this opinion of Augustine is concerned, we assert that Moses spoke in the literal sense, not allegorically or figuratively, i.e., that the world, with all its creatures, was created within six days, as the words read. If we do not comprehend the reason for this, let us remain pupils and leave the job of teacher to the Holy Spirit. . . . Disregarding these needless opinions, let us turn to Moses as the better teacher. We can follow him with greater safety than the philosophers, who, without benefit of the Word, debate about unknown matters.

Note: Luther, Lectures on Genesis, LW 1:4–6.

Matt. 28's account that Christ was resurrected on the first day of the week was an accepted literal day, so why question Genesis? Eschatologically, Luther stresses that humanity is destined for a timeless existence, where believers will enjoy eternal day while the reprobate suffer in eternal darkness.[31]

For Calvin, God in his infinite power enjoyed the ability to create the world instantaneously[32] and therefore did not *need* any amount of days to bring

31. LW 1:44.
32. Calvin interprets "in the beginning" as indicating that the earth was not perfected at the moment of its inception but began a process of moving from "empty chaos" to order. (Calvin,

creation into existence and completion.[33] Calvin reasons, therefore, that because humanity was prone to overlook the greatness of God's actions, God intentionally spent six days creating "for the purpose of accommodating his works" to human capacity.[34] By spreading out the act of creation, humanity could marvel at the handiwork of God to "fix our attention, and compel us, as if he had laid his hand on us, to pause and to reflect."[35] After all, Calvin describes creation as a "theater" of God's glory.[36]

Over the course of six days, God brought order and perfection to "the crude and formless masses"[37] that lacked solidity and distinction. Calvin describes this material as an "abyss" or "confused emptiness"[38] brought into existence by God. He reasons that although Moses could have chosen to use the Hebrew term *yāṣar* ("frame" or "form"), the term *bārā'* ("create") was intentionally employed to convey that God created the world out of nothing, or ex nihilo.[39] With this affirmation, Calvin denies the Aristotelian assertion that the physical world is eternal.[40] Previously, Luther also rejected Aristotle on this point and claimed that a general reading of the text showed that the world had a beginning,[41] that it was created out of nothing,[42] and that it was 6,000 years old.[43] For both Reformers, textual reference to the world as created out of nothing is a critical indicator of creation's total dependence on the power of God for life. As Luther teaches, life is created and preserved by God's Word alone as it follows the mandate to grow and multiply.

On the sixth day, then, God's work is completed. Luther and Calvin teach that the completion of God's work and his satisfaction with the results are signals of creation's perfection at that point.[44] Nothing needed adding or

---

Genesis, 1:70). The apocryphal text Sir. 18:1 was most often used to affirm an instantaneous creation. "He who liveth for ever created all things at once." Luther cites Hilary as advancing this perspective: LW 1:11, 37.

33. Calvin, *Genesis*, 1:103.
34. Calvin, *Genesis*, 1:78.
35. Calvin, *Genesis*, 1:78.
36. Calvin, *Institutes*, 1.5.1; 1.5.8; 1.6.2.
37. LW 1:6–7. Calvin describes the matter as "empty and confused" as well as "rude and unpolished, or rather shapeless chaos" (*Genesis*, 1:73).
38. Calvin, *Genesis*, 1:73.
39. Calvin, *Genesis*, 1:70.
40. Thompson argues that the debate over the eternity of the world was primarily an opportunity "to observe the failings to which secular pagan philosophy is liable on account of its ignorance or neglect of the revelation possessed by Christians in the Bible." RCS: OT 1:lvi.
41. LW 1:13.
42. Luther references Rom. 4:17 in support of this doctrine. LW 1:21.
43. LW 1:5.
44. LW 1:75.

SIDEBAR 9.2

John Calvin, Comments on Genesis 2:2

The question may not improperly be put, what kind of rest this was. For it is certain that inasmuch as God sustains the world by his power, governs it by his providence, cherishes and even propagates all creatures, he is constantly at work. Therefore that saying of Christ is true, that the Father and he himself had worked from the beginning hitherto, because, if God should but withdraw his hand a little, all things would immediately perish and dissolve into nothing, as is declared in Psalm 104:29. And indeed God is rightly acknowledged as the Creator of heaven and earth only whilst their perpetual preservation is ascribed to him. The solution of the difficulty is well known, that God ceased from all his work, when he desisted from the creation of new kinds of things. But to make the sense clearer, understand that the last touch of God had been put, in order that nothing might be wanting to the perfection of the world. And this is the meaning of the words of Moses, *From all his work which he had made*; for he points out the actual state of the work as God would have it to be, as if he had said, then was completed what God had proposed to himself. On the whole, this language is intended merely to express the perfection of the fabric of the world; and therefore we must not infer that God so ceased from his works as to desert them, since they only flourish and subsist in him. Besides, it is to be observed, that in the works of the six days, those things alone are comprehended which tend to the lawful and genuine adorning of the world. It is subsequently that we shall find God saying, Let the earth bring forth thorns and briers, by which he intimates that the appearance of the earth should be different from what it had been in the beginning. But the explanation is at hand; many things which are now seen in the world are rather corruptions of it than any part of its proper furniture. . . . In all these, I say, there is some deformity of the world, which ought by no means to be regarded as in the order of nature, since it proceeds rather from the sin of man than from the hand of God. . . . Moses is not considering God as armed for the punishment of the sins of men; but as the Artificer, the Architect, the bountiful Father of a family, who has omitted nothing essential to the perfection of his edifice.

Note: Calvin, *Genesis*, 1:103–4.

changing since all things were repeatedly deemed "perfectly good."[45] This point is strongly defended by Luther against those who deny that the Gen. 1 account of the created order does not reflect current reality. To critics, creation

45. Calvin, *Genesis*, 1:100. Calvin's claim that God perfected creation is stressed in opposition to the claim of "the Jews" that God left certain animals with imperfections (1:107). Calvin responds that God gives his creatures being and preserves them "that nothing should be wanting to their perfection; or the creation has proceeded to such a point, that the work is in all respects perfect" (1:108).

was flawed, ever changing, and often far from good as evidenced by vicious beasts, disease, and bugs. Chronology, however, is key to a proper hermeneutic, and the two worlds vastly differed due to the entrance of sin,[46] since the state and fate of the world were inextricably linked to humanity.[47] Consequently, Luther stresses the watershed moment of the fall attested to in Gen. 3 in order to interpret Gen. 1–2.[48] He explains that in Gen. 1, Moses is referring to "the time the world was pure and innocent because man was pure and innocent."[49] The good news, therefore, is that the renewal of humanity will also mean the renewal of creation, and in this way Gen. 1 provides a window into the origins of life as well as the eschaton.[50]

The nature of God's rest on the seventh day and the ongoing maintenance of creation was also a matter of great theological concern. Luther reasons that God's rest, when interpreted as ceasing from work, appears to contradict John 5:17, which teaches that the work of the Father and Son is always ongoing. According to this reference, Luther determines that the completion of creation could not mean ceasing from governance since life continued to thrive, and he denies that God turned governance over to the angels.[51] Similarly, Calvin grapples with the meaning of God's rest while simultaneously explaining that since God "sustains the world by his power, governs it by his providence, cherishes and even propagates all creatures, he is constantly at work."[52] Calvin stresses that creation's dependence on God's providence means that God could not withdraw his hand even a fraction without destroying the world.[53] He concludes, "We must not infer that God so ceased from his works as to desert them, since they only flourish and subsist in him."[54] Yet if even God's rest necessitated the work of sustaining the world, what was the meaning of the Sabbath for Luther and Calvin?

Luther teaches that humanity was created for the purpose of worshiping God, and the Sabbath is a day set apart by God for such worship to take place. In the state of perfection before the fall, Luther believes that humanity would have automatically observed the Sabbath without need of command, and that

46. LW 1:78.
47. LW 1:78.
48. LW 1:82.
49. LW 1:77.
50. LW 1:77.
51. LW 1:30.
52. Calvin, *Genesis*, 1:103.
53. Calvin, *Genesis*, 1:103. Calvin cites Ps. 104:29 to convey how everything would turn to dust if the Lord took his Spirit away (*Genesis*, 1:74).
54. Calvin, *Genesis*, 1:104. God was presented as "the Artificer, the Architect, the bountiful Father of a family, who has omitted nothing essential to the perfection of his edifice" (1:105).

this observance played a critical role in enabling human immortality.[55] After the fall and the loss of immortality, observance of the Sabbath through the preaching and hearing of the Word of God becomes the means by which hope in the promise of eternal life is preserved.[56] Thus, even though the knowledge of God is lost at the fall, God still grants the Sabbath to the church so that the spiritual life might be restored through Christ.[57] For Calvin, although Christ fulfilled the ceremonial requirements of the Sabbath, the Sabbath is established from the very beginning of time for all of humanity and not merely for the Jews.[58] To him, Sabbath rest is not a holiday but a "sacred rest" that is set apart until the end of time for reflection on the perfection of God's work, for mortification of the flesh, and to inspire humanity to glorify God in all things.[59] In this manner, the Sabbath offers a reminder that believers should daily practice reflection on "the infinite goodness, justice, power, and wisdom of God, in this magnificent theatre of heaven and earth."[60]

Finally, exploring the days of creation led Luther and Calvin to consider the nature and work of the Godhead. Both discuss the evidence for the Trinity in the grammatical construction of the text itself. *Elohim* (the name for God) as a noun in the plural form was customarily interpreted as confirming the plurality of persons in the Godhead. Though admitting that the fullness of the doctrine—three distinct persons in one—was absent until the teaching of the gospel, both oppose alternate Jewish interpretations (i.e., angels and judges)[61] and the idea that the plural form was a mere rhetorical device customary of royalty.[62] Luther's analysis identifies explicit engagement of the economic Trinity in terms of the doctrine of appropriations. He teaches that God the Father created the heavens and the earth through the Son known as the Word.[63] Christ, as the Second Person of the Trinity, worked "to adorn and separate the crude mass which was brought forth out of nothing."[64] Since wind did not yet exist, Luther concludes that the Holy Spirit hovered over the waters, bringing creation to life like a hen broods over her eggs.[65] When

---

55. LW 1:79–80, 82.
56. Immortality is not granted to animals. LW 1:80–81.
57. LW 1:80.
58. Calvin, *Genesis*, 1:106–7.
59. Calvin, *Genesis*, 1:106–7.
60. Calvin, *Genesis*, 1:106.
61. LW 1:57. On this point, Luther mentions with affirmation the scholastic William of Occam. Calvin, *Genesis*, 1:93.
62. Luther regards this manner of speaking as too limited to German custom (LW 1:12, 58), and Calvin views this interpretation as anachronistic (Calvin, *Genesis*, 1:92).
63. Luther references Heb. 1:2 and Col. 1:16 in support (LW 1:18).
64. LW 1:9.
65. LW 1:9. Luther engages with Augustine and the Nicene Creed.

God called light into existence, Luther claims that the Hebrew text denotes more than an utterance but an object, which he determines to be a sign of the distinction of persons since "the uttered word . . . is something distinct from him who is speaking and there is distinction between him who speaks and that which is spoken."[66] Luther continues to point out evidence in the text that affirms the plurality of the persons and the unity of the essence.[67] Using Scripture to interpret Scripture, Luther references the prologue of John to confirm Genesis's teaching on the Word and the distinction of the persons.[68]

In fact, identifying trinitarian evidence within the Genesis account was customary for commentaries well before the Reformers. As Thompson points out, "Arguments for the Trinity are common among the fathers, medieval and Reformers, and if not all Christian interpreters felt justified in finding Father, Son and Holy Spirit in Gen. 1:1, there was more agreement that the plural 'let us make' in Gen. 1:26 signals a plurality of persons in God."[69] Nonetheless, Calvin expresses reticence toward embracing this classic Christian interpretation.[70] He argues that while appeal to the plural grammatical construction for God could be used to prove the divinity of the Son and the Spirit in opposition to Arianism,[71] the question of Sabellianism (or the heresy of Modalism) persists since no clear distinction between the three persons is represented in the term. Faced with this dilemma, Calvin claims that the plural form signifies "those powers which God exercised in creating the world."[72]

Cosmology

Several shared cosmological issues occupied the attention of the Reformers, particularly in cases when Moses's explanations did not align with the theories of contemporary astronomers. Rather than assuming error in the text, Luther and Calvin valued authorial purpose and accommodation.[73] Calvin explains, "Moses wrote in a popular style things which, without instruction, all ordinary persons, endued with common sense, are able to understand; but astronomers investigate with great labour whatever the sagacity of the human mind can

---

66. LW 1:16.
67. LW 1:20–21.
68. LW 1:16–17.
69. Thompson, RCS: OT 1:lvi.
70. Calvin, *Genesis*, 1:71–72.
71. Luther contends with Arius in his discussion of Gen. 1:2 regarding the full divinity of Christ. LW 1:13–14.
72. Calvin, *Genesis*, 1:72.
73. Calvin, *Genesis*, 1:80; LW 1:43.

comprehend."[74] Additionally, Luther points out that God is not bound by the rules that govern natural order, "even if by His Word God has established and created all these things."[75] Consequently, when astronomers claimed that Saturn was larger than the moon, Calvin acknowledges that this dynamic appears differently to the human eye.[76] He also defends Moses's description of the greater and lesser lights as a reference to the sun and the moon. He denies that Moses was ignorant of the fact that the moon borrowed light from the sun since Moses's purpose was to speak plainly regarding human perceptions of creation.[77] To Calvin, God should be glorified even when creation is not perfectly understood.[78]

When the creation account defied common sense, theological purpose was at hand. For example, Luther observes that although plants naturally require seed in like kind to bloom, the power of God's Word is evident in that the first creation was brought about without seed, as a onetime miracle.[79] This serves as one of many indications to Luther of God's ability to act contrary to nature's order.[80] Calvin also explores how light could exist before the sun and the stars were created, claiming that this backward ordering was intended to teach that light resides in the power of God's hand without dependence on any created agent. For him, the stars can "teach us that all creatures are subject to his will, and execute what he enjoins on them."[81] Luther also grapples with questions about the creation of light. In considering why the sun, moon, and stars were not created until the fourth day though light was given on the first day, Luther concludes that the first light was a "crude" level of light created ex nihilo,[82] which was then perfected with God's creation of the sun, moon, and stars on the fourth day. Neither of these lights would rival the light of the last day.[83] Although Luther grapples with questions over the size and magnitude of their light according to current astronomical perceptions, ultimately he neither accepts nor rejects philosophical explanations. Above all, Luther

74. Calvin, *Genesis*, 1:86. Luther stresses this point as well. LW 1:19.

75. LW 1:27.

76. Calvin claims that Saturn is a star (*Genesis*, 1:86). He explains that Moses "adapts his discourse to common usage" (1:87).

77. Calvin, *Genesis*, 1:86. Calvin explains that the "lesser" nature of the moon was about its emission of light as compared to the sun. He regards the moon as a "fiery body."

78. Calvin, *Genesis*, 1:87.

79. LW 1:36–37.

80. LW 1:27.

81. Calvin, *Genesis*, 1:83. Calvin assumes that stars reflected the light that was already created by the sun as the dispenser of "diurnal light." He denies Plato's ascription of reason and intelligence to the stars (1:87).

82. LW 1:18–19.

83. LW 1:40. In reference to Isa. 30:26 and the last day: LW 1:20.

celebrates the theological purpose of the text, which taught God's goodness in preserving life.[84]

The division of the waters seems to be another example of the text defying the common sense of the era for the Reformers. Though acknowledging Moses's intention that even the "rude and unlearned may perceive,"[85] the firmament used to divide the "waters from the waters" leaves both Luther and Calvin puzzled. Luther declares, "Here I, therefore, take my reason captive and subscribe to the Word even though I do not understand it."[86] Similarly for Calvin, the idea that there would be waters above heaven opposed "common sense."[87] Both evaluate the text according to Aristotelian logic, wherein the four elements, including air and water, were governed by their naturally weighted position.[88] Since water was determined to be circular and heavier than air (though lighter than earth),[89] its natural position was to cover the entire circumference of the earth. The fact that the earth is not overwhelmed by the water is therefore "an illustrious miracle" by God,[90] one that he would repeat for the children of Israel at the Red Sea.[91] In this, God's providence is clear: "The heaven which cannot stand firm by means of its bounds (for it is watery), stands firm through the Word of God."[92] To Calvin, clouds also defy the laws of nature and particularly reveal God's providence since they are held above by God's power, to prevent them from engulfing humans below, "since no other barrier is opposed to them than the liquid and yielding air, which would easily give way unless this word prevailed."[93] Therefore, only by God's goodness and power does humanity have room to dwell at all.[94]

In matters of cosmology, Luther and Calvin agree that God's power and care as Creator is the true story of Genesis. Luther emphasizes the fact that even before man and woman existed, God was making a home for humanity.[95] Luther also interprets this eschatologically since before humanity came to know Christ in faith, God began to prepare mansions for his believers in

84. LW 1:141.
85. Calvin, *Genesis*, 1:80.
86. LW 1:26.
87. Calvin, *Genesis*, 1:79.
88. Calvin does not resort to angels to explain the text, as was the custom (*Genesis*, 1:79).
89. Luther explains Aristotle on these matters. LW 1:26–27.
90. Calvin, *Genesis*, 1:81.
91. LW 1:34–35.
92. LW 1:25.
93. Calvin, *Genesis*, 1:80–81.
94. Calvin, *Genesis*, 1:80–81. Calvin cites Pss. 33:7; 78:13; Jer. 5:22; Job 38:8.
95. LW 1:39.

heaven (John 14:2). By way of a typological argument, Luther explains that the world before the fall is a "type and figure of the future world; and so let us learn the kindness of God, who makes us rich and gives us wealth before we are able to concern ourselves with ourselves."[96] For Calvin, because God is not bound by the rules of nature, he is able to show humanity extraordinary care and inspire wonder.[97] For the Reformers, this reason and more indicated that the creation account is above all a story of God's grace from the start.

Astronomy and Astrology

In matters of cosmology, Luther and Calvin exhibit an intentional desire to navigate and distinguish theological knowledge gained from Scripture and philosophical knowledge assessed from the study of the world. After all, this is an era not just of ecclesiastical reform but also of scientific revolution. Although Luther and Calvin do not embrace Copernicus's hypothesis of a heliocentric universe, their many references to the natural philosophy of their time within the Genesis commentaries should not be overlooked.

At the time, astronomy and astrology were not always clearly distinguished from each other. Both Luther and Calvin reject astrology for using the celestial realm to predict the future. Luther denies its status as a true science,[98] and Calvin regards it as an "abuse" of the gifts of God.[99] Their debate revolves around Gen. 1:14, where the term "signs" is used in reference to the sun and the moon and as a means of legitimating the practice of astrology.[100] In opposition, Calvin argues that Moses was referencing the common use of the stars to mark time, seasons, and festivals.[101] Astronomy, meanwhile, enjoyed an altogether different reception.

Although Luther notes Augustine's disdain for astronomical inquiry, despite some "superstitious elements,"[102] he nevertheless values astronomy as the art of observing God's divine activity.[103] Calvin likewise speaks highly of astronomy as "pleasant" and "useful" in revealing the depths of God's

---

96. LW 1:39.

97. Calvin writes, "He is the Author of nature, yet by no means has followed nature as his guide in the creation of the world, but has rather chosen to put forth such demonstrations of his power as should constrain us to wonder" (*Genesis*, 1:88–89).

98. LW 1:45.

99. LW 1:85.

100. Calvin, *Genesis*, 1:84; LW 1:44–45.

101. Calvin, *Genesis*, 1:85.

102. LW 1:31.

103. LW 1:32.

wisdom.[104] They both show concern that astronomy and Scripture be respected in their purposes and approaches. The terminology of the astronomer
(i.e., spheres and epicycles) is not the terminology of the Holy Spirit and
Holy Scripture, but "let each of the two speak in his own terminology; . . .
they should put their achievements at one another's disposal."[105] Calvin is
concerned that Genesis might curb astronomical study out of respect for the
explanations of the text[106] when neither should suffer: "this study is not to
be reprobated, nor this science to be condemned."[107] It seems that Luther's
and Calvin's appreciation for the doctrine of accommodation allows the
text to speak truth to the common person without disproving the natural
philosophy of the period.[108]

Creation and Nature of Humanity

In their reading of the text, both Luther and Calvin identify the creation
of humanity as the apex of God's work. While the world was created ex
nihilo, all creatures—both humans and animals—were given form out of
the universal matter that God made out of nothing.[109] Nonetheless, Luther
and Calvin agree that special dignity was bestowed on humanity when God
created humanity not by "bare command" as with all other living creatures
but according to self-consultation.[110] The painstaking process of humanity's
creation was theologically intentional since God could have created humanity in an instant, but he chose to proceed slowly.[111] With echoes of Luther,
Calvin describes this as an indication of the "dignity of our nature, he, in
taking counsel concerning the creation of man, testifies that he is about to
undertake something great and wonderful."[112] For both Luther and Calvin,
human dignity is rooted in the image of God.

Luther's understanding of the image of God was shaped by his comparison of humanity with the state of animals, his reflection on Adam before the

104. Calvin, *Genesis*, 1:86–87.
105. LW 1:48. Luther points out that theologians evaluate causality differently than philosophers.
106. Calvin, *Genesis*, 1:86–87.
107. Calvin, *Genesis*, 1:86.
108. As Calvin explains, "Since the Spirit of God here opens a common school for all, it is
not surprising that he should chiefly choose those subjects which would be intelligible to all"
(*Genesis*, 1:86–87).
109. Calvin, *Genesis*, 1:89.
110. LW 1:56. Again, no angels were consulted over human creation. Calvin, *Genesis*, 1:92–93.
111. LW 1:69.
112. Calvin, *Genesis*, 1:92; LW 1:55.

fall, and his reading of Peter Lombard's *Sentences*. In the first regard, Luther teaches that although Adam and the animals share most everything before the fall—sleep, food, and life together—God sets humanity apart from animals by creating them with a "special plan and providence."[113] Animals are consequently subjected to the desires and appetites of the physical life,[114] while humans engage in wisdom, justice, knowledge, and understanding of their world and of God himself.[115] Though original sin wrought its destruction, the gospel brings restoration of eternal life, freedom from fear, and goodness.[116] The Sabbath was given to humans for the purpose of restoration, and in these ways the human state is far "better" than the state of animals since humanity alone[117] was given the gift of hearing God, knowing his will, and being called "into a sure hope of immortality."[118]

Calvin's evaluation of the image of God is heavily dominated by common issues from throughout the Christian tradition. Calvin stringently denies that humanity was made in the image of angels since humans were made greater than angels.[119] He, along with Luther, rejects any hermeneutical difference between the terms "image" and "likeness,"[120] and he criticizes the "Anthropomorphites" for identifying image and likeness too closely with the physical human body.[121] Calvin also opposes Augustine's interpretation from *The City of God* that assumes a trinity is identifiable within humanity.[122] He gives partial credence to Chrysostom's belief that the image of God relates to human dominion over the earth as God's vicegerent.[123] In evaluating this matter, Calvin reasons that since the image of God was destroyed by the fall,[124] the restoration of humanity according to the gospel should give insight into the true nature of the image of God.

113. LW 1:56.
114. Luther criticizes an Epicurean view of humanity in this regard (LW 1:26, 56).
115. LW 1:68.
116. LW 1:64.
117. LW 1:56–57.
118. LW 1:81.
119. Calvin, *Genesis*, 1:92.
120. LW 1:68; Calvin, *Genesis*, 1:94. Distinction between the terms "image" and "likeness" was widely affirmed starting in the patristic era.
121. Calvin, *Genesis*, 1:94.
122. Calvin, *Genesis*, 1:93. Calvin writes, "For in laying hold of the three faculties of the soul enumerated by Aristotle, the intellect, the memory, and the will, he afterwards out of one Trinity derives many."
123. Calvin, *Genesis*, 1:94.
124. To Calvin, the image of God was so corrupted that it might as well have been obliterated by the fall. "Although some obscure lineaments of that image are found remaining in us; yet are they so vitiated and maimed, that they may truly be said to be destroyed. . . . No part is free from the infection of sin" (*Genesis*, 1:95).

In contrast with the times, for Luther and Calvin the dignity of the image of God is also bestowed on women. In an era that still promoted Aristotelian views of women as "maimed men,"[125] Luther is complimentary of women for his time. He describes Eve as an "extraordinary creature" and "a most beautiful work of God."[126] He denies that man was split in half to make woman and affirmed that she was a distinct creation by citing Gen. 2 and Adam's rib in support. Acknowledging the reference in Gen. 1 to humanity as both male and female, Luther discerns that Moses intended to show that Eve was "a partaker of the divine image and of the divine similitude, likewise of the rule over everything."[127] Luther also teaches that woman is promised the future life with man as "joint heirs," citing 1 Pet. 3:7 (RSV). Furthermore, she partners in the management of the household and shares a "common interest" in the children and the property. In Gen. 1:27, he seems to qualify these points by describing Eve as "inferior" to Adam insofar as she was "not the equal of the male in glory and prestige."[128] Nonetheless, in Gen. 2:17, he explains that Eve was subjected to Adam only after the fall: "Hence it follows that if the woman had not been deceived by the serpent and had not sinned, she would have been the equal of Adam in all respects."[129]

Calvin's reflection on women and the image of God leads him to question the common interpretation of 1 Cor. 11:7, which seemed to deny that women were made in God's image. Calvin contends with this view, boldly declaring, "Moses honours both, indiscriminately, with this title."[130] Instead, Calvin reasons that Paul must have been referring to the domestic circumstances for women, a solution that he determined according to his evaluation of Gen. 2. Calvin concludes that for Paul, the image of God was reserved for "government" and an indication of the superiority of man over woman in terms of degree (i.e., not denying that woman is without honor). Both Reformers, in these ways, grapple with the text over the image of God as it pertained to women.[131]

---

125. LW 1:70.

126. LW 1:69.

127. LW 1:69.

128. LW 1:69

129. LW 1:115.

130. Calvin, *Genesis*, 1:96.

131. Douglass explains, "The reader senses that Calvin remains troubled by Paul's way of dealing with Eve. He regularly refutes an interpretation of Paul that would deny woman's share in the image of God; he points out that Paul in many passages teaches that Adam sinned along with Eve; but in the end his reading of Gen. 2 represents an attempt to harmonize that account with Gen. 1 and with Paul. And so Eve's subjection predates the Fall, and Eve's share in the image of God is not entirely equal." Jane Dempsey Douglass, *Women, Freedom, and Calvin* (Philadelphia: Westminster, 1985), 60–61.

Celibacy and Clerical Marriage

During the Reformation consideration of human creation and the relationship of humanity was coupled with contentious discussion over celibacy and whether clergy should marry. Blatant disregard for the vows of celibacy, even at the highest level of church governance, was a persistent stumbling block for the medieval church from the Carolingian Renaissance on. Despite efforts to curb sexually immoral behavior, medieval reform efforts were ineffective in the long run. Even into the early modern period, clerical culture continued to permit the frequenting of prostitution houses, the maintaining of concubines, and the fathering of children out of wedlock. Celibacy propaganda pamphlets frequently demonized women in the effort to promote abstinence. Of course, these views had a longer history than the medieval period. Luther references Aristotle's description of woman as a "maimed man" and a "monster" in his Gen. 1 lectures, and he responds, "But let them themselves be monsters and sons of monsters—these men who make malicious statements and ridicule a creature of God in which God Himself took delight as in a most excellent work, moreover, one which we see created by a special counsel of God."[132]

Calvin also interprets God's creation of humanity as "male and female" through the lens of marriage and as proof that God established the conjugal bond as the central building block of human society. In Calvin's view, Gen. 1 shows that man is incomplete alone. Consequently, woman was added as a "companion" so that the two might become one, and Calvin believes that Gen. 2 provides a fuller explanation of this dynamic.[133] In fact, this was the very term that Calvin used to describe his own wife, Idelette de Bure, in 1549 after her passing.[134] Thus in their promotion of marriage, Reformers countered common disparagement of women with the textual help of Gen. 1.[135] Calvin also addresses the practice of polygamy in his interpretation of the text, which he describes as an affront to conjugal fidelity. He offers a literal reading of the passage as expressly commending a pair in the following ways. "For the purpose of correcting this fault, he calls that pair, consisting of man

---

132. LW 1:70.

133. Calvin, *Genesis*, 1:97. Calvin cites Mal. 2:15 as further confirmation. According to Douglass, "Here there is no hint in Calvin's comments of any subjection of the woman to the man. Rather, Calvin sees the whole human being as requiring both male and female, and the woman is a companion." Douglass, *Women, Freedom, and Calvin*, 60.

134. Elsie McKee, *John Calvin: Writings on Pastoral Piety*, Classics of Western Spirituality (New York: Paulist, 2002), 53.

135. See Marjorie Elizabeth Plummer, *From Priest's Whore to Pastor's Wife: Clerical Marriage and the Process of Reform in the Early German Reformation*, St. Andrews Studies in Reformation History (New York: Routledge, 2012).

and woman, which God in the beginning had joined together, *one man*, in order that every one might learn to be content with his own wife."[136] Although Calvin is pointedly criticizing Jewish OT practices here, bigamy continued to be a matter of controversy during the early modern period when the Lutheran Prince Philipp of Hesse received secret permission from Martin Luther and Martin Bucer to marry a second wife in 1540.[137] Since bigamy was considered a capital offense in the Holy Roman Empire, this approval proved disastrous for the Protestant cause politically in many regards.

Another key point of the passage for the Reformers is the idea that legitimate union should lead to legitimate offspring. Calvin asserts that it is by God's blessing alone that humanity is fruitful since God could have chosen to fill the earth with humanity apart from Adam and Eve. Yet God chose that humanity should "proceed from one fountain, in order that our desire of mutual concord might be greater, and that each might the more freely embrace the other as his own flesh."[138] By this reasoning, God gave his blessing to humanity to be fruitful, multiply, and fill the earth in the context of "holy and chaste marriage."[139] One should interpret these points in light of Protestant efforts to legitimate the pastoral family, beginning with Wittenberg Reformer Andreas Karlstadt's marriage to Anna von Mochau in 1522. In his exegesis of Gen. 2:18, therefore, Calvin asserts in no uncertain terms that "solitude is not good" for humanity and the messages that malign marriage come from Satan rather than from God:

> Many think that celibacy conduces to their advantage, and, therefore, abstain from marriage, lest they should be miserable. Not only have heathen writers defined that to be a happy life which is passed without a wife, but the first book of Jerome, against Jovinian, is stuffed with petulant reproaches, by which he attempts to render hallowed wedlock both hateful and infamous. To these wicked suggestions of Satan let the faithful learn to oppose this declaration of God, by which he ordains the conjugal life for man, not to his destruction, but to his salvation.[140]

Through these interpretive moves, clerical marriage became a hallmark of the Protestant cause.

---

136. Calvin, *Genesis*, 1:97.
137. See David Whitford, *A Reformation Life: The European Reformation through the Eyes of Philipp of Hesse*, Praeger Series on the Early Modern World (Santa Barbara, CA: Praeger, 2015), 117–20.
138. Calvin, *Genesis*, 1:97.
139. Calvin, *Genesis*, 1:98.
140. Calvin, *Genesis*, 1:128.

Interpretive Peculiarities

Trinity

In every significant case, theological debates from the early Christian period were rehashed in the sixteenth century, and the doctrine of the Trinity was one such revived debate. As mentioned above, trinitarian readings of Gen. 1 were typical of Reformation commentaries. The interpretive particularity is not the fact that they pointed out the Trinity in the text but the number of reasons why Reformation scholars searched for affirmations of the orthodox view of the Trinity from the Genesis text when this was a traditional consensus.

In the wake of Renaissance humanism's attention to the original languages of the Bible, a newly emerging Christian Hebraism swept the universities of Europe. Christian scholars were increasingly engaging with Hebrew texts and scholarship, and in so doing they wrote in conversation with and in opposition to Jewish interpretations of Scripture. Consequently, uncovering evidence for the Trinity from within Hebrew Scripture became an important practice distinguishing Christian from Jewish exegesis. Meanwhile, after defeating the Hungarians at the Battle of Mohács in 1526, the Ottoman Empire stood on the doorstep of Western Europe at the Siege of Vienna (1529), and this had a profound effect on Reformation Europe. Theologically, a Trinitarian understanding of God was highlighted as the demarcation point between Christians and Turks. Thus Luther writes about the Trinity in Gen. 1: "These evidences should be precious to us and welcome. Even though both Jews and Turks laugh at us because we are convinced that there is one God and that there are three Persons, nevertheless unless they are brazen enough to deny the authority of Scripture, they are compelled by this passage and also by those quoted above to adopt our conviction."[141] Additionally, the Reformers were mindful of addressing this debate in light of Erasmus's discovery that the portion of the verse from 1 John 5:7 known as the Johannine Comma—which in Latin explicitly references the Trinity as Father, Son, and Spirit—was not found in Greek manuscripts.[142] Finally, discussion over Trinitarian theology was also revived due to a group of radical Reformers, described as the Evangelical Rationalists, who rejected the scriptural basis for the Trinity. Calvin is especially known for conflict with Michael Servetus, one of the key antitrinitarian voices of the period, who was convicted of heresy and burned

141. LW 1:59.
142. Erasmus controversially removed the scribal addition from his New Testament but then returned it to the third edition of the text. See Grantley MacDonald, *Biblical Criticism in Early Modern Europe: Erasmus, the Johannine Comma, and Trinitarian Debate* (Cambridge: Cambridge University Press, 2016).

at the stake in Geneva in 1553. Thus in his *Institutes*, Calvin references Gen. 1:2 in order to prove that the Holy Spirit is an "essential power of God," in opposition to the antitrinitarian views of Servetus.[143] In 1554, Calvin published his *Defense of the Orthodox Faith on the Trinity, against Prodigious Errors of Michael Servetus.*

For these reasons, the doctrine of the Trinity was particularly subject to critical scrutiny during the sixteenth century, and a right interpretation of Genesis was at the heart of the matter.

Satan and Demons

In Heiko Oberman's famous biography of Luther, he describes Luther as a "man between God and the devil."[144] This characterization aptly encapsulates the way in which Luther viewed his life and ministry as in conflict with the seemingly ceaseless trials and temptations of the devil. Though elaborate theories and beliefs regarding the activity of Satan and demons were a normative facet of the early modern world, Luther's views exhibit interpretive peculiarity from his time by claiming that the pursuit of righteousness, rather than the practice of sin, leads to the attacks of the devil.[145] By his reasoning, faith in Christ is what attracts the rage of Satan.

Luther's view of the Christian life as lived in direct conflict with Satan appears in his Genesis lectures in significant ways. First of all, he does not underestimate Satan and considers even whether he might be made in the image of God because of his superior memory, will, and mind.[146] Luther emphasizes that Satan was the true cause of evil in the world, rather than exclusively blaming Eve, by explaining in her defense, "They do not know the cause of evil, namely, Satan, who has so vitiated and corrupted this creation."[147] Moreover, in discussing Gen. 2:1, Luther argues from a Hebrew word study that Moses employed military language in order to convey the completion of heavens and the earth, and he notes that the common practice of the prophets to mention the "heavenly host" came from Moses's example. Luther then extrapolates how God cast Satan from his presence due to sin and that Satan henceforth sought the destruction of all creation. The language in 2:1 communicates, in Luther's estimation, that all of creation is "to be in active

143. Calvin, *Institutes* 1.13.22.
144. Heiko Oberman, *Luther: Man between God and the Devil* (New Haven: Yale University Press, 1989).
145. Oberman, *Luther*, 106.
146. LW 1:61.
147. LW 1:67.

military service, to fight for us continually against the devil, as well as against men, and to serve us and be of use to us."[148] In this manner, Luther argues that creation in its most perfected and finished form before the fall was itself God's army against Satan.

It was only fitting, Luther speculates, that the fall occurred on the Sabbath day just as "Satan disturbs the Sabbath of the church when the Word is being taught."[149] Not coincidently, the early modern witch craze that engulfed most of Europe was known to identify witch and demoniac activity with the evening of the Sabbath as a stark corruption of the intended purpose of the day.[150] Certainly there were many layers to Luther's point then. Christ was resurrected on the Sabbath; the Sabbath was given to the church to bring spiritual restoration, and this would ultimately lead to eternal life, as was first intended before Satan caused the fall.[151]

Conclusion

In their teachings on Gen. 1–2, Luther and Calvin never turn a blind eye to the exegetical conversations of the past. They engage with ancient philosophy, church fathers, medieval scholastics, and their contemporaries. At the same time, they prioritize a hermeneutic influenced by the historical and grammatical methods of Renaissance humanism in their quest to reroot theology in the scriptural text first and foremost. And out of this approach emerge two overarching themes regarding Gen. 1–2: the sufficiency of the scriptural text to meet its purpose and the inextricable link between God's providence and paternal goodness.

First, although Protestant Reformers stress the supremacy of Scripture, it is evident in their work on Genesis that they believe neither that Scripture is clear in the sense that all truth is accessible to human reason[152] nor that complete human understanding of Scripture is necessary for salvation.[153] Thus, one of the dominant themes of Luther's Genesis commentary is that "human reason is far too inadequate to be able to gain a perfect knowledge of these matters."[154]

---

148. LW 1:74.
149. LW 1:70.
150. See Brian P. Levack, ed. *The Oxford Handbook of Witchcraft in Early Modern Europe and Colonial America* (Oxford: Oxford University Press, 2013), 99.
151. LW 1:80.
152. LW 1:19.
153. Luther is critical of scholasticism for speculation over unnecessary matters such as angel folklore. LW 1:18, 22–23.
154. LW 1:42.

The supremacy of scriptural truth over human understanding is particularly evident in their interpretations where Luther teaches that incomprehensible matters should lead the reader to "admit our lack of knowledge rather than either wickedly deny them or presumptuously interpret them in conformity with our understanding."[155] Luther models this approach on more than one occasion.[156]

Additionally, while Luther consistently engages with the interpretations of philosophers like Aristotle and the church fathers, he is also not afraid to evaluate them as outside the bounds of Moses's teaching and of Scripture.[157] The limits of the text are to be respected. In this way, Luther's engagement with Genesis provides an illustration of the Reformer's larger mission that theology be ultimately bound to Scripture. Regarding the Trinity, he declares, "These are difficult matters, and it is unsafe to go beyond the limit to which the Holy Spirit leads."[158] In fact, the theme of God's incomprehensibility runs throughout his commentary and serves to stress that Scripture offers "sufficient knowledge" for salvation.[159] For that reason, authorial purpose is more valuable than minutiae, since Moses's goal was to communicate God's immeasurable care for humanity from the first days to eternity.[160]

Indeed, the theme of God's providence and goodness is a thread woven through every point of their commentaries on Gen. 1–2. God holding the waters back miraculously on the second day for human life to emerge and thrive is just the beginning of the unfolding salvation story. As Luther would say, "For what is our entire life on this earth but a passage through the Red Sea, where on both sides the sea stood like high walls?"[161] Calvin's emphasis on God's providence and goodness was particularly developed after his debate with Jerome Bolsec in 1551, which propelled him to publish his treatise on eternal predestination in 1552, mentioned in his commentary on Gen. 3. Numerous examples from his commentary reveal how God's sovereign will and paternal care are linked. Thus, though the sun is normally required to bring forth vegetation from the earth,[162] God's power is shown in that reproduction could not have happened apart from the command of God's

155. LW 1:30.
156. Luther acknowledges his lack of knowledge about the movement of light (LW 1:19) and division of the waters (LW 1:28).
157. LW 1:28; cf. LW 1:19.
158. LW 1:17. The incomprehensibility of God was an important theme here. See also LW 1:18 and LW 1:33.
159. LW 1:18.
160. LW 1:36.
161. LW 1:35.
162. Calvin, *Genesis*, 1:82.

Word. Vegetation, meanwhile, provides for the sustaining of life.[163] Thus God's paternal care of humanity is manifest in the fact that the world is filled with everything humanity could ever need, and even so before humanity was created.[164] In fact, in their description of creation, Luther and Calvin use the metaphor of a well-built house sourced with everything sufficient for living.[165] From the very first acts, God's goodness is revealed as the all-powerful source of all good things.

Although Luther and Calvin cannot escape the looming impact of the fall in Gen. 3, nonetheless, Gen. 1–2 taught them that by God's power and his goodness, human life is sustained, restored, and promised anew. In the words of Calvin, "Thus we are instructed to seek from God alone whatever is necessary for us, and in the very use of his gifts, we are to exercise ourselves in meditating on his goodness and paternal care."[166]

For Further Reading

Gordon, Bruce. *Calvin*. New Haven: Yale University Press, 2009.

Hillerbrand, Hans J. *Oxford Encyclopedia of the Reformation*. Oxford: Oxford University Press, 1996.

Kolb, Robert. *Martin Luther and the Enduring Word of God: The Wittenberg School and Its Scripture-Centered Proclamation*. Grand Rapids: Baker Academic, 2016.

Maxfield, John A. *Luther's Lectures on Genesis and the Formation of Evangelical Identity*. Sixteenth Century Essays and Studies 80. Kirksville, MO: Truman State University Press, 2008.

McKim, Donald K., ed. *Calvin and the Bible*. Oxford: Oxford University Press, 2006.

McNutt, Jennifer Powell, and David Lauber, eds. *The People's Book: The Reformation and the Bible*. Downers Grove, IL: IVP Academic, 2017.

Schreiner, Susan E. *The Theater of His Glory: Nature and the Natural Order in the Thought of John Calvin*. Grand Rapids: Baker Academic, 1995.

Selderhuis, Herman J., ed. *The Calvin Handbook*. Grand Rapids: Eerdmans, 2009.

Wengert, Timothy. *Reading the Bible with Martin Luther: An Introductory Guide*. Grand Rapids: Baker Academic, 2013.

163. The creation of the sun and moon is evidence of God's "unbounded goodness." Calvin, *Genesis*, 1:85.
164. Calvin writes, "Thus man was rich before he was born." *Genesis*, 1:26.
165. LW 1:72. Calvin uses the same metaphor to stress the abundance of God's blessing "as if the whole house were well supplied and filled with its furniture" (*Genesis*, 1:103).
166. Calvin, *Genesis*, 1:98.

Primary Texts in Print

Calvin, John. *Commentaries on the First Book of Moses, Called Genesis*. Translated by John King. Calvin's Commentaries 1. Repr., Grand Rapids: Baker Books, 2003.

Calvin, John. *Institutes of the Christian Religion*. Edited by John T. McNeil. London: SCM, 1961.

Luther, Martin. *Lectures on Genesis: Chapters 1–5*. In LW 1:v–387.

Luther, Martin. *Martin Luther's Basic Theological Writings*. Edited by Timothy E. Lull and William R. Russell. 3rd ed. Minneapolis: Fortress, 2012.

Thompson, John L., ed. *Genesis 1–11*. Reformation Commentary on Scripture: Old Testament 1. Downers Grove, IL: IVP Academic, 2012.

Primary Texts Online

1. John Calvin, *Institutes of the Christian Religion*
   http://oll.libertyfund.org/titles/calvin-the-institutes-of-the-christian-religion
2. John Calvin, *Commentary on Genesis*
   http://www.ccel.org/ccel/calvin/calcom01
3. Martin Luther, *Commentary on Genesis*
   https://archive.org/details/commentaryongene02luth
   http://www.gutenberg.org/files/27978/27978-h/27978-h.htm

See Also

4. Digital Library of Classic Protestant Texts
   https://alexanderstreet.com/products/digital-library-classic-protestant-texts
5. Early English Books Online
   https://eebo.chadwyck.com/home
6. Internet Archive Digital Library
   https://archive.org/
7. Post-Reformation Digital Library
   http://www.prdl.org

10

Rediscovery of the Ancient Near East and Its Implications for Genesis 1–2

David T. Tsumura

Among ancient languages, Greek, Hebrew, Aramaic, and their close relatives were never forgotten. This became especially important in nineteenth-century Europe when Egyptian and Mesopotamian texts were copied or brought to Europe and deciphered and read. The most important languages deciphered were Egyptian and Akkadian (the Semitic language of Babylonia and Assyria that was the lingua franca of the second millennium BCE). This provided a direct source for examining the thoughts of ancient Near Eastern (ANE) peoples.[1]

The cuneiform texts from Mesopotamia are particularly important for the study of Genesis. In 1872 George Smith noticed "references to the Creation" on one text fragment in the British Museum and allusions to it in other fragments. Intrigued, Smith embarked on a search to find other "mythological tablets," as he called them. His persistence paid off. Smith soon found half of a curious tablet of the "Chaldean account of the deluge" in an Akkadian

---

1. See Cyrus H. Gordon, *Forgotten Scripts: Their Ongoing Discovery and Decipherment*, rev. ed. (1968; repr., New York: Basic Books, 1982).

text known as the Gilgamesh Epic.[2] He presented his findings to the Society of Biblical Archaeology, pointing out that the epic had many affinities to the account of the deluge in Gen. 6–9. For comparison with Gen. 1–2, the most important text is the Babylonian creation myth, Enuma Elish.[3] Such discoveries could not be ignored by OT studies. Some made hasty uncritical comparisons that emphasized only similarities, as did Delitzsch's "Babel und Bibel" lectures of 1902, characterized by "Pan-Babylonianism," the idea that everything in the OT came from Mesopotamia.[4]

Many Christians were shocked by the similarities between the ANE literatures and the OT, and some scholars—often in reaction to the excesses of the "parallelomania"—downplayed the parallels to the point of ignoring clear, informative correlations, producing a type of "parallelophobia."[5] However, one cannot ignore the fact that those ancient literatures came from the same cultural context (milieu) as Genesis. We must recognize that though these texts arose from a variety of cultural conditions, much of the ANE shared many cultural concepts, including family, life, death, kingship, labor, war, and relationship with the divine.

Genesis and Ancient Near East Mythology

However, though there are indeed similarities, a careful examination of each in its own context shows that the relationship is superficial in many cases. Ever since Hermann Gunkel's famous book *Schöpfung und Chaos in Urzeit und Endzeit* (1895),[6] many scholars have taken it for granted that Gen. 1 was

2. George Smith, *The Chaldean of Genesis: Containing the Description of the Creation, the Fall of Man, the Deluge, the Tower of Babel, the Times of the Patriarchs, and Nimrud; Babylonian Fables, and Legends of the Gods; From the Cuneiform Inscriptions* (New York: Scribner, 1876), 3.

3. The most thorough treatment of the Mesopotamian creation texts, including Enuma Elish, is W. G. Lambert, *Babylonian Creation Myths*, Mesopotamian Civilizations 16 (Winona Lake, IN: Eisenbrauns, 2013).

4. A school of thought trumpeted principally by Hugo Winckler, Peter Jensen, and Alfred Jeremias: Winckler, *Geschichte Babyloniens und Assyriens* (Leipzig: Pfeiffer, 1892); Jensen, *Assyrisch-Babylonische Mythen und Epen*, Keilinschriftliche Bibliothek 6 (Berlin: Ruether & Reichard, 1900); Jeremias, *Das Alte Testamente im lichte des alten Orients* (Leipzig: Hinrichs, 1916).

5. See K. Lawson Younger, "The 'Contextual Method': Some West Semitic Reflections," in *Archival Documents from the Biblical World*, vol. 3 of *COS*, ed. W. W. Hallo and K. L. Younger (Leiden: Brill, 2003), xxxvi–xxxvii. See also Samuel Sandmel, "Parallelomania," *JBL* 81 (1962): 1–13.

6. Hermann Gunkel, *Schöpfung und Chaos in Urzeit und Endzeit: Eine religionsgeschichtliche Untersuchung über Genesis 1 und Ap. Jon 12* (Göttingen: Vandenhoeck & Ruprecht, 1895).

SIDEBAR 10.1

Enuma Elish on Creation and Marduk

[1]When on high no name was given to heaven,
[2]Nor below was the netherworld called by name,
[3]Primeval Apsu was their progenitor,
[4]And matrix-Tiamat was she who bore them all,

[5]They were mingling their waters together,
[6]No cane brake was intertwined nor thicket matted close.
[7]When no gods at all had been brought forth,
[8]None called by names, none destinies ordained,
[9]Then were the gods formed within them (the two).[a]

                                                      1.1–9

[103]He subdued her and snuffed out her life,
[104]He flung down her carcass, he took his stand upon it.

[105]After the vanguard had slain Tiamat,
[106]He scattered her forces, he dispersed her host.[b]

....

[126]Valiant Marduk having attained what Nudimmud desired,
[127]He made firm his hold over the captured gods,
[128]Then turned back to Tiamat whom he had captured.
[129]The Lord trampled upon the frame of Tiamat,

[130]With his merciless mace he crushed her skull.
[131]He cut open the arteries of her blood,
[132]He let the North Wind bear (it) away as glad tidings.
[133]When his fathers saw, they rejoiced and were glad,
[134]They brought him gifts and presents.

[135]He calmed down. Then the Lord was inspecting her carcass,
[136]That he might divide (?) the monstrous lump and fashion artful things.
[137]He split her in two, like a fish for drying,
[138]Half of her he set up and made as a cover, heaven.

                                                 4.103–6, 126–38

a. Hallo and Younger, *COS* (Leiden: Brill, 1997), 1:391, lines on tablet 1.
b. Hallo and Younger, *COS*, 1:398, lines on tablet 4.

based on the Babylonian creation myth Enuma Elish. Others, even if they do not go so far, accept some relationship. The main basis for this claim is Gunkel's assumption that the Hebrew word *təhôm*, "the deep," in Gen. 1:2 was borrowed from the name of the *chaos* dragon of the myth, Tiamat. In it, the storm god Marduk, the chief Babylonian deity, battles and defeats the sea goddess Tiamat and her hoard of creatures, establishing the cosmos.

However, linguistically speaking, such a borrowing is impossible. The word *təhôm* could not have been derived from the name *Tiamat*. Rather, the Hebrew *təhôm*—together with the Ugaritic *thm*, the Akkadian *tiāmtu*, the Arabic *tihāmat*, and the Eblaite *ti-à-ma-tum/tihām(a)tum*—is simply a reflection of the common Semitic term **tihām*, meaning a large body of water,[7] while the name *Tiamat* is just a personified Akkadian form of the term *tiāmtu*. So Gen. 1 and Enuma Elish, which was composed primarily to exalt Marduk in the pantheon of Babylon, have no direct relation to each other.

It is sometimes claimed that just as Marduk made the cosmos out of Tiamat's carcass, which could be called "creating order out of chaos," Genesis also portrays creating order out of chaos. However, the very different creation by divine fiat, as in Genesis, is unique in the ANE; furthermore, the creation of light as the first act of creation appears only in Genesis.[8]

It should be noted that the so-called chaos sea-dragon, Tiamat, of Enuma Elish was not *chaotic* in the real beginning. Enuma Elish depicts a harmonious mingling of Apsu and Tiamat at the beginning of the story, and there is nothing "chaotic" or "in confusion" until the storm god Marduk fights with Tiamat.[9] It seems the word "chaos" first became associated with Genesis in a negative way when Gunkel used the term *Chaoskampf* ("chaos combat") with reference to the conflict between Marduk and Tiamat.[10]

In my opinion we should stop using the term "chaos" when dealing with the biblical concept of "creation," meaning cosmic origin, because neither *təhôm* ("the deep") nor *tōhû wābōhû* (traditionally "without form and void")

7. See David T. Tsumura, *The Earth and the Waters in Genesis 1 and 2* (Sheffield: Sheffield Academic, 1989), 45–52; Tsumura, *Creation and Destruction: A Reappraisal of the* Chaoskampf *Theory in the Old Testament* (Winona Lake, IN: Eisenbrauns, 2005), 44–47.

8. W. G. Lambert, "A New Look at the Babylonian Background of Genesis," *JTS* 16 (1965): 287–300.

9. W. G. Lambert, "Creation in the Bible and the Ancient Near East," in *Creation and Chaos: A Reconsideration of Hermann Gunkel's* Chaoskampf *Hypothesis*, ed. JoAnn Scurlock and Richard H. Beal (Winona Lake, IN: Eisenbrauns, 2013), 46.

10. See Hermann Gunkel, *Creation and Chaos in the Primeval Era and the Eschaton: A Religio-historical Study of Genesis 1 and Revelation 12*, trans. K. William Whitney (Grand Rapids: Eerdmans, 2006), 76–77. Whitney notes that Gunkel himself did not use the term *Chaoskampf* in his original edition.

in Gen. 1:2 has anything to do with the concept of *chaos*.[11] In fact, the LXX translator(s) did not use χάος for Gen. 1:2 even though he (they) could have.[12] Furthermore, in Enuma Elish, Tiamat is split into the heaven and earth, while Gen. 1:2 is concerned *only* with "the earth." It is inconsistent to at times use "chaos" for the undistinguished initial state of the cosmos (as in Greek[13] and Chinese[14] myths as well as in Enuma Elish) and at other times to use "chaos" only for the initial state of the earth (as in Gen. 1:2). Moreover, the motif of the storm-sea conflict as the conflict between the storm god Baal and the sea god Yam seems to be West Semitic in origin.[15]

The main argument for seeing conflict between God and chaos in Gen. 1 seems to be this: In Enuma Elish, creation was the result of battle, so there must be a battle in the background of Gen. 1:2 also. There are myths involving battles among gods (*theomachy*), as in the Canaanite Baal myth; but in the ANE, creation and battle (conflict) are associated *only* in the *Chaoskampf* of Enuma Elish, so there is no reason they should be associated in Genesis.[16]

Sometimes one hears that rather than being derived from a myth, the creation account of Gen. 1 functions as an antimythological polemic in its use of the terms (1) *təhôm*, "deep" (Gen. 1:2); (2) *tannînîm*, "the great sea creatures" (Gen. 1:21); (3) "two great lights" for the sun and the moon, and so forth (Gen. 1:16). Nicolas Wyatt particularly promotes a polemic interpretation for the term *təhôm*. According to him, Gen. 1:2 was "a counter" to the claims for Marduk made in Enuma Elish, and the Hebrew *təhôm* was "a deliberate counterpart to Ti'āmat" of Babylonian cosmology.[17] However, this is doubtful.

---

11. Tsumura, *Earth and the Waters*, 17–65; Tsumura, *Creation and Destruction*, 9–57. See Rebecca S. Watson, *Chaos Uncreated: A Reassessment of the Theme of "Chaos" in the Hebrew Bible* (Berlin: de Gruyter, 2005). Mark S. Smith now agrees that the translation "chaos" should be avoided. *The Priestly Vision of Genesis 1* (Minneapolis: Fortress, 2010), 234.

12. David T. Tsumura, "The Doctrine of Creation *ex nihilo* and the Translation of *tōhû wābōhû*," in *Pentateuchal Traditions in the Late Second Temple Period: Proceedings of the International Workshop in Tokyo, August 28–31, 2007*, ed. A. Moriya and G. Hata (Leiden: Brill, 2012), 18, 18n49.

13. E.g., Hesiod's "chaos," which is "a moving, formless mass from which the cosmos and the gods originated." See Karen Sonik, "From Hesiod's Abyss to Ovid's *rudis indigestaque moles*: Chaos and Cosmos in the Babylonian 'Epic of Creation,'" in Scurlock and Beal, *Creation and Chaos*, 5–12.

14. The Chinese word is *hundun* (混沌).

15. See Tsumura, *Creation and Destruction*, 38–41.

16. David T. Tsumura, "The 'Chaoskampf' Motif in Ugaritic and Hebrew Literatures," in *Le Royaume d'Ougarit de la Crète à l'Euphrate: Nouveaux axes de recherche*, ed. Jean-Marc Michaud (Sherbrooke, QC: GGC, 2007), 499.

17. Nicolas Wyatt, "Distinguishing Wood and Trees in the Waters: Creation in Biblical Thought," in *Creation, Chaos, Monotheism, Yahwism: Conversations on Canaanite and Biblical Themes*, ed. R. S. Watson and A. H. W. Curtis (New York: de Gruyter, forthcoming); Gerhard Hasel, "The Polemic Nature of the Genesis Cosmology," *EvQ* 46 (1974): 81–102; also Peter

One wonders why the Hebrew author would use *thm*, the Northwest Semitic (e.g., Hebrew and Ugaritic) term for the subterranean "fresh" water,[18] to correspond to *ti'amatum*, the Akkadian term for the sea. For a Hebrew native who knew something of Canaanite mythology, the term for a god-defying sea monster was *yām*, "sea," as we can see in Ps. 74:13, where the sea (*yām*) is described as a sea dragon. This is "Canaanite," not "Mesopotamian," since *yām*, *tannînīm*, and *Leviathan* (Ps. 74:13–14) are all Canaanite terms, as can be seen by their Ugaritic cognates *ym*, *tnn*, and *ltn* (*KTU* 1.5 i 1–3). The term *təhôm* does not appear in the psalm at all. If Gen. 1 were a polemic against Tiamat, its author would have used a form such as *t'mh* or *t'mt* based on the Akkadian proper noun directly, or perhaps have used *yām*, "Sea," the enemy of the storm god Baal, who was the counterpart of Marduk. But instead he used the meaning-wise unrelated *təhôm*.[19]

Another claim is that the term *tannînīm* (v. 21, "sea creatures" [ESV]; "sea monsters" [NRSV]) is a polemic against Canaanite mythological traditions, for the Ugaritic *tnn* ("dragon")[20] refers to a sea monster who is an associate of the sea dragon Yam ("Sea") in the Ugaritic Baal myths. This is possible, but I think it more likely that *tnn* is essentially a natural reality—a large sea creature, such as a whale—and is used in this meaning in Gen. 1, while the dragon in the Ugaritic myth is a personification. In Ps. 74:14, on the other hand, *tnn* may be a metaphorization of the originally Canaanite mythological term. In other words, the meaning of the term in myths had been ossified,[21] or fossilized, and here the term is used metaphorically for explaining poetically a completely different reality, that is, the Lord's enemy in the *divine battle*.[22]

The use of the term "two great lights" in Gen. 1:16 instead of the ordinary terms for the sun and moon, *šemeš* and *yārēaḥ*, seems to be intentional for a different reason. It does seem that the description of the sun in Ps. 19:4–6, for instance, is polemic. But in Gen. 1:16 the author may have used "lights"

Enns, *The Evolution of Adam: What the Bible Does and Doesn't Say about Human Origins* (Grand Rapids: Brazos, 2012), 41.

18. See Tsumura, *Creation and Destruction*, 52–53, 136, 139.

19. See D. T. Tsumura, "Response to N. Wyatt, 'Distinguishing Wood and Trees in the Waters: Creation in Biblical Thought'" in *Creation, Chaos, Monotheism, Yahwism*, forthcoming.

20. *DULAT*, 873.

21. Arthur Gibson, *Biblical Semantic Logic: A Preliminary Analysis* (Oxford: Blackwell, 1981), 110–25, 133–39.

22. David T. Tsumura, "The Creation Motif in Psalm 74:12–14? A Reappraisal of the Theory of the Dragon Myth," *JBL* 134 (2015): 547–55, here 551–53. For a detailed description of "Chaoskampf," "theomachy," and "divine battle," see D. T. Tsumura, "Chaos and Chaoskampf in the Bible: Is 'Chaos' a Suitable Term to Describe Creation or Conflict in the Bible?," in *Creation, Chaos, Monotheism, Yahwism*, forthcoming.

apologetically or defensively because "sun" and "moon" would have been associated with the deities in the Semitic world.

But in general, use of originally mythological terms in the Bible does not necessarily indicate the introduction of mythological motifs. In a language semantically dominated by polytheistic thinking, any description of biblical truths or even natural phenomena will reflect some polytheistic terms. For example, even a monotheist Japanese Christian will use the fossilized word *kami-nari* (lit., "god's sounding") for the natural phenomenon of "thunder."

The Relationship between Genesis 1 and 2

The historical-critical approach to the Bible[23] has long advocated that Gen. 1–2 contains a "doublet" of creation stories of different origins, with two independent and mutually contradictory cosmologies. The first is the priestly (P) account from the postexilic period, characterized by use of the divine name Elohim, while the second is an earlier account (J), characterized by use of Yahweh.[24]

However, when one takes a closer look at both accounts, it is evident that they are not two "parallel" versions of the same or similar "creation" stories: the theme and purpose of each is unique. Castellino distinguishes Gen. 1, "un vrai recit de creation" ("a true story of creation"), from Gen. 2, which in a strict sense is not a creation story but "un texte d'organisation" ("an organizational text") and serves as an "introduction" to Gen. 3.[25] A story without any reference to the sun, the moon and the stars, or the sea is not a true cosmological account. Genesis 1, which locates the creation of humanity as the grand climax of the creation of the cosmos, is not of the same literary genre as Gen. 2–3, which is concerned with the immediate situation of humanity on the earth.

Both chapters, however, do reflect essentially the same cosmology. In Gen. 1:2 the initial situation of the "world" is described in linguistically positive terms as an unproductive and uninhabited (*tōhû wābōhû*)[26] "earth," totally

23. In the special issue of *VT* in 2013, republishing ten major articles in the history of the journal, editor-in-chief Jan Joosten writes, "The days of the hegemony of one school—German historical criticism during much of the nineteenth and early twentieth centuries—are gone."

24. For a useful summary of critical discussions, see Gordon J. Wenham, *Genesis 1–15* (Waco: Word, 1987), xxv–xlii; see also Wenham's response to Kenton L. Spark's article "Genesis 1–11 as Ancient Historiography," in *Genesis: History, Fiction, or Neither? Three Views on the Bible's Earliest Chapters*, ed. C. Halton (Grand Rapids: Zondervan, 2015), 101–9.

25. G. Castellino, "Les origines de la civilisation selon les textes bibliques et les textes cunéiformes," in *Volume du Congres: Strasbourg 1956* (Leiden: Brill, 1957), 128–29.

26. See the following discussion under "Treatment of Days: Desolate and Empty."

covered by an expanse of water, while in 2:5–6 the initial state of the "earth" is described by the negative expressions "no vegetation" and "no man." The traditional critical (diachronic) view is that the earth-waters relationship in Gen. 1:2 ("watery chaos") is totally different from that in 2:5–6 ("dry chaos").[27] However, in Gen. 2:6 the underground *ʾēd*-water was flooding the whole area of the "land" (*ʾădāmâ*), but not the entire earth (*ʾereṣ*) as in Gen. 1:2,[28] so it describes a stage, as in Gen. 1:9–10.

The creation of humanity is described similarly in Gen. 1 and 2. It is sometimes argued that these two accounts are contradictory. For example, it appears that in Gen. 1 the woman was created at the same time and in the same manner as the man, while in Gen. 2 the woman was created later. However, Gen. 1:27, which constitutes a three-line poetic parallelism, describes human beings, both male and female, simply as created in the *imago Dei*, not necessarily as being created at the same time.

> So God created man in his own image,
>   in the image of God he created him;
>   male and female he created them. (ESV)

The two stories view the creation of human beings from two different perspectives. The first presents their nature and function in the framework of the entire creation of the world and as the Creator's representatives on earth; the second explains their relationship with each other and with the other creatures in their physical environment.[29] This is the discourse-grammatical phenomenon of "scope change," that is, "zooming in from an overall perspective to a close-up, with a corresponding shift in reference."[30] Therefore, the flow of discourse runs from Gen. 1 to Gen. 2–3. Since biblical narratives such as Gen. 1–2 were aural discourses, written to be heard, it is not surprising that they are characterized by repetition and correspondence, like poetic literature.

27. See Gerhard von Rad, *Genesis* (Philadelphia: Westminster, 1961, 1963, 1972), 76–77; see also Benedikt Otzen, "The Use of Myth in Genesis," in *Myths in the Old Testament*, ed. Benedikt Otzen, Hans Gottlieb, and Knud Jeppesen (London: SCM, 1980), 40–41.

28. Tsumura, *Creation and Destruction*, 196.

29. Umberto Cassuto, *A Commentary on the Book of Genesis: From Adam to Noah* (1944; repr., Jerusalem: Magnes, 1961), 89–92; see also Kenneth A. Kitchen, *Ancient Orient and Old Testament* (Chicago: InterVarsity, 1966), 116–17. For the pattern in the genealogical doublets, see Richard S. Hess, "Genesis 1–2 in Its Literary Context," *TynBul* 41 (1990): 146–47.

30. Joseph E. Grimes, *The Thread of Discourse* (Hague: Mouton, 1975), 46–47. See also Robert E. Longacre, *The Grammar of Discourse* (New York: Plenum, 1983), 119, 122; Longacre, *Joseph: A Story of Divine Providence; A Text Theoretical and Textlinguistic Analysis of Genesis 37 and 39–48* (Winona Lake, IN: Eisenbrauns, 1989); Robert D. Bergen, ed., *Biblical Hebrew and Discourse Linguistics* (Dallas: SIL, 1994).

Treatment of Days

How one should explain the meaning of the "days" of creation has been a contentious issue, especially in its relationship with scientific fact since the era of evolution. It may be wise to distinguish between the exegetical issue, what the term *yôm* means, and the apologetic issue of what the term refers to, either twenty-four hours or a longer term. It is not helpful for understanding the meaning of the text if we ask a wrong question of the biblical text.

In the Beginning

The Hebrew *bərēʾšît* in 1:1 corresponds to the *en archē* of John 1:1 (both literally "in beginning"), yet here it is not the absolute beginning but the beginning of the created world. Traditionally, the Hebrew phrase has been taken as an absolute phrase, "In the beginning God created" (KJV, RSV, ESV, NIV, REB, etc.).[31] However, the Hebrew *rēʾšît* without a definite article (cf. Hosea 9:10) should be taken as a construct noun followed by a finite verb *bārāʾ*, like the so-called *awat iqbu* ("a word he said") construction found in Akkadian and Ugaritic.[32] Literally, it may be translated, "In the beginning of God's creating the heavens and the earth."

Creation accounts in the ANE often began with subordinate, temporal clauses, as in the case of Enuma Elish. Hence translations such as "When God began to create heaven and earth" (NJPS), though not wrong, have created the wrong impression that Gen. 1:1 has a close similarity to the initial part of Enuma Elish. But the grammatical argument that Gen. 1:1 can be taken as a temporal clause[33] ("In the beginning when . . .") does not support any conceptual affinities between Enuma Elish and Gen. 1. It simply means that the *awat iqbu* construction is a common Semitic phraseology. God created, that is, caused to exist, the entire cosmos (merismus: *heavens and earth*) in the beginning. So time began, or was created, together with the cosmos.[34] Since Gen. 1:2 is a parenthetical verse, Gen. 1:1 ("in the beginning of God's creating . . .") depends on the main clause, which begins with the first narrative

---

31. For the various views, see Wenham, *Genesis 1–15*, 11–13; Claus Westermann, *Genesis 1–11: A Commentary* (Minneapolis: Augsburg, 1984), 93–97; John Day, *From Creation to Babel: Studies in Genesis 1–11* (London: Bloomsbury, 2013), 6–7.

32. See Cyrus H. Gordon, *Ugaritic Textbook* (Rome: Pontifical Biblical Institute, 1965), §8.16 (56 and note).

33. For this view, see the most recent argument: Robert D. Holmstedt, "Restrictive Syntax of Gen i, 1," *VT* 58 (2008): 56–67.

34. See Augustine, *Conf.* 11.

past form ("and he said") in Gen. 1:3. The phrase "God created the heavens
and the earth" appears in Gen. 2:1–3 in reverse order: "the heavens and the
earth—God created." This marks Gen. 1:1–2:3 as a literary unit. The merismatic word pair the *heavens and the earth* (1:1) refers to the entire cosmos,[35]
and this verse is a summary statement for the subsequent narrative. In other
words, the author does not intend to suggest that "the heavens and the earth"
in Gen. 1:1 is something different from the "heaven" (1:8) and the "earth"
(1:10) in the following narrative.

The First Day

The "first day" (*yôm 'eḥād*) is literally "day one." Here "one" is used for
"first," as it is in Gen. 2:11 and in a Ugaritic ritual text.[36] From the second day
onward, the numbers are ordinal ("second," etc.). This unusual use of "one"
may reflect some kind of liturgical practice. C. John Collins even suggests
that the purpose of Gen. 1:1–2:3 is "almost liturgical."[37] He explains that
the passage "celebrates as a great achievement God's work of fashioning the
world as a suitable place for humans to live." This view may be supported by
the six days' framework of creative activities and the ceasing (*šbt*) of these
activities on the "seventh" day, which is to become the Sabbath day (see *šabbāt*
in Exod. 20:10). On this day human beings as the *imago Dei* are invited to
worship the Creator, sanctifying the day.

While there were seven-day festivals in Israel (Exod. 12; 23; 29; 34; Lev.
8; 23; Num. 28; 29; 31; Deut. 16; 2 Chron. 7; 30; 35, and so on),[38] this does
not necessarily mean that Gen. 1 is a late writing, since seven-day liturgies
are well known in the ANE, as in the Emar ritual calendars of the second
millennium BCE.[39] Thus, although the Sabbath became a major concern of
Judaism, one cannot conclude that Gen. 1 was written to teach the Jewish
people about the Sabbath.

Creation Framework

The six-day framework of creation seems to have the following literary
structure.

35. See Tsumura, *Creation and Destruction*, 63–69.
36. See J.-M. de Tarragon, *Le Culte à Ugarit* (Paris: J. Gabalda, 1980), 89–90.
37. C. John Collins, *Did Adam and Eve Really Exist? Who They Were and Why You Should
Care* (Wheaton: Crossway, 2011), 53–54.
38. Also note that the funeral ritual lasted for seven days in Gen. 50:10, *KTU* 1.161, etc.
39. Daniel E. Fleming, "The Israelite Festival Calendar and Emar's Ritual Archive," *RB*
106 (1999): 161–74.

Creation of		Creation of
Day 1 *light*		Day 4 *two great lights and stars*
Day 2 *heavens*		Day 5 *sea creatures and birds*
Day 3 *land and seas*	Day 6	*land creatures and human beings*

According to one theory, places are created on days 1 through 3, and their corresponding inhabitants are created on days 4 through 6.[40] However, such correspondences do not work well, for sea creatures (day 5) live not in the *heavens* (day 2) but in the *seas* (day 3). More important is the fact that in day 3 the *land* (*'ereṣ*) is created, and in day 6 its inhabitants are created, namely, "plants," "animals," and "human beings." On both days the announcement of the divine word "and God said" is made twice.[41] So day 3 is the climax of preparing the ideal setting for humankind, and day 6 the grand climax of God's creative activities. Thus, as the result of six days of creation, the earth becomes a productive and inhabited land with vegetation and animals, on which human beings are finally created and placed as the *imago Dei*.[42]

The Seventh Day

The ANE poets sometimes describe temples as a place for the deity to rest. Batto therefore sees in Gen. 2:2–3 a theme of God's "resting after completing the work of creation."[43] However, the Hebrew verb *šbt* of Gen. 2:2 normally means "to cease," here from creation activities, not "to rest," though in Exod. 20:11 God is said to have rested (*nwḥ*), which is the result of the cessation.

Cosmology

While the ancient Hebrews held a cosmology different from the modern scientific view, they seem to have had one similar to the ANE cosmologies. Yet their similarities are sometimes overemphasized.[44] The similarities are often

40. See Wenham, *Genesis 1–15*, 7. It was W. H. Griffith Thomas who formalized Aquinas's observations of three days of forming and three days of filling. Thomas's outline has found its way into many study Bibles and commentaries. *Genesis: A Devotional Commentary* (Grand Rapids: Eerdmans, 1946), 29.

41. Wenham, *Genesis 1–15*, 6.

42. See below under the heading "Imago Dei: *Royal Figures.*"

43. Bernard F. Batto, "The Sleeping God: An Ancient Near Eastern Motif of Divine Sovereignty," in *In the Beginning: Essays on Creation Motifs in the Ancient Near East and the Bible*, Siphrut 9 (Winona Lake, IN: Eisenbrauns, 2013), 148.

44. Enns, *Evolution of Adam*; John H. Walton, *Genesis 1 as Ancient Cosmology* (Winona Lake, IN: Eisenbrauns, 2011).

due to linguistic similarities with a metaphorical purpose, as in the case of *tnn* and "fossilized" expressions such as "to crush the heads of Leviathan" (cf. Ps. 74:14 NJPS). Furthermore, terms such as "foundations" and "pillars" of the earth appear only in poetical texts of the Bible, and we see the term "Sheol" only in a collocation with verbs such as "to descend" (*yrd*). They are not to be taken as indicating the Hebrew understanding of the structure of the cosmos. They are simply idioms in which the original meaning of each element is already "ossified" or fossilized.[45]

The Meaning of Bārā'

The Hebrew term *bārā'* is usually understood as "created," but recently E. van Wolde and her followers have claimed that it means "to separate."[46] Based on this, Nicolas Wyatt holds that *bārā'* "implies, in the process of separation, the pre-existence of that thing or those things that are separated."[47] Similarly, John Walton's "functional" theory holds that the Gen. 1 creation story has nothing to do with material origins but simply describes the functional origins of the cosmos. He interprets Gen. 1:1 as, "In the initial period, God brought cosmic functions into existence."[48] However, Wardlaw's recent detailed study concludes that the *qal* and *niphal* of *br'* (*bārā'* is *qal*) mean "to create, do (something new)," while only the *piel* means "to cut, hew."[49] Furthermore, the use of *bārā'* with terms such as *'śh*, "to make," and *yṣr*, "to form," in Amos 4:13; Isa. 43:1; 45:18, and so forth, hardly supports van Wolde's semantic argument, and her etymological argument has gained little support among scholars.[50] Therefore, Walton's functional theory has no firm basis.

---

45. Similarly, in Japanese Christian terminology, the term *yomi* (= Sheol) in the phrases *yomi-gaeri* (lit., "return from Sheol") and *yomi-ni-kudaru* (lit., "to go down to Sheol") is used with the case of Jesus's death and resurrection. The term *kami-nari*, mentioned above, and the phrase in the hymn "Daredemo tadorituku ookawa" ("the great river [= the Styx] which all eventually reach") do not mean that Japanese Christians are under the influence of Shinto or Buddhist cosmology.

46. E. van Wolde: "to separate" (see "Why the Verb *bārā'* Does Not Mean 'to Create' in Genesis 1.1–2.4a," *JSOT* 34 [2009]: 3–23), as opposed to B. Becking and M. C. A. Korpel's suggestion "to construct" in "To Create, to Separate or to Construct: An Alternative . . . in Gen 1:1–2:4a," *JHebS* 10, no. 3 (2010): 1–21. Walton has a detailed analysis of the verb *bārā'* in *Genesis 1 as Ancient Cosmology*, 127–33.

47. Nicolas Wyatt, "Distinguishing Wood and Trees in the Waters," in *Creation, Chaos, Monotheism, Yahwism*, forthcoming.

48. Walton, *Genesis 1 as Ancient Cosmology*, 133; see my review: David T. Tsumura, review of *Genesis 1 as Ancient Cosmology*, by J. H. Walton, *JAOS* 135 (2015): 356–57.

49. Terrance R. Wardlaw, "The Meaning of ברא in Genesis 1:1–2:3," *VT* 64 (2014): 502–13.

50. For example, Day supports the traditional view "to create" in *From Creation to Babel*, 5–6.

Desolate and Empty

With the phrase "and the earth" (Gen. 1:2), the narrator focuses on the "earth," putting the "heavens" aside for the time being. The *təhôm*-water ("deep") is part of the "earth" of Gen. 1:1. The OT describes the cosmos as either bipartite, "heaven and earth" (e.g., Gen. 1:1; Ps. 148), or tripartite, "heaven, earth, and waters" (e.g., Exod. 20:11; Neh. 9:6; Ps. 96:11; 146:6; Hag. 2:6)—but in the latter case the "water(s)" is always "the sea" or the like, never the underground fresh *təhôm*-water. So the *təhôm*-water is part of the "earth"[51] and so is also created by God and under his control. There is no hint of any conflict between God and the *təhôm*-water as there was between Marduk and Tiamat.

The expression *tōhû wābōhû*, which is traditionally translated into English as "without form and void" (RSV) or the like, is often taken as signifying the primeval "chaos" and thus in direct opposition to the "creation." However, the phrase has nothing to do with the primeval chaos; it simply means "emptiness" and refers to the earth in a "bare" state, without vegetation, animals, or human beings. The term *tōhû* basically means "desert" or "wilderness," as in Deut. 32:10. When used to describe locations, it means a "desert-like," "desolate" state. Thus the phrase *tōhû wābōhû* refers to the unproductive and uninhabited earth, the not yet normal earth. The translation "without form and void" (KJV, RSV, NEB), however, is via the LXX ("invisible and unformed") and seems to have been influenced by Platonic philosophy.[52] The Hebrew phrase simply conveys to the audience that the earth was not yet like the earth they knew by experience. Genesis 1:6–10 suggests that the water of *təhôm* in Gen. 1:2 covered all the "earth."[53] This water-covered "earth" is described as empty and dark, but it was not "chaotic."

According to the "gap theory," Satan fell between the first creation (1:1) and the second creation (1:3–5) and as a result the earth became *tōhû wābōhû*. But this lacks exegetical support and furthermore has to take *tōhû wābōhû* as something evil. Similarly, the so-called chaos theory often assumes that *tōhû wābōhû* is a negative element, "chaos," involved in creation. This chaos is, according to Waltke, a "surd" evil that existed before the beginning of the "moral" evil, that is, sin in the human history, and causes natural phenomena

---

51. For this relationship between the "earth" and the *təhôm*-water, see David T. Tsumura, "A 'Hyponymous' Word Pair, *'rṣ* and *thm(t)*, in Hebrew and Ugaritic," *Bib* 69 (1988): 258–69.

52. Plato renders it "invisible and unshaped." Plato, *Tim.*, 50–51. See also Tsumura, "Doctrine of Creation *ex nihilo*," 12, 12n33; Tsumura, *Creation and Destruction*, 9–35.

53. See Tsumura, *Earth and the Waters*, 78–79.

such as tsunamis and volcanic eruptions.[54] However, proposing the existence
of evil on the earth before the "moral" evil is difficult and leads to introducing
some sort of cosmic dualism into the biblical doctrine of creation.

Creation of Waters

The phrase "division in the midst of the waters" (Gen. 1:6) suggests that
water had been created earlier on the second day. The mention of the *təhôm*-
water in Gen. 1:2 does not imply that the water existed before the light,
since any linguistic description is *monodimensional*, in contrast to the *multi-
dimensional*, spatiotemporal reality. The division of water in Gen. 1:7 is often
compared with Marduk's splitting Tiamat's carcass, but that was made into
heaven and earth, not two waters. If there is a parallel to the division of water,
it might be in the description of the residence of the Ugaritic god El as being
in the confluence of "two *thmt*-waters," that is, the boundary between the
sky and the ocean, the ocean horizon.[55]

Creation of the Sea and the Land

And God said, "Let the waters . . . be gathered together into one place, and let
the dry land appear." (Gen. 1:9)

These two events were two sides of the same coin. The uniqueness of Genesis is in its order of commands: the waters' gathering together and the dry
land's appearing, not the other way around as in the cosmogonic myths in
Egypt[56] and Japan, in which a hill or an island appears out of the oceans. In
the creation of the earth, God completely controls the movement of waters.
In Gen. 1:10, the term "seas," *yammîm*, refers to a huge body of waters rather
than to many oceans. This is the first occurrence in the Bible of the term *yām*,
though in its plural form, *yammîm*.

Cosmology and Temple Theology

Recently Walton, following Weinfeld and Levenson, has claimed that as
in the ANE, "the cosmology of Genesis 1 is built on the platform of temple

---

54. Bruce K. Waltke, *Genesis: A Commentary* (Grand Rapids: Zondervan, 2001), 68–69.
For a similar view, see, e.g., Sjoerd L. Bonting, *Chaos Theology: A Revised Creation Theology*
(Ottawa: Saint Paul University Press, 2002).
55. Note that "heaven" and "*thmt*-water" are a Ugaritic word pair (e.g., the compound deity
name, *šmm w thm*, "Heaven-and-Ocean"); *DULAT*, 864.
56. See Westermann, *Genesis 1–11*, 120.

theology: both of these ideas—rest [Gen. 2:2] and the garden [2:8–9]—are integral to the temple theology of the ancient world."[57] He holds that "in Genesis, the entire cosmos can be portrayed as a temple, because the cosmos and temple serve the same functions, that is, to house a deity."[58] Peter Enns holds a similar view, but he assumes that "God's victory over chaos" enabled him to create the world, which is his temple. But Enns makes no distinction between the so-called *Chaoskampf* motif and the *theomachy* for Baal's temple building "after his defeat of Yam."[59] One should note that in Ugaritic myths the god Baal cannot be called a "creator"; he did not make or create anything.[60]

Creation in Gen. 1 has nothing to do with temple building. Even though in poetic texts such as Pss. 18:15; 24:2; 75:3; and Job 38:4 the cosmos is sometimes described using architectural terms as "foundation" and "pillar," the only such term in Gen. 1 is *rāqîaʿ* (vv. 6–8), which can be translated as "firmament," that is, like a dome. Conversely, there is nothing garden-like about Israel's tabernacle or temple, while the main purpose of a garden is to provide food for humans. Eden is said to have become a pattern for describing the Israelite sanctuary, and even the land of Israel.[61] It is indeed possible that "the tabernacle menorah was a stylized tree of life." However, many of the suggested similarities seem suspicious, such as comparing the tunics of animal skins with which God clothed Adam and Eve to the tunics of linen worn by the priests.[62]

Even if, as Lawrence Stager holds, the Temple of Solomon were "a mytho-poetic realization of heaven on earth, Paradise, the Garden of Eden,"[63] one cannot say that the cosmos, let alone the garden of Eden, was made for Yahweh to dwell in. As the dedication prayer in 1 Kings 8 says, the cosmos is not large enough for him, and Isa. 66:1 describes heaven and earth as just God's furniture—that is, God's chair (throne) and footstool. God is said to

57. Walton, *Genesis 1 as Ancient Cosmology*, 187.
58. Walton, *Genesis 1 as Ancient Cosmology*, 189.
59. Enns, *Evolution of Adam*, 72. See *KTU* 1.2 iv 11–27. See its english translation in Hallo and Younger, *COS*, 1:248–49.
60. See Tsumura, *Creation and Destruction*, 55–56.
61. Gordon J. Wenham, "Sanctuary Symbolism in the Garden of Eden Story," in *"I Studied Inscriptions from Before the Flood": Ancient Near Eastern, Literary, and Linguistic Approaches to Genesis 1–11*, ed. Richard S. Hess and David T. Tsumura (repr., Winona Lake, IN: Eisenbrauns, 1994), 399–404. Cf. Collins, *Did Adam and Eve Really Exist?*, 59.
62. Wenham, "Sanctuary Symbolism," 401.
63. See Lawrence E. Stager, "Jerusalem and the Garden of Eden," *ErIsr* 26 (1999): 183–94; and Elizabeth Bloch-Smith, "'Who Is the King of Glory?': Solomon's Temple and Its Symbolism," in *Scripture and Other Artifacts: Essays on the Bible and Archaeology in Honor of Philip J. King*, ed. Michael D. Coogan, J. Cheryl Exum, and Lawrence E. Stager (Louisville: Westminster John Knox, 1994), 18–31.

dwell in the heavens or sometimes in the temple, but he is never said to dwell on the earth, except by "name." Walton's mistake, it seems to me, is that he tries to combine the temple motif, which he thinks is in Gen. 1, and the garden motif (Gen. 2–3).

Creation and Nature of Humanity

Human beings are God's special creatures, created *in* the image of God, or even better, *as* the image of God: they themselves are the image of God.[64] Thus the humans were to be vice-regents, ruling over creation as God would rule over it. But at the fall, they alienated themselves from the Creator and lost his way of "ruling" over creatures, eventually resulting in the present ecological crisis.

Imago Dei: *Royal Figures*

The biblical view of human beings as the image of God is unique in the ANE, where otherwise only the king, as the god's representative, is "the image of god."[65] In the Akkadian-Aramaic Fekheriye inscription,[66] "image" and "like-ness" refer to an image representing the king himself. Thus the *ṣelem ʾĕlōhîm* in Gen. 1:27 is "a royal designation, the precondition or requisite for rule."[67]

But this royal image of all humankind as the likeness of God is in sharp contrast with the Mesopotamian view of humans as created to relieve the gods of hard labor by supplying them with food and drink, as can be seen in works like the Atrahasis epic.[68] No ANE myth gives such a high position to humankind, both man and woman, as does the Bible.

Humanity as Living Beings

The biblical view of humankind as being formed "from the dust" and "the breath of life" (*nišmat ḥayyîm*)[69] being "breathed into [their] nostrils"

64. David J. A. Clines, "The Image of God in Man," *TynBul* 19 (1968): 53–103.
65. Clines, "Image of God," 85.
66. A. A. Assaf, P. Bordreuil, and A. R. Millard, *La statue de Tell Fekherye et son inscription bilingue assyro-araméenne* (Paris: Recherche sur les civilisations, 1982).
67. Phyllis A. Bird, "'Male and Female He Created Them': Genesis 1:27b in the Context of the Priestly Account of Creation," *HTR* 74 (1981): 134.
68. See the opening section of the Atrahasis epic; cf. W. G. Lambert and Alan R. Millard, *Atra-Ḥasīs: The Babylonian Story of the Flood* (Oxford: Clarendon, 1969), 15.
69. Gen. 7:22 has "the breathing of spirit of life," *nišmat-rûaḥ ḥayyîm*; cf. "the blast of the breath," *nišmat rûaḥ* (2 Sam. 22:16; Ps. 18:16). Note also that breath and spirit often appear as a word pair: Job 4:9 ("blast"); 27:3; 32:8; 33:4; 34:14; Isa. 42:5; 57:16 NJPS.

The Epic of Atrahasis on the Creation of Human Beings

189"[Belet–ili, the midwife], is present,

190Let the midwife create a human being,

191Let man assume the drudgery of god."

192They summoned and asked the goddess,

193The midwife of the gods, wise Mami:

194"Will you be the birth goddess, creatress of mankind?

195Create a human being that he bear the yoke,

196Let him bear the yoke, the task of Enlil,

197Let man assume the drudgery of god."

1.189–97

221On the first, seventh, and fifteenth days of the month,

222He established a purification, a bath.

223They slaughtered Aw–ilu, who had the inspiration, in their assembly.

225Nintu mixed clay with his flesh and blood.

<That same god and man were thoroughly mixed in the clay.>[a]

227For the rest [of time they would hear the drum],

228From the flesh of the god [the] spi[rit remained].

229It would make the living know its sign,

230Lest he be allowed to be forgotten, [the] spirit remained.

232After she had mixed that clay,

233She summoned the Anunna, the great gods.

234The Igigi, the great gods, spat upon the clay.

235Mami made ready to speak,

236And said to the great gods:

237"You ordered me the task and I have completed (it)!

238You have slaughtered the god, along with his inspiration,

240have done away with your heavy forced labor,

241I have imposed your drudgery on man.

242You have bestowed (?) clamor upon mankind.

243I have released the yoke, I have [made] restoration."

244They heard this speech of hers,

245They ran, free of care, and kissed her feet, (saying):

246"Formerly [we used to call] you Mami,

247Now let your n[am]e be Mistress-of-All-the Gods (Belet-kala-ili)"

1.221–47

Note: Hallo and Younger, COS, 1:451.
a. The phrase in < > is restored in the light of lines 212–13.

in Gen. 2:7 has some similarities with Mesopotamian views. For example, in Atrahasis 1.221–26, "Man was created from the flesh and blood of a slaughtered god mixed *with clay*." Thus in both, human beings have both an earthly and divine constituent. However, in the Bible no material part of a deity is involved, only what would come out of a person naturally, his or her breath, and it is this, not divine blood, that makes a person animate.[70] In the Bible, not only humanity (2:7) but also animals (1:20, 24, 30) are called *nepeš ḥayyāh*, "living beings." The uniqueness of humanity is "the breath of life" breathed into the nostrils.

Garden of Eden[71]

In ancient versions the term *'ēd* (Gen. 2:6) has been rendered as "spring/fountain" (e.g., LXX: *pēgē*) or as *'ănānā'* "(rain-)cloud" or "vapor, mist" (Targum). Modern versions translate it "mist," "flood," "a stream," "water," or "streams." However, no satisfactory Semitic etymology has been found, and most scholars believe it goes back to the Sumerian.[72] One view is that it is a loanword ÍD via Akkadian *id*, "river."[73] Another is that *'ēd* is connected to the Akkadian *edû*, "flood," a loanword from Sumerian.[74] But *'ēdô* in Job 36:27 is borrowed directly from *edû*. Though it is possible that *'ēd* is a shortened form of *'ēdô*, it is more likely that it was borrowed directly from the Sumerian. Both *'ēd* and *'ēdô* mean "high water" and refer to the water flooding out of the subterranean ocean.[75] The phrase "was watering" (*hišqâ*) suggests an ample supply of water, rather than just moisture. This view is in harmony with Eden as a well-watered place.

The two waters in Gen. 2:5–6, the "rain" and "the *'ēd*-water," can be compared with the two *thmt*-waters in a Ugaritic expression that seems to refer to the waters above in heaven and the waters below under the earth, as in Gen. 7:11 and 8:2, and build on "an ancient tradition about the separation of heaven-water and ocean-water as reflected in the Genesis Creation story, not in 1:2, but in 1:6ff."[76] In the Ugaritic religion this upper *thmt*-water is probably

70. Alan R. Millard, "A New Babylonian 'Genesis' Story," *TynBul* 18 (1967): 10.
71. For bibliographical references, see Westermann, *Genesis 1–11*, 178–81; Wenham, *Genesis 1–15*, 41–44.
72. For a detailed discussion, see Tsumura, *Creation and Destruction*, 85–106.
73. William F. Albright, "The Babylonian Matter in the Predeuteronomic Primeval History (JE) in Genesis 1–11," *JBL* 58 (1939): 102–3.
74. E. A. Speiser, "'ēd in the Story of Creation," *BASOR* 140 (1955): 9–11.
75. Tsumura, *Creation and Destruction*, 105.
76. Tsumura, *Creation and Destruction*, 137–38.

associated or identified with the god "Heaven," while the lower *thmt*-water may well correspond to the goddess "Ocean" (*Tahāmat*).[77]

The rain god in the ANE was considered to give other water too. For example, the Fekheriye Inscription calls him the "water-controller of all rivers." Similarly, the Lord of Gen. 2, who controls the rain (Gen. 2:5), presumably also controls the subterranean waters. When he planted a garden in a well-watered place (Gen. 2:8–14), as a divine gardener he apparently drained the *'ēd*-water there through the four rivers. However, he is more than a water controller; he is also the maker of the total universe, of "earth and heaven" (*'ereṣ wəšāmāyim*, 2:4b).[78]

Etymology of ʿĒden

Although there is a Sumerian word edin, "plain, steppe," the etymology of Eden is better explained by the Semitic word *'dn* found in Ugaritic, Aramaic, and Old South Arabic, and the Arabic verb *'adana*, which probably has the literal meaning "to make abundant in water supply." The Aramaic form is parallel to Akkadian *ṭaḫdu*, "well-watered," in the ninth-century-BCE bilingual inscription from Tell Fekheriye.[79] Certainly the garden was planted in a well-watered place: the underground water "would well up" (Gen. 2:6 NJPS) and water the "land" (*'ǎdāmâ*) (cf. Gen. 13:10).[80] The biggest problem for a gardener would be how to control the abundant waters. God drained the garden by the four rivers that flow down from it.[81] The geographical relationships are as follows: the *garden* is in *Eden*, which is in the *land*, which is in the *earth*.

Tree of Life

Despite the fact that a majority of scholars support a Sumerian connection for the "tree of life,"[82] there is no evidence for such a tree in Mesopotamian myth and cult. Its identification with trees on various Mesopotamian seals

77. Tsumura, *Creation and Destruction*, 111.

78. Tsumura, *Creation and Destruction*, 128–29.

79. Alan R. Millard, "The Etymology of Eden," *VT* 34 (1984): 103–6; Jonas C. Greenfield, "A Touch of Eden," in *Orientalia J. Duchesne-Guillemin Emerito Oblata*, Acta Iranica 23 (Leiden: Brill, 1984), 219–24.

80. Tsumura, *Creation and Destruction*, 112–25.

81. See below under the heading "Location of the Garden of Eden: Four Rivers"

82. See Samuel Noah Kramer, "Enki and Ninhursag: A Paradise Myth," in *ANET* 2:37–41; Kramer, *The Sumerians: Their History, Culture, and Character* (Chicago: University of Chicago Press, 1963), 147–49.

is a pure hypothesis.[83] Also, no phrase such as "tree of life" is attested in Canaanite mythology, though we do find the phrase "tree of death" (ʿṣ mt) in Ugaritic.[84]

While the expression "the tree of life" (Gen. 2:9) means literally "the tree that gives life," it is the Lord God, not the tree itself, who gives life. Significantly, in the Eden story the central focus is not the tree of life but "the tree of the knowledge of good and evil." Human beings were not allowed to become like "divine beings," or angels, "knowing good and evil" (Gen. 3:5). Scholars have identified four common interpretations of this knowledge: (1) sexual knowledge, (2) omniscience, (3) moral discernment, (4) divine wisdom. However, since this phrase is found only in Gen. 2:9, 17, one cannot be sure which is meant.[85] The first interpretation, however, seems least likely, because God told human beings, male and female, to "be fruitful and multiply" (Gen. 1:28), for which sexual knowledge is necessary.

Location of the Garden of Eden: Four Rivers

Genesis 2:10 says that a river went out from (or in) Eden. Since this is the river that watered the garden within Eden, the river likely came out in the garden part of Eden, which was probably the highest part of Eden, so the movement of this water is most likely vertical, like a spring (cf. ʾēd-water in Gen. 2:6), for in order for the river water to water the garden, it has to flow from the highest place in the garden. In Gen. 2:10, the adverb "there" (šām) means the garden, where the river divided into four "branches" (NJPS) and flowed downward from the garden.

Westermann holds that the author did not intend to give the location of Eden but intended to say the "life-arteries" of the whole earth have their source there.[86] Some scholars compare the garden of Eden and four rivers with the ANE motif of four rivers flowing from the temple,[87] as well as the abode of the Ugaritic god El at the "source of the two rivers" (mbk nhrm).[88]

83. A. W. Sjöberg, "Eve and the Chameleon," in In the Shelter of Elyon: Essays on Ancient Palestinian Life and Literature in Honor of G. W. Ahlström, ed. W. Boyd Barrick and John R. Spencer, JSOTSup 31 (Sheffield: JSOT Press, 1984), 219–21.

84. DULAT, 186.

85. Kyle Greenwood, "Tree of Knowledge," in Bible Odyssey, http://www.bibleodyssey.org/passages/related-articles/tree-of-knowledge.

86. Westermann, Genesis 1–11, 216.

87. See, e.g., Othmar Keel, The Symbolism of the Biblical World: Ancient Near Eastern Iconography and the Book of Psalms (Winona Lake, IN: Eisenbrauns, 1997), figs. 153a, 185, 191.

88. E. Theodore Mullen Jr., The Divine Council in Canaanite and Early Hebrew Literature (Chico, CA: Scholars Press, 1980).

However, Eden is not the Lord's abode, and the four rivers are introduced as real rivers with proper names rather than as symbolic indications of the four quarters of the earth.

The four proper names suggest that the author meant the garden to be a geographical place. For those who accept this, there are two main hypotheses as to the location. The "southern" hypothesis is that the garden of Eden was in the Sumerian Dilmun, "the land of living," which lay near the head of the Persian Gulf. This hypothesis identifies the Pishon and the Gihon with actual rivers not far from the mouths of the Tigris and the Euphrates[89] and interprets the rivers as converging at Eden. However, the problem is that Gen. 2:10 says the rivers *start* in the garden.[90]

The "northern" hypothesis is that Eden is in eastern Turkey or Armenia, understanding the four rivers in the following ways. Havilah is unknown, but the place is sometimes identified with Nubia, south of Egypt, "where there is gold." However, the additional information, "the gold of that land is good," would not be necessary for Nubia. The items *bdellium* (NIV, "aromatic resin") and *šōham* (usually, "onyx stone") are difficult to identify, but if *šōham* were rather to be identified with *lapis lazuli*, Havilah might be in Afghanistan. The second river, Gihon, is clearly not the spring of Gihon in Jerusalem. While a majority of scholars identify the term Cush with the region of the Upper Nile, some[91] hold that the term is "the eponym of the Kassites,"[92] and the only one that would fit the phrase "in the east" of Gen. 2:8.[93] Cush thus probably refers to somewhere in northern or possibly southeast Mesopotamia. The Tigris and Euphrates were well known to the readers, hence simpler descriptions. The author's vantage point is most probably near the Euphrates, looking east.

From these details, it seems the author is locating the garden somewhere in eastern Turkey or in Armenia, near the sources of the Tigris and Euphrates, and this is a long-established, widely held view.[94] Certainly the garden was not simply a Utopia in the semiheavenly place (cf. 2:15–17).

---

89. E. A. Speiser, "The Rivers of Paradise," in *Oriental and Biblical Studies: Collected Writings of E. A. Speiser*, ed. J. J. Finkelstein and M. Greenberg (Philadelphia: University of Pennsylvania Press, 1967), 28–33.

90. Wenham, *Genesis 1–15*, 66.

91. Speiser, "Rivers of Paradise," 23–24. Cf. Westermann, *Genesis 1–11*, 218.

92. The original homeland of the Kassites may be located in the Zagros Mountains, east of the Tigris River. They controlled Babylonia after the Old Babylonian Empire, from the sixteenth to twelfth centuries BCE.

93. Speiser, "Rivers of Paradise," 25–26.

94. Wenham, *Genesis 1–15*, 66.

Conclusion

Reading into the Text or out of the Text?

How to read a biblical text such as Gen. 1–2 is crucial, especially in this postmodern age, when the reader often creates the meaning of the text. For example, what does it mean that God "ceased on the seventh day from all his work that he had done" (2:2, my trans.)? Did God become tired and rest on the seventh day? But the verbs in the Genesis passage and the Fourth Commandment (Exod. 20:11) are carefully distinguished. In Gen. 2:3 *šbt* means basically "to cease from, stop (the work)," focusing on the "completion" of God's creative work, hence "cessation"; but in Exod. 20:11 *nwḥ*, "rest," emphasizes the result of the cessation.[95] Certainly one should avoid reading the Exodus idea into the creation story, ignoring this verbal distinction.

The same thing can be said with regard to reading a sanctuary or temple motif into Gen. 1–2. Did the biblical author expect his readers to read ANE religious views into these chapters? Did they combine the motifs of "rest" and "garden" to get the themes of the temple as a divine dwelling? It seems to me that many scholars see too much similarity between biblical and ANE cosmologies, while putting too much emphasis on the contrast between a modern scientific worldview and ancient cosmologies.

Contextual, Comparative, Contrastive

Any comparative study must first understand the items being compared; otherwise the comparison becomes very superficial. For example, before claiming that the "split" of the sea dragon in Ps. 74:13 is based on Enuma Elish, one must show that the verb *prr* means "split." As I have shown elsewhere,[96] it means to "break."

The Genesis account takes very different stances from the ANE toward the divine, the world, and the human being's calling, and there is a clear distinction between the divine world and the human world. The Lord is the sole divine agent and significantly is without any female consort. In fact, in the ANE only Genesis deals with the creative actions by a personal deity without any involvement of a goddess. Therefore, expressions such as "be fruitful" are similar to the fertility motif in ANE religions, but the import is totally different.

95. On Exod. 20:11, see David T. Tsumura, "The Meaning of 'The LORD Rested on the Seventh Day,'" *Exegetica* 24 (2013): 37–48 (in Japanese with an English summary).
96. Tsumura, "Creation Motif in Psalm 74:12–14?," 548–51.

The contextual approach[97] is ready to accept many similarities in language and culture. But no comparative study is meaningful unless it not only examines the similarities but also detects the differences between the similar items.

Rediscovered OT-ANE relationships and their comparison thus produced new academic practices, yet it is true that the OT-polytheism relationship had existed throughout the "reception" history of the OT since the eras of (1) the biblical religion, (2) Judaism, and (3) Christianity. But how much do the people in each era demonstrate awareness of similarities between or differences from polytheism? It seems that initially the biblical religion was clearly aware of its difference from polytheism in its cultural context. And throughout the history of Judaism and Christianity, the majority of believers accepted the Bible's uniqueness. When those ANE literatures were (re-)discovered in the nineteenth century, however, many of these people were shocked to find the Bible's similarities with the polytheistic traditions.

For the modern Western reader the similarities between the Bible and the ANE religions may be a problem. However, an ancient polytheistic reader would not be struck by the similarities but would take them for granted. As Wenham declares, "It is the differences that would surprise him: its monotheism (only one God!), God's total sovereignty over the elements, his anger at sin, his rewarding of obedience, and so forth."[98] We can see this from the reactions of later polytheists on hearing the Genesis creation story for the first time, such as the Japanese Jo Niijima and Kanzo Uchimura, at the end of the nineteenth century, when the country was opened up to Western cultural and religious influence.

For Further Reading

Collins, C. John. *Did Adam and Eve Really Exist? Who They Were and Why You Should Care.* Wheaton: Crossway, 2011.

Halton, C., ed. *Genesis: History, Fiction, or Neither? Three Views on the Bible's Earliest Chapters.* Grand Rapids: Zondervan, 2015.

Hess, R. S., and D. T. Tsumura, eds. *"I Studied Inscriptions from Before the Flood": Ancient Near Eastern, Literary, and Linguistic Approaches to Genesis 1–11.* Winona Lake, IN: Eisenbrauns, 1994.

97. William W. Hallo, "Ancient Near Eastern Texts and Their Relevance for Biblical Exegesis," in *Canonical Compositions from the Biblical World*, vol. 1 of *COS*, ed. W. W. Hallo and K. L. Younger (Leiden: Brill, 1997), xxiii–xxviii.

98. See Wenham's response to Spark's article "Genesis 1–11 as Ancient Historiography," 101–9.

Tsumura, D. T. *Creation and Destruction: A Reappraisal of the* Chaoskampf *Theory in the Old Testament*. Winona Lake, IN: Eisenbrauns, 2005.

Walton, J. *Genesis 1 as Ancient Cosmology*. Winona Lake, IN: Eisenbrauns, 2011.

Primary Texts in Print

Coogan, Michael D., and Mark S. Smith, eds. and trans. *Stories from Ancient Canaan*. 2nd ed. Louisville: Westminster John Knox, 2012.

Dalley, S. "The Epic of Creation." In *Myths from Mesopotamia: Creation, the Flood, Gilgamesh, and Others*, 233–74. Oxford: Oxford University Press, 1991.

Foster, B. R. "Epic of Creation." In *COS*, vol. 1, *Canonical Compositions from the Biblical World*, edited by W. W. Hallo and K. L. Younger, 390–402. Leiden: Brill, 1997.

Hays, Christopher H. *Hidden Riches: A Sourcebook for the Comparative Study of the Hebrew Bible and the Ancient Near East*. Louisville: Westminster John Knox, 2014.

Lambert, W. G. *Babylonian Creation Myths*. Winona Lake, IN: Eisenbrauns, 2013.

Lambert, W. G., and A. R. Millard. *Atra-Ḫasīs: The Babylonian Story of the Flood*. Oxford: Clarendon, 1969.

Primary Texts Online

1. Atrahasis Epic
   http://www.livius.org/sources/content/anet/104-106-the-epic-of-at
   rahasis/
2. Enuma Elish
   http://www.etana.org/node/581
3. Epic of Baal
   http://emp.byui.edu/satterfieldb/ugarit/The%20Epic%20of%20Baal
   .html

11

Post-Darwinian Interpretations of Genesis 1–2

Aaron T. Smith

We may conclude pretty certainly that in [the ancient world] the literal interpretation was never universally prevalent, but that there always survived a somewhat obscure but healthy feeling that the old record must not be treated as historical in our sense of the word. We have therefore no reason to maintain a stricter historical interpretation than the Hebrews themselves did in their best days.

—F. D. E. Schleiermacher[1]

If science should render it certain that all the present species of living creatures were derived by natural descent from a few original germs, and that these germs were themselves an evolution of inorganic forces and materials, we should not therefore regard the Mosaic account as proved untrue. We should only be required to revise our interpretation of the word *bara* [to create] in Genesis 1:21, 27, and to give it there the meaning of mediate creation, or creation by law.

—Augustus Hopkins Strong[2]

1. Friedrich Schleiermacher, *The Christian Faith*, ed. H. R. Mackintosh and J. S. Stewart (1830; repr., Edinburgh: T&T Clark, 1999), 151.
2. Strong did not think that biological science *had* rendered evolution by natural selection "certain." By the late nineteenth century, Darwin's ideas were in a state of "eclipse" (according

That a chapter in this volume should be dedicated exclusively to "post-Darwinian interpretations" of the Genesis creation material is, on the one hand, entirely appropriate. The "new biology" given expression in Charles Darwin's 1859 *On the Origin of Species by Means of Natural Selection* raises questions concerning the derivation, character, and rank of life-forms, which are in many respects paradigmatic.

Yet on the other hand, as the epigraphic citations by the Reformed theologian Friedrich Schleiermacher (1768–1834) and the Baptist Augustus H. Strong (1836–1921) suggest, we cannot assume that Darwinian biology so challenged Christian theology as to cause it to interpret the Bible in entirely unprecedented fashions. Schleiermacher, who died a quarter-century before publication of *Origin*, indicates that the prospect of a nonliteral reading of the Bible hardly awaited Darwin. And Strong exhibits almost a reflex latent in biblical interpretation to correct previous readings in the light of new learning.

It goes without saying that twenty-first-century church and society stand at a historical and intellectual distance from Schleiermacher and Strong and that in between their time and ours, especially in North America, discussion about Darwinism and religion has not always taken their measured tones. We will also see that certain reactionary antagonisms surfaced early in the conversation. Nevertheless, a chapter on post-Darwinian interpretations of Gen. 1–2 written in the twenty-first century might best make a contribution to the kind of ranging surveys conducted in this volume by rehearsing the fuller continuum of receptions, which Darwin's insights enjoyed, and by commending a more conciliatory approach, like that of Schleiermacher or Strong.

Evolutionary biology has progressed a good deal in the century and a half since Darwin, correcting some of his claims while firmly corroborating his central thesis that in a world of competition for finite resources, species survive by chance mutation of attributes, which enhance their ability to compete; that is, species evolve by natural selection. Theology has developed in no small part through ongoing conversation with modern biology. I would be remiss not to end this book on a constructive note, which at once echoes certain prophetically restrained voices of the nineteenth century and resonates with the more collegial and productive tones being struck today.

Many after Darwin continued the long-standing Christian practice of rereading the text from within an expanding horizon of meaning. Their interpretation of the Bible progressed with enhanced understanding of both the

---

to Darwin's own son). Still, if Darwinism in its essence would carry the day, Strong saw no necessary conflict with biblical authority. Augustus Hopkins Strong, *Systematic Theology: A Compendium and Commonplace Book Designed for the Use of Theological Students*, 5th ed. (New York: Armstrong and Son, 1896), 192.

world that the biblical authors inhabited and their own time and place. That does not mean that they uncritically saw their task to be to amend the truths of Scripture in view of the higher authority of new science. Rather, with a humility that surely ought to count for something, they allowed that their understanding and interpretation of Scripture might not fully represent the meaning of Scripture. They assumed a break between biblical interpretation and the biblical text. The text may have meaning only through interpretation, but still, meaning transcends interpretation.[3] Malleability of contemporary understanding enabled these interpreters in their own distinctive fashion to extend the practice of "translating" the biblical message into categories of discourse predominating at the end of the nineteenth century, a practice traced to the earliest manifestations of Christian faith, which as such hardly signified a unique age of biblical engagement.[4]

Earlier chapters have demonstrated that analytical methods of studying the Bible predate Darwin,[5] as do figurative, typological, and allegorical readings.

3. This principle invokes the debate in hermeneutics concerning the role of the reader in establishing meaning. At the risk of oversimplification, it is possible to sketch a continuum of three perspectives. On what we might call the "objective" end are those who contend that meaning resides in and with *authorial intent*. The reader contributes nothing but accesses meaning as a thing outside of oneself. Understanding of any composition turns on the degree of success that the reader has in penetrating into the mind of the author; for starters, see E. D. Hirsch Jr., *Validity in Interpretation* (New Haven: Yale University Press, 1973). At the opposite end of the spectrum, the "subjective," are those who argue that meaning resides entirely with the reader's response. No one approaches any text in a vacuum of knowledge and judgment, but each brings to the text a set of life experiences, fore-understandings, and pre-commitments, which act determinatively on the reader's comprehension—prefiguring points of access and interest, areas of thematic resonance, and relative weight ascribed to conclusions. On this view, see Stanley Fish, "Why No One's Afraid of Wolfgang Iser," *Diacritics* 11 (1981): 2–13. Between these two perspectives are those who locate meaning *in the text itself*. The author produces a work, which takes on a life of its own (beyond the writer's intentions) as it is read, discussed, and debated in the public sphere. The reader contributes to its meaning, but by virtue of the composition's historical trajectory of readings, beyond the individual subject, the text retains a life of meaning in itself; for starters, see Hans-Georg Gadamer, *Truth and Method*, trans. Donald G. Marshall and Joel Weinsheimer, 2nd ed. (London: Continuum, 2004). My characterization of a humility, which locates meaning in interpretation yet allows the text a freedom beyond interpretation, reflects Gadamer's account.

4. I am borrowing the expression "translating the message" from the prominent historian of world Christianity and Christian missions Lamin Sanneh, who understands Christian confession to have taken shape through a process of translation out of essentially Judaic rituals and norms into Hellenistic categories, and its key formulations to be amenable to ongoing translation into new cultural idioms. See Sanneh, *Translating the Message: The Missionary Impact on Culture* (Maryknoll, NY: Orbis, 2009).

5. The hermeneutical challenge posed by the discovery of, e.g., the Epic of Gilgamesh is similar to that posed by Darwinian science: What justification can there be for reading Gen. 1–2 as empirical and historical when everyone recognizes that reading Gilgamesh that way would pervert its meaning, and the biblical account echoes its features and themes? As Richard S.

Strong and others like him found plenty of resources in these readings to allow for robust biblical authority *and* for the prospect of creative causation within natural selection. In other words, they did not assume that biblical fidelity and a sort of causal agency thought to befit the Deity demanded immediate or semi-immediate[6] appearance of discrete life-forms by fiat decree. They understood Scripture as allowing for *mediated* creative operations, and they reconciled biological evolution to this reading as God's creative medium.[7]

Indeed, some found a loftier kind of glory in a God who exercises creative sovereignty through a gradual, interdependent derivation of life than in one beholden to an interventionist, "decree-appearance" model. As Charles Kingsley wrote to Darwin in 1859 on receiving a copy of *Origin*, "I have gradually learnt to see that it is just as noble a conception of Deity, to believe that he created primal forms capable of self development into all forms needful *pro tempore* and *pro loco* [for the time and for the place], as to believe that He required a fresh act of intervention to supply the *lacunas* which he himself had made. I question whether the former be not the loftier thought."[8] When Darwin revised *Origin* in later editions to address matters raised by his critics, he cited Kingsley's remarks.[9]

Briggs summarizes, "Readers of Genesis in the late nineteenth century thus found themselves pressed on two fronts—by Darwin et al., on the one hand, and *Gilgamesh* et al., on the other." "The Hermeneutics of Reading Genesis after Darwin," in *Reading Genesis after Darwin*, ed. Stephen C. Barton and David Wilkinson (Oxford: Oxford University Press, 2009), 57–71, here 59–60.

6. I have included the term *semi-immediate* because strict creationists generally allow for at least some derivation to take place within species (or "kinds" or other preferred boundaries) at least by a sort of Lamarckian trait inheritance over time.

7. At least they did so in an incipient way. Darwinian evolution is a brutal process: species emerge only through mortal competition. Combat to the death is of course seen regularly in the predator/prey relationship, but beyond this, one predator out-competes another by lucking into characteristics that allow it to kill more efficiently (stronger teeth for crushing bone and tearing sinew, enhanced speed for the chase, and so on). Reconciling the creative work of a loving God and evolution by natural selection takes detailed, sustained, theological reflection.

8. "C. Kingsley to C. Darwin," in *The Life and Letters of Charles Darwin, Including an Autobiographical Chapter*, ed. Francis Darwin (London: John Murray, 1888), 2:288. I was led to Kingsley's letter by S. Brian Stratton, "Genesis after the Origin: Theological Responses to Evolution," WW 29, no. 1 (2009): 7–18. This issue is dedicated to the theme "In the Wake of the Beagle: Faith after Darwin." Stratton contrasts Kingsley's perspective with the more critical views of Adam Sedgwick and uses each to sketch a continuum of responses to Darwin. He favors Kingsley, commending an approach to creation (à la Arthur Peacocke and John Haught) that understands the creative act as an immanent operation involving "chance" and "randomness," properly understood. Cf. Arthur Peacocke, *Evolution: The Disguised Friend of Faith?* (Philadelphia: Templeton Foundation Press, 2004); John Haught, *God after Darwin: A Theology of Evolution* (Boulder, CO: Westview, 2000).

9. See Charles Darwin, *On the Origin of Species by Means of Natural Selection, or the Preservation of Favored Races in the Struggle for Life*, 6th ed. (New York: Appleton, 1883),

So we have to be cautious about what it means to interpret Scripture after Darwin. In important respects, "post-Darwinian interpretation" is like pre-Darwinian interpretation: ongoing movement in the hermeneutical spiral, in which the reader brings a frame of understanding to the text, then returns from the text to their own world-picture with a fresh horizon of meaning, and so on. Certainly, for some, there was *conflict* between scriptural fidelity and commitment to divine lordship on the one hand and evolutionary theory on the other.[10] But for others, *accommodation* best characterizes the relationship between Genesis and Darwinian biology.[11] *Cautious forbearance* might explain this relationship for still others.[12]

Characterizing interpretations of Gen. 1–2 as post-Darwin is thus a complex undertaking. It requires sufficient historical patience and theological nuance to attend simultaneously to a series of interconnected issues: movements in biblical scholarship operating independently of Darwin; the diversity of reception of Darwin's work among his peers in science and the church; adjudication of theological contributions made after Darwin not only on the basis of their facility in biblical studies and the relevant science but also according to their aptitude in identifying what are and are not core Christian faith commitments; and informed awareness of the interrelationship of basic doctrinal convictions (minimally, creation and redemption, biblical

---

422. Darwin does not name Kingsley, but the quotation is close to that given above. Darwin prefaces his citation with a notable observation: "I see no good reason why the views given in this volume should shock the religious feelings of any one. It is satisfactory, as showing how transient such impressions [of a theory's antireligious implications] are, to remember that the greatest discovery ever made by man, namely, the law of the attraction of gravity, was also attacked by Leibnitz, 'as subversive of natural, and inferentially of revealed, religion'" (421–22).

10. Historians often trace the origins of the "conflict" or "warfare" model between science and religion to two publications from the late nineteenth century: John William Draper, *History of the Conflict between Religion and Science* (1874; repr., Charleston, SC: Nabu, 2010); Andrew Dickson White, *A History of the Warfare of Science with Theology in Christendom*, Great Minds (Cambridge: Cambridge University Press, 1896; repr., Amherst, NY: Prometheus, 1993).

11. A classical attempt to accommodate evolution, even integrate it into a constructive eschatology, is Pierre Teilhard de Chardin, *Le Phénomène humain* (Paris: Seuil, 1955); trans. Bernard Wall as *The Phenomenon of Man* (New York: Harper, 1959).

12. A historian of evangelical Christianity, David N. Livingstone, has suggested such a threefold typology. He observes that reception of Darwin's theory did not take place in a philosophical vacuum but came from within varying intellectual climates. The mood with which Darwin was received depended to a degree on a broader readiness, or lack thereof, to mediate between matters of faith and science. In three case studies, Livingstone detects a climate inclined to "adoption" of Darwinian thought in Edinburgh, "repudiation" in Belfast, and "toleration" at Princeton. See Livingstone, "Situating Evangelical Responses to Evolution," in *Evangelicals and Science in Historical Perspective*, ed. David N. Livingstone, D. G. Hart, and Mark A. Noll (Oxford: Oxford University Press, 1999), 193–219.

inspiration and authority, and the nature of divine sovereignty and God's work of providence).

Such an undertaking is too grand for us to finish here. But we can make what I hope will be a helpful start. In keeping with restraints of scale, and my own limits as a systematic theologian, I cannot attempt a comprehensive inventory of modern OT scholarship on Gen. 1–2. Nor can I offer an exhaustive report of the reception of Darwin's work among British, American, and Continental divines, let alone scholarship of the developing world as it has met with evolutionary biology.[13] Both the exegetical and science-reception backgrounds are critical, of course, in getting a handle on post-Darwinian readings of Genesis, so I will not neglect them entirely.

I will focus on what we might call *textual regard and associated views of God*, which properly identify an era of biblical interpretation that can be characterized as "post-Darwinian." By this I mean those conceptions of biblical character and of the God to whom the Bible bears witness, which divergent readings seem to presuppose or necessitate. Diversity of reading is hardly novel, even as the reader must now reckon with the novelty of Darwinian science.

Treatment of Days

One of the challenges posed by Darwinian biology for biblical interpretation concerns the massive time frames required for chance mutation to render known species. Humans come to exist in a differentiated form only over millions of years of gradual development. Geologically minded Christians already had been forced to try to reconcile the earth's old age with the six "days" of Gen. 1, clearing at least a footpath for those facing the same climb after Darwin. But to certain fundamentalists,[14] this attempted reconciliation

13. This is also a self-consciously Protestant account. For a broader, historical survey, which considers Catholic and Orthodox perspectives, see Jitse van der Meer and Scott Mandelbrote, eds., *Nature and Scripture in the Abrahamic Religions: 1700–Present*, vol. 1 (Leiden: Brill, 2008).

14. "Fundamentalism" is a multilayered designation. On one level, it refers to an era of theological reflection located predominantly in the Anglo world bridging the late nineteenth and early twentieth centuries. It embraced figures such as Charles Hodge, James Orr, and B. B. Warfield, each of whom represented a distinct perspective on evolution and the age of the earth. What unified the occasionally disparate foci of this period was a shared effort to identify "fundamental" points of Christian faith—e.g., the virgin birth and the deity of Christ—by which authenticity of confession might be gauged. The commonly adduced touchstone of the movement was a series of ninety essays on such topics published in twelve volumes between 1910 and 1915 titled "The Fundamentals." But fundamentalism also describes a cultural phenomenon that blends biblical literalism with social and political conservatism. Figures like George McCready Price represent the latter sort. For a classic study, which contains perspicacious conclusions

only highlighted the common threat posed by both kinds of science: they imperiled a plain reading of the Bible[15] and with it a plenary verbal model of inspiration. In so doing both kinds of science also challenged a God-concept, which sets divine and human agency in opposition, that is, which predicates the God-ness of God, if you will, on invasive, nonnatural action and address. For fundamentalists, creation is only *God's* act if creatures are *not* naturally emergent, and the Bible is only *God's* Word if it is *not* originally human speech.[16]

In his opening salvo against Darwinism, published in 1906, suggestively by Modern Heretic Company, the Seventh-Day Adventist[17] George McCready Price explicitly connected the challenge of Darwinian biology with that of modern geology:

> Darwinism . . . rests logically and historically on the succession-of-life idea as taught by geology. If there has actually been this succession of life on the globe, then some form of genetic connection between these successive types is the intuitive conclusion of every thinking mind. But if there is no positive evidence that certain types are older than others, *if this succession of life is not an actual scientific fact*, then Darwinism or any other form of evolution has no more scientific value than the vagaries of the old Greeks.[18]

Price dedicated much of his life to attacking the pervading interpretation of the fossil record, which stratified life-forms in discrete eras and implied

---

concerning the emergence of views resistant to evolution, see George Marsden, *Fundamentalism and American Culture*, 2nd ed. (Oxford: Oxford University Press, 2006).

15. In translation, of course; a common challenge posed to fundamentalist treatment of the Bible is its apparent inattention to the highly stylized language of Gen. 1–3 in Hebrew.

16. Resistance to the text's blatant humanity—however ironic in light of a *literalist* hermeneutic—was provoked in no small part by the perceived erosion of biblical authority brought about by a century and a half of textual criticism. The more the text was treated as an object of scientific study, like a lab rat, the less its claims seemed to command comprehensive obedience. Their relevance became proportional to their reasonableness. To many fundamentalists, then, preservation of biblical clout was tantamount to reestablishment of *super*natural origin, and defense of *meta*physical agency.

17. Price's Adventist background is important: this tradition's commitment to a plain reading of the Bible founds its characteristic worship on the seventh rather than first day of the week and its anticipative millennialism. This hermeneutic was endorsed by the movement's founder, Ellen G. White, and rabidly defended by Price. For a brief but well-researched and incisive treatment of Price's life and work, including its reception, see Ronald L. Numbers, *The Creationists: From Scientific Creationism to Intelligent Design*, expanded ed. (Cambridge, MA: Harvard University Press, 2006), 88–119.

18. George M. Price, introduction to *Illogical Geology: The Weakest Point in the Evolution Theory* (Los Angeles: Modern Heretic Company, 1906), https://www.gutenberg.org/files/420 43/42043-h/42043-h.htm; see also Price, *The New Geology: A Textbook for Colleges, Normal Schools, and Training Schools; and for the General Reader* (Mountain View, CA: Pacific Press, 1923), http://documents.adventistarchives.org/Books/NG1923.pdf.

hereditary continuity from one kind to the next. To the contrary, he argued that no clear link between fossils could be detected, that fossils were haphazardly and not orderly arranged, and that life-forms thought to have gone extinct before the arrival of others actually coexisted with their apparent progeny.[19] By what mechanism were the fossils deposited? Recent, catastrophic, and worldwide deluge better explained the record of death beneath our feet than the lumbering processes of uniformitarian geology and evolutionary biology.[20]

John C. Whitcomb and Henry M. Morris took their cue from Price's flood geology or "deluge catastrophism," coauthoring the highly influential work *The Genesis Flood*.[21] Whitcomb specializing in OT and Morris in engineering, they structured the book in two parts: defense of the notion that the Bible teaches a worldwide and not local flood, and exposition of selected scientific data points, drawn largely from Price,[22] which seem to challenge prevailing commitments to lengthy geologic time. These include such things as "misplaced fossils" (anomalies in the location of certain fossils as, e.g., in "fossil graveyards" where the bones of species from allegedly different eras are intermingled, suggesting a haphazard, catastrophically caused deposit) and "formations out of sequence" (geological formations such as "overthrusts," in which older rock sits on top of supposedly younger, which appear to contradict uniform construction).[23]

Although Price, Whitcomb, and Morris genuinely believed modern geology and biology to be deficient on scientific grounds, their resistance to "the succession-of-life idea" in large measure reduced, as indicated, to hermeneutical convictions. "We accept as basic the doctrine of the verbal inerrancy of Scripture," Whitcomb and Morris declared at the beginning of their book.[24] Through some kind of word-based communication, God caused a written

---

19. Perhaps Price's most infamous challenge was this: "I am willing to give a thousand dollars to anyone who will, in the face of the facts here presented, show me how to prove that one kind of fossil is older than another." Introduction to *Illogical Geology*.

20. "Man must have witnessed a cosmic geological catastrophe of some character and of some dimensions—the true nature and probable limits of this catastrophe ought to be the chief point of all geological inquiry." *Illogical Geology*, chap. 12.

21. John C. Whitcomb and Henry M. Morris, *The Genesis Flood: The Biblical Record and Its Scientific Implications* (Philadelphia: P&R, 1961). As evidence of its influence, in his endorsement of the work's latest issue (2011, celebrating the fiftieth anniversary of its initial release), the popular young-earth creationist Ken Ham credited exposure to the book as "a key event that led me to join the modern creation movement in the 1970s." Similarly, John MacArthur called it "one of the most important books of the past century." For a historical overview and estimation of the work's impact, see Numbers, *Creationists*, 208–38, here 225–38.

22. Referring to Morris, Numbers concludes that "his section read like an updated version of [Price's] *New Geology*." Numbers, *Creationists*, 227.

23. For this "evidence," see Whitcomb and Morris, *Genesis Flood*, 172–211.

24. Whitcomb and Morris, *Genesis Flood*, xx.

SIDEBAR 11.1

The Geological Record and the "Days" of Genesis 1

Geological debate about development of life on earth and what this means for a right understanding of Gen. 1–2 dates to the 1700s. The Swiss Louis Agassiz (1807–73) and Arnold Guyot (1807–84), both of whom eventually relocated to America, British Charles Lyell (1797–1875) and Hugh Miller (1802–56), and American Benjamin Silliman (1779–1864) and James Dwight Dana (1813–95) are but a handful of the more recognizable figures who attempted to reconcile an ice age (or ages), slow and carving glacial movements, the fossil record, the geologic column, and "uniformitarian" views of nature with biblical creation stories.[a]

Modern geology provided early encouragement to two means of reading Genesis with awareness that the earth was much older than the roughly 6,000 years calculated by Bishop James Ussher. These are the "Gap" and "Day-Age" theories. The first theory was made popular by the Scottish divine Thomas Chalmers (1780–1847). It contends that the great periods of time required for slow-moving geological cutting, along with most of the fossil record, can be located between the initial creative act of Gen. 1:1 and the "formlessness" and "emptiness" of Gen. 1:2. Such a rendering interjects age into the biblical record while still allowing for a "literal" reading. Each of the acts recorded after Gen. 1:2 can be understood as part of God's work of re-creation occurring in the course of six solar days.

Chalmers's views diverge from those of Miller, chief advocate of the Day-Age perspective. Miller, writes Livingstone, "simply could not agree with Chalmers's forcing the whole gamut of geological time in at the beginning of the biblical text."[b] Not that Miller endorsed a straightforwardly progressionist account; he did not think that the geological record supported so much empirical diversity of species just by way of macrolevel "development." But it did demand "many ages" to pass between periods of "elevatory fiat" (special acts by which certain new creaturely kinds were brought forth, culminating in humankind) in order for life within these kinds to emerge. The "days" of Gen. 1 refer to vast periods of time separating these acts.[c]

a. For a notably clear treatment of this essential background to the reception of Darwinian biology, see David N. Livingstone, *Darwin's Forgotten Defenders: The Encounter between Evangelical Theology and Evolutionary Thought* (Vancouver: Regent College Publishing, 1997), 1–99.
b. See Livingstone, *Darwin's Forgotten Defenders*, 12.
c. For more on Miller's perspective, see Hugh Miller, *The Foot-prints of the Creator: Or, The Asterolepis of Stromness* (London: Johnstone & Hunter, 1849; Cincinnati: W. H. Moore, 1851).

---

composition, which circularly exhibits divine origin by lacking any kind of error (including history and chronology, as well as scientific measurement and description).

No authentic *knowledge* of the world can contradict the perfect, divine account of its creation given verbally by God in the book of Genesis. This account clearly states that life did not arise by lumbering succession but arose "instantaneously."

> Any real *knowledge* of origins or of earth history antecedent to human historical records can only be obtained through divine revelation. . . . And this revelation simply says that "in the beginning God created the heaven and the earth" (Gen. 1:1). Although secondary processes are not precluded by this verse, the most obvious meaning derivable from it would be that God instantaneously, by divine omnipotence, called the universe, and particularly the earth, into being.[25]

What most irked fundamentalists was the unjustified arrogance of modern science to offer an account of origins that challenged the only kind of account that could "knowledgeably" convey such information, that is, an account that came from the other side, as it were, before and beyond the world: the account of the world's Originator. Darwinism worked backward from sparse empirical observation of the present state of things through nonempirical speculation to the beginning state of things. And it presumed to do so when the Originator's empirical account of the beginning was freely available.

Fundamentalists saw conflict over truth in its telling: either a world made by fiat, an act that was verbally communicated by the world's Maker in Gen. 1, or species generation through the randomness of natural selection derived inferentially by Darwin. The one account is based in the only possible "eyewitness" reporting, which therefore counts as *knowledge*; the other account is based in deduction, which is based on extrapolation of continuous succession and therefore counts as *conjecture*.

Obviously, this is the exact reverse of what counts for "knowledge" from the standpoint of modern science. One does not simply assume an omnipotent Source of the world because the world seems to demand it and a religious book seems to claim it, particularly, it is worth saying, in a world where other religious books make divergent claims. One does not simply assert that this book contains the Source's empirical narration of creation. And one does not buttress the credibility of that assertion with a second, circular assertion of the narration's "inerrancy." To make such an assumption and such assertions is the very definition of "conjecture." Scientific *knowledge*, by contrast, entails studiously avoiding supernaturalist inferences and working instead within what is naturally given. Despite covering itself in a veneer of scientific acumen, cultural fundamentalism is antagonistic of modern science to the core.

25. Whitcomb and Morris, *Genesis Flood*, 213, 219.

This antagonism, as indicated, involves corollary opposition between "God" and "world." "God" is whatever makes the world by virtue of a super-worldly power, whoever tells about it by virtue of a preworldly precedence, and whoever can be trusted in the telling by virtue of an otherworldly perfection (inerrancy assumes nonhumanity, since humans of course make mistakes).[26]

This opposition entangles fundamentalism in some unfortunate contradictions. Not all of the Bible requires preworldly accounting. In fact, the second creation account of Gen. 2–3, according to Whitcomb and Morris's own argument, could be "empirically" and therefore reliably conveyed without the benefit of a super-worldly perspective. Adam could have written it, or at least most of it, just by recording his own experience. But if that happened, then we can have an "inerrant" account without the very otherworldliness that inerrancy presupposes and protects.

We see the issue in the following citation from a volume edited by Morris, intended for use as a creationist textbook:

> There really are two creation accounts, the second [Gen. 2:3–5:1] written by Adam, from his viewpoint. The first (Gen. 1:1–2:3) could not have been observed by any man at all, and must have been written directly by God himself, either with his own "finger" as he also did the Ten Commandments (Exod. 31:18), or else by direct supernatural revelation. . . . In a direct and peculiar way, this constitutes the Creator's personal narrative of heaven and earth.[27]

Observation yields two distinct kinds of biblical material: that which contains information that God alone could have seen and so is produced by "direct supernatural revelation," some kind of word-based communication to a recorder who, being limited by her time and senses, could not otherwise have "knowledge" of the event (the first creation story or the Ten Commandments). More oddly, this revelation might have taken place by God scribing it as if at a desk. And we have that which humans like Adam authored[28] from their own viewpoint.

26. For Price and company, biblical revelation means the conveyance of data supplied from outside creation concerning the origin of creation. It cannot entail a world or text that originate interdependently or even that originate in a dialectical union of God and humanity (i.e., a Christ-centered account of creation and revelation).

27. Henry M. Morris, ed., *Scientific Creationism* (1974; repr., Green Forest, AR: Master Books, 2012), 206, https://books.google.com/books?id=blkuAS0qoQ8C&printsec=front cover&source=gbs_ge_summary_r&cad=0#v=onepage&q&f=false. The volume, which has enjoyed more than twenty printings, has been offered as a textbook through the Institute for Creation Research, which Morris helped found.

28. Uniquely, and without conventional justification, Morris et al. contend that Moses only edited the book of Genesis, while its various chapters were written by the patriarchs mentioned

But if Adam was without need of supernatural influence in giving "knowl-
edgeable" account of his own formation because he was witness to it (Gen.
2:7), then there is no longer a need for otherworldliness as a precondition of
textual authority. "Knowledge" of *creation*, we were told, had to come from
beyond creation, otherwise it could not have been empirically derived and
would therefore have been unreliable or, again, conjectural. Yet Adam had
the same order of knowledge of creation as God did, since he also wrote
a perfect and trustworthy account of creation alongside God's (Gen. 2–5
being part of the "verbally inerrant" Scriptures). But Adam achieved his
perfect, reliable knowledge precisely as non-God, through the restricted
perceptual apparatus of his human being, once more, from his own empirical "viewpoint." Thus, otherworldliness is no longer required to give a
trustworthy and authoritative account of creation. Natural observation, in
fact, scientific study could serve as an equally adequate means of knowing
the origins of creation to the otherworldly way of God. The opposition
between God and God's Word and creation and the creature's words, as
well as the authority of God and God's Word, which is predicated on this
opposition, lose their effect in light of Adam's authoritative, observational
self-description.[29]

Similarly, otherworldliness and empiricism do not mix well when it comes
to giving account of God's giving account. If to have "knowledge" of an event
one must observe it, then there is no way to have knowledge of God verbally
inspiring or physically scribing Gen. 1. No human actually saw the act, and
the result, God's alleged composition itself, makes no reference to the act. To
deduce that God must have written the first book of the Bible because God
alone could have observed its content presupposes another act of observation, a human observing God's observation and description, which never
happened. The deduction of divine authorship thus appears to be a much

---

in the "generations" (*toledoth* [*tôlǝdōt*]) formula. These, "in accord with the common practice
of ancient times," wrote what they experienced on tablets and handed them down "from family
to family, perhaps, finally, to be placed in a library or public storehouse of some sort." Moses
compiled the library archives, added "necessary transitional and explanatory comments," and
produced the book we now have. See Morris, *Scientific Creationism*, 205. What order of inspiration Moses experienced is not clear.

29. One might try to untangle fundamentalism's logic problem by appeal to the Holy Spirit:
Adam's viewpoint was not, actually, his own, but a perception elevated by the Spirit of God.
But this move is logically undermined by the fact that empirical observation relieves the need
for supernatural elevation, and in any case, if it was needed, then the Spirit could have simply
caused Adam in a state of elevated knowledge to perceive the elements contained in God's account of Gen. 1, relieving God of the need to write it out (as, e.g., the Spirit later would seem
to have done with certain "predictive" prophecies). Once again, Morris contends that *only* God
could have written Gen. 1, which would no longer be true.

grosser form of nonempirical, speculative conjecture than anything proffered by modern science.

Fundamentalism does not allow for the Creator's inimitable freedom to be defined by moment-by-moment, self-authorized capacity to assume creation. For Price and others, God just is God by decreeing from without all that is, in a highly concentrated weeklong period, then writing down or directly communicating the events of the week for the benefit ("knowledge") of his final creative act (humankind), only to see it corrupted by humans in their reading and transmission of it (since, technically speaking, "verbal inerrancy" only applies to the biblical autographs). God would not be God if God were to allow creation any sort of reciprocal impact, or if God were to grant to creation the corollary freedom to actualize itself (evolve). This view squares poorly with the God whose divine agency is revealed in Jesus Christ.

The gist of such criticism can be traced at least to the middle of the twentieth century. Reacting against Price and provoking Whitcomb and Morris, Bernard Ramm took issue with fundamentalism's adversarial depiction of Creator and creation, especially with its opposition between knowledge supplied by the Creator and that by creation, that is, between allegedly objective observations of revelation and conjectural inferences of modern science:

> There are two traditions in Bible and science both stemming from the developments of the nineteenth century. There is the ignoble tradition which has taken a most unwholesome attitude toward science, and has used arguments and procedures not in the better traditions of established scholarship. There has been and is a noble tradition in Bible and science, and this is the tradition of the great and learned evangelical Christians who have been patient, genuine, and kind and who have taken great care to learn the facts of science and Scripture. . . . It is our wish to call evangelicalism back to the noble tradition.[30]

Ramm diagnosed the problem of the "ignoble tradition" to be one of "hyper-orthodoxy."[31] Certain evangelicals like Price took the doctrine of divine transcendence to the unconstructive extreme, pitting the books of Scripture and nature against each other. By contrast, Ramm argued, "if the Author of Nature and Scripture are the same God, then the two books of God must eventually recite the same story. . . . *A positive relationship must exist between science and Christianity.*"[32]

30. Bernard Ramm, *The Christian View of Science and Scripture* (Grand Rapids: Eerdmans, 1955), 9–10.

31. Ramm, *Christian View*, 26–31.

32. Ramm, *Christian View*, 32–33.

The gradual developmentalism of Darwinism is not intrinsically antagonistic toward biblical revelation. The "noble tradition" of exegesis does not
find sufficient reason to oppose the two. The Bible, Ramm argues, allows for
continuity rather than discontinuity between ways and intentions of God
and the regular development of creaturely life. "If it is the intent of science
to amass all the facts about the universe in its countless facets, *it is the function of theology to give these data their purpose and teleological ordering.*"[33]
For Ramm, Darwinian biology and systematic theology are complementary
disciplines. The one supplies information about the world; the other orders
that information around God's redemptive designs for the world. Ultimately,
God is progressively bringing the world to its intended form:

> God creating fiatly and sovereignly *outside* of Nature now turns the task of
> creation over to the Holy Spirit who is *inside* Nature. The Spirit, the Divine
> Entelechy of Nature, knows the divine blueprint and *through process working
> from the level of vacancy* [the awaiting of form in Gen. 1:2] realizes the divine
> form or intention in Nature. If dry land is to appear, the Spirit sets those laws
> of geology to work which will produce dry land. . . . The laws of Nature, under
> the direction of the Holy Spirit, actualize over a period of time and through
> process, the plan of God.[34]

The upshot of Ramm's trinitarian "progressive creation"[35] is that it relieves
the burden of detail from Gen. 1–2. "The Bible tells us emphatically that God
created, but is silent as to how God created. It informs us that the stars, and
the flowers, and the animals, and the trees, and man are creatures of God,
but how God produced them is nowhere a matter of clear affirmation in
Scripture."[36] For the "how," we are free to consult the sciences.

Although Ramm's account is less problematic than the hyperorthodoxy
of Price, Whitcomb, and Morris, it has difficulties. It ascribes a cryptic and
extraneous action to the Spirit. By some undefined agency, the Spirit stirs
matter into a form that, it turns out, was already latent by law within matter,
so that in its place science might antiseptically describe the parameters and
product of the Spirit's work—creation's laws and resultant form. Then, by
another undefined agency, the Spirit reveals a hidden, eschatological meaning
of that scientific description. If I may borrow a sport illustration, this feels a
bit like declaring triumphantly that the Spirit hit the first pitch without ever

33. Ramm, *Christian View*, 34.
34. Ramm, *Christian View*, 116.
35. Ramm, *Christian View*, 113.
36. Ramm, *Christian View*, 104.

asking why the Spirit should be playing baseball. God endows the laws of nature with a regulative and generative power, then for some reason, and in some unexplained way, relies on the Spirit to effect the laws (or conversely, subjects the work of the Creator Spirit to the laws of nature).

Further, Ramm's view is too rosy. Already by the mid-twentieth century, and certainly in the decades since Ramm's treatment appeared, evolutionary biology steadfastly rejected the notion of "progression." Evolutionary development is ruthless and violent, moving "forward" only through cycles of death, apparent retrogression, and sideways trails—through trait acquisition guided by chance mutation, which ends up better outfitting certain organisms and species for survival than others. Other than, perhaps, by appealing to a general tendency over time toward increased complexity within species, there is no means of affixing "higher" and "lower" to species. It does not seem plausible to identify consensus end-state design over the arc of creaturely emergence and development.

Ramm asserts a kind of deus ex machina (God or ghost from the machine) role for the Creator, differentiating between progressive creation and *theistic evolution*. Progressive creation seeks to "avoid the arbitrariness of fiat creationism and preserve its doctrine of the transcendence of God," while trying "to avoid the uniformitarianism of theistic evolution, and preserve its sense of progress and/or development."[37] Theistic evolution introduces more distance between divine intention and any particular end-state organism. It allows even those organisms that seem "irreducibly complex" simply to be stages on the continuing march of evolution; eventually they may, by the ongoing forces of resource competition and random happenings, prove unfit for survival. To the contrary, progressive creation sees design throughout the process, positing, as indicated, teleological conditions secured by God through the agency of the Holy Spirit, which dictate evolutionary outcomes. In this, it anticipates the Intelligent Design movement.[38]

Finally, Ramm's view is hermeneutically naive. The books of Scripture and nature might ultimately align, but the noetic effects of sin (on his account,

37. Ramm, *Christian View*, 113.

38. Its arguments are echoed by, for example, Michael Behe, *Darwin's Black Box: The Biochemical Challenge to Evolution* (New York: Free Press, 2006). Baptist theologian Millard Erickson understands progressive creation to allow the possibility of "de novo" creative acts in progressive creation (i.e., to ensure progress toward the creative goal, God occasionally introduces a new kind of creature by radical intervention, then allows evolution to take place within the kind, on the "micro" scale). This view is distinct from Ramm's and differentiates between progressive creation and intelligent design. See Erickson, *Christian Theology*, 3rd ed. (Grand Rapids: Baker Academic, 2013), 352–55, 446–48. Erickson's treatment reflects that of Warfield below.

too) surely will not permit recognition of that alignment without divine aid. If the problem of fundamentalism is that it opposes revelation and science, Ramm's problem is that it seamlessly entwines them. Against both, I suggest that revelation must be free to confront and confirm human readings, biblical and scientific, or it is not revelation.

Two summary remarks at this intermission: First, we have identified predominant models of treating the matter of the earth's age in light of Scripture and modern science, especially Darwinian biology. These are Young Earth Creationism à la cultural fundamentalism (reading Gen. 1–2 without historical context and in opposition to science); the Gap Theory (introducing an indeterminate break between Gen. 1:1 and Gen. 1:2, in which geologic formation and evolutionary development took place, then reading the remainder of the text without context); the Day-Age Theory (that "day" in Gen. 1 really means an extended age within which species development has taken place); Progressive Creation (the Holy Spirit brings creation to its intended form through guided evolution, which spooky agency prefigures the teleological influences claimed by Intelligent Design); and Theistic Evolution (sometimes called Evolutionary Creation, God gives creation a share in God's creative power and allows it to unfold gradually and self-determinatively, all the while relating God's self to it redemptively).

Second, in these varied readings we have begun to detect distinct implications for the character of the biblical text, as well as divergent views of God. For Young Earth Creationists, the text is treated almost like a talisman—mystical and inerrant, inspired in such a way that God handwrote parts of it. "God," however anthropomorphically conceived in this way of thinking, stands outside of creation: as Perception beyond perception, Word before words. On the other end of the continuum, Progressive Creation (and Theistic Evolution) contends that the Bible simply does not address significant questions about creaturely origins. Scripture is situationally occasioned, dealing with the issues of weightiest concern to its authors, and so inspired in such a way as to allow a good measure of human input—including content selection, engagement with other origin stories, redacted structure, and genre variety. In this way of thinking, God is of such a mind and nature as to cede robust power to creation, allowing it a degree of self-determinacy, enabling it to exist as a bona fide counterpart to him. That includes the human creature, who *through its humanity* records the stories according to which "God" becomes known among humans (more dogmatically, who authors the words that God brings into conformity with, indeed assumes as God's Word). The Gap and Day-Age theories obviously fall between these two points on the spectrum.

Cosmology

Lengthiness of creative time frame is not the only challenge with which post-Darwinian readers of Gen. 1–2 must wrestle. The underlying structure of nature and the susceptibility of the natural world to divine influence (and in this, the character of "divine influence") also take on new weight and meaning. As human understanding of nature's productive mechanisms increases, what role is there for God's creative activity?

For Princetonian Benjamin Breckinridge Warfield, the Bible teaches of a God who is decidedly beyond nature. "The religion of the Bible is a frankly supernatural religion."[39] The Creator is not creation; thus the creative agency is outside of creation. Warfield's theology is more sophisticated than that of cultural fundamentalism, to be sure, but nonetheless shares the basic assumption of an opposition between God and nature, or more exactly, between a nonnature being constitutive of "God" (and conversely, nondeity being constitutive of nature). Whatever life-bringing quality nature may exhibit and science may describe, whatever animating action happens "here," so to speak, comes from "there," beyond nature and scientific description. Nature itself is only "nature" insofar as it is a causal outcome of a "higher" power.[40]

The cosmos is an open system. It is not self-realizing but in need, protologically and eschatologically, of divine stimulus and input. That does not mean for Warfield that creation is the immediate outcome of divine fiat. Against fundamentalists like Price, Warfield contended that God creates "mediately," that is, progressively, in and through prior acts of creation.[41] Still, Warfield identifies the key requirement of Gen. 1–2 to be in *safeguarding supersessory causation* for divine agency:

> If we condition the theory [of evolution] by allowing the . . . constant oversight of God in the whole process, and his occasional supernatural interference for the production of *new* beginnings by an actual output of creative force, producing something *new*, i.e., something not included even in posse in

---

39. B. B. Warfield, *The Inspiration and Authority of the Bible* (Philadelphia: P&R, 1948), 71.

40. Warfield thinks soteriologically: "God has intervened extraordinarily, in the course of the sinful world's development, for the salvation of men otherwise lost." The claim is of manifest cosmological relevance. Life comes from the outside, redemptively and originally. *Inspiration and Authority*, 71.

41. See B. B. Warfield, "Creation, Evolution, and Mediate Creation," in *B. B. Warfield: Evolution, Science, and Scripture; Selected Writings*, ed. Mark A. Noll and David N. Livingstone (Grand Rapids: Baker Academic, 2000), 197–210.

preceding conditions,—we may hold to the modified theory of evolution and be [Christ]ians in the ordinary orthodox sense.[42]

God may create through evolution so long as (1) God retains uninterrupted supervisory administration of the process; that is, a power beyond nature supplies some sort of catalytic impulse through natural law directed teleologically, anticipating Ramm, and (2) the same power is allowed occasionally to override natural laws with generative interferences, which transcend all potency latent within the natural system.

The break between and causal movement from Himmelsphere to Terrasphere, if you will, obtains for Warfield also in the doctrine(s)[43] of revelation and inspiration. The Spirit of God "prevails" upon, "energizes," "elevates," "directs," and "superintends"[44] the reasoning of human authors so that they rightly apprehend and communicate God's truth, in fact, so that their words are only secondarily theirs, and primarily God's:

> The Bible is the Word of God in such a sense that its words, though written by men and bearing indelibly impressed upon them the marks of their human origin, were written, nevertheless, under such an influence of the Holy Ghost as to be also the words of God, the adequate expression of His mind and will. . . . This conception of co-authorship implies that the Spirit's superintendence extends to the choice of the words by the human authors (verbal inspiration), and preserves its product from everything inconsistent with a divine authorship.[45]

That the aim of verbal inspiration is to preserve the Bible "from everything inconsistent with a divine authorship" presupposes an *Übermensch/Mensch*

---

42. B. B. Warfield, "Lectures on Anthropology," cited by David N. Livingstone, *Darwin's Forgotten Defenders: The Encounter between Evangelical Theology and Evolutionary Thought* (Vancouver: Regent College Publishing, 1997), 118–19.

43. The plural is put in parentheses because Warfield, although much more systematically precise and thorough, and much more classically instructed than Bible students like Whitcomb, is ultimately inconsistent in treating revelation and inspiration. On the one hand, he construes inspiration as but the third form of revelation (in addition to "theophany" and "prophecy"), while, on the other hand, he maintains that inspiration is *not* revelation, "seeing that it has to do with the communication of truth not its acquirement"; see his *Inspiration and Authority*, 82, 421. Warfield tries to posit a distinction, of course, in order to account for all of the ways that biblical material is ensconced in human culture and tradition. *Communication* of divine truth takes place according to human conventions, whereas *disclosure* happens according to conventions proper to God. Yet at the same time, he wishes to uphold a doctrine of strict inerrancy, indeed, to contend that the biblical words are entirely selected by the Holy Spirit in order to ensure accuracy in reporting, and so conflates communication into acquirement, revelation into inspiration.

44. Warfield, *Inspiration and Authority*, 95.

45. Warfield, *Inspiration and Authority*, 173.

conceptuality. The human is "over-directed" (*super* + *intendere*) even in word choice, however much this raises the question, absent word picking, how the human humanly coauthors Scripture. The human can reliably exercise linguistic capacity only under a prevailing influence, only at the supersessive authority of the Over-human, even as free linguistic exercise is the hallmark of creaturely authorship or evidence of the Bible's "human origin." In the end, nature is overridden by supernature. Even when God works most intimately with creation, the divine influence must come determinatively from without creation, must overcome it, or the outcome would be untrustworthy and therefore nondivine. Being of creation, it would be *erroneous*.[46]

Although Warfield might seem, then, to make conciliatory room for science and human reasoning, he is beholden finally to a conceptual pattern vis-à-vis the cosmos that denies them determinative integrity. Creation, including the biblical author, has no standing in relation to Super-creation.

Early twentieth-century NT scholar Rudolf Bultmann provides a more nuanced treatment of the God-world relation. Biographically, Bultmann was a German Lutheran, and it should be noted that twentieth-century continental European scholarship, perhaps because of its exploration of existential and linguistic ontologies, tends to conceive of the God-world relation in ways that more readily allow for organic and interdependent emergence of life than do its Anglo and especially North American counterparts. In perhaps his most often-cited writing, Bultmann squarely confronts a divergence in cosmological perspective between biblical and modern times and identifies the critical challenge posed to biblical interpretation in the modern era:

> Experience and control of the world have developed to such an extent through science and technology that no one can or does seriously maintain the New Testament world picture. What sense does it make to confess today "he descended into hell" or "he ascended into heaven," if the confessor no longer shares the underlying mythical world picture of a three-story world? Such statements can be confessed honestly only if it is possible to divest their truth of the mythological representations in which it is expressed. . . . Likewise, illnesses and their cures have natural causes and do not depend on the work of demons and on exorcising them. . . . We cannot use electric lights and radios and, in the event of illness, avail ourselves of modern medical and clinical

46. Another way of putting the matter is to say that "humanity" just is that which can produce only the flawed, and "God" is that which can produce only the unflawed. It is worth considering this formulation for a moment, because it highlights the central problem: by its definition *plenary verbal inspiration* fails to allow "humanity" as *object of divine favor* (from beginning to end) to produce, even in its flawed condition, something that God makes perfect use of in the event of its hearing.

means and at the same time believe in the spirit and wonder world of the
New Testament.[47]

For Bultmann, it is axiomatic that the three-tiered world picture of the
ancients—"with earth in the middle, heaven above it, and hell below it"[48]—
simply cannot be maintained in the light of modern cosmology. Neither can
the notion that dark supernatural powers cause, extend, intensify, or otherwise influence illness in a world aware of disease agents like germs, viruses,
genetic abnormalities, and thanks to biology post-Darwin, mutations giving
rise to self-propagating cells resistant to death-inducing protocols (cancer).

From the perspective of a spinning globe elliptically orbiting the sun, no
one who confesses with the apostles that Jesus "*ascended* into heaven" or
"*descended* into hell" has in her mind's eye precisely the upward and downward movement that the apostles envisioned. Nor do most modern Christians
think it viable to corner and extract demons in order to treat a seizure. Nor
do they consider it wise or psychologically healthy to pine or argue for the
world picture of the ancients, and to try to restore their medical practices,
as if their modern world picture and practices lacked something spiritually
critical, which was inextricably imbedded in the ancientness of the ancients.

Instinctively, modern readers fairly well operate as if it is entirely possible
to detach the essential spiritual nutrients of the Bible from their premodern,
mythological husks. Not that they know how to do this consistently, or that
they have carefully adjudicated what is and is not essential biblical teaching.
Bultmann dedicated much of his professional work to the mission of demythologizing the Bible and rendering its core truths in terms meaningful to modern
interpreters—to divesting NT "truth of the mythological representations in
which it is expressed," as the above quotation puts it.[49]

But for Bultmann, modern science supplied only secondary impetus for
such work. Primary motivation to reread and rethink biblical truth from a
new perspective came from within the text itself. "The motive for criticizing
myth, that is, its objectifying representations, is present in myth itself, insofar
as its real intention to talk about a transcendent power to which both we and

47. Rudolf Bultmann, "New Testament and Mythology: The Problem of Demythologizing
the New Testament Proclamation (1941)," in *New Testament and Mythology and Other Basic
Writings*, ed. and trans. Schubert M. Ogden (Minneapolis: Fortress, 1984), 4.
48. Bultmann, "New Testament and Mythology," 1.
49. By construing Bultmann's work as a "mission," I am endorsing the thesis of the recent
study by David Congdon, which contends in part that against the misunderstanding of so many
conservative critics, as well as certain piercing barbs from Karl Barth, Bultmann was something
of a missionary to modernity for the historic Christian faith; see Congdon, *The Mission of
Demythologizing: Rudolf Bultmann's Dialectical Theology* (Minneapolis: Fortress, 2015).

SIDEBAR 11.2

Source Criticism and Interpreting Genesis 1 and 2

Contemporary understanding of the Genesis creation accounts is indelibly stamped by textual, source, redaction, form, and literary analyses.[a] That we can speak confidently of Gen. 1:1–2:4a and Gen. 2:4b–3:24 as creation "accounts" (plural) is a legacy, indeed an achievement of such scholarship. Together with the kind of increased understanding of its ANE background addressed by David Tsumura in the preceding chapter (10), source criticism of the Pentateuch has raised the question of how to interpret Gen. 1–2 more critically than has physical science, and without necessary reference to science.

By the 1870s, when Julius Wellhausen began to publish the material that would compose his classic, *Prolegomena zur Geschichte Israels*, conclusions about the human authorship and editing of source documents had long compelled reconsideration of the doctrine of biblical revelation.[b] In what sense can the book of Genesis be considered "God's Word" when its content owes to multiple human writers and editors with distinct theological agendas (for Gen. 1–2, the Priestly and the Jahwist), its material reflects awareness of and even deliberate engagement with religious claims current in the ANE, and its divergences and repetitions suggest material reassessment over time?

Overlay this question with the mounting consensus that the primeval and patriarchal portions of Genesis offer not a report of history proper but a kind of religiously significant "history." They are "sagas" or "legends," passed down orally over generations, intended to inspire faith in Israel's God.[c] What Genesis presents is testimony to YHWH composed in the expressive, devotional language of ancient Israelites, which was transmitted across many generations and eventually written down by different authors with different points of emphasis. It is not the record of a divine oracle concerning the origin of the earth, Adam and Eve, and so on.

a. For a helpful recent overview of "modern scholarly approaches" specifically to the study of Gen. 1, see the appendix in Mark S. Smith, *The Priestly Vision of Genesis 1* (Minneapolis: Fortress, 2010), 161–92.
b. Julius Wellhausen, *Prolegomena to the History of Israel*, trans. J. Sutherland Black and Allan Menzies (1885; repr., Atlanta: Scholars Press, 1994).
c. On this, see Hermann Gunkel, *Genesis: Translated and Interpreted*, trans. M. E. Biddle, foreword E. W. Nicholson (Macon, GA: Mercer University Press, 1997). The first of three editions of this commentary were published in 1901. Most relevant is the introductory section, "The Legends of Genesis." Also important is Gunkel's *Schöpfung und Chaos in Urzeit und Endzeit: Eine religionsgeschichtliche Untersuchung über Genesis 1 und Ap. Jon 12* (Göttingen: Vandenhoeck & Ruprecht, 1895).

---

the world are subject is hampered and obscured by the objectifying character of its assertions."[50]

The mythic form treats as objects those things which are not—or at least are not in the simple and direct sense of things like trees and rocks and

---

50. Bultmann, "New Testament and Mythology," 10.

water—yet at the same time directs attention beyond its objectifications to their underlying significance. Its design is to place divine truth, power, intention, and effect into narration, not in order to collapse God's being and act into base (nondialectical) objectivity, or to suggest that God's being and act are readily available to simple historical description but quite the opposite—to show by the peculiarity of the narration the essential nonnarratability of its objects. Put simply, myth points beyond itself; it calls the reader to deeper reading by its very nature.

In "demythologizing," then, Bultmann is really "remything" myth, helping the reader to appreciate the character of the textual form in order to interpret it rightly. He says, "Myth is an objectifying kind of thinking like that of science. Myth actually talks about transcendent powers or persons as though they were immanent and worldly—contrary to its real intention. . . . Demythologizing seeks to bring out the real intention of myth, namely, its intention to talk about human existence as grounded in and limited by a transcendent, unworldly power, which is not visible to objectifying thinking."[51]

When myth is read as if its intention is disinterestedly to convey data about the nature of God and the structure of the world, the existentiality of its message becomes lost behind the expedient objectivity of its form. Or more exactly, the content of its message—God, creation, and their interrelation—becomes distorted into competitive scientific description. Contrary to this (regrettably common) happening, Bultmann calls contemporary interpretation to the restorative task of identifying the real, existential significance of the biblical text. It is the goal of the mythical form to reveal a "God" who exists in covenantal communion with creation without collapsing "God" into creation. In Christ Jesus, God is Creator among the created, even more, God exists as created without forfeiting the transformational, life-giving agency constitutive of being "Creator." The transcendent becomes immanent, yet as Source and Ground of the immanent. The creature experiences her Creator as existing with her but with the right and ability to transform her. Existentially, that is, *within* the sphere of her lived experience, she can be made new.

Thus Bultmann points beyond a simple nature/supernature dichotomy. God is not supernature occasionally interrupting nature, but rather, God's Godness is in the free action of directively and determinatively assuming nature. Similarly, humanity is not nature waiting to be overcome by supernature. Humans achieve authenticity in existential realization of their covenantal unity with

51. Rudolf Bultmann, "On the Problem of Demythologizing (1952)," in *New Testament and Mythology*, 98–99.

God, which again is predicated on the constancy of God's self-determining act of being-with-creation.

In other words, Bultmann points in two new directions at once. First, he reckons with the scientific truth that world-description assumes a closed system. The cosmos is cosmically constituting. This is not just a way of saying that science is uninterested in extracosmic discourse, or that the scientific magisterium encompasses questions of empirical value, whereas the philosophical and theological magisteria adjudicate nonempirical subject matter such as ethics (to appropriate the popular framework of Stephen J. Gould). It rather means to convey the truth that divisions are ultimately artificial between nature and supernature, cosmic and extracosmic, even empirical inquiry and ethics.

The self-determining action of God introduces a dialectical alternative: nature is that realm in which God wills fully and totally to exist even as "nature" fails utterly to capture or enframe "deity." God is at once fully present and fully absent to the cosmos, redemptively engaged in the world process and yet agentially unworldly enough to allow the world process authentic self-determination. (In this, theology shares with science a *lack of concern* for questions of origin, which assume a sequential break of any kind between precreation and creation, since such a break already assumes the sequentiality of creation.)

Second, Bultmann's dialectic affords the chance to move beyond thinking of God in mythically spatial terms, as "up there," or for someone like Warfield, "out there." Instead, we might construe divine reality in eschatological terms: God's being-with-us is "already" and "not yet." This temporally oriented way of thinking will find more detailed expression in later twentieth-century figures like Jürgen Moltmann and Wolfhart Pannenberg.

Creation and Nature of Humanity

Perhaps the most acute pressure placed on biblical faith by Darwinian biology concerns a demoted view of humankind. If creaturely development takes place via random mutation from a common ancestor over massively long periods of time, and if that mutation is not causally guided by a supernatural influence but occurs within a closed system, then in what sense is humanity specially created by God to bear God's image?

The late nineteenth-century Princeton theologian Charles Hodge expresses the challenge succinctly. "God, says Darwin, created the unintelligent living cell . . . [and] after that first step, all else follows by natural law, without purpose and without design. No man can believe this, who cannot also believe that all the works of art, literature, and science in the world are the products of carbonic acid, water, and ammonia."[52] Just as we cannot reduce products of great learning and aesthetics to the ingredients of their composition, so also we cannot reduce the human to its cells and their reproduction. There is a minimal holism, a totality that transcends humanity's parts.

For Hodge, Darwinian thought is problematic because it is reductionist. By obscuring the complexity of its mind-body-soul totality, Darwin flattens the human to the level of less sentient or even nonsentient entities. He thus removes the specialness of humanity's standing relative to other existents; emphasizing the commonness of its ancestry, Darwin downplays any quality of distinction, whereby the human is more than the beasts. Hodge defends the traditional view of a "something more," which makes the *humanum* of man and woman. The human "is the image of God, and bears and reflects the divine likeness among the inhabitants of the earth, because he is a spirit, an intelligent, voluntary agent."[53] Humans stand far above the beasts, in God's likeness, by virtue of the fact that they enjoy the sagacious esprit, which is to say the "intelligent, voluntary" agency of their Maker (over against the nonsentient instinctualism of the animals).

Because Darwinism sacrifices the qualitative superiority of humankind in its rationality, which superiority and quality Hodge understands the Genesis narrative to obligate, Hodge concludes that the theory is irredeemably "atheistic."[54] If humankind also emerged by descent from common origin, then its constitution is nearly identical to that of other animals, and its intelligent agency is merely accidental, not the necessary ground of its ability to obey the divine command to rule the earth. The human is no more designed and equipped for this special work than the anteater. And this lack of designed purpose undermines the teleology required to make room for God in evolutionary development.

For Hodge, by contrast, the primal human is the product of a deliberate, purposive act. Length of time designated for the act is not as significant as the uniqueness and intentionality of it. "Adam" is not merely general speech for an inadvertent species but a particular reference to that ordained instant of a distinctly spiritual *Homo sapiens*.

Hodge is a potent critic, but on this issue his thought lacks foresight and betrays the kind of reactionary antipathies characteristic of less-measured

52. Charles Hodge, *Systematic Theology* (1871; repr., New York: Scribner's, 1929), 2:15.
53. Hodge, *Systematic Theology*, 2:99.
54. Hodge, *Systematic Theology*, 2:15–19.

analysis. Genetically, humanity's constitution is nearly identical to that of at least some animals. In view of evidence amassing since Hodge, our intelligence may in fact be only relatively and not qualitatively distinct; selective pressure stemming from resource competition commends itself as the best explanation for the developmental impetus to larger brains.

Moreover, Hodge's attempt to safeguard the ontological singularity of human beings obscures alternative ways of interpreting the *imago Dei*, ways that are intrinsically less hostile to Darwinian thought. Perhaps in referring to the "image" and "likeness" of God, Gen. 1:26 is not referring to possession of an essential quality, a divine "attribute," that the animal world at large does not possess. On the contrary, it may be that God is imaged in freedom for authentic relationship. The Creator gives life not abstractly but personally, making life by giving a share in the Creator's own life to an other—positing an "other," a creature, opposite the Creator, yet in union with the Creator. To be "God" is to share life with another without being absorbed into the other; to be with the creature, once again, but as Creator.

The image of God may be humanity's corollary, derived freedom to have life with God yet as humanity, to exist with the Creator as creature. It may be obediently to enact in its own life the self-determined, covenantal framework of God's life. In that case, the divine image is not a fixed characteristic that separates humanity from the animals but a dynamic manner of action whereby humanity represents and relates redemptively to the animals. Rather than an "essentialist" account of the *imago Dei*, what is needed today is perhaps a "relational" account.

This line of thinking approximates the view of Karl Barth. Barth is sensitive to the impulse to preserve the uniqueness of humankind in the light of Darwinism by appeal to an essential quality of the human composition. He reviews a continuum of three perspectives, which may be thought of as Continental counterparts to Hodge: those of Otto Zöckler ("Mensch," in *Realenzyklopädie für protestantische Theologie und Kirche*, 1903), Rudolf Otto (*Naturalistische und religiöse Weltansicht*, 1904), and Arthur Titius (*Natur und Gott*, 1926).[55] Zöckler argues against Darwinian science on the terms current at the beginning of the twentieth century, citing incomplete fossil evidence and disparities in skull size between humanity and its nearest ape ancestor. "Above all," summarizes Barth, Zöckler emphasizes "the psychological gulf which exists between man and the animal."[56]

55. Karl Barth, *Church Dogmatics* III/2:80–85, *The Doctrine of Creation*, ed. G. W. Bromiley and T. F. Torrance (1960; repr., London: T&T Clark, 2004).
56. Barth, *Church Dogmatics* III/2:80.

Otto is more accepting of continuities between animal and human forms of life, but he, too, contends that "nowhere is the mental a mere function of the process of physical evolution."[57] For him, also, the psyche amounts to a de novo endowment. Titius is more nuanced but nevertheless likewise wishes to think of human psychology as constitutionally *sui generis*. "Titius . . . cannot exclude from the general process of evolution the emergence of the human psyche" but nevertheless stresses "the singularity of [humanity's] mental life."[58] Even though humankind derived by descent from an ancestry shared with the animals, including that organ by which it judges, decides, and plans, the creative potential it exhibits intellectually as well as the complexity of its cultural systems suggest a qualitative difference between this species and all others. Humanity may be protologically base, but it has become special: the *highest* life-form.

Although Barth applauds the efforts of these "apologists for man" in that they rightly appreciate the Christian significance of human nature (i.e., that redemption is founded on assumption of *human* flesh and not nature in general), he does fault them for trying to launch their defense from an abstracted, static quality or nexus of qualities. The psyche/reflective capacity or cultural faculty may not be found elsewhere, at least (so Titius) in the degree to which it is among humankind. But this fact does not alone constitute the specialness of humanity. "We have to know already that we are [human], and that as such we are characteristic and different from the animal and all other beings, if we are to recognize ourselves again in these phenomena of the human. Only those who are familiar with a thing can recognize its symptoms."[59] Perception of human uniqueness assumes prior self-knowledge that the human is unique. The human can only recognize, as it were, its own distinctiveness.

That prior self-knowledge, according to which the human confirms its special identity, comes by way of confrontation with the "genuine" or "real man," Christ Jesus:

> From the very outset we have not been prepared to recognize real man in a being which is neutral, indefinite or obscure in respect of God's attitude towards it and its own attitude to God. On a very definite ground, that of the view of the man Jesus which is normative for Christian theology, we have postulated that real man must in any event be a being which as such belongs to God, to which God turns as Savior, the determination of which is God's glory, which exists under the lordship of God and is set in the service of God.[60]

57. Barth, *Church Dogmatics* III/2:81.
58. Barth, *Church Dogmatics* III/2:82–83.
59. Barth, *Church Dogmatics* III/2:89.
60. Barth, *Church Dogmatics* III/2:121.

Barth describes authentic humanity Christocentrically, as being defined by Jesus in his specific relation to the Father. The import of this for our study is that it locates the identifying marker of human being not in a given *quality* (which is neutral and indefinite with regard to God) but in an *event* (which is partisan and concrete). What differentiates humankind from all other creatures—and at once situates it in relation to every creature as servant and custodian—is the continuing action of God to identify God's self as Savior and Lord *in a concrete person*.

What makes *'ādām* of Adam, then, is not something that he has been given or has cultivated. It is not that a discrete *'ādām* first received a rational soul at some chronological point, the identification of which correlated to achievement of *anthrōpos*. "But man becomes a living soul as God breathes the breath of life *into his nostrils*; in this most direct and most special act. To no beast does God turn in this way."[61] It is in *face-to-face* reiteration of the I-Thou *relation*, which defines God's own, triune life, that humanity comes to be what it is.

In this, Barth is able to affirm both humanity's common descent *and* its specialness as God's image bearer. He requires no mysterious agency guiding anthropological development to a designated end state because it is the action of God toward the human, *in whatever state of existence*, that secures its uniqueness. Put otherwise, Barth is able not to lose the uniqueness of humankind in the soupiness of its shared ancestry, or for that matter in the uncertainty of its future. Past and future, humanity is collectively constituted as *communicant with God*.

Conclusion

Barth supplies an appropriately constructive note on which to end, at least provisionally, as dialogue between scientists and theologians continues on a number of fronts. (Indeed, future conversation almost surely will have less to do with Darwinism, theoretically, and much more to do with concrete developments in biology after Darwin, especially in the field of genetics.) Barth recognizes that there can be no undialectical opposition between the *Christian* God and creation. On the contrary, this God just is Immanuel, *with us*. The self-giving relationality of God's triune life is not an abstract second next to the incarnation but is fully and reiteratively realized in the incarnation. In turn, God's self-disclosure or revelation cannot stand aloof from the creature.

61. Barth, *Church Dogmatics* III/2:236, emphasis added. Barth recognizes that God does give the breath-life also to the beasts, but not in a face-to-face manner. Thus it is not "having" breath (or any other capacity) that makes the human unique but the intimacy of the event of communion with the Maker.

The Bible confronts humanity in its deductive activity, yet makes that activity good and indeed in its very textual output affirms human thought and speech as a secondary locus of the divine Word.

Just as the integrity of creation at large is affirmed in the Son's assumption of specifically human flesh, so also is the humanity of the biblical authors. By their participation in revelation, they reiteratively practice the obedience of the Word and bear God's covenantal image. But we cannot stop there. As the doctrine of God informs our doctrine of Scripture, so our doctrine of Scripture reflects back on our doctrine of God. The two arise together and nourish each other. Not only in their content but also in their canonical operation, if you will, the humanly-authored Scriptures point away from themselves. They describe a God who is at once with us *and* Lord over us. Not just *what* the Bible says but also how it says it, *that* it arrests, *that* it confronts and corrects and commands obedience—in its operation as well as in its content, we encounter the self-determining action of the living, incarnational God.

Faithful reading of the Bible after Darwin is therefore the same as faithful reading before him: that which respects the freedom of the text, which respect grows organically out of encounter with, and corresponding understanding of, the God of the text. For the freedom of the text is given in the freedom of this God, the Creator who wills creation really to be his partner—in fidelity and in perpetual and indeed dynamic newness.

For Further Reading

Barton, Stephen C., and David Wilkinson, eds. *Reading Genesis after Darwin*. Oxford: Oxford University Press, 2009.

Livingstone, David N. *Darwin's Forgotten Defenders: The Encounter between Evangelical Theology and Evolutionary Thought*. Vancouver: Regent College Publishing, 1997.

Livingstone, David N., D. G. Hart, and Mark A. Noll, eds. *Evangelicals and Science in Historical Perspective*. Oxford: Oxford University Press, 1999.

Marsden, George. *Fundamentalism and American Culture*. 2nd ed. Oxford: Oxford University Press, 2006.

Numbers, Ronald L. *The Creationists: From Scientific Creationism to Intelligent Design*. Expanded ed. Cambridge, MA: Harvard University Press, 2006.

Primary Texts in Print

Bultmann, Rudolf. "New Testament and Mythology: The Problem of Demythologizing the New Testament Proclamation (1941)." In *New Testament and Mythology and Other Basic Writings*, translated and edited by Schubert M. Ogden, 1–43. Minneapolis: Fortress, 1984.

Darwin, Charles. *On the Origin of Species by Means of Natural Selection, or the Preservation of Favored Races in the Struggle for Life*. 6th ed. New York: Appleton, 1883.

Hodge, Charles. *Systematic Theology*. Vol. 2. 1871. Repr., New York: Scribner's, 1929.

Price, George McCready. *The New Geology: A Textbook for Colleges, Normal Schools, and Training Schools; and for the General Reader*. Mountain View, CA: Pacific Press, 1923.

Ramm, Bernard. *The Christian View of Science and Scripture*. Grand Rapids: Eerdmans, 1955.

Whitcomb, John C., and Henry M. Morris. *The Genesis Flood: The Biblical Record and Its Scientific Implications*. Philadelphia: P&R, 1961.

White, Andrew Dickson. *A History of the Warfare of Science with Theology in Christendom*. Great Minds. 1896. Repr., Amherst, NY: Prometheus, 1993.

Primary Texts Online

1. American Association for the Advancement of Science / Dialogue on Science, Ethics, and Religion (Templeton-funded program promoting dialogue between faith and science; includes lectures and videos by leading scientists)
   https://www.aaas.org/page/doser-video

2. Biologos (affiliation of scholars arguing for continuity between matters of faith and science, esp. evolution and Christian faith; includes videos, articles, and interviews)
   https://biologos.org

3. Darwin Online (includes full text of Darwin's writings)
   http://darwin-online.org.uk

4. Henry M. Morris, ed. *Scientific Creationism*. 1974. Repr., Green Forest, AR: Master Books, 2012.
   https://books.google.com/books?id=blkuAS0qoQ8C&printsec=frontcover&source=gbs_ge_summary_r&cad=0#v=onepage&q&f=false

5. George McCready Price. *Illogical Geology: The Weakest Point in the Evolution Theory*. Los Angeles: Modern Heretic Co., 1906.
   http://www.gutenberg.org/files/42043/42043-h/42043-h.htm

Postscript

Kyle R. Greenwood

In the present era, interpreters have at their disposal a vast arsenal of interpretive weapons: canonical, global, historical-critical, literary, narrative, postmodern, rhetorical, and theological approaches, to name a few. One of the lessons hopefully learned from following a millennia-long conversation is that reading strategies change, but the commitment to the Bible as *Scripture* has not. The interpreters we have studied did not perceive themselves approaching Gen. 1–2 in a purely subjective manner, in which the text only has meaning insofar as the reader or hearer ascribes meaning to it. Rather, each interpreter operated under the conviction that Gen. 1–2 is Scripture, and thus in some way is authoritative. As such, the text must be read closely and interpreted carefully. Nonetheless, interpretations varied markedly from generation to generation.

To some degree interpreters from every age are bound to the cultural and theological concerns of their era. At times their interpretations and appropriations of Gen. 1–2 are intertwined with the philosophies and customs of the period: early Christians and church fathers in light of Christ; medieval Jews in light of Arabic and Christian interpretations; medieval Christians in light of Aristotelian cosmology; Protestant Reformers in light of Renaissance humanism; Assyriologists in light of Enuma Elish; Bernard Ramm in light of modern science. At other times biblical exegetes adamantly oppose the spirit of the age: early Christians against apostasy; church fathers against heresy; medievalists against Neoplatonic philosophy; Protestant Reformers against

excesses in the Roman Catholic Church; Assyriologists against "parallelomania"; fundamentalists against Darwinian evolution.

Yet this is not to say that, when engaging the history of biblical interpretation, we now face a smorgasbord of interpretive options, with a hermeneutic
du jour at the top of the menu. We should not select only what agrees with our
well-formed palates. On the matter of days, for example, we cannot concur
with Nahmanides that the days of Gen. 1 are twenty-four-hour solar days
but then turn a deaf ear to his more profound explanation that these days are
emanations of the Most High. We cannot stand with Basil's "young earth"
position but then balk at his view that all the elements necessary for creation
were made instantaneously. We cannot demand a literal interpretation of
Gen. 1–2 as a higher view of Scripture but then scoff at literal readings that
treat "one day" (Gen. 1:5 MT, NJPS fn.) as the day of judgment, deduce that
God created two heavens, surmise that Adam was originally androgynous,
conclude that Adam had two wives, place Jesus (the Logos) in the garden of
Eden, or assume that Gen. 2:23 was not referring to Adam and Eve since they
did not have a father and mother.

If nothing else is gleaned from listening to the voices of the past, we should
be reminded of our own inadequacies as interpreters. We do not come to the
text tabula rasa. We are formed and informed by our cultural milieu, which
entails economic, linguistic, philosophical, political, sociological, and theological influences, among others. The questions we bring to Scripture have
likewise been shaped by those with whom we engage and debate on a regular
basis. We adopt perspectives of the like-minded, while we resist contrarians.
However, if we are to be faithful readers of Scripture, it behooves us to look
beyond our interpretive enclaves, to shed our hermeneutical hubris, and listen.
By listening to the voices of others, whether those voices spoke three years
ago or three millennia ago, we can discover models and techniques for taking Scripture more authoritatively and holding our own interpretations less
dogmatically.

Select Bibliography

Adams, Edward. *The Stars Will Fall from Heaven: Cosmic Catastrophe in the New Testament and Its World*. LNTS 347. London: T&T Clark, 2007.

Albright, William F. "The Babylonian Matter in the Predeuteronomic Primeval History (JE) in Genesis 1–11." *JBL* 58 (1939): 87–103.

Alexander, P. "Midrash." In *A Dictionary of Biblical Interpretation*, edited by R. J. Coggins and J. Houlden, 450–60. Philadelphia: Trinity Press International, 1990.

Allison, Dale. "Eschatology of the NT." In *The New Interpreter's Dictionary of the Bible*, edited by Katharine Doob Sakenfeld, 2:249–99. Nashville: Abingdon, 2007.

Anderson, Gary A. *The Genesis of Perfection: Adam and Eve in Jewish and Christian Imagination*. Louisville: Westminster John Knox, 2001.

Attridge, Harold W. *The Interpretation of Biblical History in the "Antiquitates Judaicae" of Flavius Josephus*. HDR 7. Missoula, MT: Scholars Press, 1976.

———. "Josephus and His Works." In *Jewish Writings of the Second Temple Period: Apocrypha, Pseudepigrapha, Qumran Sectarian Writings, Philo, Josephus*, edited by Michael Stone, 185–232. Philadelphia: Fortress; Assen: Van Gorcum, 1984.

———. "'Let Us Strive to Enter That Rest': The Logic of Hebrews 4:1–11." *HTR* 73 (1980): 279–88.

Baer, Richard A. *Philo's Use of the Categories Male and Female*. ALGHJ 3. Leiden: Brill, 1970.

Bandstra, Barry L. *Genesis 1–11: A Handbook on the Hebrew Text*. Waco: Baylor University Press, 2008.

Barrosse, Thomas. "The Seven Days of the New Creation in St. John's Gospel." *CBQ* 21 (1959): 507–16.

Barth, Karl. *Church Dogmatics* III/2. *The Doctrine of Creation*. Edited by G. W. Bromiley and T. F. Torrance. London: T&T Clark, 1960. Repr., 2004.

Barton, Stephen C., and David Wilkinson, eds. *Reading Genesis after Darwin*. Oxford: Oxford University Press, 2009.

Batto, Bernard F. "The Sleeping God: An Ancient Near Eastern Motif of Divine Sovereignty." In *In the Beginning: Essays on Creation Motifs in the Ancient Near East and the Bible*, 139–57. Siphrut 9. Winona Lake, IN: Eisenbrauns, 2013.

Bavinck, Herman. *In the Beginning: Foundations of Christian Theology*. Edited by John Bolt. Translated by John Vriend. Grand Rapids: Baker, 1999.

Behr, John. *The Mystery of Christ: Life in Death*. Crestwood, NY: St. Vladimir's Seminary Press, 2006.

Bellamah, Timothy, OP. *The Biblical Interpretation of William of Alton*. New York: Oxford University Press, 2011.

Bergen, Robert D., ed. *Biblical Hebrew and Discourse Linguistics*. Dallas: SIL International, 1994.

Bloch-Smith, Elizabeth. "'Who Is the King of Glory?' Solomon's Temple and Its Symbolism." In *Scripture and Other Artifacts: Essays on the Bible and Archaeology in Honor of Philip J. King*, edited by Michael D. Coogan, J. Cheryl Exum, and Lawrence E. Stager, 18–31. Louisville: Westminster John Knox, 1994.

Blowers, Paul. *Drama of the Divine Economy: Creator and Creation in Early Christian Theology and Piety*. Oxford: Oxford University Press, 2012.

Bockmuehl, Markus, and Guy G. Stroumsa, eds. *Paradise in Antiquity: Jewish and Christian Views*. Cambridge: Cambridge University Press, 2010.

Boehmer, Julius. "Wieviel Menschen sind am letzten Tage des Hexaëmerons geschaffen worden?" *ZAW* 34 (1914): 31–35.

Borgen, Peder. "Philo of Alexandria." In *Jewish Writings of the Second Temple Period: Apocrypha, Pseudepigrapha, Qumran Sectarian Writings, Philo, Josephus*, edited by Michael Stone, 233–82. Philadelphia: Fortress; Assen: Van Gorcum, 1984.

Bouteneff, Peter C. *Beginnings: Ancient Christian Readings of the Biblical Creation Narratives*. Grand Rapids: Baker Academic, 2008.

Brayford, Susan. *Genesis*. Septuagint Commentary Series. Leiden: Brill, 2007.

Brock, Sebastian. Introduction to *St. Ephrem the Syrian: Hymns on Paradise*, translated by S. Brock, 7–75. Crestwood, NY: St. Vladimir's Seminary Press, 1990.

Brown, Jeannine K. "Creation's Renewal in the Gospel of John." *CBQ* 72 (2010): 275–90.

Brown, William P. *The Seven Pillars of Creation: The Bible, Science, and the Ecology of Wonder*. Oxford: Oxford University Press, 2010.

———. *Structure, Role, and Ideology in the Hebrew and Greek Texts of Genesis 1:1–2:3*. SBLDS 132. Atlanta: Scholars Press, 1993.

Bultmann, Rudolf. *New Testament and Mythology and Other Basic Writings*. Translated and edited by Schubert M. Ogden. Minneapolis: Fortress, 1984.

Calvin, John. *Commentaries on the First Book of Moses, Called Genesis*. Translated by John King. Vol. 1. Calvin's Commentaries. Repr., Grand Rapids: Baker Books, 2003.

————. *Institutes of the Christian Religion*. Edited by John T. McNeil. Translated by Ford Lewis Battles. Philadelphia: Westminster, 1960; London: SCM, 1961.

Caputo, Nina. *Nahmanides in Medieval Catalonia: History, Community, and Messianism*. Notre Dame, IN: University of Notre Dame Press, 2007.

Carroll, John T. "Creation and Apocalypse." In *God Who Creates: Essays in Honor of W. Sibley Towner*, edited by William P. Brown and S. Dean McBride Jr., 251–60. Grand Rapids: Eerdmans, 2000.

Cassuto, Umberto. *A Commentary on the Book of Genesis: From Adam to Noah*. 1944. Repr., Jerusalem: Magnes, 1961.

Charlesworth, James H. "Paradise." In *The New Interpreter's Dictionary of the Bible*, edited by Katharine Doob Sakenfeld, 4:377–78. Nashville: Abingdon, 2009.

Chavel, Charles Ber. *Ramban: Commentary on the Torah*. Vol. 1. New York: Shilo, 1971.

Clines, David J. A. "The Image of God in Man." *TynBul* 19 (1968): 53–103.

Cochran, Elizabeth Agnew. "The *Imago Dei* and Human Perfection: The Significance of Christology for Gregory of Nyssa's Understanding of the Human Person." *HeyJ* 50 (2009): 402–15.

Cohen, Jeremy. *"Be Fertile and Increase, Fill the Earth and Master It": The Ancient and Medieval Career of a Biblical Text*. Ithaca, NY: Cornell University Press, 1992.

Collins, C. John. "Adam and Eve in the Old Testament." In *Adam, the Fall, and Original Sin: Theological, Biblical, and Scientific Perspectives*, edited by Hans Madueme and Michael Reeves, 3–32. Grand Rapids: Baker Academic, 2014.

————. *Did Adam and Eve Really Exist? Who They Were and Why You Should Care*. Wheaton: Crossway, 2011.

————. *Genesis 1–4: A Linguistic, Literary, and Theological Commentary*. Philipsburg, NJ: P&R, 2006.

————. "Reading Genesis 1–2 with the Grain: Analogical Days." In *Reading Genesis 1–2: An Evangelical Conversation*, edited by J. Daryl Charles, 73–92. Peabody, MA: Hendrickson, 2013.

Coloe, Mary L. "Creation in the Gospel of John." In *Creation Is Groaning: Biblical and Logical Perspectives*, edited by Mary L. Coloe, 71–90. Collegeville, MN: Liturgical Press, 2013.

Costache, Doru. "Approaching *An Apology for the Hexaemeron*: Its Aims, Method, and Discourse." *Phronema* 27, no. 2 (2012): 53–81.

Dahan, Gilbert. *Les intellectuels chrétiens et les juifs au moyen âge*. Paris: Cerf, 2007.

Dalley, Stephanie M. *Myths from Mesopotamia: Creation, the Flood, Gilgamesh, and Others*. Oxford: Oxford University Press, 1991.

Dan, Joseph. "Samael, Lilith, and the Concept of Evil in Early Kabbalah." *AJSR* 5 (1980): 17–40.

Darwin, Charles. *On the Origin of Species by Means of Natural Selection, or the Preservation of Favored Races in the Struggle for Life.* 6th ed. New York: D. Appleton, 1883.

Darwin, Francis, ed. *The Life and Letters of Charles Darwin, Including an Autobiographical Chapter.* Vol. 2. London: John Murray, 1888.

Day, John. *From Creation to Babel: Studies in Genesis 1–11.* London: Bloomsbury, 2013.

————. *God's Conflict with the Dragon and the Sea: Echoes of a Canaanite Myth in the Old Testament.* UCOP 35. Cambridge: Cambridge University Press, 1985.

De Beer, Wynand Vladimir. "Being Human, Becoming Like God: Patristic Perspectives on Humankind." *JTSA* 148 (March 2014): 65–82.

Dembski, William A., Wayne J. Downs, and Justin B. A. Frederick. *The Patristic Understanding of Creation: An Anthology of Writings from the Church Fathers on Creation and Design.* Riesel, TX: Erasmus, 2008.

Dennis, John. "Cosmology in the Petrine Literature and Jude." In *Cosmology and New Testament Theology*, edited by Jonathan T. Pennington and Sean M. McDonough, 157–77. LNTS 355. London: T&T Clark, 2008.

Derby, Josiah. "The Fourth Commandment." *JBQ* 22 (1994): 26–31.

DeSilva, David. "Entering God's Rest: Eschatology and the Socio-rhetorical Strategy of Hebrews." *TJ* 21 (2000): 25–43.

Doering, Lutz. "Sabbath and Festivals." In *The Oxford Handbook of Jewish Daily Life in Roman Palestine*, edited by Catherine Hezser, 566–86. Oxford: Oxford University Press, 2010.

Doron, Pinchas, trans. *The Mystery of Creation according to Rashi: A New Translation and Interpretation of Rashi on Genesis I–VII.* New York: Moznaim, 1982.

Douglass, Jane Dempsey. *Women, Freedom, and Calvin.* Philadelphia: Westminster, 1985.

Draper, John William. *History of the Conflict between Religion and Science.* 1874. Repr., Charleston, SC: Nabu, 2010.

Eder, Asher. "The Sabbath Commandment: Its Two Versions." *JBQ* 25 (1997): 188–91.

Edsall, Benjamin A. "Greco-Roman Costume and Paul's Fraught Argument in 1 Corinthians 11:2–16." *JGRChJ* 9 (2013): 132–46.

Elgvin, Torleif. "The Genesis Section of 4Q422 (4QParaGenExod)." *DSD* 1, no. 2 (1994): 180–96.

Ellington, John. "Man and Adam in Genesis 1–5." *BT* 30 (1979): 201–5.

Endo, Masanobu. *Creation and Christology: A Study on the Johannine Prologue in the Light of Early Jewish Creation Accounts.* Tübingen: Mohr Siebeck, 2002.

Enns, Peter E. *The Evolution of Adam: What the Bible Does and Doesn't Say about Human Origins.* Grand Rapids: Brazos, 2012.

Feldman, Louis. *Flavius Josephus: Translation and Commentary.* Vol. 3, *Judean Antiquities 1–4.* Leiden and Boston: Brill, 2000.

————. *Studies in Josephus' Rewritten Bible*. JSJSup 58. Leiden: Brill, 1998.

Feldman, Seymour. "Gersonides' Proofs for the Creation of the Universe." *PAAJR* 35 (1967): 113–37.

Fleming, Daniel E. "The Israelite Festival Calendar and Emar's Ritual Archive." *RB* 106 (1999): 161–74.

Foster, Benjamin R. "Epic of Creation." In *COS*. Vol. 1, *Canonical Compositions from the Biblical World*, edited by W. W. Hallo and K. L. Younger, 390–402. Leiden: Brill, 1997.

Funkenstein, Amos. *Perceptions of Jewish History*. Berkeley: University of California Press, 1993.

————. *Theology and the Scientific Imagination from the Middle Ages to the Seventeenth Century*. Princeton: Princeton University Press, 1986.

Furley, David. *The Greek Cosmologists*. Vol. 1, *The Formation of the Atomic Theory and Its Earliest Critics*. Cambridge: Cambridge University Press, 1987.

Furstenberg, Yair. "The Rabbinic Ban on Ma'aseh Bereshit: Sources, Contexts and Concerns." In *Jewish and Christian Cosmogony in Late Antiquity*, edited by Lance Jenott and Sarit Kattan Gribetz, 39–63. Texts and Studies in Ancient Judaism 155. Tübingen: Mohr Siebeck, 2013.

García Martínez, Florentino. "Creation in the Dead Sea Scrolls." In *The Creation of Heaven and Earth: Re-interpretations of Genesis I in the Context of Judaism, Ancient Philosophy, Christianity, and Modern Physics*, edited by Geurt Hendrik van Kooten, 49–70. TBN 8. Leiden: Brill, 2005.

————. "Man and Woman: Halakhah Based upon Eden in the Dead Sea Scrolls." In *Paradise Interpreted: Representations of Biblical Paradise in Judaism and Christianity*, edited by Gerard P. Luttikhuizen, 95–115. TBN 2. Leiden: Brill, 1999.

Geiger, Ari. "A Student and an Opponent: Nicholas and His Jewish Sources." In *Nicolas de Lyre, franciscain du XIVe siècle, exégète et théologien*, edited by G. Dahan, 167–203. Paris: Institut d'Études Augustiniennes, 2011.

Giller, Pinchas. *Reading the Zohar: The Sacred Text of the Kabbalah*. Oxford: Oxford University Press, 2000.

Ginzberg, Louis. *Legends of the Jews*. Translated by Henrietta Szold and Paul Radin. 1909. Repr. in 2 vols. London: Forgotten Books, 2008.

Goodacre, Mark. *The Case against Q: Studies in Markan Priority and the Synoptic Problem*. Harrisburg, PA: Trinity Press International, 2002.

Goodman, Martin. "Paradise, Gardens, and the Afterlife in the First Century CE." In *Paradise in Antiquity: Jewish and Christian Views*, edited by Markus Bockmuehl and Guy G. Stroumsa, 57–63. Cambridge: Cambridge University Press, 2010.

Gordon, Bruce. *Calvin*. New Haven: Yale University Press, 2009.

Graboïs, Aryeh. "The *Hebraica Veritas* and Jewish-Christian Intellectual Relations in the Twelfth Century." *Speculum* 50 (1975): 613–34.

Gray, Patrick. *Opening Paul's Letters: A Reader's Guide to Genre and Interpretation*. Grand Rapids: Baker Academic, 2012.

Greenfield, Jonas C. "A Touch of Eden." In *Orientalia J. Duchesne-Guillemin Emerito Oblata*, 219–24. Acta Iranica 23. Leiden: Brill, 1984.

Greene-McCreight, K. E. *Ad Litteram: How Augustine, Calvin, and Barth Read the "Plain Sense" of Genesis 1–3*. New York: Peter Lang, 1999.

Greenwood, Kyle. *Scripture and Cosmology: Reading the Bible between the Ancient World and Modern Science*. Downers Grove, IL: IVP Academic, 2015.

Grimes, Joseph E. *The Thread of Discourse*. The Hague: Mouton, 1975.

Grossman, Avraham. *Pious and Rebellious: Jewish Women in Medieval Europe*. Waltham, MA: Brandeis University Press; Hanover, NH: University Press of New England, 2004.

Grypeou, Emmanouela, and Helen Spurling. *The Book of Genesis in Late Antiquity: Encounters between Jewish and Christian Exegesis*. Leiden: Brill, 2013.

Gunkel, Hermann. *Creation and Chaos in the Primeval Era and the Eschaton: A Religio-historical Study of Genesis 1 and Revelation 12*. Translated by K. William Whitney Jr. Grand Rapids: Eerdmans, 2006. Translation of *Schöpfung und Chaos in Urzeit und Endzeit: Eine religiongeschichtliche Untersuchung über Genesis 1 und Ap. Joh. 12*. Göttingen: Vandenhoeck & Ruprecht, 1895.

———. *Genesis: Translated and Interpreted*. Translated by M. E. Biddle. Foreword by E. W. Nicholson. Macon, GA: Mercer University Press, 1997.

Hagner, Donald A. "Jesus and the Synoptic Sabbath Controversies." *BBR* 19 (2009): 215–48.

Hallo, William W. "Ancient Near Eastern Texts and Their Relevance for Biblical Exegesis." In *COS*, vol. 1, *Canonical Compositions from the Biblical World*, edited by W. W. Hallo and K. L. Younger, xxiii–xxviii. Leiden: Brill, 1997.

Halton, C., ed. *Genesis: History, Fiction, or Neither? Three Views on the Bible's Earliest Chapters*. Grand Rapids: Zondervan, 2015.

Harding, Mark. "Josephus and Philo." In *Prayer from Alexander to Constantine: A Critical Anthology*, edited by Mark Kiley, 86–91. London and New York: Routledge, 1997.

Harris, Jay M. *How Do We Know This? Midrash and the Fragmentation of Modern Judaism*. New York: State University of New York Press, 1995.

Harris, Robert A. "Medieval Jewish Biblical Exegesis." In *A History of Biblical Interpretation: The Medieval through the Reformation Periods*, edited by Alan J. Hauser and Duane F. Watson, 141–71. Grand Rapids: Eerdmans, 2009.

Harvey, Anthony E. "Genesis versus Deuteronomy? Jesus on Marriage and Divorce." In *The Gospels and the Scriptures of Israel*, edited by Craig A. Evans and W. Richard Stegner, 55–65. JSNTSup 104. Sheffield: Sheffield Academic, 1994.

Hasel, Gerhard F. "The Polemic Nature of the Genesis Cosmology." *EvQ* 46 (1974): 81–102.

Haught, John F. *God after Darwin: A Theology of Evolution*. Boulder, CO: Westview, 2000.

Hendel, Ronald. *The Book of Genesis: A Biography*. Lives of Great Religious Books. Princeton: Princeton University Press, 2013.

———. *The Text of Genesis 1–11: Textual Studies and Critical Edition*. New York: Oxford University Press, 1998.

Hess, Richard S. "Genesis 1–2 in Its Literary Context." *TynBul* 41 (1990): 143–53.

———. "Splitting the Adam: The Usage of ʾĀDĀM in Genesis I–V." In *Studies in the Pentateuch*, edited by J. A. Emerton, 1–15. VTSup 41. Leiden: Brill, 1990.

Hess, Richard S., and David T. Tsumura, eds. *"I Studied Inscriptions from Before the Flood": Ancient Near Eastern, Literary, and Linguistic Approaches to Genesis 1–11*. Winona Lake, IN: Eisenbrauns, 1994.

Hill, Edmund P. Introduction to *The Literal Meaning of Genesis*. In *On Genesis*, 155–66. Works of Saint Augustine: A Translation for the 21st Century. Hyde Park, NY: New City Press, 2002.

Hill, Robert C. "*Akribeia*: A Principle of Chrysostom's Exegesis." *Australian and New Zealand Theological Review* 14, no. 1 (1981): 32–36.

———. Introduction to *Homilies on Genesis 1–17*, by John Chrysostom, 1–19. Washington, DC: Catholic University of America Press, 1986.

———. Introduction to *The Questions on the Octateuch*, by Theodoret of Cyrus, xix–lix. Washington, DC: Catholic University of America Press, 2007.

———. "On Looking Again at *Synkatabasis*." *Prudentia* 13 (1981): 3–11.

Hillar, Marian. *From Logos to Trinity: The Evolution of Religious Beliefs from Pythagoras to Tertullian*. New York: Cambridge University Press, 2011.

Hillerbrand, Hans J. *Oxford Encyclopedia of the Reformation*. Oxford: Oxford University Press, 1996.

Hodge, Charles. *Systematic Theology*. Vol. 2. New York: Scribner, 1871. Repr., 1929.

Holmstedt, Robert D. "The Restrictive Syntax of Genesis i 1." *VT* 58, no. 1 (2008): 56–67.

Holsinger-Friesen, Thomas. *Irenaeus and Genesis: A Study of Competition in Early Christian Hermeneutics*. Winona Lake, IN: Eisenbrauns, 2009.

Idel, Moshe. "We Have No Kabbalistic Tradition on This." In *Rabbi Moses Nahmanides (Ramban): Explorations in His Religious and Literary Virtuosity*, edited by Isadore Twersky, 68–73. Cambridge, MA: Harvard University Press, 1983.

Jackson, Ryan T. *New Creation in Paul's Letters: A Study of the Historical and Social Setting of a Pauline Concept*. Tübingen: Mohr Siebeck, 2010.

Jacobsen, Anders L. "The Importance of Genesis 1–3 in the Theology of Irenaeus." *VC* 62 (2008): 213–32.

Jaki, Stanley. *Genesis 1 through the Ages*. 2nd rev. ed. Edinburgh: Scottish Academic Press, 1998.

Jervell, Jacob. "Imagines und *Imago Dei*: Aus der Genesis-Exegese des Josephus." In *Josephus-Studien: Untersuchungen zu Josephus, dem antiken Judentum und dem Neuen Testament*, edited by Otto Betz, Klaus Haacker, and Martin Hengel, 197–204. Göttingen: Vandenhoeck & Ruprecht, 1974.

———. *Imago Dei: Genesis 1,26f. im Spätjudentum, in der Gnosis und in den Paulinischen Briefen*. FRLANT. Göttingen: Vandenhoeck & Ruprecht, 1960.

Jobes, Karen H., and Moisés Silva. *Invitation to the Septuagint*. 2nd ed. Grand Rapids: Baker Academic, 2015.

Johnson, Luke Timothy. "Life-Giving Spirit: The Ontological Implications of Resurrection." *Stone-Campbell Journal* 15 (2012): 75–89.

Jones, C. W. *Libri quattuor in principium Genesis usque ad nativitatem Isaac et eiectionem Ismahelis adnotationum (sive Hexaemeron)*. CCSL 118A. Turnhout: Brepols, 1967.

Kalman, Jason. "Rabbinic Exegesis." In *The Oxford Encyclopedia of Biblical Interpretation*, edited by Steven L. McKenzie, 2:177–89. New York: Oxford University Press, 2014.

Kamin, Sarah. "Rashbam's Conception of the Creation in Light of the Intellectual Currents of His Time." *Scripta Hierosolymitana* 31 (1986): 91–132.

Kasher, Rimon. "Scripture in Rabbinic Literature." In *Mikra: Text, Translation, Reading, and Interpretation of the Hebrew Bible in Ancient Judaism and Early Christianity*, edited by Martin Jan Mulder and Harry Sysling, 547–94. Assen: Van Gorcum; Philadelphia: Fortress, 1988. Repr., Peabody, MA: Hendrickson, 2004.

Klein-Braslavy, Sara. *Maimonides as Biblical Interpreter*. Boston: Academic Studies Press, 2011.

Kolb, Robert. *Martin Luther and the Enduring Word of God: The Wittenberg School and Its Scripture-Centered Proclamation*. Grand Rapids: Baker Academic, 2016.

Kramer, Samuel Noah. *The Sumerians: Their History, Culture, and Character*. Chicago: University of Chicago Press, 1963.

Kreitzer, L. J. "Adam and Christ." In *Dictionary of Paul and His Letters*, edited by Gerald F. Hawthorne, Ralph P. Martin, and Daniel G. Reid, 9–15. Downers Grove, IL: InterVarsity, 1993.

Kugel, James. *The Bible as It Was*. Cambridge, MA: Belknap, 1999.

Kvam, Kristen E., Linda S. Schearing, and Valarie H. Ziegler, eds. *Eve and Adam: Jewish, Christian, and Muslim Readings on Genesis and Gender*. Bloomington: Indiana University Press, 1999.

Lambert, Malcolm. *The Cathars*. Oxford: Oxford University Press, 1998.

Lambert, W. G. *Babylonian Creation Myths*. Winona Lake, IN: Eisenbrauns, 2013.

————. "Creation in the Bible and the Ancient Near East." In *Creation and Chaos: A Reconsideration of Hermann Gunkel's* Chaoskampf *Hypothesis*, edited by JoAnn Scurlock and Richard H. Beal, 44–47. Winona Lake, IN: Eisenbrauns, 2013.

Lambert, W. G., and A. R. Millard. *Atra-Ḥasīs: The Babylonian Story of the Flood.* Oxford: Clarendon, 1969.

Lambrecht, Jan. "Paul's Christological Use of Scripture in 1 Corinthians 15:20–28." *NTS* 28 (1982): 502–27.

Levine, Michelle J. *Nahmanides on Genesis: The Art of Biblical Portraiture.* BJS 350. Atlanta: SBL Press, 2009.

Lewis, Jack P. "The Days of Creation: An Historical Survey of Interpretation." *JETS* 34, no. 2 (1989): 433–55.

Liebes, Yehuda. *Studies in Jewish Myth and Messianism.* Albany: SUNY Press, 1993.

Lim, Richard. "The Politics of Interpretation in Basil of Caesarea's *Hexaemeron.*" *VC* 44 (1990): 351–70.

Lincoln, Andrew T. "Sabbath, Rest, and Eschatology in the New Testament." In *From Sabbath to Lord's Day: A Biblical, Historical, and Theological Investigation*, edited by D. A. Carson, 197–220. Grand Rapids: Zondervan, 1982.

Livingstone, David N. *Darwin's Forgotten Defenders: The Encounter between Evangelical Theology and Evolutionary Thought.* Vancouver: Regent College Publishing, 1997.

Livingstone, David N., D. G. Hart, and Mark A. Noll, eds. *Evangelicals and Science in Historical Perspective.* Oxford: Oxford University Press, 1999.

Loader, William. *The Septuagint, Sexuality, and the New Testament: Case Studies on the Impact of the LXX in Philo and the New Testament.* Grand Rapids: Eerdmans, 2004.

Loepp, Dale. "The Adamic Creation Tradition in the Seventeenth Demonstration of Aphrahat." In *Exegesis and Hermeneutics in the Churches of the East*, edited by Vahan S. Hovhanessian, 9–21. New York: Peter Lang, 2009.

Louth, Andrew. "The Fathers on Genesis." In *The Book of Genesis: Composition, Reception, and Interpretation*, edited by David L. Petersen, Joel N. Evans, and Craig A. Evans, 561–78. Leiden: Brill, 2012.

Louw, Theo van der. *Transformations in the Septuagint: Towards an Interaction of Septuagint Studies and Translation Studies.* CBET 47. Leuven: Peeters, 2007.

Luther, Martin. *Lectures on Genesis: Chapters 1–5.* In LW 1:v–387.

Luttikhuizen, Gerard P. *Gnostic Revisions of Genesis Stories and Early Jesus Traditions.* Leiden: Brill, 2006.

————, ed. *Paradise Interpreted: Representations of Biblical Paradise in Judaism and Christianity.* Leiden: Brill, 1999.

Macaskill, Grant. "Paradise in the New Testament." In *Paradise in Antiquity: Jewish and Christian Views*, edited by Markus Bockmuehl and Guy G. Stroumsa, 64–81. Cambridge: Cambridge University Press, 2010.

Maimonides, Moses. *The Guide of the Perplexed*. Translated and with an Introduction and Notes by Shlomo Pines. 2 vols. Chicago: University of Chicago Press, 1963.

Manekin, Charles H. "Conservative Tendencies in Gersonides' Religious Philosophy." In *The Cambridge Companion to Medieval Jewish Philosophy*, edited by Daniel H. Frank and Oliver Leaman, 304–42. Cambridge: Cambridge University Press, 2003.

Mangenot, E. "Hexaméron." In *Dictionnaire de Théologie Catholique*, edited by E. Mangenot et al., 6:2325–54. Paris: Letouzey, 1947.

Marsden, George. *Fundamentalism and American Culture*. 2nd ed. Oxford: Oxford University Press, 2006.

Martens, Peter. *Origen and Scripture: The Contours of the Exegetical Life*. Oxford: Oxford University Press, 2012.

———. "Origen's Doctrine of Pre-existence and the Opening Chapters of Genesis." *ZAC* 16 (2013): 516–49.

Mathewson, David. *A New Heaven and a New Earth: The Meaning and Function of the Old Testament in Revelation 21:1–22:5*. JSNTSup 238. Sheffield: Sheffield Academic, 2003.

Maxfield, John A. *Luther's Lectures on Genesis and the Formation of Evangelical Identity*. Sixteenth Century Essays and Studies 80. Kirksville, MO: Truman State University Press, 2008.

May, Gerhard. *Creatio ex Nihilo: The Doctrine of "Creation out of Nothing" in Early Christian Thought*. Translated by A. S. Worrall. Edinburgh: T&T Clark, 1994.

McDonough, Sean M. *Christ as Creator: Origins of a New Testament Doctrine*. Oxford: Oxford University Press, 2009.

McIver, R. K. "'Cosmology' as a Key to the Thought-World of Philo of Alexandria." *AUSS* 26, no. 3 (1988): 267–79.

McKim, Donald K., ed. *Calvin and the Bible*. Oxford: Oxford University Press, 2006.

McNutt, Jennifer Powell, and David Lauber, eds. *The People's Book: The Reformation and the Bible*. Downers Grove, IL: IVP Academic, 2017.

Meer, Jitse M. van der, and Scott Mandelbrote, eds. *Nature and Scripture in the Abrahamic Religions: 1700–Present*. Vol. 1. Leiden: Brill, 2008.

Mermelstein, Ari. *Creation, Covenant, and the Beginnings of Judaism: Reconceiving Historical Time in the Second Temple Period*. JSJSup 168. Leiden: Brill, 2014.

Mettinger, Tryggve N. D. *The Eden Narrative: A Literary and Religio-historical Study of Genesis 2–3*. Winona Lake, IN: Eisenbrauns, 2007.

Meyers, Carol L. *The Tabernacle Menorah: A Synthetic Study of a Symbol from the Biblical Cult*. Missoula, MT: Scholars Press, 1976.

Millard, Alan R. "The Etymology of Eden." *VT* 34 (1984): 103–6.

Moore, Nicholas J. "Jesus as 'The One Who Entered His Rest': The Christological Reading of Hebrews 4:10." *JSNT* 36 (2014): 383–400.

Morris, Henry M., ed. *Scientific Creationism*. San Diego: Creation-Life Publishers, 1974. Repr., Green Forest, AR: Master Books, 2012.

Navon, Chaim. *Genesis and Jewish Thought*. Jersey City, NJ: KTAV, 2008.

Neusner, Jacob. *Confronting Creation: How Judaism Reads Genesis; An Anthology of Genesis Rabbah*. Columbia: University of South Carolina Press, 1991.

Neusner, Jacob, and William Scott Green. *Rabbinic Judaism: Structure and System*. Minneapolis: Fortress, 1995.

————. *Writing with Scripture: The Authority and Uses of the Hebrew Bible in Formative Judaism*. Eugene, OR: Wipf & Stock, 2003.

Nielson, J. T. *Adam and Christ in the Theology of Irenaeus of Lyons*. Assen: Van Gorcum, 1968.

Noll, Mark A., and David N. Livingstone, eds. *B. B. Warfield: Evolution, Science, and Scripture; Selected Writings*. Grand Rapids: Baker, 2000.

Novak, David. *The Theology of Nahmanides Systematically Presented*. BJS 271. Atlanta: SBL Press, 1992.

Numbers, Ronald L. *The Creationists: From Scientific Creationism to Intelligent Design*. Expanded ed. Cambridge, MA: Harvard University Press, 2006.

Orbe, Antonio. "Cinco exegesis Ireneanas de Genesis 2:17b: *Adv. haer.* V 23, 1–2." *Greg* (1981): 75–113.

Osborn, Ronald E. *Death before the Fall: Biblical Literalism and the Problem of Animal Suffering*. Downers Grove, IL: IVP Academic, 2014.

Osiek, Carolyn. "The Bride of Christ (Ephesians 5:22–33): A Problematic Wedding." *BTB* 32 (2002): 29–39.

Oyen, Geert van. "The Character of Eve in the New Testament." In *Out of Paradise: Eve and Adam and Their Interpreters*, edited by Bob Becking and Susanne Hennecke, 14–28. Sheffield: Sheffield Phoenix, 2011.

Painter, John. "Earth Made Whole: John's Rereading of Genesis." In *Word, Theology, and Community in John*, edited by John Painter, R. Alan Culpepper, and Fernando F. Segovia, 65–84. St. Louis: Chalice, 2002.

Peacocke, Arthur. *Evolution: The Disguised Friend of Faith?* Philadelphia and London: Templeton, 2004.

Pope, Marvin. "Adam (אָדָם)." *EncJud* 1:371–72.

Porter, Stanley E., ed. *Hearing the Old Testament in the New Testament*. Grand Rapids: Eerdmans, 2006.

Powell, Mark Allan. *Introducing the New Testament: A Historical, Literary, and Theological Survey*. 2nd ed. Grand Rapids: Baker Academic, 2018.

Presley, Stephen O. *The Intertextual Reception of Genesis 1–3 in Irenaeus of Lyons*. Leiden: Brill, 2015.

Price, George McCready. *Illogical Geology: The Weakest Point in the Evolution Theory*. Los Angeles: Modern Heretic Co., 1906.

———. *The New Geology: A Textbook for Colleges, Normal Schools, and Training Schools; and for the General Reader.* Mountain View, CA: Pacific Press, 1923.

Provan, Iain. *Discovering Genesis: Content, Interpretation, Reception.* Discovering Biblical Texts. Grand Rapids: Eerdmans, 2015.

Rabin, Chaim. "The Translation Process and the Character of the Septuagint." *Textus* (1968): 1–26.

Rad, Gerhard von. *Genesis: A Commentary.* Translated by J. H. Marks. Rev. ed. OTL. Philadelphia: Westminster, 1973.

Radice, Roberto. "Philo's Theology and Theory of Creation." In *The Cambridge Companion to Philo*, edited by Adam Kamesar, 124–45. New York: Cambridge University Press, 2009.

Ramm, Bernard. *The Christian View of Science and Scripture.* Grand Rapids: Eerdmans, 1955.

Ray, Roger. "Who Did Bede Think He Was?" In *Innovation and Tradition in the Writings of the Venerable Bede*, edited by Scott DeGregorio, 11–35. Morgantown: West Virginia University Press, 2006.

Reed, Annette Yoshiko. "From 'Pre-Emptive Exegesis' to 'Pre-Emptive Speculation'? *Ma'aseh Bereshit* in *Genesis Rabbah* and *Pirqei de-Rabbi Eliezer*." In *With Letters of Light: Studies in the Dead Sea Scrolls, Early Jewish Apocalypticism, Magic, and Mysticism in Honor of Rachel Elior*, edited by Daphna Z. Arbel and Andrei A. Orlov, 115–32. Ekstasis 2. Berlin: de Gruyter, 2011.

Reid, Barbara E., OP. "Sabbath, the Crown of Creation." In *Earth, Wind, and Fire: Biblical and Theological Perspectives on Creation*, edited by Carol J. Dempsey and Mary Margaret Pazdan, 67–76. Collegeville, MN: Liturgical Press, 2004.

Rösel, Martin. *Übersetzung als Vollendung der Auslegung: Studien zur Genesis-Septuaginta.* Berlin: de Gruyter, 1994.

Rosik, Mariusz. "Discovering the Secrets of God's Gardens: Resurrection as New Creation (Gen. 2:4b–3:24; John 20:1–18)." *Liber Annuus* 58 (2008): 81–98.

Rudavsky, T. M. *Time Matters: Time, Creation, and Cosmology in Medieval Jewish Philosophy.* Albany: State University of New York Press, 2012.

Ruiten, J. van. "The Creation of Man and Woman in Early Jewish Literature." In *The Creation of Man and Woman: Interpretations of the Biblical Narratives in Jewish and Christian Traditions*, edited by Gerard Luttikhuizen, 34–62. TBN 3. Leiden: Brill, 2000.

Runia, David T. *Philo of Alexandria: On the Creation of the Cosmos according to Moses; Introduction, Translation and Commentary.* PACS 1. Leiden: Brill, 2001.

Sæbø, Magne, ed. *Hebrew Bible / Old Testament.* Vol. 1, *From the Beginnings to the Middle Ages (until 1300).* Part 2, *The Middle Ages.* Göttingen: Vandenhoeck & Ruprecht, 2000.

Samuel ben Meir. *Rabbi Samuel ben Meir's Commentary on Genesis: An Annotated Translation*. Translated by Martin I. Lockshin. Jewish Studies 5. Lewiston, NY: Edwin Mellen, 1989.

Samuelson, Norbert Max. *Judaism and the Doctrine of Creation*. New York: Cambridge University Press, 1994.

Sarason, Richard. "Interpreting Rabbinic Biblical Interpretation: The Problem of Midrash, Again." In *Hesed ve-Emet: Studies in Honor of Ernest S. Frerichs*, edited by Jodi Magness and Seymore Gitin, 135–54. Atlanta: Scholars Press, 1998.

Sarna, Nahum. *Genesis: The Traditional Hebrew Text with the New JPS Translation*. Philadelphia: Jewish Publication Society, 1989.

Schachter, Lifsa. "The Garden of Eden as God's First Sanctuary." *JBQ* 41 (2013): 73–77.

Schleiermacher, Friedrich. *The Christian Faith*. Edited by H. R. Mackintosh and J. S. Stewart. 1830. Reprint, Edinburgh: T&T Clark, 1999.

Schreiner, Susan E. *The Theater of His Glory: Nature and the Natural Order in the Thought of John Calvin*. Grand Rapids: Baker Academic, 1995.

Schuele, Andreasa. "Sabbath." In *The New Interpreter's Dictionary of the Bible*, edited by Katharine Doob Sakenfeld, 5:3–10. Nashville: Abingdon, 2009.

Scurlock, JoAnn, and Richard H. Beal, eds. *Creation and Chaos: A Reconsideration of Hermann Gunkel's* Chaoskampf *Hypothesis*. Winona Lake, IN: Eisenbrauns, 2013.

Sedley, David. *Creationism and Its Critics in Antiquity*. Berkeley: University of California Press, 2007.

Seeskin, Kenneth. *Maimonides on the Origin of the World*. New York: Cambridge University Press, 2005.

Selderhuis, Herman J., ed. *The Calvin Handbook*. Grand Rapids: Eerdmans, 2009.

Seufert, Matthew. "The Presence of Genesis in Ecclesiastes." *WTJ* 78 (2016): 75–92.

Siliezar, Carlos Raul Sosa. *Creation Imagery in the Gospel of John*. LNTS 546. London: Bloomsbury, 2015.

Sim, David C. "The Meaning of παλιγγενεσία in Matthew 19:28." *JSNT* 50 (1993): 3–12.

Sjöberg, A. W. "Eve and the Chameleon." In *In the Shelter of Elyon: Essays on Ancient Palestinian Life and Literature in Honor of G. W. Ahlström*, edited by W. B. Barrick and J. R. Spencer, 219–21. Sheffield: JSOT Press, 1984.

Slifkin, Natan. *The Challenge of Creation: Judaism's Encounter with Science, Cosmology, and Evolution*. Brooklyn, NY: Zoo Torah and Yashar Books, 2006.

Smalley, Beryl. *The Study of the Bible in the Middle Ages*. Notre Dame, IN: University of Notre Dame, 1978.

Smith, J. M. Powels. "The Syntax and Meaning of Genesis 1:1–3." *AJSL* 44, no. 2 (1928): 108–15.

Smith, J. P. "Hebrew Christian Midrash in Irenaeus Epid. 43." *Biblica* 38 (1957): 24–34.

Smith, Mark S. *The Priestly Vision of Genesis 1*. Minneapolis: Fortress, 2010.

Speiser, E. A. "ʿēd in the Story of Creation." *BASOR* 140 (1955): 9–11.

———. *Genesis: A New Translation with Introduction and Commentary.* AB 1. New York: Doubleday, 1964.

Stadelmann, Luis. *The Hebrew Conceptions of the World.* AnBib 39. Rome: Biblical Institute, 1970.

Stager, Lawrence E. "Jerusalem and the Garden of Eden." *ErIsr* 26 (1999): 183–94.

Staub, Jacob J. *The Creation of the World according to Gersonides.* BJS 24. Chico, CA: Scholars Press, 1982.

Steenberg, Matthew. "Children in Paradise: Adam and Eve as 'Infants' in Irenaeus of Lyons." *JECS* 12, no. 1 (2004): 1–22.

———. *Of God and Man: Theology as Anthropology from Irenaeus to Athanasius.* New York: T&T Clark, 2009.

———. "To Test or Preserve? The Prohibition of Genesis 2:16–17 in the Thought of Two Second-Century Exegetes." *Greg* 86 (2005): 723–41.

Stegmüller, Freidrich. *Repertorium Biblicum Medii Aevi.* Vol. 5. Madrid-Barcelona: Matriti, 1955.

Stern, David. Introduction to *The Book of Legends = Sefer Ha-Aggadah: Legends from the Talmud and Midrash*, edited by Hayim N. Bialik and Yehoshua H. Ravnitzky, translated by William G. Braude, xvii–xxii. New York: Schocken, 1992.

Stolz, Fritz. "Die Bäume des Gottesgartens auf dem Libanon." *ZAW* 84 (1972): 141–56.

Stordalen, Terje. "Heaven on Earth—or Not? Jerusalem as Eden in Biblical Literature." In *Beyond Eden: The Biblical Story of Paradise (Genesis 2–3) and Its Reception History*, edited by Konrad Schmid and Christoph Riedweg, 28–57. Tübingen: Mohr Siebeck, 2008.

Stratton, S. Brian. "Genesis after the Origin: Theological Responses to Evolution." *WW* 29, no. 1 (2009): 7–18.

Strickman, H. Norman, and Arthur M. Silver. *Ibn Ezra's Commentary on the Pentateuch.* 5 vols. New York: Menorah, 1988.

Strong, Augustus Hopkins. *Systematic Theology: A Compendium and Commonplace Book Designed for the Use of Theological Students.* 5th ed. New York: A. C. Armstrong & Son, 1896.

Talmage, Frank. "Apples of Gold: The Inner Meaning of Sacred Texts in Medieval Judaism." In *Apples of Gold in Settings of Silver: Studies in Medieval Jewish Exegesis and Polemics*, edited by Barry Walfish, 108–50. Toronto: Pontifical Institute of Medieval Studies, 1999.

Talmon, Shemaryahu. "The Community of the Renewed Covenant: Between Judaism and Christianity." In *The Community of the Renewed Covenant: The Notre Dame Symposium on the Dead Sea Scrolls*, edited by Eugene Ulrich and James VanderKam, 3–24. Christianity and Judaism in Antiquity 10. Notre Dame, IN: University of Notre Dame Press, 1994.

Teske, Roland J. Introduction to *St. Augustine: On Genesis*, translated by R. J. Teske, 1–38. FC 84. Washington, DC: Catholic University of America Press, 1991.

Thompson, John L., ed. *Genesis 1–11*. Reformation Commentary on Scripture: Old Testament 1. Downers Grove, IL: IVP Academic, 2012.

Tishby, Isaiah. *The Wisdom of the Zohar: An Anthology of Texts*. Translated by David Goldstein. 3 vols. Oxford: Littman Library and Oxford University Press, 1989.

Tov, Emanuel. "The Septuagint." In *Mikra: Text, Translation, Reading and Interpretation of the Hebrew Bible in Ancient Judaism and Early Christianity*, edited by Martin Mulder and Harry Sysling, 161–88. Peabody, MA: Hendrickson, 2004.

———. *The Text-Critical Use of the Septuagint in Biblical Research*. JBS 8. Jerusalem: Simor, 1997.

Tsumura, David Toshio. "The 'Chaoskampf' Motif in Ugaritic and Hebrew Literatures." In *Le Royaume d'Ougarit de la Crète à l'Euphrate: Nouveaux axes de recherche*, edited by Jean-Marc Michaud, 473–99. Sherbrooke, QC: GGC, 2007.

———. *Creation and Destruction: A Reappraisal of the* Chaoskampf *Theory in the Old Testament*. Winona Lake, IN: Eisenbrauns, 2005.

———. "The Creation Motif in Psalm 74:12–14? A Reappraisal of the Theory of the Dragon Myth." *JBL* 134 (2015): 547–55.

———. "The Doctrine of *creatio ex nihilo* and the Translation of *tōhû wābōhû*." In *Pentateuchal Traditions in the Late Second Temple Period: Proceedings of the International Workshop in Tokyo, August 28–31, 2007*, edited by A. Moriya and G. Hata, 3–21. JSJSup 158. Leiden: Brill, 2012.

———. *The Earth and the Waters in Genesis 1 and 2*. JSOTSup 83. Sheffield: Sheffield Academic, 1989.

Van Winden, J. C. M. "In the Beginning: Some Observations on the Patristic Interpretation of Genesis 1:1." *VC* 17 (1963): 105–21.

Vogels, Walter. "'And God Created the Great *Tanninim*' (Gen. 1:21)." *ScEs* 63 (2011): 349–65.

Wakeman, Mary K. *God's Battle with the Monster: A Study in Biblical Imagery*. Leiden: Brill, 1973.

Walfish, Barry. "Medieval Jewish Interpretation." In *The Oxford Jewish Study Bible*, edited by Adele Berlin and Marc Zvi Brettler, 1876–1900. Oxford: Oxford University Press, 2005.

Wallace, William. *Thomas Aquinas: Summa Theologiae, Cosmogony*. Vol. 10. Appendixes 1–11. Cambridge: Cambridge University Press, 1967.

Waltke, B. *Genesis: A Commentary*. Grand Rapids: Zondervan, 2001.

Walton, John H. *Genesis 1 as Ancient Cosmology*. Winona Lake, IN: Eisenbrauns, 2011.

Wardlaw, Terrance R. "The Meaning of ברא in Genesis 1:1–2:3." *VT* 64 (2014): 502–13.

Ware, James. "Paul's Understanding of the Resurrection in 1 Corinthians 15:36–54." *JBL* 133 (2014): 809–35.

Warfield, Benjamin Breckinridge. *The Inspiration and Authority of the Bible*. Philadelphia: P&R, 1948.

Watson, Rebecca S. *Chaos Uncreated: A Reassessment of the Theme of "Chaos" in the Hebrew Bible*. BZAW 34. Berlin: de Gruyter, 2005.

Watson, Rebecca S., and A. H. W. Curtis, eds. *Conversations on Canaan and the Bible: Creation, Chaos, Monotheism, Yahwism*. Berlin: de Gruyter, forthcoming.

Weiss, Harold. "The Sabbath in the Fourth Gospel." *JBL* 110 (1991): 311–21.

Wellhausen, Julius. *Prolegomena to the History of Israel*. Translated by J. Sutherland Black and Allan Menzies. Edinburgh: A. & C. Black, 1885. Scholars Press Reprints and Translations. Atlanta: Scholars Press, 1994.

Wengert, Timothy. *Reading the Bible with Martin Luther: An Introductory Guide*. Grand Rapids: Baker Academic, 2013.

Wenham, Gordon J. *Genesis 1–15*. WBC 1. Waco: Word, 1987.

———. "Sanctuary Symbolism in the Garden of Eden Story." In *"I Studied Inscriptions from Before the Flood": Ancient Near Eastern, Literary, and Linguistic Approaches to Genesis 1–11*, edited by Richard S. Hess and David Toshio Tsumura, 399–404. Winona Lake, IN: Eisenbrauns, 1994.

Westermann, Claus. *Genesis 1–11: A Commentary*. Minneapolis: Augsburg, 1984.

Whitcomb, John C., and Henry M. Morris. *The Genesis Flood: The Biblical Record and Its Scientific Implications*. Philadelphia: P&R, 1961.

White, Andrew Dickson. *A History of the Warfare of Science with Theology in Christendom*. Great Minds. Cambridge: Cambridge University Press, 1896. Repr., Amherst, NY: Prometheus, 1993.

Wise, Michael, Martin Abegg, and Edward Cook. *The Dead Sea Scrolls: A New Translation*. San Francisco: HarperSanFrancisco, 1996.

Wright, N. T. *The New Testament and the People of God*. Vol. 1 of *Christian Origins and the Question of God*. Minneapolis: Fortress, 1992.

———. *The Resurrection of the Son of God*. Vol. 3 of *Christian Origins and the Question of God*. Minneapolis: Fortress, 1994.

———. *Surprised by Hope: Rethinking Heaven, the Resurrection, and the Mission of the Church*. New York: HarperOne, 2008.

Young, Frances M. "Adam and Anthropos: A Study of the Interaction of Science and the Bible in Two Anthropological Treatises of the Fourth Century." *VC* 37 (1983): 110–40.

Younger, K. Lawson. "The 'Contextual Method': Some West Semitic Reflections." In *COS*, vol. 3, *Archival Documents from the Biblical World*, edited by W. W. Hallo and K. L. Younger, xxxvi–xxxvii. Leiden: Brill, 2003.

Younker, Randall W., and Richard M. Davidson. "The Myth of the Solid Heavenly Dome: Another Look at the Hebrew רקיע (*rāqîaʿ*)." In *The Genesis Creation Account and Its Reverberations in the Old Testament*, edited by Gerald A. Klingbeil, 31–56. Berrien Springs, MI: Andrews University Press, 2015.

Zachman, Randall C. "Calvin as Commentator on Genesis." In *Calvin and the Bible*, edited by Donald K. McKim, 1–29. Oxford: Oxford University Press, 2006.

Contributors

Joel S. Allen (PhD, Hebrew Union College–Jewish Institute of Religion)
Associate Professor of Religion, Dakota Wesleyan University.

Timothy Bellamah, OP (PhD, École Pratique des Hautes Études, Paris)
Assistant Professor in Systematic Theology, Pontifical Faculty of the Immaculate Conception, Dominican House of Studies.

Ira Brent Driggers (PhD, Princeton Theological Seminary)
Professor of New Testament, Lutheran Theological Southern Seminary of Lenoir-Rhyne University, Columbia, South Carolina.

Kyle R. Greenwood (PhD, Hebrew Union College–Jewish Institute of Religion)
Previously served as Associate Professor of Old Testament and Hebrew Language, Colorado Christian University.

Jason Kalman (PhD, McGill University)
Gottschalk-Slade Chair in Jewish Intellectual History, Professor of Classical Hebrew Literature and Interpretation, Hebrew Union College–Jewish Institute of Religion, Cincinnati, Ohio; Research Fellow, University of the Free State, Bloemfontein, South Africa.

Michael D. Matlock (PhD, Hebrew Union College–Jewish Institute of Religion)
Professor of Inductive Biblical Studies, Old Testament, and Early Judaism, Asbury Theological Seminary.

Jennifer Powell McNutt (PhD, University of St. Andrews)
Associate Professor of Theology and History of Christianity, Wheaton College.

Stephen O. Presley (PhD, University of St. Andrews)
  Associate Professor of Church History and Director of the Center for Early
  Christian Studies, Southwestern Baptist Theological Seminary.

C. Rebecca Rine (PhD, University of Virginia)
  Assistant Professor of Biblical and Religious Studies, Grove City College.

David T. Tsumura (PhD, Brandeis University)
  Professor of Old Testament, Japan Bible Seminary.

Aaron T. Smith (PhD, Marquette University)
  Adjunct Professor of Theology, United Lutheran Seminary and Bethel Seminary; Term-Call Pastor, Trinity Evangelical Lutheran Church, East Berlin, PA.

Scripture and Ancient Sources Index

Ecclesiastes Rabbah

7:13 92n42

Genesis Rabbah

1:1 93
1:3 85n25
1:4 87n31
1:5 86, 86n30
1:8 87n32
1:10 82nn15–16
3:5 84n20
3:6 84nn21–22
3:7 84n23
3:8 84n23
4:1 85n27
4:3 86
4:5 85n28
8:10 87n34
16:6 91n41
19:3 89n39
19:3–5 89
19:4–5 88n37
19:14 159

Leviticus Rabbah

on Gen 12:2 162

Mishnah

Ḥagigah
2:1 83n18, 88n35, 148
2:12 87n33

Josephus and Philo

Josephus

Jewish Antiquities
1.1 30
1.27 32
1.30 32
1.31 32
1.33 30
1.34 36
1.35 36
1.38 39
1.41 41
1.46 39

Philo

Allegorical Interpretation
1.2 30
1.4 29
1.19 31
1.31 35
3.96 40
3.161 36

On the Cherubim
21–22 32

On the Creation of the World
8–9 40
13–14 28, 29
22 40
25 41
29 32
35 30
48–49 29
69 36
72 41
151–52 36
154 38

That the Worse Attacks the Better
82–84 36

Who Is the Heir?
221 32
224 32

Apostolic Fathers

Barnabas

6.12 113n77, 113n81
6.13 113n82
15.3–5 107n42
15.8 107n41

1 Clement

33 104n26, 112n68

Church Fathers

Ambrose

Paradise
294–95 127n20
296–98 128n22
302–3 137n52

Six Days of Creation
1 173n12, 176n25
3–4 130n26

Athanasius

Orations against the Arians
2 175n20

Augustine

Confessions
3.5 184n58
7.1–2 184n58
7.19–21 184n58
11 223n34
13.33 176n26

On Christian Teaching
27 128n23

On Genesis Literally Interpreted
49 176n26

Two Books on Genesis against the Manichaeans
2 176n26

Basil

Exegetic Homilies
3 134
33–34 131n32
39–41 133n40
51–52 134n41
53–54 134
136 142n72

Subject Index

Abelard, Peter, 173
Acts, 46
'ādām/Adam
  author of Genesis, 249–50
  as a child, 117–18
  descendants, 14
  and Eve, 34, 35, 36, 37, 61, 65, 66, 87–89, 111, 114–15, 162, 176–77, 184–86
  garden of Eden, 137, 139–40
  and God, 87–88
  humanity, 12–13, 14, 16, 125, 162, 264
  and Jesus Christ, 67–69, 113–14
  proper name (Adam), 12–13, 125, 162
  sin, 14–15, 16, 19
  two genders, 162–63
  See also Eve; humanity
Akkadian, 216–17, 230
Albert the Great, 180–81
Alexander of Hales, 180
allegory, 105, 106–7, 126–27, 128–29, 156
Ambrose of Milan, 127, 130, 137, 176
Amoraic period, 78
Angel, Marc, 147, 165
angels, 28, 84–85, 87–88
animals, 10–11, 36, 41, 162, 204–5, 262, 263
anthropology, 106, 111, 174
Antiochene school of thought, 175–76
Aphrahat, 138
apocalyptic, 60
Apocrypha, 24–25, 26–27, 31, 33, 37
apologists, 99
Apostolic Fathers, 99

Arabic works, 170, 171, 181
archē. See beginning
Aristotle, 39n3, 178, 181, 185, 196
Assyria, 19
astrology, 203–4
astronomy, 158, 200–201, 203–4
Augustine, 124, 131, 132–33, 139, 176, 181–83, 203

Baal, 219, 220, 229
bārā', 226
Barnabas, 107, 112–13
Barth, Karl, 263–65
Basil of Caesarea, 133–35, 176
Bavinck, Herman, 4
Bede, Venerable, 124, 173, 176–77
beginning, 109, 156, 223–24. See also bərē'šit
Behemoth, 31
ben Gershom, Levi. See Gersonides
ben Isaac, Solomon. See Rashi
ben Nahman, Moses. See Nahmanides
Ben Sira, 33
bərē'šit, 3, 82–83, 156–58, 223–24
bêt (Hebrew), 82
Bialik, Hayim, 78
biology, 240, 244
Blowers, Paul, 98
Bonaventure, 180
Bouteneff, Peter, 126
Brenz, Johannes, 190
Briggs, Richard S., 241n5
Bultmann, Rudolf, 257–61

Cajetan, 173
Calvin, John, 192, 193–94, 195–96, 198, 199,
    200–201, 202, 203–4, 205, 206, 207–8,
    209–10, 212–13
canon, 24
cataclysm, 58–60. *See also* eschatology
Cathars, 174–75. *See also* Manichaeism
celibacy, 207–8
chaos. *See* creation: chaos; *tōhû wābōhu*
chiliasm, 117. *See also* eschatology
Christianity, 47, 97, 98–99, 122–23
Christology. *See under* Jesus Christ
Chrysostom, John, 123, 130, 136–37, 142
church, 50, 102–3, 129, 135
church fathers, 98n3, 100–101, 103, 107–11,
    117, 121–25, 126, 127, 128, 129–30, 132–
    35, 138, 169–70
Clement of Rome, 104
Collins, C. John, 4, 15, 16, 19, 224
commentaries on Genesis, 77–78, 98n3, 124,
    170, 175–78
comparative study, 236
Congdon, David, 258n49
contextual study, 237
contradictions, 150–51
cosmology
    ancient Near Eastern, 5–6, 55–56, 225–26
    biblical, 5–8, 221–22
    in church fathers, 107–11, 132–35
    cosmic order, 8
    in New Testament, 54–61
    post-Darwinian, 255–61
    in rabbinic Judaism, 85–87
    Reformation, 200–203
    in Second Temple Judaism, 30–33
    tripartite, 7–8
covenant, 15, 33
creation
    chaos, 86–87, 218–19, 227. See also *tōhû
        wābōhu*
    in church fathers, 103, 123–25
    creationism, 242n6, 246n21, 254
    division and ornamentation, 172
    "evening," 131
    ex nihilo, 85, 87, 108, 155, 177
    in Genesis
        first account, 6–11, 37, 112, 221–22
        literary structure, 1, 2–4
        second account, 32–33, 36, 37, 112, 221–22,
            249

in Hebrew Bible, 4–5, 8–9
in Jubilees, 33–34
in medieval Judaism, 148
in New Testament, 48–54
perfect, 28–29, 31, 86–87, 196–97, 247
in Philo, 28–29
and Platonism, 40, 101, 156
progressive, 251–53, 254
in rabbinic Judaism, 82, 84–85
renewal, 48–50, 60, 74
See also God: Creator
cross, tree of the, 139
cuneiform texts, 215–16
Cyril of Alexandria, 175

Damascus Document, 35
Darwin, Charles, 239n40, 240, 242, 243, 244,
    245, 262, 265
Day-Age Theory, 254
days of creation
    in the ancient Near East, 223–25
    in church fathers, 103–7, 117, 129–32
    in Hebrew Bible, 2–5
    in medieval Christianity, 175–78
    in medieval Judaism, 153–61
    post-Darwinian, 244–54
    in rabbinic Judaism, 82–85
    in Reformation, 194–200
    in 2 Enoch, 40
    in Second Temple Judaism, 26–30
    See also Hexaemeron
Dead Sea Scrolls, 26–27, 31, 38. *See also*
    Qumran
Decalogue. *See* Ten Commandments
demons. *See* Satan
divorce, 61–62
Documentary Hypothesis, 2

earth, 7, 31–32
education, 122–23, 129
elements, 142
Eliyashiv, Sholom, 147, 148
Enns, Peter, 229
Enuma Elish, 216, 218, 219, 223
Ephrem the Syrian, 124n6, 125, 131–32, 137,
    139–41
Epic of Gilgamesh, 216, 241n5
epistles, 46
Erickson, Millard, 253n38